AF255793

Exposition
Of The
Minor
Prophets

Exposition Of The Minor Prophets

George Hutcheson

Sovereign Grace Publishers, Inc.
P.O. Box 4998
Lafayette, IN 47903

*Printed In the United States of America
By Lightning Source, Inc.*

EPISTLES DEDICATORY

From the Licenser to the Reader

Christian Reader,

This book, which God's providence puts into your hand, contains a brief exposition upon six of those divine prophecies which are called the small or lesser prophets; not because their authority or excellence is lesser than those who are called the greater prophets, but because of the brevity and littleness of their books. All the lesser prophets put together do but contain sixty-seven chapters, whereas one of the greater (viz. Isaiah) consists of sixty-six. Hence it was that these books were anciently put into one volume and called one book, lest by their smallness any of them should be lost. These prophets are in number twelve, according to the twelve tribes, to which they were sent.

Now though it cannot be denied that there are many excellent commentaries already extant upon these lesser prophets (which may deter some men from buying this), yet I desire such to take notice:

1. That such is the profundity and inconceivable depth of the divine scriptures, that they cannot be exhausted by any writers or commentators whatsoever. When men have dug out of this precious mine all the spiritual gold and silver they can, there will be enough left behind for others to gather.

2. That this reverend author has gone in a way unusual and almost untrodden, and has a peculiar excellence in him which others have not. For his chief scope is, after a short and yet full analysis and exposition, to collect choice and pithy observations out of every chapter. And in this undertaking he is very successful.

Now though the work itself is sufficient to commend the author, yet (because there are many in our days who prize books for their authors' sake, not authors for their books' sake) I was desired to write something to make this reverend minister known to this nation, to which he is altogether a stranger. And for this purpose, I have a testimony concerning him from those whom I dare trust, that he is a man of singular abilities, and deservedly in high esteem in his own country for his learning, godliness, modesty, peaceableness, and humility; and that he was earnestly entreated by some of his learned brethren (especially those in Edinburgh, where he is minister) to make this work public for the good of the churches. The truth is, the book itself represents him to the world in a very fair and beautiful character; for it comprehends much in a little, and breathes out much of God and godliness. His observations are so excellent and so useful, and sometimes so unexpected, and yet so natural, that I verily believe they will be very acceptable, not only to private Christians, but also and especially to ministers, affording them many rare and unconsidered doctrines, for the spiritual edification of their congregations. That which was said of Socrates, "Whosoever knew him, loved him and honoured him; and they that did not do so, it was because they did not know him," may truly be said of this book. They who know it prize it.

My prayer to God shall be that the learned and religious author of this short and brief commentary upon these six prophets, may find such good success of his endeavours herein that he may be much encouraged to make a further progress in this way, and that other able men may be stirred up by his example to do the like upon other scriptures, which no doubt will tend much to the glory of God and the profit and edification of his people. I am

Your servant in the work of the
Lord,

Edmund Calamy.

To The Most Noble and Truly Religious Lady,
Anne, Duchess of Hamilton, etc.

Madam:

Grace, Mercy, and Peace, through Jesus Christ, be multiplied.

It is the verdict, not only of the wisest of men, but of the unerring Spirit of God, concerning all things under the sun,

"Vanity of vanities, all is vanity" (Eccl. 1:2), and that not only as the creation is made subject to the vanity of corruption, because of men's sin (Rom. 8:20) but also and chiefly in respect of men, who are not content with the lawful use of things, for which they are appointed and are very good; but study to place their happiness in them, neglecting God, the only fountain of true felicity. As the creatures cannot answer the expectations of such, nor satisfy their vast desires, they provoke the Lord by their acts to reveal to them the folly of their choice, whether in mercy to his own or in justice to the wicked, that they may be no better for all their endless endeavours than they who voluntarily mortify their affections to those things; and that all may see the folly and madness of their way.

And though this way has been tried and not found by him, and though experience in all ages reveals what a sandy foundation they build upon, who seek by these means to satisfy their own souls, made after the image of God; yet how few will believe this truth. "This their way is their folly, yet their posterity approve their sayings" (Ps. 49:13). Yea, when we find this truth verified, we hardly trust our eyes and senses; or if we are put from that hope, yet often we are little the better, but sit down in bitterness, as if all happiness were lost if we do not find it where we expected it; and thus do we neglect the true remedy of our grievances and provoke God to consume our days in vanity and our years in trouble (Ps. 78:33).

What great cause then do we have to lament the folly of the children of men, who err, and upon their error do forsake their own mercy, unto which they would be led by discovering the emptiness of all things besides God. They quarrel with the wise and holy dispensations of God, by which a foundation might be laid for much good, if they were wisely considered, when yet their quarrelings can avail or help them nothing; and they do not improve such dispensations for the end for which they are appointed, but either sit down stupidly under them, or grow worse that such pains are taken on them, or pine away under the punishment of their iniquity and howl upon their beds for corn and wine and oil, but do not return to the Most High (Hos. 7:14, 16). And on the other hand, we have cause to admire the mercy of God toward his own chosen ones, in that he will (so to speak) make them happy against their wills. When they would destroy themselves with a vain show, he in mercy to them will smash their idols and

drive them from snares, as he did Lot out of Sodom. And
when the Lord has dealt so hardly with them that many times
in their bitterness they have no language to express it, yet
he will let them see their mistake by giving them meat even
out of the eater, and by setting them to mind their heavenly
country more, and to see the commandments exceeding
broad, when they have seen an end of all perfection (Ps.
119:96). And he will reveal the riches of his grace, and the
fullness of his spiritual comforts, by making his people
bless him, and acknowledge the mercy of those dispensations
which sometimes they were so startled at (Ps. 119:71, 75),
and causing the voice of rejoicing and salvation, even in the
pilgrim tabernacles of the righteous (Ps. 118:15).

Herein, madam, your Ladyship has cause to observe the
loving kindness of the Lord toward you, who from your ten-
derest years have been exercised with difficulties of many
kinds, and have experienced this truth of the vanity of all
things; yet your Ladyship has obtained mercy to be led
thereby, (and much more by the Law, and by the love and
hope of mercy through Jesus Christ) to seek after a more
enduring substance, and after Christ that pearl of price.
This is indeed a token for good, even in lots wherein God
seems to write most bitter things, when they set hearts
to work this way. It has been refreshing to such of the Lord's
servants and people as know your Ladyship's way and exercise, to see your sweet submission under the Lord's hand,
and your desire and care to have afflictions rather blessed
than removed, and to make sure of your interest in Christ,
when the thong of other things might rather have put flesh
and blood to other exercise; and it has laid a special obligation upon myself (as having been a witness unto it at
several occasions) to be instrumental, as the Lord shall
enable, in your Ladyship's furtherance and encouragement
therein, and to make some acknowledgement of the many
respects it has pleased your Ladyship to show unto me for
the truth's sake.

This has induced me to make bold, in dedicating unto your
Ladyship this piece upon some of the Lesser Prophets, who
were the faithful interpreters of the Law of God, applying the
same unto the sins of several times, and who do point out the
infallible and true cause of calamities, with the use to be
made thereof, and the true remedy thereof; to wit, Christ.
The hope of Christ to be manifested in the flesh for the redemption of lost man was the godly's life in those days, and

much more ought to be so now, for the substance has come, and that abundance of grace and truth treasured up in him has been brought to light by the gospel. If these my weak endeavours may prove serviceable to any of the Lord's people in their exercises and journey toward heaven, and in special to your Ladyship, that shall be more than abundant recompence unto

Your Ladyship's obliged
Servant in the Gospel,

George Hutcheson.

TO THE READER

Christian Reader,

I do here present you with an exposition of some of the lesser prophets; concerning which, and my undertaking, I give this brief account.

I have looked upon a short exposition of holy scripture joined with the principal doctrines flowing therefrom, after the mould of the Reverend Mr. David Dickson's late piece upon Matthew, as a special means (through God's blessing) for promoting truth and piety, and for preventing errours; but I little thought to have undertaken any such thing myself, when so many godly, able and experienced ministers of the gospel did not (for reasons known to themselves) put hand to it.

But being some years ago seriously invited with others, by the reverend author of that Exposition of Matthew, to concur with him in prosecuting that purpose which he had begun, and has since made further progress into, upon the Book of Psalms, I then essayed some of these prophets, being at that time recommended unto me. Of late, at his desire (living now through God's providence in one city) I have looked upon them again, and have adventured to present these to public view, if it may invite others who have more ability and leisure to mind and help forward such a work upon the whole Bible; which is a study (besides the profit the Church of God might reap thereby) which will, I am confident, richly recompence the undertakers in their own bosom.

As this recommendation led me to the choice of these prophets in this undertaking, the narration thereof may shorten my account concerning the mould of this piece, since I have conformed myself (so far as my weakness could reach, or the nature of the subject, often very dark and obscure, would admit) to the mould followed in the Exposition of Matthew formerly mentioned. I have found it necessary (besides a short summary of each chapter) to permit some short exposition of the words before the doctrines, which is enlarged when needed in clearing the deductions of each doctrine. In the exposition I have pointed, upon occasion, to other scriptures helping to clarify the place; but for the doctrines, I did not set myself to bring scriptures confirming them, since it is my desire that no more should be admitted or received here than such as clearly flow from the text. It cannot be avoided in a piece containing so many doctrines, and on so many subjects, that the same doctrines, at least in substance, will recur often; but the reader will consider that every time it occurs, it is confirmed anew, from a new reason; and God's way of teaching often calls on us to hear and consider them much. If any man thinks the doctrines sometimes too prolix, he should consider that in this sort of writing it is required to say much in little bounds; and sometimes two truths flowing from one reason will speak more fully when conjoined than if every one of them were made a doctrine alone; and some doctrines could not satisfy unless they were either limited or cleared a little.

As the doctrines will be found, I hope, to arise naturally from the text explained, in exposition I have studied to keep by the rule of faith, and set down that exposition which is most agreeable to the context itself -- and where diversity of interpretations could agree together, I have conjoined them, and but seldom have held forth different interpretations of one place where there was no such affinity between them.

There is only one thing of which I would advise you in a word, and that is concerning some promises made not only to the church of the Jews, but to all Israel, in which their conversion and future restitution to their own land seem to be held forth. I am not ignorant how peremptory many have been of old, and of late, in determining such future events from the word. Many who have asserted the restitution of Israel to their land, have asserted also a reign of Christ, not only in his spiritual government but in his person also on earth, and that the church shall flourish and be glorious for a thousand years. But for these assertions they have no sure footing in scripture. Indeed the first speaks little comfort to the church; for if Christ has a circumscribed body, he can be in but one place at once; and it is more comforting to the church in all quarters of the world to be governed by his Spirit, than by deputies employed by him while he remains in one corner of the world, as that opinion must insist he will.

And for the second: though the church may have some glimpses and breathings of tranquillity and prosperity, yet that happy condition which many speak of, seems at odds even with common sense; for if the church and particular saints have corruption even in that time, that fire will necessarily produce sparks of trouble; and how any trouble can be consistent with the condition which these men speak of, I see not. The experience of the Jews at the first coming of Christ, and of the church in all ages, may show us how many carnal conceptions of the glory of Christ's kingdom have been disappointed.

Yet this would seem probable: many passages scattered in the prophets do not have their full accomplishment until all Israel is converted, as the apostle explains (Rom. 11), citing a more obscure place to clear it, and giving us warrant to make use of other places that speak more clearly. So there are also many passages in the prophets, which (however they may be applied to a spiritual restitution of every true church) yet in their full accomplishment seem to take in the restitution of the nation of Israel.

This interpretation seems to have Christ's own warrant: "They shall fall by the edge of the sword, and shall be led away captive into all nations, and Jerusalem shall be trodden down by the Gentiles, until the times of the Gentiles are fulfilled" (Luke 21:24). He seems to set the same term-day to their captivity and the desolation of Jerusalem (including the land), that the apostle sets to their conversion (Rom. 11: 25, 26). And indeed, if the conversion of Israel will be national (Rom. 11:25, 26; Hosea 3:4, 5), it is agreeable to right reason that they will get a land for habitation as a nation; and what better land than their own, which God gave to their fathers of old? And of this there are plain promises, spoken not only to Judah, but to Jacob, Ephraim, and Israel (Jer. 30:18; Jer. 31:17; Ezek. 37:16-25; Hosea 11:9-11; and many others).

I take no pleasure in singular opinions, nor in being peremptory in those things, which time will be the best commentary unto; so, as there is so much to this purpose spoken in the word, I could not but briefly point at such passages in any of these following prophets, so that the godly may be stirred up to pray more earnestly for the conversion of Israel, at which time the Lord will by performance give his own commentary to these and many other promises.

I shall detain you, Christian reader, no longer in the entry. That this present piece may be blessed unto you, and that you may more and more fall in love with God speaking to you in scripture, shall be the prayer of

Your servant in the Gospel,

George Hutcheson.

Christian Reader,

It cannot be denied on the one hand, that the Lord in this last age has manifested unto Britain, more than in any former time, the riches of his grace, in the clear and long continued offer of righteousness, reconciliation, peace, sanctification and salvation, freely to be had by heartily embracing his Son Jesus Christ; and that, for the long slighting of this gracious and rich offer, he is now manifesting his just indignation and wrath against this unthankful and froward generation, not only by inflicting many sad bodily judgments, but also by sending upon the spirits of many, who have not received the love of the truth, strong delusions, that they should believe a lie and be damned, all of them who will not believe the truth, but have pleasure in unrighteousness, as it was foretold (2 Thess. 2:11, 12).

And it cannot be denied on the other hand that in the midst of this great wrath, the Lord remembers his tender mercies toward us, by continuing the open preaching of the offer of his rejected grace; and by stirring up from time to time the spirits of many of his servants to open still more and more clearly the little book of holy scripture, by pious and learned annotations, larger commentaries, shorter paraphrases, brief explications, and other sorts of fruitful writings. By these and all other means he testifies his lothness to depart altogether from this isle, which is engaged unto him by all sorts of obligations, and wherein, besides those who are already converted blessed ones, he has many elect souls to bring home from their pernicious wanderings.

His gracious purpose appears in this, that as Satan is be-
stirring himself in the maddest manner that any age has
ever heard of, to darken the light held forth in scripture,
by the hellish smoke of so many pernicious errours, so the
Lord is daily revealing more and more fully the folly and
vileness of these vessels of dishonour and of those abominations vented by them; thereby giving hope that when they,
with Jannes and Jambres, have done their worst to with-
stand the truth of God in the mouth of his ministers, they
shall proceed no further than to carry away with them the
uncleanness of the household to their own shame and perdi-
tion (2 Tim. 3:1-9; 2 Tim. 2:16-21). This hope has inclined
the author of this piece, among others, to offer his service
unto the church.

I need not commend him unto you, nor speak of the measure of the grace of God bestowed upon him, because his work
will speak for itself. After perusing any part of it, you will
readily allow unto him more than his modesty will allow
me to say of him. Therefore let the prefixing of my name to
this book be judged to be no more than my presuming to
come forth, making his acquaintance with you; praying God,
the Father of lights, to bless to you this his first essay, and
his intention, by the grace of God, to do more service to
you in this sort; and for this end to increase his talents and
lengthen his life, and to stir up other able labourers to take
part in this service, till it be perfected for your edification.
In this petition let me entreat you to join with

Your servant in the Gospel,

David Dickson.

OBADIAH

THE ARGUMENT

This prophet, among others, is raised up by God to denounce and foretell the judgments that were to come upon the posterity of Esau, because of their cruelty against Judah in the time of their distress -- which accordingly were executed (as histories record) by the Chaldeans some years after the destruction of Jerusalem -- and to comfort the church of the Jews, unto whom it could not but be a sad temptation and addition to their sorrows, to see those who had been ordained to serve them (Gen. 25:23) so prosperous and insolent, while they were sharply afflicted.

We need not curiously inquire who this Obadiah was, since that adds nothing to the authority of his message; and although the time he lived and prophesied is not expressly set down, yet considering the substance of his doctrine, and its affinity with that of Jeremiah (chap. 49) and of Ezekiel (chap. 25), it appears that he prophesied after the captivity of Judah under Jehoiachin (2 Kings 24:10-12), if not after the captivity under Zedekiah, at which time especially their neighbouring enemies were cruel and insolent, and Edom among, if not above, the rest (Ps. 137:7).

The prophecy (omitting the inscription) may be taken up in two parts.

1. The Lord threatens Edom with destruction by war (ver. 1, 2) notwithstanding their pride and conceit of their country's situation (ver. 3, 4), or of their treasures (ver. 5, 6), confederates (ver. 7), wisdom (ver. 8), valour (ver. 9); and that because of their injurious dealing with their brethren of Judah (ver. 10, 11), which they ought not to have done (ver. 12-14). Because of this a day of vengeance upon enemies was certainly approaching, in which they would have a share (ver. 15, 16).

2. The Lord comforts his afflicted church with a promise of deliverance, of holiness and restitution (ver. 17), of victory over their enemies (ver. 18), of enlargement of their border (ver. 19, 20), and of fitted instruments and rulers with their king (ver. 21).

> Ver. 1. The vision of Obadiah. Thus says the Lord God
> concerning Edom: We have heard a rumour from the
> Lord, and an ambassador is sent among the heathen.
> Arise, and let us rise up against her in battle.

The authority of this prophet and his doctrine is asserted;
and the judgment of Edom is summarily set down; that God,
who is its author, has all things in readiness; that the prophets and church had received some intimation of the Lord's
dark counsel concerning Edom; and that as men by their
ambassadors, so the Lord by his effectual providence was
about to stir up the nations that served Nebuchadnezzar,
and make them willing to come against them.

1. The prophets of God did not speak, nor are ministers
to speak, the dreams of their own brain, but what they have
received in commission from God. This doctrine is "the
vision of Obadiah," that is, what he received by prophetic
revelation, represented either to the senses or understanding; and "thus saith the Lord" is prefixed to it.

2. The word of the Lord (and especially threatenings
against impenitent sinners) will have greatest weight when
it is received as indeed the word of God, and proceeding
from such a dreadful majesty. "Thus saith the Lord Jehovah," he who has an established dominion and lordship over
all creatures, and who can give being and performance to
what he says, and who therefore is not to be slighted.

3. Those who defect from God and renounce their interest
in heaven for their belly and sensual pleasures, it is righteous with God to brand them with infamy, and to make them
bear the prints of it unto all generations; for not only Esau
but his posterity bear the name of Edom to perpetuate
the memory of his selling his birthright for red pottage (Gen.
25:29, 30).

4. The counsel and providence of the Lord extends itself
and is exercised not only about his church, but even among
enemies. He who reigns in the midst of enemies has somewhat to say concerning Edom.

5. Though the enemies of God and his people are little
sensible of their own condition and what God intends against
them, yet the church is not left ignorant of what God will do
with these enemies, but in his sanctuary and from his word
it may be seen. "We," he says; that is, I and my fellow-
prophets, Ezekiel and Jeremiah, and by our ministry the
church of God, "we have heard a rumour from the Lord

concerning Edom," that is, some taste of his dark counsel before it breaks forth in effect.

6. It is a comfortable and useful doctrine to the church, to be instructed concerning God's judgments to come upon her enemies; partly that she may be comforted in her troubles, in expectation that God will clear his affection toward her by plaguing those that wronged her, and partly that she may hereby see what sins especially God is angry at, to avoid them. For these ends a prophet is raised up to teach, not in Seir, but in Judah, concerning Edom.

7. War is one of the sharp scourges by which God punishes wicked nations; and it comes upon a people not accidentally, but by the special providence of God, who has peace and war in his own hand, and who, when he has any work to do, can make instruments (however led by their own principles and ends) active and willing. For it is from the Lord that "an ambassador is sent among the heathen," who not only stirs them up but makes them mutually to excite one another: "Arise, and let us rise up against her in battle."

Ver. 2. Behold, I have made you small among the heathen; you are greatly despised.

The greatness of Edom's calamity by this war is held forth from its effects: hereby the Lord would diminish their number, power, wealth, and reputation, and put them beneath all other nations, and load them with contempt and ignominy.

1. Whatever instruments are employed in inflicting any judgment, yet God is to be eyed as having chief hand in them all. "I have made you small," says the Lord.

2. The Lord pursuing for sin, can bring down the greatest person and people in the world, and lay them in the dust, and pour contempt upon the most honourable: "I have made you small and greatly despised."

3. The Lord's judgments upon enemies are not readily foreseen or expected by them; so when they come, they are remarkable. This much does this word "behold" imply.

4. Things undertaken by God, and foretold by him in his word, ought to be reckoned as certain as if they had already come to pass. "I have made you small, you are despised," says he.

5. To be singular in afflictions or judgments, or in the measure of them, adds to the weight and renders them more grievous. To be "small among the heathen," or nations,

implied not only that Edom was reckoned among the heathen nations and not of the church, but that God by his judgments would make him one of the smallest of them, and that none should be so far brought down as he; and this is told him as an aggravation of his stroke.

6. As the Lord's showing mercy upon any makes way for man's mercy towards them also, insofar as may be for their good (Jer. 42:12), so when the Lord becomes a party in anger, men's affections and respects will dry up; for however Edom was esteemed before, yet when God deals with him, he is "greatly despised."

> Ver. 3. The pride of your heart has deceived you; you who dwell in the clefts of the rock, whose habitation is high, who says in his heart, Who shall bring me down to the ground?
>
> 4. Though you exalt yourself as the eagle, and though you set your nest among the stars, I will bring you down from there, says the Lord.

For further confirmation of the judgment, the Lord enlarges and amplifies the former sentence from several considerations, overturning all their vain confidences with which they were puffed up, supposing by them to be exempted from the stroke. The Lord reveals their pride and conceit because of these, to be one of the causes of his controversy against them; and he explains further the judgment to come upon them, by threatening to pull down every one of these confidences, and so make them completely miserable and contemptible. The first vain confidence is the situation of their hilly country and their cities built upon inaccessible rocks; of which (as the rest) they were intolerably proud, as conceiving their country to be inaccessible, and their cities to be invincible. Against this the Lord threatens that though they dwelt as high as the eagle builds her nest, yea, as the stars toward which eagles mount, yet he should reach them and debase them, and so their country should be invaded and their cities taken.

1. Outward advantages and accommodations, concurring with a natural heart, usually produce pride, self-confidence and insolence. Edom, whose habitation is high, is proud and says in his heart, Who shall bring me down to the ground? -- whereas a renewed heart in all these is poor and depends on God.

2. The Lord judges of men's pride, not so much by their outward carriage, which may be masked over with a show of humility, as by looking to their heart and discerning the conceit and lofty imaginations that reign there. He sees the pride of Edom's heart.

3. Of all the deceits that men are deceived with, self-deceiving is one of the greatest, when they are given up to delude themselves with vain imaginations and confidences; "your heart has deceived you."

4. Pride and conceit, however they muster up men's excellencies before them, are but deluders, and make a show of what will prove nothing, being either an evidence of being nothing in reality, or that what they are conceited of is blasted and withered. In particular, however presumption promises great things to make sinners secure, and contemn God's threatenings, yet it deceives and feeds with vain hopes, and will prove a deceiver in the end, when there is most need of what it promised. "The pride of your heart has deceived you."

5. Pride in the creature is looked upon by God as a stroke against him, as striking eminently at his glory, in not depending on him, and as affecting his throne; and therefore it provokes God, though there were no other quarrel or enemy, and engages him to prove his power in abasing it. Therefore that general defiance, "Who shall bring me down to the ground," is answered by God, as especially concerned: "I will bring you down, says the Lord."

6. The Lord is able to reach man and bring him down in his most eminent strength and greatness imaginable; and he cannot only make strongholds a vain refuge in a day of vengeance, but he is able to overturn more confidences than man can build up for his own security. To dwell in the clefts of the rock is but a small thing for God's power to reach, and yet it was the height of that which Edom had to boast of; for "though you exalt yourself as the eagle, and though you set your nest among the stars, I will bring you down."

> Ver. 5. If thieves come to you, if robbers by night (how you are cut off!), would they not have stolen until they had enough? If the grape-gatherers came to you, would they not leave some grapes?
>
> 6. How are the things of Esau searched out! How are his hidden things sought up!

A second vain confidence is their wealth and treasures, with which men help themselves in their extremities. The Lord threatens to make these a prey to their enemies, who after their victory, without fear of ambushes, should at leisure seek and carry away even their hidden treasures; and so their spoiling should not be ordinary, but complete, even to admiration. From this, learn:

1. Riches treasured by those with whom God has a quarrel, are so far from helping or delivering them in a day of wrath, or from doing the owners good, that they are justly given as a prey to their enemies: "Edom's things are searched out and sought up."

2. As the children of the Lord are to read the mercy of their trials by considering how moderate they are in respect to judgments upon enemies, so the wicked may see the severity of God in what their strokes are beyond ordinary. For this end Edom's spoiling is set before him, as being beyond what thieves and robbers by night do; for they do not take away all, but what may suffice; not being able to carry all, or not daring for fear to stay and search out all. It is likewise beyond what grape-gatherers do in vineyards, for according to the law (Lev. 19:10) they must leave some grapes; but the things of Esau are searched out, and his hidden things sought up.

3. The strokes that God has appointed for those who not only live wickedly, but also turn enemies and persecutors of his church, are complete and far beyond the ordinary visitations that come upon the children of men. This comparison between Esau's stroke and the stroke of robbers imports that the one would have been in some way a mercy and deliverance from the other.

4. However the wicked are senseless and fearless when God threatens them, yet his stroke will make them feel and awake them; for this expression, "How you are cut off! How the things of Esau are searched out!" implies no pity in the Lord or his prophet toward them, but that the judgment should admonish and affect them when it came upon them.

Ver. 7. All the men of your confederacy have brought you even to the border. The men who were at peace with you have deceived you and prevailed against you. They who eat your bread have laid a wound under you; there is no understanding in him.

8. Shall I not in that day, says the Lord, even destroy the wise men out of Edom, and understanding out of the mount of Esau?

The third vain confidence is the help of their confederates, the nations round about them, and especially Egypt, whose interest it was to engage the Edomites, who lay in their frontiers, against the Chaldeans. The Lord threatens to make these the occasion and instruments to promote their ruin, for all their confederates would engage them to oppose the Chaldeans at the border of their country, which was in effect to cast them out of it; as the phrase also in the original signifies. Their friends and intimate familiars by subtlety and fair pretences should ensnare them to their own hurt and ruin, as if they had given them a bed to lie on and yet hidden a dagger in it, with the point upward to slay them.

And this is more fully cleared by reading the words as the original has it, without addition of any words which are put in the translation: "They have laid your bread a wound under you," signifying that their bread which they had from Egypt was the snare that drew them on to their ruin.

1. According to the sin of a person or nation, so ordinarily is their judgment. Edom broke off that brotherly amity that ought to have been between his brother Jacob and him, and therefore he is paid in his own coin, for his heathen confederates are his ruin. He sinned in breaking bonds, and he is plagued in that other bonds break him and are broken to him. "All the men of your confederacy have brought you even to the border."

2. God can make those to be instruments of sinners' ruin who are in appearance very near friends; he can make confederacies in which men confide, the short cut to their destruction. Edom was ruined by his confederates, and the men who were at peace with him.

3. The confederacies and alliances of political men are not to be trusted in, because they are led only by their own state interests, and mind only their own advantage. So did Edom's confederates: the men who were at peace with him, deceived him; they gave him bread for a wound under him, to put him between themselves and the dint of the enemy.

The fourth vain confidence is their wisdom and prudence, by which they might think to manage their affairs dexterously, and to the best advantage, as it seems they have been famous for this (Jer. 49:7). Concerning this the Lord foretells that for all their wisdom, they should not be able so much as to discern and prevent the treachery of their confederates; and because when they were ready for the stroke, the Lord would deprive them of wisdom, either by taking away such as were wise or by turning their wisdom into folly. Hence learn:

1. When the Lord has ruin to bring upon a people, their wisdom and policy will not avert it. He can deprive men of wisdom to manage their affairs; he can make the wisest to be overreached and outwitted, and can make what they think their wisest course to prove greatest folly in the issue; for Edom is wise, and many confederacies seemed a wise course to strengthen himself, and yet in all this "there is no understanding in him," to discern the snares in it.

2. That in which men are most eminent and are ready to confide most in, will prove vain when they have most need, that the pride of all glory may be stained; for "the wise men are destroyed out of Edom, and understanding out of the mount of Esau," who were a wise people. Excellencies confided in are a disadvantage.

3. Whatever wisdom or excellencies are in men, they are all God's gift and dependent on him, who gives or takes them away at his pleasure, and according as he has a people to raise or to ruin; for "he destroys the wise men" when he will.

4. Men's wisdom and prudence are ordinarily looked upon by God as an enemy to him, and ground of a controversy, because men's conceit of their wisdom is the reason why they give God little, and do not acknowledge his providence, but take all upon themselves. This question, "Shall I not, says the Lord, even destroy the wise men out of Edom?" imports that there is some necessity for doing so.

5. It is a singular demonstration of God's sovereignty and providence in the world, when he overturns the wisdom of the wise, brings all their well-contrived projects to nought, snares them in their own works and counsels, makes eminent fools of them, and causes them to reel like drunken men. When there is no wisdom in him, the Lord declares himself the author of it, that we may see his hand in it and give him the glory of it, and may believe his power to do the same when the wisdom of adversaries is the church's fear; "shall I not, says the Lord, destroy the wise men?"

6. No matter how improbable the threatenings of God's word may seem when they are pronounced, yet in the Lord's

time the accomplishment will be remarkable. Though Edom retains his former wisdom, notwithstanding the Lord's threatening, yet "in that day," to wit, the day of his calamity, "shall I not destroy these wise men, says the Lord?"

> Ver. 9. And your mighty men, O Teman, shall be dismayed, to the end that every one of the mount of Esau may be cut off by slaughter.

The fifth vain confidence is their valour and strength, for which also that nation was eminent, as living by their sword, as was foretold (Gen. 27:40). Concerning this, the Lord threatens to confound with terror the mighty men of their country, or some part of it most renowned for valiant men, called Teman, from Esau's grandchild (Gen. 36:15) or from its location southward (as the word signifies) from Judea. And so these being laid by, there should be a universal slaughter of the inhabitants of the country, at least of every one of note (as the word in the original signifies, and is translated so, Ps. 49:2, 62:9, and elsewhere) as was usual for the Chaldeans to do where they prevailed (2 Kings 24:15).

1. Natural men are in a way endless in their carnal confidences, and hard to be put wholly from them; when one fails, they will have another to fly to. Therefore all this pain is taken to show the vanity of Edom's refuges. If the situation of his country fails him, he has treasures to gather forces with; and failing that, he has confederates, and if they are lacking, prudence, which has delivered people in great extremities; and if he is yet put to it, he has mighty men to run on all hazards. And every one of these needs to be particularly threatened, to make them sure of vengeance.

2. The terror of God is sufficient to crush and overthrow the mightiest of men. Man's valour is not terror-proof, when the terror is from God. "Your mighty men, O Teman, shall be dismayed, and broken with terror," as the word also signifies.

3. As terror upon a people is an ordinary forerunner of great desolation, so where the Lord has a judgment to go through a land, no probable or promising circumstances will turn it away, but what would hinder it shall be made useless. "The mighty men shall be dismayed," to the end that he may reach his purpose and cut off every one.

> Ver. 10. For your violence against your brother Jacob, shame shall cover you, and you shall be cut off forever.

The Lord, having pronounced sentence against Edom, proceeds to show its justice from the cause procuring it. In general, God's quarrel against them is for their violent carriage towards Judah, for which they are again threatened.

1. As the Lord does not strike a people unless he has a just quarrel, so the stupidity of men, in not laying sin to heart, and their blindness and self-love is such that God's quarrel will not be taken up until he himself reveals it. Therefore the Lord himself reveals it here.

2. Of all the injuries and evil deeds committed by wicked men, none are to remarked, or so suddenly and severely punished, as the injuries they do to the church and people of God. The Lord threatens Edom for violence against Jacob, as if he had committed no other fault and yet as filling his cup speedily.

3. The Lord will not forget the interest and obligations of enemies to the people of God, whom they oppress; thereby he aggravates their guilt and doubles their punishment. Therefore the Lord reckons Edom's kindred to Jacob, that his unnaturalness might appear as a ground for the sentence. "Your brother Jacob."

4. Much ignominy and shame abides those especially who ought to be friends and are foes to the church of God; partly in that they shall be disappointed of their expectation to see the church's ruin, and partly in that judgments from God shall make them base and contemptible, if not also confound them with horror, that they should have taken part against the church with those who ruin themselves; for "shame shall cover Edom" when he is destroyed by the Chaldeans, with whom he joined against Judah.

5. Judgments upon the troublers and enemies of the church are without moderation and hope of recovery, as coming from the hand of justice and of a jealous God. "You shall be cut off forever"; for, though there may be some relenting under this or that particular stroke, yet (unless repentance prevails) justice makes what they get but an earnest of more, and pursues them to all eternity, as this stroke of Edom is expounded (Mal. 1:4).

> Ver. 11. In the day that you stood on the other side, in the day that the strangers carried away captive his forces, and foreigners entered into his gates and cast lots upon Jerusalem, you were as one of them.

Edom's violence is more particularly described by showing positively what he had done. In the day of the church's trouble, he was not only an idle spectator, forbearing to assist his brother, but he concurred with the enemy as one of them to help forward the affliction.

1. Many sad afflictions may come upon the privileged people of God when God is provoked; not only sufferings for truth, which have comfort, but judgments full of bitterness and calamity; for here "strangers carry away their forces, enter the gates" by force, "and cast lots upon Jerusalem," or divide their prey by lots, as Joel 3:3; Nahum 3:10.

2. Though the Lord in great severity punishes his people, yet he has an eye upon the carriage of every instrument of their calamity, to requite them accordingly, and would have his humbled people comforted in believing that his love is to those who do so; yet afterward he reckons with Edom for his behaviour, as that which he had closely marked, and he now reveals this doctrine to the church for her comfort.

3. An idle beholder or onlooker on the people of God's distress, as not concerned with it, is in God's account an enemy, especially one who is obliged to do otherwise; for it is a part of Edom's violence and cruelty that "he stood upon the other side," stayed aloof and did not come near to comfort, as the same word in the original is used (Ps. 38:11).

4. It is horrible wickedness before God, and will be specially marked by him, when false brethren not only countenance but actively concur and partake with enemies in oppressing the church of God. "Even you were as one of them" in their hostility, and a remarkable hostility, as being not only a brother and they but "strangers and foreigners," but as being a most active instrument in setting on the rest (Ps. 137:7).

> Ver. 12. But you should not have looked on the day of your brother, in the day that he became a stranger; neither should you have rejoiced over the children of Judah in the day of their destruction; neither should you have spoken proudly in the day of distress.
>
> 13. You should not have entered into the gate of my people in the day of their calamity; yea, you should not have looked on their affliction in the day of their calamity, nor have laid hands on their substance in the day of their calamity.

> 14. Neither should you have stood in the cross way
> to cut off those of his that did escape; neither should
> you have delivered up those of his that remained in
> the day of distress.

Edom's violence is yet further described by showing
negatively, what he ought not to have done and yet did.
In the day of Judah's calamity by the Chaldeans, he a
brother, who is born for adversity (Prov. 17:17) ought not
to have looked on their condition with delight, nor insulted
nor spoken blasphemously against God and his people (as
this is expounded, Ezek. 35:12, 13), nor entered the city
with the enemies and spoiled them of their goods, nor have
laid wait for the Jews who fled, to cut them off or to deliver
them into the enemy's hand.

1. The hour of the church's trial and correction is a very
sharp, dark, and violent blast. It is a day of calamity, destruction, and distress, a day in which he becomes a stranger
(that is, not dealt with as a privileged people, but as strangers) and is sent to a strange country in exile, and exercised
with strange lots. The church's heinous sins, and God's
jealousy over his confederate people, causes this; and the
Lord, in order to hasten over the church's afflictions, sends
it thick on.

2. The church of God suffering much must not therefore
think to be exempted from more trial; but must, by what
they suffer, be taught submission to yet further exercise
if the Lord will. Judah, in their distress and calamity, must
yet have more from Edom.

3. Though wicked men walk after the lusts and passions
of their own hearts, and stick at nothing, yet the Lord will
let them know that they stand obliged by a law to duty; and
its violation God will note, aggravate, and punish. Though
Edom satisfied himself and his passion in what he did against
Jacob, yet the Lord tells him, "you should not" have done
thus and thus, but were obliged by the law to do otherwise,
being both a brother and a neighbour.

4. To add affliction to the afflicted is great cruelty, especially when it is done by those from whom comfort might
in reason be expected. "You should not have looked on the
day of your brother." This adds to Edom's sin, that he chose
such a time to let out his hatred.

5. As a careless or greedy look on the affliction of the
people of God, as if it were a pleasant spectacle, is a further degree of their trial and affliction, so it is Esau-like,

and the badge of a reprobate disposition, to take pleasure in such a sight; for it is twice marked that he looked on the day of his brother, as an evidence of his cruelty in adding that to their affliction (Ps. 22:17).

6. Rejoicing of enemies and their blasphemies against God, his truth, and his people's privileges in him, is an unusual and sore trial of the church when she is in affliction; and to become insolent with success is the badge of wicked men, and a cause for which God will plead against them; for it is another challenge that "Edom rejoiced over Judah in the day of their destruction, and spoke proudly in the day of distress."

7. The Lord will not forget the least injuries done by any to the church, even when greater wrongs are being done to them, which might seem to hide the lesser. Though the Chaldeans were now bringing all to ruin, yet the Lord takes notice of an insolent eye, proud looks, entering into the gate, and laying hands on substance.

8. Apostates and false brethren are most cruel enemies and persecutors of those whom they desert. Edom the brother, besides all his insulting and joining with the enemy, did yet more, and "stood in the cross way to cut off those who did escape," and "delivered up the remnant" when it seems the Chaldeans had given over.

9. Even when God is afflicting his church and setting loose the reins to the fury of men against them, yet he does not quit his interest in them. In the midst of all this storm from the Chaldeans and Edom, the Lord gives them the covenant-title, "My people." Sin may procure affliction, but every provocation will not make void the covenant.

> Ver. 15. For the day of the Lord is near upon all the heathen. As you have done, it shall be done unto you; your reward shall return upon your own head.
>
> 16. For as you have drunk upon my holy mountain, so shall all the heathen drink continually. Yea, they shall drink, and they shall swallow down, and they shall be as though they had not been.

The Lord repeats the threatening, and shows that whereas no brotherly obligation or sense of duty to God had moved Edom to desist, yet there is another reason more touching, why he should not be so insolent — the heathen would have their day of it, and shortly, and particularly Edom. It is just with God to recompence their injuries done to the church; and as his own people had drunk of the cup of affliction, so he will make Edom (with others) drink of his judgment to their own destruction.

1. God by his universal providence is sovereign Lord and Judge of all men, even of those who do not know him nor acknowledge him, to take trial of their ways and punish them; for there is a day of the Lord upon all the heathen, a day of judicial cognition and recompence, and a day in which he will prove himself God upon them.

2. The Lord's correcting of his church is a presage and pledge of vengeance to come on the world and enemies. When Judah is in distress, the day of the Lord on all the heathen is near; when they have drunk, the heathen shall drink.

3. The Lord will not be owing his enemies anything for afflicting his people, but will pay them in their own coin and make them scholars at the school they bred the church with, for such is Edom's doom: "As you have done, it shall be done unto you; your reward shall return upon your own head."

4. No external privilege exempts a people from affliction, when it is for their good and their sinful temper calls for it. "You have drunk upon my holy mountain," says the Lord to Judah; but still he afflicts her.

5. It is the church's advantage to get the first measure of trials and judgments, that they may be easiest. The nearer the bottom of the cup of God's wrath, the more dregs, which are reserved for the wicked to destroy them. "They have drunk upon my holy mountain," and are yet preserved and spoken to, but "the heathen shall drink continually, and swallow down, and be as if they had not been," that is, utterly confused.

6. The Lord's correcting of his people is a means to endear them the more to him, and to make them more precious in his eyes. This sentence against the heathen is given to comfort and assure the church, and make her confident of his good will, in that he will avenge her quarrel.

> Ver. 17. But upon mount Zion shall be deliverance, and there shall be holiness, and the house of Jacob shall possess their possessions.

The rest of this prophecy contains comfortable promises to the church now in trouble, of which however Judah had some taste at their return from the captivity and afterwards.

And though the church of the gospel are getting continual performance of them in a spiritual way, yet at least some of them seem to point more especially to the time of the conversion and saving of all Israel (Rom. 11). In this verse there is promised to the church deliverance and evasion from all her troubles, holiness, and restitution to their former possessions; not only what they were deprived of by the captivity, but the whole house of Jacob, to what was given them by covenant made with their fathers, which is yet unaccomplished.

1. Though the Lord, in the time of the church's trouble, withholds from her the possession of her pleasant things, yet his thoughts and purposes of love are then as large and sure to her as ever, as she may read from the word, though she see it not in dispensations. The time of Judah's trouble is a time in which he makes many promises.

2. Not only is there in the greatest afflictions of the church still some to escape, since it is impossible that she should totally perish; but the church may expect complete deliverance from all her evils in due time, for "upon mount Zion shall be deliverance."

3. Holiness is the inseparable companion of blessed deliverance, and is a means to secure it to the church, for where there is deliverance "there shall be holiness." Holiness is an evidence of God's dwelling in the church, and a token that he will establish his own habitation and preserve them as his consecrated people, and not allow them to be profaned and polluted with invasion of the enemies as formerly; and thus also holiness is sometimes to be taken (Joel 3:17; Isa. 52:1), as the fruit of the holy Lord's dwelling among them and setting them apart for himself.

4. Holiness is not only the church's duty, to seek after it, but it is the promise of the Lord, who undertakes to work it in her. It is a promise, "there shall be holiness"; they shall be a holy people, enjoy God's presence in holy ordinances, and be preserved from violence of enemies.

5. The mercies of the church, whether spiritual or temporal, are sure, and will be recovered after they have been suspended from the comfort and use of them for a long time. "The house of Jacob shall possess their hereditary possessions," as the word is, after long captivity and exile.

Ver. 18. And the house of Jacob shall be a fire, and the house of Joseph a flame, and the house of Esau for stubble, and they shall kindle in them and devour

> them, and there shall not be any remaining of the house
> of Esau, for the Lord has spoken it.

The next promise is of the utter ruin of Edom for the
church's sake; and of all the inveterate enemies of the
church, especially of the church of converted Israel, who
shall be the occasion and cause, if not also the instruments,
of their enemies' destruction.

1. The church of God will never lack inveterate and cruel
enemies, nor difficulties, while she is in the world. Not only
Judah in the time of her captivity, but the church in her
restoration by Christ, when they share of this deliverance,
have a house of Esau against them. When the church has
corruptions, let her look for difficulties in them as well.

2. Opposition of enemies to the church only contributes
to make way for God's letting out many proofs of his love
in helping and delivering her; as this promise teaches

3. Opposition to the church is a certain pledge of the utter
destruction of opposers; and the Lord is able, when he
pleases, to make his weak people strong to bring it about.
This promise that Jacob shall be a fire implies not only
that Edom shall be utterly consumed as flame devours a
stubble, but that their meddling with the church shall be the
cause of their ruin, as if stubble attempting to put out a
fire were burned itself. This was in part accomplished
when the Jews after their captivity destroyed the Edomites,
as history records.

4. The word of God and the omnipotence and fidelity of him
who speaks it, are sufficient to confirm the church's faith in
the certainty of most improbable things. Whatever unlikeli-
hood there is in this promise, it is removed by this: "For
the Lord has spoken it."

> Ver. 19. And they of the south shall possess the mount
> of Esau, and they of the plain, the Philistines; and they
> shall possess the fields of Ephraim, and the fields of
> Samaria, and Benjamin shall possess Gilead.
>
> 20. And the captivity of this host of the children of
> Israel shall possess that of the Canaanites even unto
> Zarephath, and the captivity of Jerusalem which is in
> Sepharad shall possess the cities of the south.

It is further promised that the church shall not only have
restitution, but enlargement of their possessions, enjoying
all their own, and possessing what had been their enemies'.

The Jews in the south shall take in Edom with their portion; they who dwell in the plain shall enjoy the Philistines' land, as lying nearest them; and all their own borders shall be recovered, not only Ephraim, Samaria, and Benjamin, but Gilead also beyond Jordan. And for further confirmation, the Lord foretells that the numerous captivity of Israel should possess their northern border to Zarephath, or Sarepta, toward Sidon (1 Kings 17:9), and that the captives of Jerusalem and Judah in Sepharad (conceived to be a place in Chaldea) should possess their south border. Now concerning the accomplishment of this promise it cannot be said that anything done by the Maccabees and their successors, or obtained by Herod and his successors from the Romans, was the full performance, since these things come far short of what was here foretold. Besides, the children of Israel, the ten tribes, are expressly mentioned in this prophecy. Nor does the taking of the place in a spiritual sense fully exhaust the meaning, as there are such express designations of places to be possessed, and of several troops of captives to possess the several places; and therefore it seems to point further to the restitution of Israel to their own land and the enlargement of their border, when they shall turn to Christ in the latter days (Rom. 11:25, 26). However, the promise may teach us:

1. The afflictions of the church, through God's blessing, tend to their advantage and gain; for the captivity are to get not only their own land, but the mount of Esau and the Philistines, which they had not had before their captivity.

2. Christ in his church will gain ground on his enemies, and possess and reign over them, either by their voluntary conversion or by violent subjection and destruction; for so much does this promise, spiritually taken, imply.

3. The privileges of the people of God are irrevocable and immutable, and will break forth in comfortable fruits after long and sad interruptions. This is again signified and taught by Israel's possessing the fields of Ephraim, and Samaria and Benjamin with Gilead (as the original has it), of which they have been so long deprived.

4. The Lord marks every distress and captivity of his people, and what becomes of them, and may manifest much of his goodness to those whom he has sorely afflicted and brought down with corrections. Though the captivity was sent away with much ignominy, and carried far off, yet the Lord knows where they are, and will restore them to their lands and cause them to possess the gates of their enemies.

> Ver. 21. And saviours shall come up on mount Zion to
> judge the mount of Esau, and the kingdom shall be
> the Lord's.

The Lord further promises fit instruments to be raised up in the church to deliver her and manage the cause of God against enemies, as of old, when the Lord raised up judges to deliver Israel. By this we are to understand, not only spiritually, that Christ will send to the church his apostles and messengers, who instrumentally save the elect (1 Tim. 4:16) by holding forth Christ in the word of salvation, and who by their doctrine condemn the world; but that in all ages, and especially in the church of converted Israel, God will raise up instruments of deliverance to the church, as he did also in the times between the captivity and coming of Christ.

1. The church of Christ will not lack fit instruments to promote her happiness, for saviours shall come up on mount Zion.

2. The allowance of the church of God is salvation eternal and temporal also, insofar as is fit for her to receive. Therefore the instruments sent to her are called saviours, to wit, in an instrumental way.

3. The doctrine of the gospel in the mouth of Christ's servants does reprove, judge, and condemn the world and all the enemies of Christ; and this judgment is seconded with spiritual plagues, and sometimes temporal, until the day comes when the word shall judge them, and they shall receive a complete recompence according to it. Thus do some of Christ's instruments judge the mount of Esau.

4. The Lord is sovereign in all the world, even over his enemies; so when he raises up instruments for the church's good, he will bless them and by them bring his enemies to an account, and execute his sentence against them. These instruments of the church's temporal deliverance do judge the mount of Esau, when God delivers enemies into their hand as his delegates to pour his vengeance upon them.

The last and great promise is that God in his Christ shall have a kingdom in his church and among their enemies.

1. Where Christ sets up his church, there he sets up his kingdom also, and will be acknowledged as such; for the kingdom shall be his.

2. No dominion or sovereignty is to be acknowledged in the true church, but Christ's alone; he alone has power to

make laws binding the conscience, to institute ordinances, enjoin censures, appoint officers, by his own courts to judge his own house. "For the kingdom shall be the Lord's"; all other saviours, or instruments of deliverance, must serve him, and his officers must content themselves with a ministry.

3. The kingdom of Christ is matter of comfort to the true church and godly, it being sweet to live under his yoke and protection; for it is a promise. "The kingdom shall be the Lord's."

4. Christ holds his kingdom by a certain and firm tenure, as being made sure to him by the infallible promise of God, as here is recorded in holy Scripture; and upon this ground may the church, notwithstanding all opposition, expect the day when the kingdoms of this world shall become the kingdoms of our Lord and of his Christ, and he shall reign forever and ever (Rev. 11:15).

JONAH

The Argument

Jonah had prophesied in Israel, in or a little before the days of Jeroboam the son of Joash (2 Kings 14:25), but with little success, as may be gathered from a consideration of the times in which he lived. He is sent to preach to Nineveh, the chief city of the Assyrian Empire; but disobeying the command, he is sharply punished by God until he is humbled for his folly. And being brought to follow the second call, upon Jonah's preaching and Nineveh's repentance God spares them. The prophet, repining at this, is reproved by God. In sum, the prophet's frailty is a message to all, and especially to disobedient servants; and the repentance of the Ninevites, and God's dealing with them, holds out his riches in mercy, and may convince all who are unfruitful under the plenty of preaching. Though this is a history, it is justly reckoned among the prophets, since the penman was a prophet, and since the chief subject of it is a prediction of things to come. Though Jonah was in some things a type of Christ (Matt. 12:37, 40), yet the consideration of that is to be remitted to its proper place; to speak of him as a type further than is opened by Christ, is unsafe.

Chapter I

The parts of this chapter are: 1. Jonah's disobedience to the Lord's call; he essayed to fly to Tarshish when he should have gone to Nineveh (ver. 1-4). 2. The correction of his disobedience; the Lord by a mighty storm at sea pursues him till, by lot and his own confession, he is found guilty and gives out his own doom, which is executed by the mariners, though with much reluctance (ver. 5-17). 3. His preservation in his correction by a fish prepared to swallow him (ver. 17).

Ver. 1. Now the word of the Lord came to Jonah the son of Amittai, saying,

2. Arise, go to Nineveh, that great city, and cry against it; for their wickedness has come up before me.

Here Jonah gets a commission and calling to go and preach against that great city Nineveh, and stoutly accuse and threaten them for their great wickedness, which was crying unto God for vengeance. From this learn:

1. The servants of God are not to be at their own disposing, but to be employed in service as the Lord thinks fit; for Jonah, after his employments in Israel, is put upon strange service of leaving his country and going to a barbarous and wicked people to carry hard tidings, which might be full of hazard.

2. Great and flourishing places ordinarily have great and crying sins; for the wickedness of that great city came up before God.

3. As abounding sin is not in a cold way to be spoken against, but with all zeal and urgency, so the Lord's servants having commission from him may and ought boldly to plead his controversy, and for him, against greatest persons or places; for Jonah is sent to cry against the great city and their wickedness.

4. Greatest sinners are ordinarily most secure and insensible; thus Nineveh, whose sins have come up before God, needs that the prophet should cry.

5. The Lord's reason for sending Jonah there to preach, was not only to show that God is Lord of all the earth and a punisher of sin even among pagans, or to give some instance of sending his word unto the gentiles, but was more especially: (a) To leave a standing witness in the repentance of Nineveh, against all who obstinately contemn the gospel, as this passage is commented upon by Christ (Matt. 12:41). (b) To forewarn all of the removing of the Lord's messengers, when their message is not received. Therefore Jonah was sent away from Israel, which was now desperate in its backsliding (Matt. 21:43). (c) To convince all that he takes no pleasure in the death of sinners; though Nineveh's wickedness has come up before God, yet Jonah is sent to warn them before the stroke comes on.

> Ver. 3. But Jonah rose up to flee unto Tarshish from the presence of the Lord, and went down to Joppa, and found a ship going to Tarshish. So he paid the fare, and went down into it, to go with them to Tarshish from the presence of the Lord.

Here we have Jonah's disobedience to this call. He was surprised with the novelty of such a command, and fearing hazard or lack of success, or, as may be gathered from 4:2, that if the threatenings should not be executed, he might be reputed a false prophet and so be exposed to contempt (1 Kings 22:8, 18; 2 Kings 9:11), therefore he resolves to flee from God to Tarshish in Cilicia; not that he denied his universal presence in all the world, but (as the original bears) he fled "from before the face of the Lord," that is, from the land where God usually manifested himself to the prophets, and from obeying the Lord, as a rebellious servant fleeing from his master in whose presence he stood. He follows this resolution; and finding at Joppa a ship, he sets to the journey, it being safer and nearer to travel by sea than by land.

1. It is a usual fault in men to examine God's command by their own wisdom or will, and to obey or disobey as they judge; so does Jonah here. "He rose up to flee," and so do all who look more to a reason for God's commands satisfactory to them, than to the will of the commander.

2. Even the precious servants of the Lord have so much unmortified corruption that (being left to themselves) they may be driven on in very high fits of disobedience; Jonah, a prophet, resists the will of God.

3. Rebellion in the children of God may not only be a sudden temptation or a fit shortly shaken off, but they may go on long in it, and with great deliberation; for all the while Jonah was going to Joppa, lading the ship and launching out (all the while the Lord trying his determination), he continues in his resolution.

4. Men in their rebellion are ordinarily so addicted to their own will, that they are blind and inconsiderate, not pondering any inconvenience that may ensue, but will hazard all rather than be crossed in their purposes. This appears in Jonah; knowing the Lord, he will rather disobey him and yet think to prosper. He will rather lose the great privilege of standing before the Lord to receive prophetic revelations, than to lose his own will. This is twice noted, to show his great madness. Yea, he will rather be at charges to pay the fare, and hazard to sea with pagan men, than go among pagans at God's command.

5. Success in a way of rebellion against God is a snare, leading the rebel on to sadder corrections. Therefore Jonah found a ship ready, and had opportunity to launch out, that he may get a sharper rod at sea, where pagans should be witnesses, and not Israel.

> Ver. 4. But the Lord sent out a great wind into the sea,
> and there was a mighty tempest in the sea, so that the
> ship was like to be broken.

Now follows Jonah's correction. The Lord by a violent tempest, likely to break the ship, pursues him until he is found guilty and cast into the sea. Whence learn:

1. A storm will sooner or later overtake those who rebel against God, though they were his own people; for Jonah went his own way, but the Lord sent out a great wind.

2. God is sovereign Lord of the winds, in the sea as well as the dry land, and can arm any creature he pleases against a rebel. The Lord sent out the great wind and caused a mighty tempest in the sea.

3. To be in company with wicked men, or with men in a wicked way of rebellion against God, is dangerous, and may involve society in hazards with them; for the ship was like to be broken, and all the rest were in danger of perishing with Jonah.

> Ver. 5. Then the mariners were afraid, and cried each
> man unto his god, and cast forth the wares that were
> in the ship into the sea to lighten it of them; but Jonah
> had gone down into the sides of the ship, and he lay
> and was fast asleep.

In the next place, we have some effects and consequences of this tempest, by which at last God's purpose in it is brought forth. The first effect upon the mariners is fear, stirring them up to do all that is usual in such desperate cases for their own relief, both such means as they accounted divine, in calling on their gods, and such as were human, in casting out their commodities to lighten the ship; all which is amplified from Jonah's security, for he in the meantime was sleeping.

1. God can shake the hearts of stoutest men and make them afraid; for the mariners, otherwise stout at sea, are afraid.

2. Men may be afraid and much exercised about troubles, when the Lord does not intend them to be hurt by them; the mariners are afraid of the storm sent out to pursue Jonah and not them, though they had their own gross sins.

3. Even nature's light may teach men to ascribe things to the hand of a sovereign Lord, and teach them that without

acknowledging this there can be no safety in dangers; for so does these pagans' practice teach us, for they in their fear cried each man to his god.

4. As nature's light in corrupted man will mislead him in taking up the true God, so when men turn their back upon the true God and the knowledge of him, they become vain in their imaginations, and endless in seeking out false gods and confidences. Therefore among pagans, even in one ship, there are more false gods than one: "They cried every man to his god." There is no certainty when the true God is forsaken.

5. Although men ought not to be unwilling to yield up their life to God, when or wherever he in his providence shall be pleased to call for it, yet life is so precious that nothing worldly is too dear to be employed to preserve it. Nature's light teaches this to the mariners, who cast out all the wares that were in the ship as a means of preserving their lives.

6. Ordinarily those who are most guilty, and whom affliction is pointing at, are most secure under it; for all this while Jonah, the guilty man, was fast asleep.

7. The conscience of a renewed man may, after it is wounded by a gross sin, be very dead and stupefied for a time; for fleeing from his master, Jonah lay fast asleep in the midst of the storm, and had gone down to the sides of the ship for that end.

8. It is ordinary for guilty consciences to shift and sleep away challenges, without finding the true remedy; Jonah had gone down to the sides of the ship to sleep away his trouble.

> Ver. 6. So the shipmaster came to him and said to him, What do you mean, O sleeper? Arise, call upon your God, if so be that God will think upon us that we perish not."

To the end that the Lord may reveal the guilty man, the shipmaster is set on work to waken Jonah, that he might try his interest with his God (whom they knew not yet to be the true God), if possibly he had more power or good will to his worshippers than theirs had. This was the first step to Jonah's being revealed.

1. A child of God may sometimes miscarry so far through infirmity, negligence, and temptation, that even a pagan by nature's light may see him reproveable and blameworthy; so Jonah is reproved by the shipmaster.

2. It is deeply censurable and absurd, even to nature's eyes, to be secure in trouble. "What meanest thou, O sleeper? Arise!"

3. Variety of false gods hold men in great suspense and uncertainty; though every man had cried to his god (v. 5), yet they are not settled, but will have Jonah to persuade his God also, if he is better than the rest. This is implied in that doubtful speech, "if so be that God will think upon us."

4. Nature's light will acknowledge that the true God has power to deliver in most extreme dangers, for in this great tempest they assert it: "if God thinks upon us, we will not perish."

5. Though in a calm day nature's conceit will boast of merit, yet in a strait even natural men are forced to have recourse to the favour of God alone; for this pagan has no ground of hope that they shall not perish except in God's thinking (or shining, as the word also signifies; that is, looking favorably) on them.

> Ver. 7. And they said each one to his fellow, Come and let us cast lots, that we may know for whose cause this evil is upon us. So they cast lots, and the lot fell upon Jonah.

The second effect of this tempest tends to a further discovery of Jonah as the guilty man. Being awakened and not confessing his sin, the tempest continues notwithstanding all they had done. Therefore the mariners, instead of searching each man into himself and finding his own guilt, began to suspect that God was pursuing some notorious guiltiness in some of them. Since none voluntarily confessed it, they resolve with common consent to seek it out by lot. Whatever fault there was in this, yet God's providence ordered it so that the lot fell upon Jonah, to awaken his conscience.

1. Nature may lead men in great difficulty to consider sin as the cause, as this consultation imports; it was true in this case, and it is always true that sin is the root which affliction springs from. Yet nature goes not so far as to lead men to lay sin to heart in common and ordinary crosses, or to look on common and ordinary sins as provocation sufficient to bring on saddest trials; for they must seek some unusual cause here, so far from looking on afflictions as trials of faith, or to prevent sin.

2. Men in nature do not so much become sensible of sin from the law of God having authority in their heart, as grope

for it in some trial and difficulty. We hear nothing of their sense of guilt before, but now in their trial they begin to ask for whose cause this evil is upon them.

3. Prayer in a day of distress will not avail until sin procuring it is searched out and dealt with; so much do these pagans acknowledge, when along with prayer they set themselves to seek out the guilty and to know for whose cause this evil is upon them.

4. Afflictions sharply pursuing may put men, otherwise careless, to seek out sin, and not to let those sleep who gladly would and would have been insensible of sin. These men are so put to it that they are willing to have the quarrel sought out, and to submit themselves to a lot for that effect. Afflictions will command men to turn from iniquity, who would not hear such a charge in any other language (Job 36: 10).

5. The Lord's all-seeing eye perceives every secret sin, and his providence overrules most contingent and uncertain events, and holily orders the rash actions of men so as to bring about his own purposes by them. These men acknowledge that the guilty is known, though not to them, and that the determination of a contingent lot, overruled by a deity, is a true evidence for whose cause this evil is. And though it was a fault in them not to search themselves, and to consult by lots without special warrant, yet God overrules the lot to reveal Jonah.

6. The Lord's controversy is sometimes greater and more severely prosecuted against his own children for their miscarriages, than against pagans and gross idolaters among whom they may be. The lot, guided by God, fell upon Jonah, signifying his rebellion to be the cause of all their danger, rather than their idolatry, though openly practiced in the height of their calamity; for: (a) Rebellion is as idolatry (1 Sam. 15:23), and so much the grosser, since it is in a child of God. (b) Although they had worshipped that which was no god, yet none of them had behaved themselves toward a supposed deity as he had done toward the true God (Jer. 2:10, 11). (c) God may wink at sins in pagans, but will not let his own child go on unreclaimed (Amos 3:2); it is mercy to pursue them for their folly, and amend them.

> Ver. 8. Then they said unto him, Tell us, we pray you, for whose cause this evil is upon us. What is your occupation, and whence do you come? What is your country, and of what people are you?

The guilty man, being now discovered by God, is examined by the mariners to find out the particular fact, but very discreetly, as they supposed the sin might be something of which his nation and people were guilty, and not particularly himself. And therefore concerning himself they inquire of his calling and journey, if they were unlawful, and of his country and place, if they were accursed.

1. Men have need of full information before they give out sentence upon any; for, though Jonah was taken by a lot and these men might in passion have shortly rid themselves of him, the occasion and cause of their trouble, yet they will further inform themselves, and very meekly: "Tell us, we pray you."

2. Charity, even in refined nature, does not easily admit of a hard construction of any, or without sure grounds. Therefore they first inquire, "Tell us for whose cause this evil is upon us," desiring to be more particularly informed, and not being willing to hold him for a wicked man until they should hear further.

3. In men's callings, employments, country, and people there is hazard of sin; so by those circumstances much of men's faults may be found out. Therefore Jonah is questioned concerning all these, for besides unlawful callings and places, every particular country and people have their own temptations to particular sins, from which sins of a generation or calling it is hard to keep free.

4. Men often, following their own ends, engage in courses without all consideration, until a day of trouble sets them to trace back and make inquiry; for these mariners, minding their own gain, put none of these questions to Jonah when they took him aboard, till the storm led them to see their folly and rashness.

5. The Lord, in pursuing for sin, knows how to order challenges so as to make sin most bitter to the guilty. Therefore he orders the mariners' moving of the questions, every one of which might be a sting to Jonah's conscience, that he a prophet should be fleeing from God, coming from the holy land and the church, going on a way without a warrant from God for it, etc.

Ver. 9. And he said unto them, I am an Hebrew, and I fear the Lord, the God of heaven, who has made the sea and the dry land.

10. Then the men were exceedingly afraid, and said to him, Why have you done this? (For the men knew

> that he fled from the presence of the Lord, because he
> had told them.)

Jonah's confession in answer to their question, clears up the matter for which God was pursuing him. Thereat the idolaters (dazzled with the apprehension of the majesty of God) are astonished through fear, amazed at and reproving his presumption. Hence learn:

1. God will not allow iniquity, no matter how well concealed, to lurk, but will bring it out to light, especially where he has a purpose of mercy to the sinner. Therefore Jonah is pursued until he confesses his sins, even before pagans: "he told them that he fled."

2. Sin is not barely to be confessed, but ought to be aggravated by every person who would be approved as sensible of it; for this speech, "I am an Hebrew, and I fear the God of heaven," implies that it was a great sin in him, a member of the church, to dally, and that with such a great God.

3. The true God is to be commended by all his children, and set forth, as they are able, before natural men, that they may have no occasion to think basely of him; for this much does his description of God, who has made the sea and the dry land (intimating that he had raised that tempest) import.

4. It is a fearful condition to be found in a way of rebellion against the great and mighty God; therefore these pagans, hearing of the greatness of God and of Jonah's sin, "were exceedingly afraid, and said unto him, Why have you done this?"

5. The more men see of God's hand in judgments, especially that he is pursuing for sin, the more they are affected. They were afraid before of the tempest (v. 5); but now, when they see God pursuing rebellion by it, they are exceedingly afraid.

6. The light and judgment of natural men may be clearer in many things than the light of a child of God under temptation; for they feared exceedingly, though Jonah himself did not. "Why have you done this?"

> Ver. 11. Then said they unto him, What shall we do unto
> you, that the sea may be calm unto us? (For the sea
> wrought and was tempestuous.)
>
> 12. And he said unto them, Take me up and cast me
> forth into the sea; so shall the sea be calm unto you;
> for I know that for my sake this great tempest is upon
> you.

Being found out, and by his own confession convicted of guilt, Jonah now pronounces his own sentence against himself. He, the cause of all their trouble, should be cast into the sea, since the sea still raged, testifying that God's anger was not appeased:

1. Confessing, yea, and repenting for scandalous sins, will not sometimes exempt from such corrections as may make the guilty see more of God's displeasure and of the desert of sin. Though Jonah had confessed his sin, and that with remorse, as may appear from the confession and that which follows here, yet "the sea wrought and was tempestuous," as if seeking him.

2. It is a kindly fruit of affliction when men are taught tenderness and humanity, and a greater subjection of spirit to follow the revealed will of God under it. Therefore the mariners consult with him, "What shall we do unto you?", as minded in humanity and compassion to do nothing without his own consent, and intending to reverence what he should say, as a prophet of God.

3. A sinner truly humbled will be sensible of the huge desert of sin, and will submit and reverence the righteousness of God in saddest punishments. So Jonah counsels: "Take me up and cast me into the sea"; not out of any bitterness, hatred, or weariness of his own life, but from a prophetic spirit, knowing God's mind, and from the sense of sin, acknowledging the equity of the sentence in his conscience.

4. It will be most sad and bitter to a humbled sinner to be accessory, by his provocation, to the afflictions of others, and to draw on common calamities. "Cast me forth," says he; "so shall the sea be calm unto you."

Ver. 13. Nevertheless the men rowed hard to bring it to the land, but they could not; for the sea wrought and was tempestuous against them.

14. Therefore they cried unto the Lord and said, We beseech thee, O Lord, we beseech thee, let us not perish for this man's life, and lay not upon us innocent blood; for thou, O Lord, hast done as it pleased thee.

15. So they took Jonah and cast him forth into the sea, and the sea ceased from her raging.

As Jonah had pronounced sentence against himself, the mariners execute it. But first, out of compassion toward him, they used their utmost endeavours to get to any land by rowing, but to no purpose, for God made the sea fight against them. Therefore they pray and protest that their execution of the sentence might not be imputed to them as bloodshed, he being innocent in respect to them, and what they were now to do being undertaken only in obedience to God's sovereign providence and will revealed by Jonah himself. And on these conditions they proceed to execute the sentence, upon which follows their deliverance from their difficulty.

1. Even humanity in natural men will be tender and compassionate toward those who are in trouble, though justly procured; especially if they know them to have relation to God and to be sensible of their condition. Though Jonah had been the cause of their trouble, yet they looked on him as a prophet of God; and pitying him when they heard his confession and sentence against himself, "they rowed hard to bring it to land," and would trouble themselves to exempt him.

2. Even refined nature has an antipathy against bloodshed and manslaughter, if in justice it could be avoided. This appears in their endeavours and earnest protestations before they execute a just sentence.

3. The utmost endeavours of men will not frustrate the purposes of God, nor free a guilty sinner from his stroke. "They rowed hard" to exempt him, "but the sea wrought and was tempestuous against them," as pursuing him, and them also, if they did not do what God revealed to be their duty.

4. God in his sovereignty disposes of all things at his pleasure and will; this they acknowledge and see in his sentence. "Thou, O Lord, hast done as it pleased thee."

5. Extremest necessities give no latitude to men to do anything except what is warranted by God, for they judge that no necessity could free them from the guilt of innocent blood in casting out Jonah, but only God's revealed will.

6. In obedience to the sovereign will and pleasure of God revealed to them, men are to go about actions which otherwise their inclinations are much averse from; for in obedience to the Lord's will "they took up Jonah and cast him forth," much against their own hearts.

7. As God is a severe chastiser of rebellion in his own dearest children, so rebellion against him deserves that the rebel should be cut off in a violent way, and that the Lord's earth or sea should not carry him; for so is Jonah cast forth into the sea.

8. The execution of justice upon the guilty in a society is a means of turning away judgments from the rest; when Jonah

was cast forth, "the sea ceased from her raging." (See Ps. 106:30.)

> Ver. 16. Then the men feared the Lord exceedingly, and offered a sacrifice unto the Lord, and made vows.

All these events are amplified from the effect they had upon the mariners. Observing all that was done, and no doubt having heard Jonah preach more of God than is recorded (as appears from ver. 10), they were moved to tremble and fear the true God, and testified it by sacrificing unto him (whether presently, for they were ignorant as yet, or at Jerusalem, we will not determine) and making vows for the future, they show that they would dedicate themselves to God and profess the true religion.

1. In one work the Lord may have more holy purposes than one, and besides what we see, may be doing many other things. While he is pursuing Jonah, he is also setting himself forth and preaching his power and justice to pagans, when Jonah refused to go to Nineveh and do it.

2. The Lord can in a short time, and by few means, produce strange effects and changes upon the children of men, though they had not heard of him before. Though it cannot be determined with certainty whether these mariners were indeed converted, or whether it was Jonah's doctrine or their apprehension of God in this work which wrought most upon them, yet it is certain that in this short while there was made in them a great change; "they feared the Lord exceedingly."

3. As the Lord can easily make up men's losses which they sustain in his providences, so it is his way sometimes to make up temporal losses with some spiritual advantage. These men, whose ship and lives were in hazard, and their goods lost, are made up by having a prophet among them and by being brought to know something of the true God, which made it a rich voyage.

4. The Lord's dispensations among a people, especially when they are accompanied by any of his word, call for them to improve them to some spiritual advantage; this their practice impresses upon us. By considering what they saw, felt, and heard, "they feared the Lord exceedingly."

5. God rightly considered and taken up, as he has revealed himself, and as he appears in some special acts of providence, is exceedingly dreadful and to be stood in awe of. They feared him exceedingly.

6. It is not a sufficient proof of men's receiving the fruit of God's dispensations toward them when they merely draw to some acknowledgement of him for the present, but grow negligent for the future. This they acknowledge in their practice: "they offered a sacrifice unto the Lord, and made vows" for the time to come, and engaged themselves to God.

> Ver. 17. Now the Lord had prepared a great fish to swallow up Jonah; and Jonah was in the belly of the fish three days and three nights.

The chapter closes with the narration of Jonah's preservation (though thus pursued by justice) in a fish's belly, where in a miraculous way he was kept three days and three nights.

1. When God is pursuing the rebellion of his children in a most severe way, yet he does not altogether cast off his mercy toward them, but out of its abundance he moderates their affliction. Though pursuing Jonah, yet the Lord had prepared a great fish to swallow him up.

2. God's providence overrules and directs the motions of irrational creatures and sea-monsters as pleases him. The Lord had prepared the fish, though it knew nothing but to range up and down in the sea, and swallow him as any other prey.

3. God may have a mercy and proof of love waiting upon his people in a time and place where it would be least expected. Jonah meets a mercy in the heart of a raging sea, into which he is cast in anger as if to be destroyed.

4. Though the mercy of God will not destroy his guilty people in their afflictions, yet his wisdom does not see it fitting wholly to deliver them at first; he will have their faith exercised. Jonah is here arrested three days and three nights between hope and perplexity, to exercise him further.

5. God can, when he sees fit, preserve his people from ruin in an incredible and miraculous way. Jonah is not only swallowed whole by the fish, not being hurt by its teeth, but is preserved in its belly three days and three nights, where he was in danger of choking for lack of breath, or of being digested by the fish into its own substance.

CHAPTER II

This chapter contains: 1. Jonah's exercise in the fish's belly (v. 1). 2. An ample declaration of his exercise, penned

after his deliverance, with an addition of praise; in which
he rehearses his trouble, exercise, and deliverance (v. 2)
and more fully enlarges the narration of his trouble and
exercise, and how by faith he obtained victory while he
was yet in the strait (ver. 3, 4). 3. Again he declares how
his temptation assaulted him afresh because of his hopeless
condition, that he may set forth God's great bounty in his
actual deliverance (ver. 5, 6). 4. This is all summed up
again (ver. 7). 5. By way of conclusion, he condemns men's
following of crooked ways (ver. 8) and promises praise (ver.
9). 6. A declaration of the way of his deliverance out of the
fish's belly (ver. 10).

> Ver. 1. Then Jonah prayed unto the Lord his God, out of
> the fish's belly.

From Jonah's exercise in his prison, learn:
1. It is a kindly fruit of sanctified exercise in trouble to
overcome insensibleness, bitterness, quarrelling, and the
like, and to set about humble prayer. "Jonah prayed."
2. It is requisite for the right performance of prayer in
a strait, that the supplicant take up God in the covenant of
grace, as his own, that so he may pray with humble confidence. "Jonah prayed unto the Lord his God."
3. The Lord's correcting of his people for their sins is no
evidence of his breaking covenant with them, nor should it
hinder a convinced saint from claiming an interest in God
as a ground of his approach unto him. Being under this sad
stroke, yet by faith Jonah prayed unto the Lord his God.
4. As no condition or state ought to discourage from
prayer, as if it were vain to use it, so rebels against God
may sue for his favour in hard conditions, because they
would not otherwise study to please him. Jonah prayed "out
of the fish's belly," where for disobedience to God he is put
to prayer with much disadvantage.

> Ver. 2. And he said, I cried by reason of my affliction
> unto the Lord, and he heard me; out of the belly of hell
> I cried, and thou didst hear my voice.

The issue of his trouble, as he records it after his deliverance, is that being brought to his grave by affliction, and
under the dominion of death, he yet prayed and was heard.
1. The exercises and experiences of the children of God
ought to be communicated one to another, as they have a

calling and opportunity, for mutual instruction and edification; for so does Jonah here. His prayer is not to be understood as if he had said it in the fish's belly, for it is not a prayer but rather a thanksgiving; but it rather shows what he expressed after his deliverance, and that he made a rehearsal of his whole condition for the edification of others.

2. Great afflictions or temptations arising from them, are so far from being just cause of discouragement to hinder our praying, that they ought to stir us up to more fervency and earnestness. Jonah cried because of his affliction, when he was so beset on every hand (as the word signifies) that he could not flee nor find relief; he took this as a call to seek help in God, and to turn to him, and to sharpen, as on a whetstone, his (otherwise) sluggish desires.

Out of the belly of hell he cried, when he was buried alive and put as it were under the dominion of death in the fish's belly; and when he felt the anger of God in all this, as a hell on earth, yet faith directs him to God. And when he was as far as heaven from hell, from his own sense of God and his favor, yet he looked on that as only an argument to move him to cry the louder.

3. As God can help in greatest distresses, so the prayers of the children of God in their deep afflictions, flowing from real indigence and need, will get a good answer. Jonah's faith, strengthened by God, saw the great distress when he cried in affliction and in the belly of hell; and in his experience he found the good answer, that he did not pray in vain: "He heard me." Prayer speeds best when necessity instructs its sincerity; and when it is spoken out of the dust, then faith will by prayer bring help from heaven to one little better than in hell.

4. The Lord's seasonable answering of his people's needy desires in their extremity will not only ease their griefs, but will be refreshing afterwards to think upon. Jonah repeats and dwells upon this mercy; "I cried and he heard me," twice over; and the oftener he looks upon it, the more he sees in it. The more it is thought on, the more it ought to enlarge our hearts with affection toward God, that our voices should be heard from the belly of hell, as is implied in his directing his last speech to God. "Thou didst hear my voice"; he speaks as one overcome with the kindness of God in it.

> Ver. 3. For thou hadst cast me into the deep, in the midst
> of the seas, and the floods compassed me about; all thy
> billows and thy waves passed over me.

Jonah is not content to have spoken so briefly of so rich a purpose, but to glorify the grace and mercy of God in supporting him in his strait and delivering him from it; but that he may edify the church, he enlarges the narration and speaks more particularly of every step of it. And first he shows the greatness of his trial, in that he had to do with an angry God, pursuing him in anger, who had taken and cast him into the sea, and into the depth and midst of it, where waves of seas without and waves of temptations within, overwhelmed him. Hence learn:

1. Serious thoughts and apprehensions of trouble are needful, not only when we are in it, to stir us up to prayer, but when delivered also, to set forth the greatness of mercy, for all this variety of expressions in setting out his trouble tend to this purpose. "I cried, for thou hadst cast me into the deep," to show also from what great danger he had been delivered, and what a mercy he thought it to be heard of God even when he was so dealing with him.

2. Much of God seen in our troubles will hide those who have been most instrumental and active in it; there is no word of the mariners, but "thou hadst cast me into the deep."

3. Unto the child of God, afflictions are nothing to bear in comparison to the displeasure of God who afflicts, and to the temptations which are raised. "All thy billows and waves," not only the billows raised by thee in the sea, to pursue me a rebel, but tides of tossing temptations, begotten by the sense of thy displeasure, "passed over me," so that I was overwhelmed and run down by one of them after another.

4. It may commend the rich mercy of God toward his children, and furnish rich matter of praise to him, that he does not allow them to quit him, but causes them to follow him when he seems to forsake them, and to flee to him, when he is pursuing in hot displeasure. The scope of Jonah's account of his trial and temptation tends also to set forth the grace of God, which had enabled him to cry to him in all this extremity. It was an admirable power of faith, supported by grace, to call on an angry God, to follow after him when he went away, to lay hold of him when he smote, to pray to him to desist from anger when he was threatening him with worse, and to look and seek for better tidings when he was run down with the current and tide of temptations.

> Ver. 4. Then I said, I am cast out of thy sight; yet I will
> look again toward thy holy temple.

He rehearses further his exercise upon this trial, that there was a conflict between unbelieving despair, concluding his rejection from God's favour and care, and faith, looking to God in heaven and to the covenant made in Christ with the elect, a sign of which was his presence on the mercy-seat in the temple at Jerusalem, toward which the godly were to direct their prayers (1 Kings 8). This gave him yet ground of hope.

1. It is the usual lot of the Lord's children to have not only outward afflictions to wrestle with, but spiritual temptations and sad conclusions, gathered from their troubles, which are sorer to endure than many simple afflictions; for so it was with Jonah while he was in the sea.

2. The children of the Lord in their troubles may be so tossed and divided between hope and despair that faith and unbelief will be striving for mastery; "I said, I am cast out; yet I will look again."

3. In a time of temptation, unbelief's word is usually first out, until faith comes and corrects it. Ordinarily what is said in haste is unbelief's language, and is to be unsaid again; for this comes out first: "I am cast out of thy sight."

4. A child of God may not only be assaulted with fits of despair, but may for a time be overcome with it and yield to it, and yet for all that recover his feet again; for Jonah once concluded and said, "I am cast out of thy sight."

5. It is ordinary under temptation to judge all of God's respect, care, and love, by our sense of his present dealing; so to be cast off by God as one whom he will not favour nor care for, nor take notice of, is the sorest of trials, especially to the child of God, who lives by God's favour. This is Jonah's apprehension and saddest complaint: "I am cast out of thy sight."

6. It is no new thing to see a child of God and vessel of mercy apprehending reprobation and rejection from God, in his sad and dark hour; for this is also Jonah's temptation.

7. Nor is it strange to see the children of God exercised and sadly afflicted with that which has never been nor will be, save in their own fearful apprehensions; for Jonah thinks himself to be cast off. When we reckon by our own deservings and by probabilities in a strait, and not by God's love and all-sufficiency, we cannot but draw sad conclusions, and our own spirits will make us work enough.

8. Temptations, even when they have overcome for a season, are not to be laid under and given way to, by the children of God, but ought to be resisted and set against, though they should (if it were possible) perish in the attempt. This is the way to honor God and get deliverance; for vanquished Jonah will not leave it so. "Yet will I look again."

9. That by which the children of the Lord must oppose all troubles, inward and outward, and resist temptations, is naked faith closely adhering to the covenant of grace made in Christ, and gathering hope of better dealing, which is imported in Jonah's looking again toward the holy temple, which was a sign of the covenant. To cast away confidence as useless in a strait; or not to venture faith until we are brought on by sense; or to lie by in willful unbelief, thinking that to be the way to get sense to lose our doubts; or to seek any footing for faith except in God's covenant and free grace in Christ, is the height of folly.

10. The weakest act of faith may do much good in a day of greatest need; for in all this extremity Jonah could do no more than "look again," as a poor banished man.

11. Faith in a time of need will find a way through many a dark impediment to find God. Therefore Jonah, enclosed in the sea, and not knowing where the Temple (toward which they were to pray) stood, will let faith and need seek it out.

12. It speaks much of God's praise that when his people are laid by with their temptations, yet he will not lose them, but recover them out of their deepest faints, and will make vanquished faith yet again to triumph over difficulties which they had judged insuperable. This is also recorded to his praise, not only that he persevered in crying when his trouble was great (ver. 2, 3), but that after he had once yielded to the temptation, he was strengthened to believe and look again.

> Ver. 5. The waters compassed me about, even to the soul; the depth closed me round about; the weeds were wrapped about my head.
>
> 6. I went down to the bottoms of the mountains; the earth with her bars was about me forever; yet thou hast brought up my life from corruption, O Lord my God.

He rehearses further how his temptation left him not so, but gathered strength anew from his hopeless condition in his trouble, seeing no deliverance, but as a condemned man cast into the prison of hell; for the waters (drunk by the fish, or by himself before he got into the fish, or the huge sea in which his life was endangered) had closed him in on every hand, and the sea-weeds were wrapped about him (either when the fish swallowed them down, or when the fish went down with him among them). The fish went with him to the very bottom of the sea, to the roots of the hills; and if he had gotten out of the fish and could have swum out of the sea, yet the steep rocks on that shore where the fish ranged with him, as so many bars, would have held him as in a perpetual prison. He here records all these grounds of fear, to set forth the mercy of God, who brought him out in safety when neither depth of sea nor steepness of shore could allow him any hope; as if he had been revived and brought out of the grave.

1. It is no unusual trial of a child of God in temptation, after he has resolved to adhere to God and hope in him, to see his resolution fail. By casting his eye upon his trouble and poring on it, he judges himself yet to be in a hopeless condition, and that he has been a fool ever to think otherwise; and yet for all this he may be happy. Jonah, now delivered, gives an account how after his resolution to believe (ver. 4) temptation set upon him again, and made him conclude himself a lost man and a perpetual prisoner.

2. The sense of an afflicted and sad condition is not soon to be forgotten, but to be kept fresh and carried along with every sight of mercy. Therefore the Lord allowed Jonah to take a second view of his condition, and Jonah now testifies that he is yet more sensible of what he would have been without God's help.

3. The more we study the difficulties of our afflicted conditions, the more we see reasons why we should admire and magnify the Lord in his deliverance of us; for after his former sight of his troubles (ver. 3), when he takes this other view of it, he sees yet more impossibility of being delivered without God.

4. It is the Lord's way with his people to let them see their difficulties to be past hope and irrecoverable, before he appears for them, that he may be the more eminently seen; for Jonah's aggravation of his trouble from hazard of life, depth of seas, and steepness of shore, implies that deliverance was impossible in his eyes.

5. Whatever may be the fears and apprehensions of saints under their troubles, yet in due time all that they will have to say of their greatest trials is that they have made way for God's manifesting himself in them. Therefore that sweet

return is subjoined to his hopeless trouble: "yet thou hast brought up my life."

6. Though the Lord would have his people enjoying an escape in the midst of their trouble, in living by faith, and will have faith tried to find how it will follow its look, yet it is his way also, when he sees fit and has tried their faith, to refute all their doubting thoughts with real deliverance. Therefore after the former breathing (ver. 4) and Jonah's fresh assault, he gets actual deliverance to end the controversy.

7. The Lord can give deliverance from deadly extremities, and can restore his people in safety, and their mercies to them, when they are no better in their own eyes than dead and rotten in their own graves. "For thou hast brought up my life from corruption," that is, his body from the fish's belly, where it was as in a grave ready to rot, and his soul from those terrors that would have consumed him.

8. In God's working for his people, much of his power and love is to be seen and acknowledged; this is imported in that sweet compellation, "O Lord my God."

> Ver. 7. When my soul fainted within me, I remembered the Lord, and my prayer came in unto thee, into thy holy temple.

Jonah's exercise and deliverance is again summed up in this, that when his spirit was ready to faint under a burden of affliction and terrors of conscience, he called God to mind, found encouragement to pray, and was heard. Learn hence:

1. The spirits of men, no matter how stout and courageous, yet will soon be overthrown and faint when left alone in trouble and temptation; for his soul fainted (or was overwhelmed with anxiety) within him.

2. Before the Lord works for his people, he usually lays them and their courage aside, that he may stain the pride of their glory and that no flesh may glory in his presence; for says Jonah, "my flesh fainted within me."

3. Much unbelief and discouragement flows from our infirmity and weakness, in not fixing our hearts to meditate on God, casting off other perplexing thoughts which we cannot resolve, and in not pondering seriously what God is and will be to his people, or has at any time been to ourselves. Jonah's remedy and antidote against fainting is, "I remembered the Lord."

4. Remembering and serious apprehension of God by

faith is a notable encouragement to prayer, and gives a good account of prayer's success; whereas to the unbeliever's sense his prayers wander, and they go he knows not where: "I remembered the Lord, and my prayer came in unto thee."

5. God's mercy is to be much seen and magnified in his answering of his peoples' prayers in their distress. "My prayer," says he, "came into thy holy Temple," that is, into heaven, the habitation of God's holiness. It was a wonder that such a rebel's prayers should be admitted; they were accepted by virtue of the covenant and promise made in Christ, not for any worth in them.

6. God's manifestation of himself in any place calls for holiness; therefore not only heaven but the temple at Jerusalem is called "thy holy temple," or "the temple of thy holiness"; not only because he is holy, but his presence here calls for holiness in all who approach him.

7. To be delivered from fainting in trouble, and to get access unto God by prayer, is the child of God's greatest mercy in trouble, as speaking special love, whatever his outward issue may be; therefore Jonah insists in commending this mercy of enlargement of soul (ver. 2, 4, 7).

> Ver. 8. They who observe lying vanities forsake their own mercy.

From all his exercise and deliverance, he gathers some conclusions by way of instruction and use from it. First he gives out his verdict of all by-ways, as depriving man of true happiness, and disappointing him in the end; by which we are not only to understand the courses of gross idolaters, but more generally all courses which men lay down for attaining happiness in anything besides God; and more particularly his own former folly and rebellion, in which he imagined himself to have found happiness and content; but on the contrary he ran from it and plunged himself in misery.

1. The experience of saints, from many changes and variety of conditions, ought to imprint in their hearts more serious and settled thoughts concerning true happiness and the right way of attaining it. Therefore Jonah, thus exercised and daunted, gathered this conclusion as a certain truth: "They who observe lying vanities forsake their own mercy."

2. When anything besides God, though lawful in the use for which God appointed it, is made the source of supreme happiness or confidence, it will not be able to answer the

expectation of the creature. Being observed as man's happiness, they are vanities because of their emptiness to supply the creature's need or to satisfy its desire; and they are lying vanities because for the present, if we are not attentive, they delude us with a vain show, and in the end they miserably disappoint.

3. Though things stand thus, yet men are so deluded and doted that they will place their confidence and look for happiness in those things which will disappoint them; there are those who "observe (esteem, care for, expect, depend upon, and pursue after) lying vanities."

4. By pursuing happiness apart from God and his way, men do indeed deprive themselves of happiness and consequently run upon their own ruin; therefore they forsake mercy. Since happiness is to be found only in God, they who follow vain courses do in effect renounce and forsake God, who will not be joined with idols, and who is provoked to plague things which we put in his place.

5. The portion of those who seek happiness in God and in his way only, is mercy, and the mercy an all-sufficient God can give. Therefore those who take another way forsake this mercy, that is, their happiness flowing from the infinite mercy of God, as all happiness to lost man is mercy's gift.

6. By forsaking God, men can take nothing from him, but all the ruin comes back to them; for they forsake their own mercy, but they do not deprive him of happiness.

7. Men in their forsaking of God can have no just challenge or accusation against him for putting them away, but they must take all the blame upon themselves, for it is their own mercy which they forsake; their own by offer, for notwithstanding his secret purpose, God yet excludes none from mercy to whom the offer is made, until they exclude themselves.

> Ver. 9. But I will sacrifice unto thee with the voice of thanksgiving; I will pay that which I have vowed. Salvation is of the Lord.

The second conclusion that Jonah gathers is that since the Lord had thus in his folly reclaimed him, and in his deep distress delivered him, he will testify his thankfulness by offering praise and performing what he had vowed in his trouble; and he will learn by this experience that deliverance can be expected from God only, and may be expected from him.

1. Mercy received calls for praise at the receiver's hand, as a testimony of his thankfulness for the mercy, and of his esteem of God who gave it. Jonah, thus delivered, will sacrifice.

2. The Lord's crossing and afflicting us in our wanderings, until we are brought back to obey the will of God, is to be acknowledged as a mercy and matter of praise; for such is the subject of Jonah's song, compared with the former verse. He will bless the Lord not only for deliverance, but that he had not been permitted to prosper in a wrong way.

3. Praise is that true sacrifice pointed at in the law by the thanksgiving offerings in the temple; therefore he gives praise the name of that sacrifice which shadowed it; "I will sacrifice with the voice of thanksgiving." See Heb. 13:15.

4. The truly godly under the law were taught by God not to rest upon these outward performances and offerings, but to press and seek after the spiritual duty and substance, and to make use of Christ, in whom alone even our best moral actions are accepted. Jonah holds forth that the voice of thanksgiving (that is, affectionate praise) was the sacrifice indeed. See Ps. 69:30, 31; Hos. 14:2. And by joining sacrifice with the voice of thanksgiving, he shows that his praise was offered up in and by that true sacrifice.

5. The Lord's people in their afflictions and deliverances will be made to see great necessity for making vows and binding themselves more firmly to their duty; for Jonah in his trouble had vowed, that is, bound himself with his own consent, more accurately to observe and follow the will and commandments of the Lord. The reason for this engagement is that they will find in a strait much shortcoming and little fervour in their ordinary walking, which needs upstirring; they will find also much obligation laid upon them by the Lord's merciful remembering of them in trouble, to take on his yoke voluntarily; and they will find much sense of their own instability, needing such bonds and ties.

6. It is the duty of the Lord's children, when delivered, not to forget their condition in trouble nor their resolutions and obligations following upon it, as though once out of trouble they were out of God's majesty, but to study to walk in their calm day according to that which they resolved in greatest extremity. Therefore Jonah says, "I will pay that which I have vowed."

7. Salvation and deliverance of all kinds is God's royal prerogative; none can save or give peace when he commands

trouble, and he has the prerogative to save and deliver, when reason, probability, the sentence of the law, and all things else have condemned and given over for lost, and in spite of all opposition whatsoever. And it is the duty of those who have had any experience of this, to cling to it as an undeniable truth in all following extremities; for Jonah, having found this in his present case, lays it down as a fixed ground of faith in all extremities, that "salvation is of the Lord"; the force of the Hebrew word comprehends salvation both temporal and eternal.

> Ver. 10. And the Lord spoke to the fish, and it vomited out Jonah upon the dry land.

In the last part of the chapter, after his miraculous support by faith, Jonah rehearses the way of his deliverance, that the Lord by his effectual providence (as by a commanding speech) made the fish to vomit him out upon the land. Whence learn:

1. The Lord, by the afflictions of his people, is but schooling and bettering them, and not seeking to destroy them; of this he gives proof by setting them in freedom and safety. When Jonah was humbled, the Lord spoke to the fish, and it vomited him out safe upon the dry land.

2. The most insensible of creatures have an ear to their Maker's speech, and do (at least by obedient subjection) obey his will, and will not hinder but will help his purposes of love toward his people. The Lord spoke to the fish, and it vomited out Jonah upon the dry land.

3. In the ordinary paths and motions of creatures, God may be bringing about special purposes and providences. As this fish is made to deliver Jonah when it is intending to do no such thing, but merely to swim back and forth, so much more it may be so in the ordinary ways of men; as Joseph went to Bethlehem (Matt. 2:5, 6; Luke 2:4-6).

CHAPTER III

In this chapter we have, first, Jonah's second calling to go to Nineveh, and his obedience in going there and denouncing God's judgment against them (ver. 1-5). 2. The success of his preaching there, appearing in a general and solemn humiliation, countenanced and enjoyed by authority (ver. 6-10). 3. The Lord's acceptance of this, and his revocation of the sentence given out against them (ver. 10).

> Ver. 1. And the word of the Lord came to Jonah the second
> time, saying,
>   2. Arise, go to Nineveh that great city, and preach
> unto it the preaching that I bid you.

Humbled for his rebellion and delivered from his affliction, Jonah is again called to go and preach against Nineveh. It was needful to have his calling repeated, for if he
had gone on the first call, which he had disobeyed, it might
have fared with him as with Israel, who repented of their
disobedience and would go up into the land without the Lord
(Numb. 14:40, 41). Hence learn:

1. As sin justly deprives men of all their privileges which
they enjoy of God's free favor, so a true penitent will not
only obtain pardon, but may also be restored to his former
dignities; Jonah is not deprived of his prophetic office, of
which he was so careless (1:3), but "the word of the Lord
came to him the second time."

2. No endeavours or strugglings of men will free them
from such exercises and lots as God has to exercise them;
for Jonah, resisting the first call, is brought to obey; his
duty which he had refused is enjoined upon him again.

3. The servants of the Lord ought to stick close by their
commission and ought faithfully to publish it, without adding
or diminishing; for so is Jonah commanded: "Go to that
great city and preach the preaching which I bid you."

> Ver. 3. So Jonah arose and went to Nineveh, according to
> the word of the Lord. Now Nineveh was an exceeding
> great city, of three days' journey.
>   4. And Jonah began to enter into the city a day's jour-
> ney; and he cried and said, Yet forty days, and Nineveh
> shall be overthrown.

In the next place we have Jonah's obedience, and a description of the greatness of Nineveh, where he was to
preach. It was of three days' journey in circuit, or if one
would go through all the streets of it. Recorded also is a
brief summary of his preaching, which for a whole day (going
from place to place, as God directed him) or going through a
third of the city (it being three days' journey in all) he proclaimed. We are not to understand by this that he preached
no more regarding the causes of this judgment, or of God in
whose name he threatened; but the result of all was that
Nineveh was to be destroyed. Nor yet are we to understand

that he preached no more in any more of the city during
the forty days, but the meaning is that before he got any
farther his word took effect with those who had heard it,
and by their means it reached the rest of the city, as appears in ver. 5, 6. Hence learn:

1. Obedience to God in a calling and commanded duty is
a sure evidence of an humbled man; for Jonah, before rebellious, now arose and went to Nineveh.

2. It is our duty to obey the will of God, not because of our
inclination, but with an eye to the command of him to whom
our wills and inclinations ought to stoop, unto whom we
should study to approve ourselves in all things, and from
whom we may expect help in following his way. Jonah went
to Nineveh "according to the word of the Lord," being taught
now to look more to God's will than to his own.

3. God's servants, following his commandment and trusting in him, have been and will be enabled to oppose and denounce vengeance against the wickedness of greatest persons
or places; for though Nineveh was an exceeding great city,
yet Jonah cried with zeal and courage.

4. God is able to reach and utterly overthrow greatest
persons or places, when he prosecutes a controversy against
them; for Jonah in his name denounces Nineveh and declares
that the great city will be overthrown.

5. The Lord often sees fit in great wisdom to conceal any
thoughts of love toward a people, and hold out only threatenings and severity, to induce them more seriously to repent.
For this cause the sentence is absolute: "Yet forty days, and
Nineveh shall be overthrown," without any mention of a
condition that by their repentance they should be spared,
as afterwards he did spare them. But indeed the grant of forty
days to them carried in its bosom an invitation to repent.

Ver. 5. So the people of Nineveh believed God and proclaimed a fast, and put on sackcloth, from the greatest
of them even to the least of them.

6. For word came to the king of Nineveh, and he
arose from his throne, and he laid his robe from him,
and covered himself with sackcloth and sat in ashes.

7. And he caused it to be proclaimed and published
through Nineveh (by the decree of the king and his nobles), saying, Let neither man nor beast, herd nor
stock, taste anything; let them not feed nor drink water.

8. But let man and beast be covered with sackcloth
and cry mightily unto God; yea, let them turn every one

from his evil way, and from the violence that is in their hands.

The success of Jonah's preaching among the Ninevites is their reception of the message, and humbling of themselves before God. Being generally stated in ver. 5, this is more fully enlarged in the following verses. The king, hearing of this threatening (even before Jonah came unto him) set in his own person about this duty of humiliation; and by his authority with his nobles he ordained a public fast, in which not only rational creatures, but even beasts (which they decked in times of peace) should for a time be deprived of food, and clothed with sackcloth, so that by this sad sight men might be set on edge to cry fervently to God, and that with their repentance they should reform their evil ways and oppression.

Though it cannot be said that all who were employed in this exercise had true faith and repentance unto conversion, yet since Christ calls it repentance (Matt. 12:41), we may safely conclude that there was no gross dissimulation in it, but that at least they had legal faith and contrition.

1. The word of the Lord may, when he accompanies it, have strange and speedy effects among those whom men would look for very little from. When Israel is despising the word, Nineveh is affected by it, and that so speedily that before Jonah had gotten through the city (ver. 4) the word is begun, and report from hearers sets others to work. Word comes to the king, and he repents.

2. To believe the truth of God's word when it is spoken is the ready way to make it effectual; it is ordinarily slighted because it is not credited. Nineveh's reformation begins with her believing.

3. What is spoken by messengers in the name of the Lord must be received as God's message before it can be effectual. The people of Nineveh, hearing Jonah, believed God in whose name he spoke.

4. Extraordinary cases of a people under wrath imminent or incumbent for sin, call them to extraordinary courses and remedies for averting the same. In this strait the Ninevites count it not enough to use an ordinary way of dealing with God, but "proclaim a fast and put on sackcloth."

5. In a time of great extremity, it becomes those who would approve themselves to God, to carry themselves in a way which may testify most sense of their desert of sin, of their abjection and low condition before the Lord, and which

may stir them up to earnest prayer. These things contained in the king's edict, sackcloth and fasting in man and beast, tend to these ends; for hereby they declare how all sorts had offended God and abused the creatures in sin. They testify also of their sense of their own deserving; the Lord might cut them all off, and their beasts for their sake, and because of this they were in an abject and deplorable condition in their own eyes. And with this mournful face in all things, they would stir themselves up to entreat the face of the Lord.

As for the external performances, they were never of any worth, but abominable, if they were rested upon, without the substance; and they (especially sackcloth) were more called for under the shadows of the law, when the promises were not so clear as under the gospel, and when the people were trained in their duty by that pedagogy. Abstinence is still required in solemn humiliations insofar as may be subservient to spiritual duties, and might be more practiced in warm countries than in colder climates.

6. A lively sense of God's authority, and of his wrath kindling against sin, may well make a king quit his throne and robes, and take a place in the dust with the meanest of his subjects; for "the king of Nineveh arose from his throne, and laid his robes from him, and covered himself with sackcloth, and sat in ashes."

7. Kings are obliged to promote piety among their people, not only by their authority but by their example as well. The people had informed the king, and he, in his person, "arose from his throne" and by his authority "caused it to be proclaimed and published." Authority and law without example will not avail much.

8. Though men in authority cannot compel the consciences of their subjects to faith and obedience, yet they may by their authority enjoin them to perform the external duties of religion. The king of Nineveh made a proclamation and decree to this purpose, whereby he testified his own repentance and promoted it in others.

9. Men in highest authority are not to rule and do all by themselves, but with the advice and concurrence of those who ought to have authority next to them. He caused the proclamation to be made "with his nobles"; so much did these heathens know of human frailty that they saw even the greatest of men needed such assistance.

10. All external ceremonies and performances, as fasting and putting on sackcloth, are no sufficient means of averting the anger of God unless there is fervent prayer to God.

Therefore it is subjoined in the decree, "and cry mightily to God"; all these other performances ought to stir up to that as the climax and height of repentance.

11. Prayer, though ever so apparently fervent, is not acceptable without an endeavour of reformation. Therefore they are also exhorted and enjoined to "turn each one from his evil way, and from the violence that is in their hands." Their idolatry (being convicted by the true God) may be comprehended in that general statement, "evil ways"; and they name "violence" in particular, because all men by nature are more clear in duties of the second table than of the first.

> Ver. 9. Who can tell if God will turn and repent, and turn away from his fierce anger, that we perish not?

The exhortation and injunction in the decree is seconded and encouraged by this motive. There was some hope that if the Lord were instantly sought, he would be reconciled to them and would in mercy avert his judgment.

1. Even when God is solemnly threatening, there may be some sight of his mercy attained by those who are sensible of sin and who acknowledge the justice of God's correction. Notwithstanding Jonah's preaching (ver. 4), there is a possibility seen of God's turning and repenting, even by those who apprehend his fierce anger. The act of taking pains to threaten and warn forty days before sentence was executed, might give ground for such a hope, that his purpose was held back until he saw their repentance.

2. Sensible sinners under feared or felt judgments look on God's being reconciled with them as the fountain of their happiness, and only from that can they expect any comfort in their calamities. Therefore their eye is chiefly upon God's repenting and turning away from his fierce anger, for only from this can they gather hope that they "perish not."

3. Those who are most earnest with God, under the sense of sin and judgment, will be ready to see most of his grace and free love in showing favour toward them. Therefore all their hope, when they cry mightily, is built on God's turning and repenting; grace and compassion must be eminently active if the peace can be made up at all.

4. This way of speech, "Who can tell if God will turn?" is used likewise by the church in the same extremities (Joel 2:14). Sensible sinners may have many sad tossings between the expectation of God's mercy and the sense of

their own deservings; though the promise is most absolute to such, yet perhaps they can neither speak the pure language of faith, nor yet wholly the language of unbelief, but mixed and made up of both. Though it is beyond controversy that God will be reconciled with a penitent, and no doubt Jonah had preached much concerning God, yet they cannot make themselves certain of his good favour. They can rise no higher than questioning and hope: "Who can tell if God will turn away?"

5. It is no small difficulty to get free from a stroke, where provocations are great and where God has severely threatened. Though exemption from them is to be looked for by the penitent, with very great submission, considering his guilt; yet God is not always pleased upon repentance to keep off temporal punishments, when iniquity has come to a height, and happiness is not to be placed therein, if God is otherwise minded. Therefore this suspended hope looks chiefly not so much to remission as to temporal preservation: let God turn away from his fierce anger "that we perish not."

6. The Lord, by keeping our minds in suspense between hope and discouragement, would stir us up to more diligence. Therefore this doubtful hope is subjoined as a reason why they should cry mightily to God and reform their ways (ver. 8).

7. Those who are convinced of sin ought not to be deterred from duty, though it seems hopeless, but ought to resolve to follow it, get what they will; therefore they will cry to God, though they are not certain of deliverance.

> Ver. 10. And God saw their works, that they turned from their evil way; and God repented of the evil that he had said he would do unto them, and he did it not.

God is graciously pleased to accept this, and recalls the sentence; this is expressed in terms taken from among men.

1. The Lord's most peremptory and absolute threatenings are always to be understood as implying that the penitent may yet look for God's acceptance. Notwithstanding the absolute threatening in ver. 4, "God saw their works and repented."

2. God chiefly takes notice of and rewards men's practices, and real endeavours of reformation, and not their external performances of religious exercises. "God saw their works," rather than their fasting and sackcloth.

3. Though the Lord is not debtor to any, nor can they merit at his hand, yet free grace will so reward weak endeavours that all may be encouraged to seek him; yea, he will reward them with temporal favours, even temporary repentance, as an image of true repentance, to show how he loves and how he would graciously reward true repentance. "He saw their works," both the works of those who were truly converted and of those who did not come to that length.

4. When God is said in scripture to repent, we are not to conceive any change in God or in his external purposes, but only a not executing of his revealed threatenings. His purposes include the exception of repentance, which God decrees to give those whom he spares. God's "repenting of the evil" is expounded to be, "he did it not." This is not a changing of his purpose, but a not executing of what he said, i.e. conditionally.

CHAPTER IV

This chapter contains: 1. Jonah's murmuring at God's dealing with Nineveh, and his wish to be dead (ver. 1-3). 2. The Lord's reproving of him; first by words (ver. 4) and then by deed; for by a gourd (in whose shadow he delighted, being gone out of the city, ver. 5, 6, and at the lack of which he repined, ver. 7-9), he is reproved, that he should be so much taken up with so small a thing, and yet be angry at God's sparing so populous a city (ver. 10, 11).

Ver. 1. But it displeased Jonah exceedingly, and he was very angry.

2. And he prayed unto the Lord, and said, I pray thee, O Lord, was not this my saying when I was yet in my country? Therefore I fled before unto Tarshish; for I knew that thou art a gracious God, and merciful, slow to anger, and of great kindness, and repentest of the evil.

Jonah is discontented with this mercy of God toward Nineveh, and expostulates with him about it, applauding himself in his former rebellion, as having done more wisely in it than in obeying God's call. The ground of all this distemper, as later appears, was that God's sparing of Nineveh (which it seems he knew by revelation, or gathered from their repentance, or from the standing of the city after forty days had expired) was a ready means, he thought, to make his ministry and God's name and authority to be vilified; or (as temptation is full of invention) perhaps he repined that such an enemy to the people of God had not been cut off.

1. Corruptions may lurk and remain alive in those who have gone through many straits, and so might have had them mortified; for Jonah after many difficulties is yet passionate and impatient. "He was displeased exceedingly, and very angry."

2. It is great iniquity in the children of men, to seek to have God's dispensations framed after the mould of their mind; for it is Jonah's sin to be very angry and exceedingly displeased with what God did.

3. Corruption may sometimes so prevail with the children of God that it shall not only be a temptation smothered within their breast, out of love to him, but may also break out with their own consent against God for a season. Jonah vents his passion: "he prayed unto the Lord, and said."

4. Much of that which we vent under the name of prayer, may indeed be our raving in our fevers, and a letting loose of our corruption and passion; for what is called prayer here is in effect a bitter expostulation with God, and a venting of his passionate desire to die.

5. Crooked ways, for which the people of God have been corrected, and which they have been made to condemn, may yet again in an hour of temptation be approved and liked by them; for Jonah applauds himself in his former way of rebellion, which he had condemned (2:8), and thinks he had done well.

6. It is a temptation inherent in Adam's posterity to presume that they would guide things better, if they had their will, than God guides them. This much does this expostulation imply, that he thought it better to go on to Tarshish than to have come to Nineveh, as things were.

7. A person under temptation will not lack his fair pretences, with which he may think to justify his way, and to make it seem reasonable. Jonah seems to have such reasons that he dares appeal to God himself, whether he did not foresee in his own country that God's mercy would make his threatening vain and bring his ministry in contempt, and whether he did not therefore do well in fleeing. "Was not this my saying?" says he to God; but our reasonings must submit to God's sovereign will, and give place to his infinite wisdom.

8. The mercy of God toward lost man is so far beyond man's mercy, that it may sometimes be a discontent to his dearest children that he is so merciful. God's mercy to

Nineveh, and that he is so "gracious and merciful," is Jonah's eyesore.

9. God is so gracious that, as he is not easily provoked by sins, so when provoked he is easily reconciled again to them. Jonah knew this in his heart, that he is "a gracious God, and merciful, slow to anger, and of great kindness, and repented of the evil"; and this he now sees verified.

10. It is a great mistake to think that mercy manifested to humble sinners should make them scorn God or his servants; it is rather a most effectual means to produce fear of God, and respect to his ordinances and messengers (Ps. 130:4). Therefore Jonah's reasoning against God's mercy is grounded upon a mistake, and is an evidence of his being carried headlong with passion.

> Ver. 3. Therefore now, O Lord, take, I beseech thee, my
>   life from me; for it is better for me to die than to live.

Jonah subjoins to his expostulation an impatient wish, that God would take him away by death, since he did not get his own will and could not endure the infamy which he expected to come upon him. Hence learn:

1. Death (not as a release from sin, or a chariot to convey us to the place where we will be with God forever, but as it takes away a present imagined or real bitterness) is the ordinary refuge of embittered spirits, and the back door unto which, out of impatience, weariness of life, pride, and contest with providence, they seek; so Jonah now prays, "take my life from me."

2. It is the fruit and evidence of an embittered spirit that any condition, however ill, seems better than the present to them; Jonah thinks it "better to die than live," without any affectionate eye to glory but rather looking to his rest from present trouble (as appears from God's reproving his request); whereas it ought rather to have affrighted him, to think of going out of the world in such a bitter frame.

3. The children of God under temptation may be very ardent in expressing the dross of their own heart, and in seeking that which is altogether wrong; Jonah in his passion beseeches the Lord to take away his life. Great is the mercy of the saints in having a Mediator to reform their petitions.

4. It is a sign of great corruption and self-love in men, to seek their own contentment and satisfaction in dying or living, rather than in being subject to the will of God; and it is

baseness and cowardice to seek passionately to be out of life, because of any trouble we may meet in it because we follow God. Such is Jonah's infirmity, and this is his reason in his passion; take my life from me, "for it is better for me to die than to live."

Ver. 4. Then said the Lord, Do you do well to be angry?

The Lord first reproves Jonah's passion by word, and appeals to himself, whether he thought it seemly so to repine. Hence learn:

1. The Lord himself, in greak meekness and patience, bears with the infirmities of his servants while they are in a distemper and while there is hope of recovery; so much does this gentle reproof of great passion and stubbornness teach. And so the mercy of God which he envied when shown to Nineveh, is the cause of his own safety.

2. Gentle reproofs from God, and his tender dealing with his children, ought to make deepest impression on them. Therefore the Lord chooses this way, so that Jonah, seeing therein his goodness to him though he was so often out of course, might be more deeply convinced.

3. The children of God, when they cool of their sins, will be most severe against themselves for their impatience and miscarriage. Therefore the Lord appeals to Jonah himself when sober, to judge of his own way. "Do you do well to be angry?" as if he were the fittest judge to pass a hard censure upon himself.

4. It is a great iniquity and presumption in the creature to be angry at, or quarrel with, any of God's ways; for he is absolute and unsearchably deep in his counsels. Says he, "do you," a worm, a potsherd and an owl, who cannot discern my ways, "do you do well to be angry?"

Ver. 5. So Jonah went out of the city, and sat on the east side of the city. And there he made himself a booth, and sat under it in the shadow, that he might see what would become of the city.

Not pacified with this reproof, Jonah now perseveres in his ill humour and goes forth out of the city, and eases himself as best he may from the sun's heat, until he may see what becomes of the city. Hence learn:

1. A child of God under temptation may be very hard to convince of his errour, and may go on in his course, even

when God reproves him for it; for Jonah, thus reproved (ver. 4), goes on and is intent upon the ruin of the city.

2. Immediate affections may not only carry men to show themselves in opposition to the will of God, but are a ready way to draw them to delusion; as men will not believe truth, but according as they fancy and wish, so will they still expect and look that things should be so. Though the forty days were expired, and though Jonah was informed of God's will, yet he expected the satisfying of his own desire. "He went out to see what would become of the city," possibly judging that since the precise day of Nineveh's ruin, after the forty days, was not fixed, therefore they might perish yet, or possibly they might fail in their repentance, or that since God's sentence of judgment had been altered, so might his purpose of mercy be.

3. Even the children of God, in the hour of temptation, may vent dispositions which are monstrous among men, so much of old Adam there is in the most mortified, and so much need to pray that we be not led into temptation. Whereas Jonah, a prophet, ought to have rejoiced at the success of his ministry and the repentance of sinners, his mind is bent only upon the destruction of penitents, and it is his great eyesore to see that city standing. "He sat to see what would become of it," as daily wishing its destruction and grieving that he saw it not.

4. Smaller contentments and accommodations are to be chosen, rather than greater delights by abiding in a place where God's judgments are imminent; therefore does Jonah, who expected and wished the ruin of Nineveh, do well in this respect. He will rather sit under the shadow of a booth than abide in the city. By this also the Ninevites might take occasion to repent yet more seriously, since his removal might tell what he expected.

> Ver. 6. And the Lord God prepared a gourd, and made it to come up over Jonah, that he might be a shadow over his head, to deliver him from his grief. So Jonah was exceeding glad of the gourd.
>
> 7. But God prepared a worm when the morning rose the next day; and it smote the gourd that it withered.
>
> 8. And it came to pass when the sun arose, that God prepared a vehement east wind, and the sun beat upon the head of Jonah, that he fainted and wished in himself to die, and said, It is better for me to die than to live.

Here the Lord first gives Jonah matter of delight, in a plant miraculously raised up to cover his booth and keep him from the heat which increased his grief; and then again his passion is stirred up by the Lord's sudden removing of the gourd, and raising of such a wind that the sunbeams might effectually beat upon him. By all this the Lord lays a reason for more sensibly reproving Jonah for his former bitterness.

1. A spirit once broken and embittered with troubles is more easily grieved and stirred up; to Jonah heat is a grief from which he must be delivered, and which he cannot bear.

2. The Lord, in healing the infirmities of his people, sometimes first lances their sores and reveals more of their putrefaction, before he applies healing plasters. Therefore Jonah's passion is more kindled before the former distemper is healed.

3. God in his holy providence may ensnare men who are willfully given to passions, with more occasions to make them vent more of their corruptions; for so he deals with Jonah. He gave him delight in a gourd, and then took it from him, and sent the beating sun, to cast (as it were) oil in the flame of his passion; so dangerous is it to walk contrary to God, or to be violently carried on with any corruption.

4. From this sending of the gourd, and the worm, and the effects of it in Jonah, we may see: (a) The vanity of all earthly delights, in that they all carry a worm of instability in their root, which in short time will turn upside down all the expectations which men have from them. There is here one day a flourishing gourd, and "the next day it is withered." (b) Much delight in earthly contentments is ordinarily a forerunner of much sorrow in their removal; Jonah was exceeding glad of the gourd, but when it withered, he fainted. (c) Passion, when given way to, will soon make men furious and absurd. Jonah upon the least discontent would be gone: "he wished in himself to die, and said, It is better for me to die than to live," when the sun beat upon him, and the gourd was gone, as if he should be exempted from bearing anything; so little are men themselves in their passions.

> Ver. 9. And God said to Jonah, Do you do well to be angry for the gourd? And he said, I do well to be angry, even unto death.

Before the Lord makes use of all this to his holy purpose, he challenges Jonah concerning this discontent, that he,

after confession of his passion, may be prepared for the
reproof.

1. In every action it is our duty to look on ourselves as
accountable to God for it, and to examine how it is done,
whether well or not. So we are taught by God's challenge,
to give an account and to examine: "do you do well?"

2. To be excessively discontented at providences, especially for small matters, is not becoming in the servants
of God; this also is imported in the challenge, that it was
not right for him, a prophet, to be angry (yea, "exceedingly
angry," as the words may be read) for the gourd.

3. The pride of man's heart is such that it will justify
itself, and stand it out even against the verdict of God, if
he be given over to temptation; so does Jonah's answer to
the Lord teach. "I do well," says he (or, 'I am greatly angry'),
"even unto death." Nothing will please him but death, by it
to be rid of these troubles.

> Ver. 10. Then said the Lord, You have had pity on the
> gourd, for which you have not laboured, neither made
> it grow; which came up in a night and perished in a night.
>
> 11. And should I not spare Nineveh, that great city,
> in which are more than six-score thousand persons,
> who cannot discern between their right hand and their
> left hand, and also much cattle?

The Lord now applies all that is past to his present purpose; and from this discontent of Jonah he lets him see the
absurdity of his former murmuring. If he had given way to
himself so passionately to commiserate so small a thing
as a gourd (in producing which he had no hand, which was of
short continuance, and which needed no pity), and that only
because he received some profit and refreshment by it, why
did he so much stumble that the Lord spared Nineveh, which
was his handiwork and in every way considerable? There
were many in it who justly called for pity, for they were not
sensible of anything, neither had they by gross actual transgressions provoked the Lord to denounce that judgment. So
here the Lord is not approving Jonah's passion, but convin-
cing him of selfishness in unjustly approving in himself
that mercy which he condemned in God, when done most
rightly.

1. Self-love will easily blind men so far as to make them
approve themselves in doing worse things than those they
condemn in others; for this is the scope of this reproof, to

show Jonah that he would not allow the Lord, on just causes, to be merciful; and yet he could allow himself his self-passion.

2. Much more latitude ought to be allowed to God in his way of working, without our quarreling, than we may take to ourselves. The Lord says, "you," who may be blinded with fancy and humour, "had pity," and allowed it in yourself; "and should not I," a wise and sovereign Lord, "spare Nineveh?" since I am he to whom you owe absolute submission of spirit, though I cannot reason you out of your folly.

3. The Lord can easily take off the veil from fair pretexts of selfish men, and let them be seen in their own colours. Whatever Jonah might pretend as the cause of his grief that Nineveh was spared, the Lord by this demonstrates that his bitterness flowed indeed from love to himself, as might be seen in the matter of the gourd.

4. Men under temptation and in an ill way are not easily convinced that they are wrong; therefore the Lord uses all these means to take Jonah with his reproof.

5. The Lord is so constant in his good-will, that he will not only show mercy, but will maintain his so doing against all who oppose it; here he pleads against Jonah for his mercy to Nineveh: "should I not spare Nineveh?"

6. By his practice, the Lord teaches us to let out our affections upon objects according to their worth in themselves. Though nothing can be of worth to him, yet he represents Jonah's pity on the gourd, a thing of small worth, coming up in one night and perishing in another, as far worse employed than his mercy in sparing Nineveh that great city.

7. The Lord has created men; this may give ground of hope to the awakened sinner that God does not delight in his destruction, but that upon repentance he will be willing to spare. While he reasons from Jonah's pity upon the gourd, for which he "had not laboured, neither made it grow," he teaches that he could not destroy repenting Nineveh, as it was his own handiwork.

8. Not even persons in maturity, coming to God, but even their children, yea, and cattle, who cannot sensibly acknowledge him, do concur to plead for pity to the penitent at God's hands. And his mercy will look on their condition and number as a reason for sparing; for he knows what infants are in Nineveh, how innocent they were of gross provocations, and that there was much cattle there; and from that he pleads that so great a city, in which are so many infants and cattle, should be spared.

9. The children of the Lord will at last be cleared and satisfied with all the Lord's dispensations, and will submit to God's way in them, as only right and wise, however they repine under their fits of temptation. The Lord gets the last word in this debate, and therefore it is evident from Jonah's silence, and not answering again, that he submitted at last. In testimony of this, and of his unfeigned repentance, he glorifies God in registering all these passages for the edification of the church.

By this also is held forth the infallible certainty of holy scripture, in that the penmen of it were so little their own in writing it that they did not spare, at God's command, to register their own infirmities, that he may be glorified.

MICAH

THE ARGUMENT

This prophet, living almost in the same time as Isaiah (only he was sent out a little after him, and his commission is also extended to the kingdom of Israel) is much like him in matter, and is recorded afterwards to have been a faithful man in declining times (Jer. 26:18). If we compare the beginning of the first and sixth chapters, which are almost one and the same, we may take up the whole prophecy in two solemn sermons.

In the first of these, he foretells the captivity of the ten tribes, and the calamity of Judah by the Assyrians, because of idolatry (chap. 1), and because of covetousness, oppression, and contempt of the messengers of God (chap. 2), and the wickedness of rulers both in church and state, for which Judah is yet further threatened (chap. 3). Then he arms the godly against the Babylonian captivity, then approaching, with the promise of restitution under the Messiah (some taste of which is mixed with the threatenings, chap. 2:12, 13), chap. 4; and he sets forth the Messiah's birth and government (chap. 5).

In the second sermon he challenges and threatens Israel in the Lord's name for ingratitude, hypocrisy, injustice, and idolatry (chap. 6). Having lamented the general defection of the time, he comforts himself and all believers, in their troubles of all sorts, by many ample promises; concluding all with one solemn acknowledgement of the mercy and fidelity of God (chap. 7). Many particulars in this prophecy will be best understood by considering the times in which the prophet lived; see 2 Kings chap. 15; 16:7; chap. 18; 2 Chron. chaps. 26-31.

CHAPTER I

In this chapter, after the title (ver. 1) the prophet sets forth the Lord, as in a solemn court day, appearing with great power, severity, and majesty, to judge Israel and Judah for their sins, especially idolatry (ver. 2-5). Then he particularly foretells the desolation of the kingdom of Israel (ver. 6, 7), the greatness of which, together with Judah's stroke by the same Assyrian, is particularly and pathetically held forth by the prophet, from his own sorrow for it (ver. 8, 9),

from enemies' rejoicing at it (ver. 10), from a declaration
of the calamity of particular places where the enemy should
come (ver. 10-15), and from the mournful face that then
should be upon all things (ver. 16).

> Ver. 1. The word of the Lord that came to Micah the
> Morasthite, in the days of Jotham, Ahaz, and Hezekiah,
> kings of Judah, which he saw concerning Samaria and
> Jerusalem.

The inscription or title of the prophecy contains a description of the messenger employed, from his name and
the city where he was born (conceived to be the Mareshah in
the tribe of Judah, Josh. 15:44, 2 Chron. 11:8, 2 Chron. 14:
9, 10, which is here threatened, ver. 15); as likewise his
commission from God; the time of his prophesying under
several kings of Judah; and a declaration that his commission extended to both the kingdoms of Israel and Judah, and
especially to the chief cities thereof. Hence learn:

1. Men are not to run unsent on public employments in
God's house, but to wait upon a call and commission, and
having received it, to cleave closely to it; for "the word of
the Lord came to Micah," and he published only "the word
of the Lord which came to him, which he saw."

2. The messages and challenges sent by the Lord's servants to the church are to be considered as sent from him;
whose challenge the conscience cannot flee, as being from
more than one party, and as being most certain and infallible.
Therefore this doctrine is held out to be "the word of the
Lord," and Micah "saw" this, in vision or prophetic revelation; implying that what he said was as certain as if it were
seen already accomplished.

3. The Lord, in his great mercy and long-suffering, is
pleased not to withhold a testimony from his backsliding
people; but by multiplication and long continuance of prophets, he is pleased to forewarn them of ruin, if perhaps they
will turn and repent from it. Therefore not only backsliding
Israel is honoured with prophets, but there are many at
once in both kingdoms, and these prophesying long in the
time of many kings. Not only is Isaiah prophesying in Judah
at the same time as Micah, but Hosea, if not also Amos in
Israel; as may be gathered from the inscription of their
prophecies. Frequent sending of prophets and messengers
is either a means of stirring up to reformation, as when

(Hagg. 1:1; Zech. 1:1; cf. Ezra 5:1,2), or a presage of speedily approaching ruin where their message is not received (2 Chron. 36:15-17).

4. The servants of God must not expect to have always sweet times and fair weather in the service of their generation, but they ought to look for variety of times and conditions to wrestle with; such was the lot of this prophet. He lived in the days of Jotham, Ahaz, and Hezekiah; he had not only a pious Hezekiah to deal with, but a wicked Ahaz, and a Jotham in whose days reformation was not so thorough as under Hezekiah or Josiah; and he saw the total ruin of Israel and the affliction of Judah by the Assyrians.

5. As the Lord will not spare his own people when they provoke him, so does he in equity deal with them according to the degrees of their provocation. Therefore there is a sad message concerning Jerusalem, and they must not take it ill in the process to be joined with Samaria, whom they hated as vile apostates. Yet it is so ordered that Samaria is placed first (being first and chief in the provocation, which is a poor preferment) and consequently first and deepest sharers in the punishment; they get threatenings only, whereas Judah is comforted at this time and punished with greater leniency.

> Ver. 2. Hear, all ye people; hearken, O earth, and all that is therein; and let the Lord God be witness against you, the Lord from his holy temple.

To bring authority to the ensuing doctrine, the prophet summons all the creatures and all people to be witnesses to this legal proceeding against Israel and Judah, and to one solemn court day, in which the Lord would judge and witness against his people, and by his judgments vindicate the sentence of his servants against sin, from all contempt of unbelievers. Hence learn:

1. The word of the Lord ought to be gravely and with all authority delivered by his messengers. By this solemn charge to all creatures to appear, Micah declares that his message was a grave purpose, not to be slighted; and that it was with the Lord, who has command of all creatures, and not with men only that they had to do.

2. It is usual for the visible church, not only to slip through inadvertance, but especially to drown herself in apostasy; and having once fallen away, to prove so void of all sense of piety, so selfish and so obstinate that she is not

likely to be convinced, and so stupid in sin as to be insensible
of approaching wrath. Therefore there must be a solemn
citation of all nations, as if there were need of a daysman,
to awake them from their sleep; and "the Lord must be a
witness against them" before they will be convicted.

3. God is a witness whose testimony may and will convince
of sin; not only because he knows all things perfectly, but
when he declares this with power, either inwardly to the
conscience or outwardly by corrections, he will convince
the most obstinate. Let the Lord be witness against you, and
he will carry his point.

4. When sin has come to a height in the church, and they
will not take with it nor strive to amend it, then publicly,
in view of all the world, the Lord will convince and correct
them by his strokes. Therefore he calls "all people, the
earth, and all that therein is," to hear and see the Lord
witnessing against his church; and this is a bitter case,
when our betrothed Lord is provoked to go out of doors to
the streets with his beloved's faults.

5. The justice and equity of the Lord's dealing with his
people, even when he proceeds to severity in correction, is
so uncontrovertedly clear that it may be seen and read of all.
Therefore also the creatures are called to appear, as witnesses of his proceedings, and that affliction is justly procured by Israel.

6. If this passage, "from his holy temple," be understood
of heaven, it teaches that no matter how obstinately men may
bear out against all convictions from men, yet the glorious
majesty of God, when he lets forth any rays of it from heaven
(as ver. 3, 4) in his works, it will so dazzle them that they
shall not be able to stand out. If we understand it of the
temple at Jerusalem, it teaches that the Jews' confidence in
the temple should not exempt them, but rather be a part
of their charge, that the mercies of God manifested there
unto them, should effectually convince them of sin, and aggravate it, for they have not walked accordingly; and that
Israel's renouncing of that temple and the worship of God will
be matter of sad challenge, which they will not be able to
answer. In all these respects "the Lord God will be witness
from his holy temple."

 Ver. 3. For behold, the Lord comes forth out of his place,
  and will come down and tread upon the high places of
  the earth.

4. And the mountains shall be molten under him, and the valleys shall be cleft, as wax before the fire, and as the waters that are poured down a steep place.

To stir them up yet more, and make them heed the message, he declares in general God's purpose concerning them: that he would manifest himself in his glory from heaven, and trample under his feet whatever is most eminent, and make high and low feel the effects of his presence and justice, according to his infinite power, which (when he pleases to set forth) will make mountains to tremble and resolve into dust, and valleys to cleave as wax melts before a fire, and as waters run with violence down a steep place.

1. Though the Lord reveals his glory most clearly in heaven, and atheists and carnal men think he is shut up there, yet he is everywhere filling heaven and earth, and will, when he pleases, manifest his presence on earth in glorious effects of providence. This much does this speech import: "the Lord comes forth out of his place." Though heaven is in a peculiar way his habitation, yet he will from thence appear in glorious majesty on earth.

2. The glorious manifestations of God in the world ought to be looked upon with reverence, admiration, and humble wondering. This is imported by "behold," prefixed to this manifestation.

3. It is quite beside the expectation of a backsliding church that God should appear in severity against them, and therefore such a dispensation surprises them. This much also does this "behold" teach; to them who still dream of peace with God, notwithstanding their wicked way, it should be an unexpected and sudden thing to see him appear in glory to punish.

4. The greatness and majesty of God ought to be well studied and considered by all those who oppose him and reject his will; not to drive them yet farther from him, but rather to crush their obstinacy and induce them to repent. God's majesty is here held forth to make them tremble, to be found in a way disapproved by his word.

5. Men in their declinings from God seek false refuges for themselves, whereby they think to shelter themselves against God's vengeance; but they are deluded in this. There are "high places of the earth," by which are signified their idols worshipped on these high places, in whom they trusted, or their strongholds, or high and lofty men, who thought to

be exempted from all common judgments, or generally their high and lofty imaginations, all which, or whatever else they can oppose, the Lord is potent to crush. "He will come down and tread upon the high places of the earth."

6. Greatness of opposition against God contributes to manifest him more eminently by crushing it. "He treads on the high places"; that is, not only crushes and commands them, but is more eminently seen in so doing, in that they are high; their height makes him conspicuous from afar when he stands upon them.

7. The Lord is able to overturn what is greatest and most stable in the world, and to make all creatures feel his power and indignation in an effectual way. This is held forth in that "the mountains shall be molten under him, and the valleys cleft as wax before the fire."

8. Sin in the people of God makes that which otherwise might be comforting to be matter of terror to them. Whereas the majesty and power of God are comforting to the church, in that she has such a God to crush her enemies and to be above them in that wherein they deal proudly, yet now, because of sin, it is the matter of her terror. Yet it is comforting in that all this is done to drive her to mercy.

> Ver. 5. All this is for the transgression of Jacob, and for the sins of the house of Israel. What is the transgression of Jacob; is it not Samaria? And what are the high places of Judah; are they not Jerusalem?

Now follows the Lord's quarrel, or the cause of his appearing thus in glorious severity; which is the heinous transgression of his people, who came of Jacob, otherwise called Israel. He declares that the origin and rise of this transgression in Israel was from its chief city, Samaria, where Omri and Ahab erected idolatry; and this idolatry had now, in process of time, spread through the kingdom, and had daily influence from the court and chief city. The Lord further charges that in Judah the city Jerusalem had been an example to all the land, not only in sins against the second table, but in corrupting the worship of God with their high places, which Jotham tolerated; and his son Ahaz proceeded to greater abominations (2 Kings 16:10, 11; 2 Chron. 28:24, 25), and so drew the people on to imitate their ways.

1. The provocations of the Lord's privileged people may bring on very remarkable and heavy strokes; "all this,"

that is, all this severity, "is for the transgression of Jacob."

2. Though the Lord in his great mercy looks over the infirmities of his people, yet rebellion, idolatry, and corrupting of his worship, especially when multiplied, he will not tolerate; this stroke is for their transgressions (or rebellions), their sins, and their high places.

3. In times of defection and controversy, the Lord has a special eye upon, and a chief quarrel against, those who have a leading hand in bringing on or carrying on the apostasy. These questions, "What is the transgression of Jacob? What are the high places of Judah?" import that God observes, and would have made known, the cause of all the defection and who began it.

4. In universal defections, eminent places and persons are ordinarily most guilty, as misleading others by their example and authority; for the transgression of Jacob is Samaria, and the high places of Judah are Jerusalem. That is, iniquity abounds most in these cities, and the sins of the land have their rise and countenance from them.

5. The Lord has a special eye upon his own church and people, to whom he manifests himself, and marks their declinings closely, especially in the matter of his worship; "Judah's high places" are especially pointed at, whereas all Israel's desperate defection is contained in general transgression.

> Ver. 6. Therefore I will make Samaria as an heap of the field, and as plantings of a vineyard; and I will pour down the stones thereof into the valley, and I will uncover the foundations thereof.

The Lord pronounces a more particular sentence against Israel for these sins, and particularly against Samaria, that when the ten tribes should be led captive, that city (as being chief in the sin) should have a very remarkable stroke; her buildings should be rased to the very foundation, and her stones cast down from the hill on which she stood, to the valley, to lie as the heaps of stones which are gathered by the labourers of the ground; and the place should be suitable only for the planting of vineyards.

1. Iniquity entertained will lay most eminent and strong places desolate, for "therefore I will make Samaria as an heap of the field." Though the city endured a siege of three years (2 Kings 17:5), yet this sentence takes effect at the last.

2. Eminence in sin causes eminence in judgments. "Samaria is made an heap, her stones are poured down"; yet other cities of that kingdom were not thus ruined, but there are some cities of Samaria, or the country around, to be inhabited (2 Kings 17:24) when Samaria itself lies desolate.

3. Wicked men, prosecuting their wicked and ambitious ends, may be used by God in a holy manner, as instruments to execute his judgments upon his backsliding people; and they are so to be considered by all who would have the use of their condition. Therefore, for the people's instruction and direction, the Lord claims the stroke as his, though inflicted by the Assyrians: "I will make Samaria as an heap of the field."

> Ver. 7. And all her graven images shall be beaten to pieces, and all her hires shall be burnt with the fire, and I will lay all the idols desolate; for she gathered it of the hire of an harlot, and they shall return to the hire of an harlot.

Samaria is threatened with further ruin, for not only her private things but her supposed sacred things should be destroyed; her graven images broken, that the metal of them might be carried away, and her gifts given to idols (as harlots do to their paramours) or her riches, out of which she gave these gifts, and which she accounted to be the reward of her idolatry, shall either be burnt by the furious soldiers, or go as they came and perish as they are purchased; and so her idols shall be desolate.

1. It proves the vanity of all idols, that they are obnoxious to destruction and desolation; so in days of vengeance God's special quarrel is against them, to show their frailty and the folly of all who cling to them. Therefore "all the graven images shall be beaten in pieces, and I will lay all the idols desolate," by withdrawing respect, worship, and gifts from them.

2. Idolatry is in God's account spiritual harlotry and adultery; for their gifts given to idols are "hires," given unto or by harlots, as the word signifies; and their riches are "the hire of an harlot." Idolaters break that covenant between God as their husband and them as his spouse, and pour out on idols that affection due only to God; and therefore he is provoked in his jealousy to punish.

3. As men may through God's permission prosper in an evil way, so they are ready to sacrifice their prosperity to

a wrong cause, and by it to harden themselves in their way. Samaria bestowed gifts on her idols, as her great riches enabled her to offer. "She gathered it of the hire of an harlot"; that is, she did not acknowledge God for her riches, but conceived that they came to her for her unlawful leagues and treaties with idolaters, and as a reward for her idolatry and defection from the tribe of Judah and the worship of God; and therefore she persevered in it. See Hosea 2:5; Jer. 44:17, 18.

4. Riches purchased in a wrong way, or abused to confirm men in a sinful course, shall come to nought; for "the hire thereof shall be burnt with fire, and they shall return to the hire of an harlot." By this we are not to understand that the Assyrian idolaters should take the riches and gifts of Samaria, and abuse them as Israel had done by putting them in the temple of their idols; but it is a proverb, signifying that as these riches were ill purchased by Israel, so they should go as they came, and should do them no good, but vanish; for an harlot purchases her hire ill, and ordinarily it is as ill spent.

> Ver. 8. Therefore I will wail and howl, I will go stripped and naked; I will make a wailing like the dragons, and a mourning like the owls.

The sentence being pronounced, the prophet proceeds to set forth the greatness of the judgment, together with that which was to come on Judah, so that they might be stirred up to lay it more seriously to heart in time. First he declares what their calamity shall be, by his own sorrow for it. His sorrow was extremely bitter, as of dragons and owls, whose horrible howling in desert places is used in scripture to express the condition of men sensible of great calamities (Job 30:29; Ps. 102:6). Further, he will go naked and stripped of his upper garments, as a sign of total desolation (Isa. 20:2, 3). By all this the Lord does not declare his favour upon any bitter carnal mourning in trouble, but by the prophet's practice the Lord would teach:

1. When his people provoke him, the Lord can send affliction beyond expression, and sorrows which no outward signs can sufficiently show; for this howling, wailing, and going naked imports this in the prophet foreseeing the storm, and he foretells that it shall be so with the people when they feel it.

2. It is the duty of faithful ministers not only to denounce judgment against sin and sinners, but to do it in the way which may make them most sensible of their danger before they feel it in reality. Therefore Micah wails and howls, that they might thereby read the reality and weight of the threatening, and might study to prevent the execution.

3. A most effectual way of making people sensible of threatenings is when the messengers themselves are affected with them when they deliver them; for therefore Micah, who carried this message, wails and howls.

4. Threatenings from the Lord ought to be denounced with great affection and sympathy in the messengers, so that they may show that it is no revengeful and bitter spirit in them which makes them speak so sharply, and so that their affection thus shown may make way for the unpleasant message. "Therefore I will wail and howl," says he, as a sympathiser with the people of God; but as the Lord's messenger, I must carry the hard tidings.

> Ver. 9. For her wound is incurable, for it has come to Judah. He has come unto the gate of my people, even to Jerusalem.

In giving a reason for his sorrow, he describes the calamity yet farther from its universality. As Samaria is desperately sick of provocations, without any hope that she would ever amend, so her stroke is incurable; after the Assyrians had destroyed them, fire should burn through all Judah even to Jerusalem, the mother city and seat of justice to all the Jews, of whom the prophet was one, and whom he loved dearly.

And so he comes to the second branch of the threatening, which is against Judah, as was likewise foretold by Isaiah (8:7, 8) and accomplished (2 Kings 18:13). Hence learn:

1. It is a bitter cause of complaint when strokes inflicted by God are irremediable, whereas a stroke is easy if there is hope of deliverance; therefore Micah wails, for "her wound is incurable."

2. Though the Lord begins his punishments for sin where it pleased him, yet when he lifts up his hand, those who are guilty of the same sins may not think to escape. When the wound is begun at Samaria, it comes to Judah; "it has come unto the gate of my people." Jerusalem was thus called because it was the seat of justice, which was administered publicly in the gate.

3. The Lord may suspend his corrections upon his church for her backsliding until a time of reformation, and then afflict them; for though Ahaz had his own fears from Rezin king of Syria (Isa. 7; 2 Kings 16), yet the correction for the high places of Judah (ver. 5) is by the Assyrian, who destroyed Samaria, and that in the days of Hezekieh the reformer (2 Kings 18). "It has come," i.e. from Samaria, "into Judah." The reason for this is partly because reformation had not been set about sincerely and cordially (as it was in Josiah's time, Jer. 3:6, 10), and thus the Lord was provoked so much the more to punish for former apostasy. Partly the Lord chooses such a time of reformation to punish in, that when a people is at such a time sensible of the sin procuring a stroke, the affliction may be blessed to make them reform the more throughly; and partly the Lord chooses this time that the stroke may be the more moderate, there being some standing in the gap, and no total backsliding; and accordingly we find Jerusalem preserved, though threatened.

4. The affections of the Lord's servants, in a time of distress, ought to be set to sympathise chiefly with those who are most dear to God. Micah says, "he has come to the gate of my people," not his so much because he was their countryman (which should not sway ministers in public administrations, Deut. 33:8, 9, though otherwise to be tender even in that respect is commendable), but because they were more upright in religion than Samaria; and therefore when the enemy comes even to Jerusalem, where the temple stood, it is most bitter.

> Ver. 10. Declare it not at Gath; weep not at all; in the house of Aphrah roll yourself in the dust.

In the next place the calamity of the people, and the cause of the prophet's sorrow, is held to be so great that it were to be wished that their enemies (such as the Philistines in Gath) never knew of it, and so might not insult over them in their misery to add to their affliction; and therefore in a figurative way (usual in lamentations and borrowed from 2 Sam. 1:20) they are enjoined to conceal their affliction from them by suppressing their weeping, lest they should hear it.

1. There are still some in the world waiting for matter of joy in the church's calamities, whose gladdest day will be to see her in trouble; for so much is imported in this prohibition not to declare it in Gath.

2. Of all enemies, those are most inveterate who are nearest to the people of God and yet do not partake of their mercies; such were these of Gath, lying hard upon the borders of Judah, from whom especially they desired to conceal their grief.

3. It is a new grief, and great addition to the afflictions of the godly, that by reason of their calamities enemies take occasion to reproach them, their God, and their religion; and it would be a deliverance in part to have their case concealed from such, and an ease to smother their grief if that would conceal it. This charge shows the church's wish that such knew it not, and her relief if it were so.

4. The church of God must resolve not only to have afflictions, but also to have them noted and observed by enemies, and to lie under all their insolencies and reproaches because of them, until their trial is perfected; for while in a figurative way the prophet thus prohibits, he intimates that it could not be hidden, and that the church had this added to her trial.

In the rest of this chapter to the last verse, the greatness of this stroke and cause of the prophet's sorrow is yet further set forth in a particular and pathetic enumeration of the places (especially those in Judah) which would feel the calamity of war, and what their calamity should be. Though we find no mention elsewhere of the places named here, and especially those in ver. 11, 12, yet we are to conceive that they are either proper names of places (though unknown to us) chosen out from among other places because of the signification of their names, which illustrates their condition by the war; or that they are appellative and borrowed names given to some places from their qualities, properties, or conditions, to illustrate their calamity in the ensuing tempest, as may be seen in the particulars.

And so here by Aphrah, signifying "dust," we are to understand either that city in Benjamin (Josh. 18:23) where the Assyrian was to come (and which was far from the Philistines' hearing), or generally, a place brought to the dust and made dusty by affliction, who therefore are to roll themselves in the dust, taking great sorrow for their dusty and afflicted condition (Jer. 6:26).

1. As the children of God by their behaviour in times of trouble are to give no occasion of reproach unto enemies, so they are before the Lord to evidence that they are sensible of his hand. They are "not to weep at all in Gath,"

or where the Philistines may hear it, yet notwithstanding "in the house of Aphrah," among themselves, they are to express their sorrow.

2. Great afflictions will be very grievous and bitter, making men wallow in dust and ashes without any regard to themselves; so the sweet use of trouble is when men stoop to their condition and to what it calls unto, i.e. when Aphrah, made dusty by affliction, descends to dust.

3. Our kindly bed in trouble is dust, for we are dust by our origin, and the end of affliction is to let us know we are such. "In the house of Aphrah," the house of dust, "roll yourself in the dust."

> Ver. 11. Pass away, you inhabitant of Saphir, having your shame naked; the inhabitant of Zanaan came not forth in the mourning of Bethezek; he shall receive of you his standing.

The next place mentioned is Saphir, the signification of which leads to this description. Those who dwelt beautifully and pleasantly (as is signified by "inhabitant of Saphir") would either flee or be carried into captivity by the enemy, in much ignominy and reproach; this manner of speech is used to express great ignominy put upon captives by licentious soldiers (Isa. 20:4; Isa. 47:3; Jer. 13:22). It teaches us that as as pleasures and delectable situations and dwellings will be no guard against God's pursuing a controversy for sin, so pleasures abused will lead to double ignominy, and will embitter the cup of affliction. "The inhabitant of Saphir passes away, having her shame naked"; her glory does not keep her from ignominy, and it is so much the sadder that she had been an inhabitant of Saphir.

The next place, Zanaan, signifies a place of concourse, as of flocks, and Beth-ezek signifies a place that is near. This leads us to the exposition of the rest of the verse: a place of great concourse and many people shall not come out to help or comfort, when their closest neighbours are mourning. The reason for this is subjoined in these words, "he shall receive of you his standing"; that is, either Zanaan shall not appear in Bethezek's trouble, for they have indeed their own difficulties, and they have learned by the example of their neighbours that there is no resisting of the enemy; or else they dare not express compassion, for they expect that the enemy will settle his camp among them, and will take of them a sore recompence if they make him continue in a

long siege against their confederates, whom they helped.
Hence learn:

1. Human helps and greatest probabilities will prove but
vain in a day of vengeance; a place of repair (such as Zanaan)
will not be able to help, nor will a place near them, though
their number, or the vicinity of the place afflicted, might
seem to prophesy other ways.

2. It is a usual thing in a day of calamity to see men
selfish and taken up with their own grievances, without
regarding others, and to see the Lord give every man and
place so much to do that they shall have no leisure to look
around them. "Zanaan came not forth in the mourning of
Beth-ezek"; see Jer. 47:3.

3. Universal discouragement ordinarily goes before an
instrument of God's vengeance, especially once prevailing,
to make way for his further success; one place learns by
the example of another that there is no resistance. This is
taught by the first interpretation of that passage, "he shall
receive of you his standing."

4. Though it is lawful and necessary for a people to bestir
themselves in their own defence in danger, yet such is the
fierceness of God's anger pursuing for sin that all opposition made to its instruments, and all loss of time, means,
or men, is made up by their spoil and further ruin. This is
imported by the other interpretation of that passage, which
agrees also with the principal scope.

> Ver. 12. For the inhabitant of Maroth waited carefully for
> good, but evil came down from the Lord unto the gates
> of Jerusalem.

This verse contains another evidence that there shall be
no standing against that calamity, and therefore it comes in
as a further clearing of the end of the former verse; this
appears by the particle, "for." The signification of Maroth
("bitterness") and of the original word rendered "waited"
(which also signifies "to be grieved"), and of the word
rendered "but" (which signifies chiefly, "because") leads
to this interpretation of the verse. Those whose condition
is made bitter by affliction are earnestly to expect some
good; but in vain. Yea, they should be grieved more for lack
of it and for disappointment of these expectations, and that
because the trouble should overspread and reach to the
gates of the royal city where the temple was. Hence learn:

1. When the Lord arises to plead against sinners, he can put them in a very disconsolate condition and make all their pleasures end in bitterness; for in this calamity there is "the inhabitant or Maroth," or "of bitternesses," even many of them. See Ruth 1:20.

2. No matter how afflicted people usually look out for some issue, yet grief may often be but growing when they who have felt some bitterness are expecting an end of it; for "the inhabitant of Maroth was grieved for good," which they wanted, though "they waited carefully" for better, as the word also signifies (Jer. 14:19).

3. Sometimes the only comfort left to a people in trouble may be this, that a greater trouble is coming to make them forget the lesser; this evil comes "to Jerusalem," to make them forget particular grievances, and "from the Lord," to make them digest the Assyrians' fury.

4. Afflictions sent from God upon the church are to be observed and laid to heart, not only as being sad in themselves, but as being presages of great anger to come on the rest of the world besides; for they were "grieved for good, because evil came down from the Lord unto the gate of Jerusalem"; that added to their grief, and was an evidence of their own hopeless condition.

> Ver. 13. O inhabitant of Lachish, bind the chariot to the swift beast; she is the beginning of the sin of the daughter of Zion; for the transgressions of Israel were found in you.

Lachish, a city in the tribe of Judah (Josh. 15:21, 39; Jer. 34:7) is threatened; they should endeavour speedily to flee from the enemy, but to no purpose, as accordingly it was besieged by Sennacherib (2 Kings 18:14, 17; 2 Kings 19:8). The reason for the judgment is that they first, of those in Judah, received the idolatrous worship of the ten tribes, and occasioned its spread even to Jerusalem.

1. The Lord in his wisdom has so ordered the writing of holy scripture that every passage and book has in it something for our further information, something which would not be so clearly gotten elsewhere, so that we may be allured to study it much. Here we have Lachish's receiving idolatry first, which is not mentioned in the books of sacred history.

2. As sin will drive men from their habitations, so flight will perish from the swift when God has judgments to bring

on. This saying, "bind the chariot to the swift beast," implies that they would have been glad to flee from their city on any terms, and that they could not be saved by flight.

3. To be the first occasion and a chief stumbling-block in a land's defection, brings an exemplary judgment; Lachish is shut up in her enemies' hands, because "she is the beginning of sin to the daughter of Zion; for the transgressions of Israel were found in you."

> Ver. 14. Therefore you shall give presents to Moresheth-Gath; the houses of Achzib shall be a lie to the kings of Israel.

Lachish's further judgment is that when they should send presents and gifts to some town or country called Moresheth, belonging to Gath of the Philistines (and so distinguished from Moreshah in Judah); or (as the word signifies) to the "inheritance" (and people) of Gath, for aid and assistance against the enemy, they should disappoint them, as the kings of Israel were disappointed by some other confederates. This Achzib, with some other cities, was not at first subdued by the tribe of Asher (Judg. 1:31, 32). And it seems the kings of Israel had covenanted with them for aid against the Assyrians, but were deceived as Lachish was by the Philistines. Only Achzib is named, either because the rest depended on it (and are called "the houses of Achzib") or because the signification of its name ("a lie") serves to illustrate the disappointing of their friends.

1. Wicked men had rather employ any means in their straits than seek to God, and so they provoke God to disappoint them; "you shall send presents to Moresheth-Gath," but to no purpose.

2. The Lord has given many experiences of the vanity of all human helps when he is angry, though men will not be wise to make use of them; for the disappointment of Lachish is illustrated from another, which might have taught them wisdom: "the houses of Achzib are a lie."

3. The vanity of all refuges, when God is provoked, is conspicuous to an observant eye, as if it were their very name and written on their forehead. The houses of Achzib are houses of a lie, answerable to their name.

> Ver. 15. Yet I will bring an heir unto you, O inhabitant of Mareshah; he shall come unto Adullam, the glory of Israel.

He threatens Mareshah in Judah (Josh. 15:44), which seems to have been his own city, that according to the significance of the name, the Lord should bring the enemy to be their heir and to possess their goods. And then he summarily sets forth the extent of this stroke, that it should reach to Adullam, which lay southward of Jerusalem, toward the border of Judah (Josh. 15:21, 35). That which is subjoined, "the glory of Israel," may be understood of Adullam, as a strong city in which Israel glories; or that in coming to Adullam he should come to Jerusalem, the glory of all Israel, as Adullam was beyond Jerusalem to the Assyrians, who came from the north; or, by way of exclamation, that the glory of Israel is now stained by this universal overflowing scourge, which went from the north to the very south border of Judah.

1. The messengers of God ought not to set forth the mind of God partially, as affection and interest direct them; but they are to publish it freely and fully, without respect to friend or foe; the prophet spares not his own city Mareshah.

2. Provocation against God makes men's purchase unsure, and may make their enemies their heirs; for "I will bring an heir to you, O inhabitant of Mareshah."

3. When God raises up instruments to scourge a land for sin, men are not to expect that lying afar off and out of the way will exempt them; but God will find out those whom he is to chastise, wherever they be: "he shall come to Adullam," which was the remotest border to the Assyrians.

4. No matter which of the ways above we understand this expression, "the glory of Israel," it teaches that though the visible church enjoy the great privilege of God's presence in his pure ordinances, of which they glory and boast, yet when God is provoked and these privileges abused, they will not keep off corrections. The glory of Israel will be laid in the dust for her sins.

> Ver. 16. Make yourself bald, and poll yourself for your delicate children; enlarge your baldness as the eagle, for they have gone into captivity from you.

In the last place, the greatness of the calamity is summarily comprehended in the mournful face that shall be when it comes to pass; to this the body of the people, or chief cities, are invited and called, as it were, from their vices, to hearken rather to the bitterness which awaits them and to consider what ruin they cast upon themselves by sin. Their sorrow to come is expressed in such signs as were usual in those times, such as making themselves bald as the eagle when she casts her feathers, and polling their hair (of which see Ezra 9:3; Job 1:20; Isa. 22:12; Ezek. 27:31). And the cause of their sorrows is foretold, that their pleasant children were to be carried into captivity, as Asshur dealt with Israel and (it seems) with some of Judah. For this cause they who are left are to mourn. Hence learn:

1. It is fitting that men in a sinful time think on the bitterness that may ensue, and of the wormwood which God will pour in among their delights, to mar their mirth. Therefore he calls them to make bald and to poll. See Isa. 10:3.

2. Sin will in the end result in bitterness; and as calamity for sin will be grievous on the church, so sin procuring it, and lack of reconciliation with God under it, will make it sad and intolerable. This is signified by these expressions, "make yourself bald, poll yourself, enlarge your baldness as the eagle."

3. Captivity from the place of our habitation, and restraint of outward liberty, is a sharp trial and matter of sorrow to those who are so dealt with; and it ought to be considered so by others, as matter of sympathy, and by the body of a people as matter of affliction, in diminishing their number and leaving those who remain weak and contemptible; for this is the cause of baldness and sorrow to the body of the people. "Your delicate children, they have gone into captivity from you."

CHAPTER II

In the first part of this chapter, the Lord prosecutes his controversy against his people for several sins. First, he accuses them for assiduousness in sin, especially covetousness and oppression (ver. 1, 2), and threatens them with insuperable and lamentable difficulties and with being cast out of their land (ver. 3-5). 2. He threatens and expostulates with them for their opposition to his messengers (ver. 6, 7). 3. He again accuses them for cruel robbery, not sparing so much as women and children (ver. 8, 9), and threatens them with exile (ver. 10). 4. He accuses them for their approbation of and delight in false prophets (ver. 11). In the second part of the chapter he comforts believers with promises of restitution by Christ (ver. 12, 13).

> Ver. 1. Woe unto those who devise iniquity and work evil
> upon their beds; when the morning is light, they prac-
> tice it, because it is in the power of their hand.

The judgment of God is declared to be already upon them, and yet further to be inflicted, for their assiduousness and activity in plotting and practicing evil; hereby showing us how to discern a condition plagued of God, and which without repentance will be pursued with more plagues. (This "woe" implies that such a condition is itself a plague, and that it will receive further plagues.) Of such a state there are these evidences:

1. Evil ways become habitual to men, so that they are never out of them; by night as well as by day they are carried away with them; for it is "on their beds," when they should rest or examine themselves (Ps. 4:4), or be instructed by their reins (Ps. 16:7), or meditate upon God (Ps. 63:6), as well as "in the morning," when they should direct their prayer unto God (Ps. 5:2) and go forth to their lawful callings (Ps. 104:22, 23), that they are thus employed; then sin sleeps not.

2. Men not only sin through infirmity, being surprised and made to stumble in a fit of temptation, but their wits are bent to project and plan sin; for "woe to those who devise iniquity."

3. Men's spirits are so taken up with wickedness that they delight themselves with acting it in their imaginations. "Woe to those who work evil on their beds"; that is, are so transported that their spirits and fancy imagine themselves as acting those wickednesses which they cannot for the present get really acted, and thus think to delight themselves.

4. Men's hearts are so far engaged in their premeditated wickedness that without taking leisure between deliberation and practice, they run eagerly about the execution of their purposes, which is the woeful fruit of giving sin too much room in the heart; being master there, it violently and effectually commands our practice. Not only do they devise iniquity on their beds, but "when the morning is light they practice it." See Jer. 8:6; Eph. 4:19.

5. Men ill-affected have power to effect their desires and succeed in them, as God lays no impediment in their way to stop their progress in sin; for it is a woe upon them that "it is in the power of their hands" to practice the ill they have devised.

6. It is also an evidence of woe upon men when, having power and lacking external restraints, they have no inward principle or tenderness of conscience, to make them hate an ill way, as Joseph had (Gen. 42:18), but count everything right which they are able to effect, and go on as far as their power will reach; for "they practice it because it is in the power of their hand."

> Ver. 2. And they covet fields and take them by violence; and houses, and take them away; so they oppress a man and his house, even a man and his heritage.

He gives an instance of his general challenge of ver. 1 and of the evils they plotted and acted. When they saw houses and fields that they desired, they coveted them and violently deprived their true owners of them; by this not only a man's self but his family and posterity were oppressed, by taking away not only some of his means, but his very heritage, which belonged to him by the law of God and man.

1. Covetousness is a root of much evil and wickedness, and it will embark men in desperate and violent courses; "they covet and take by violence."

2. It is a high aggravation of oppression when the oppressor is not compelled by hunger and want, but when his covetous disposition is the only cause of his miscarriage; for here the quarrel is that simply because "they covet," therefore "they take by violence."

3. Covetousness, given way unto and entertained in men's hearts, will drive them beyond all bounds and moderation; for "they covet fields and houses." Everything they get serves only as a bait to draw them on farther, so dangerous is it once to transgress the bounds of contentment prescribed by God.

4. Though covetousness is a lawless sin, and though oppressors think everything theirs which they can encompass, yet in God's account violent usurpation and possession is no right. Though they "take it away," yet it is still "the man's heritage."

5. Not only the wants of those who are presently oppressed, but all the wants of their posterity, will be laid to the charge of the oppressors and will cry to God against them; for "they oppress a man and his house." They ruin him, his family, and his offspring, by taking away his house and heritage, which are a constant livelihood.

> Ver. 3. Therefore thus saith the Lord: Behold, against
> this family do I devise an evil, from which you shall
> not remove your necks; neither shall you go haughtily;
> for this time is evil.

The Lord pronounces sentence against them for these sins, and explains that woe which he had threatened in ver. 1, showing that the Lord is about to bring on such a judgment and sad time as should effectually and irresistibly seize upon them, and lay their pride, and bring them down.

1. In times of violent oppression, the Lord is not to be looked upon as one not regarding, or as an idle spectator, but as a Lord, ready to appear for the oppressed in a remarkable way; for "therefore thus says the Lord, behold, I devise an evil."

2. The Lord's word ought to be received and believed as a true evidence that he will so appear, though the performance seems to be delayed; for "thus says the Lord." We ought to judge according to what he says, and not according to what we think.

3. The Lord will recompence all his delays in executing vengeance for sin, by its severity when it comes. In opposition to their devising iniquity (ver. 1), the Lord devises an evil; that is, it shall be as sore and sharp an evil as if it had been most seriously devised, and as if all the time of delay had been employed for that end.

4. Sin publicly committed, without control, will bring judgment against a whole people. "Therefore," i.e. because oppression was committed publicly, "I devise an evil against this nation," against the whole nation (Amos 3:1, 2). Even the notorious sins of private persons (much more of public ministers of justice), being unpunished, or the universality of such sins, cannot but bring judgments upon a whole land.

5. Though oppressors may think to shift the Lord's visitations, yet when they come they shall seize upon them, and their violence shall be met with afflictions which they cannot shake off. It is "an evil from which you shall not remove your necks."

6. Though men dream that if they cannot avoid judgments, they will courageously and undauntedly bear out under them, yet the Lord by his rods will make the most haughty to stoop; "neither shall you go haughtily."

7. God has our times so completely in his power that he can thereby, when he will, cause the stoutest to fall before

him. Therefore it is subjoined as a reason why they shall
not walk haughtily: "this time is evil"; God shall make the
times to crush them.

8. By their transgressions men provoke the Lord to make
their time bitter and evil unto them, whereas otherwise they
might comfortably serve their generations. Because they
had oppressed and wronged, therefore "this time is evil."

> Ver. 4. In that day shall one take up a parable against
> you, and lament with a doleful lamentation, and say,
> We are utterly spoiled; he has changed the portion of
> my people; how he has removed it from me; turning
> away, he has divided our fields.

Their calamity is further set forth, that it should not be
ordinary, but should be the matter of a proverb in all men's
mouths, and of a bitter lamentation, either composed by
themselves to bewail their calamities, or by their enemies
to counterfeit their sorrow. They should bewail their utter
desolation, in that the Lord had transferred the possession
of the holy land (which he had given as a portion to his people) to their enemies; and he had not only cast his people out
of it, but turning away in anger, he had given it to the enemies
to divide it among them; and so he had put them out of hope
to return to it again. All this relates especially to the case
of the ten tribes, whose lands were thus possessed by the
Assyrians (2 Kings 17:24).

1. Sinning against God with a high hand will at last make
the sinner a remarkable spectacle of justice, and will end
in bitterness and lamentation. "In that day one shall take up
a proverb against you, and lament."

2. The sinner's desert is to be utterly ruined without hope
of restitution, and to be left in that condition to bewail his
want and misery. This is the sum of their lamentation, that
they are utterly ruined and put away from their land, their
enemies dividing it as their own inheritance.

3. Seeing God as a party, and affliction as flowing from
his anger, may make the afflicted's lamentation more bitter;
for so they lament. "He has changed and removed; turning
away, he has divided."

4. The Lord's judgment upon a sinful people will surprise
them with astonishment, and will be more sad than anything
they expected or dreamed of, when they were wallowing in
their iniquities; for such does their admiration import: "how
he has removed it from me!"

Ver. 5. Therefore you shall have none that shall cast a cord by lot in the congregation of the Lord.

Their utter desolation is here positively denounced by God in confirmation of their lamentation, that being cast out of their land, they should lack the benefit of dividing their inheritances by lot, before the Lord in his congregation, as Joshua had done of old (Josh. 18:4, 6, 10); but they should remain exiled, and their enemies in possession of their country.

1. It is a bitter case when a hard condition is not only feared or apprehended by us, but proves in reality as sad as we imagine; for here the Lord confirms their lamentation, apprehending desolation by a positive sentence. "You shall have none to cast a cord by lot."

2. Iniquity will make a land spue out even a covenant people, and will detain them in exile, desitute of their former privileges. This is imported in the threatening, "you shall have none to cast a cord."

3. The causes procuring judgments are to be taken along in our thoughts with the judgment. "Therefore," because of the sins mentioned, "you shall have none." This will make us justify God in his afflicting, and will set the afflicted to repentance, to make up their outward losses in God.

4. Afflictions will be more bitter if the mercies of which they deprive us have been given by special providence, and as a sign of God's favour; for so the land from which they are to be banished is a land divided to them by the special providence of God, and the land in which the congregation of the Lord was. See Ps. 47:4; Ps. 137:1.

Ver. 6. Prophesy not; say to those who prophesy, They shall not prophesy to them, that they shall not take shame.

The second accusation is for their contempt of and oppression to God's word and ministers. The sense of the words (which in the original are concise and short) is, when the wicked heard the prophets of God threaten sin so sharply, they could not endure this sound doctrine, but either would have them silent (Amos 7:10-13) or would limit them to preach only what they pleased, as their false prophets did; and so some read the words, "Prophesy not; let these (the false prophets and their followers) prophesy." Upon this the Lord threatens to add this to their judgments, that he will take away his prophets, and hereby give them up as dogs, to whom holy things are not to be cast, and prevent the shame and ignominy which his prophets suffered at their hands, as Matt. 7:6; or (as the words may be read as an interrogation), "If they shall not prophesy unto these, shall they take no shame?" Although they were rid of faithful messengers to warn them, yet that would not hold off judgments, nor exempt them from shame and confusion.

1. The Lord's word in the mouth of his messengers ought to be refreshing, and a means of fructifying unto the church, and will prove so in all but those who are nigh unto cursing. Therefore "prophesying" is in the original called "dropping," as rain, which refreshes and fructifies the earth.

2. A declining time and a faithful ministry will be at odds and contending. Decliners would either be rid of the word and ministry altogether, or if they think that too gross, yet they will allow none but those who are made to their mind, not those who may be instrumental to frame them according to God's mind. "Prophesy not, they say to those who prophesy," or, "prophesy not; let these prophesy."

3. The Lord will have his truth published, as long as he sees fit, or has use for it, oppose who will; and so the words may be read; when the wicked said, "prophesy not," the Lord answers, "they shall prophesy!" Further, when men become so desperately wicked as not only not to care for the word, but to study to affront and injure its messengers, it is righteous with God to deprive them of it, for a judgment to them and for the good of his wronged servants. "They shall not prophesy to them, that they shall not take shame"; see Ezek. 3:26, 27.

4. Though wicked men think all sure enough if they are freed from that eyesore of a reproving and threatening Word and ministry, yet that would put them no farther from judgments for sin. This is imported in the other reading: "If they shall not prophesy, shall they take no shame?" As if he had said, will that exempt them from judgments, that the word is removed? No verily, for it is a judgment itself, and a presage of more following.

> Ver. 7. O you who are named the house of Jacob, is the Spirit of the Lord straitened? Are these his doings? Do not my words do good to him who walks uprightly?

To this accusation the Lord subjoins a sad expostulation with his people, who are now so far degenerated as to scorn and oppose his messengers, as if they might limit his Spirit to speak only what pleased them, or as if his Spirit were limited in doing good and preaching comforts, since they were not fit for them, but must only threaten. He asks them if their ways and doings were approved of God, and if they called for comforting doctrine; and he questions them further, if they could allege that threatenings and judgments were his usual way of dealing with his people, in whom he delighted, if he were not provoked by their sin. He appeals to them, asking if his words did not both speak and perform good things, and would prove so to them if they were holy; and consequently it was not he nor his prophets, but themselves who were to blame, that the word spoke hard things unto them and that accordingly they were punished.

1. It is a deplorable case, and sadly to be lamented, when men stand in opposition to the word of God and its carriers; so this expostulation and these pressing interrogations imply.

2. Men may both think and do many things with great boldness, which they would be forced to condemn and find a witness against in their bosoms; for these questions, put to their consciences, imply that God had a witness for him there, and they dared not say or do as they did if their consciences were put to it, as in his sight.

3. Many have, and study to keep up a name which they are ill worthy of. "O you who are named the house of Jacob," says he, but in no way like that which Jacob was and should be; see John 8:40; Hos. 12:3.

4. God can discern between show and substance, and will see a fault in those who glory in fair titles, for he calls them as they are: "you are named the house of Jacob," and you have only a name.

5. It is an evidence that a visible church is degenerated, whatever show they have, when they turn opposers of the word of the Lord in the mouth of his servants, and of his servants for their message's sake; for it is the true glory of the church to have messengers carrying God's mind to them, and to entertain the message and messengers as is becoming.

6. Those who oppose and fight against the word of God and his messengers, do in effect fight against the Spirit of the Lord, whose word it is; for these oppressors are challenged as "straitening the Spirit of the Lord."

7. It is a high presumption and injury done to the Spirit, to think to imprison and deny him liberty in the mouths of his servants to speak anything but what men please; for

the question, "is the Spirit of the Lord straitened?" imports
that it was not seemly that they should limit him in giving
commission to his servants.

8. The Lord has a storehouse of spirit to bring forth comforts, and a storehouse of power to produce mercies, if his
people are fit for them; "is the spirit of the Lord straitened?"
This imports also that it was not for lack of fullness in his
Spirit to publish or perform the good things, that the prophets were commissioned only to threaten. See Isa. 50:2.

9. When the Lord sends forth sad threatenings in the mouth
of his servants, it becomes a people seriously to examine
their ways, to see them disapproved of God and deserving
such entertainment. Therefore he leads them from quarreling
with the Spirit of God or with his servants, seriously to consider, "are these his doings?" -- that is, whether their own
ways were agreeable to the law, or whether they were such
as the Spirit of God works in his people.

10. The Lord's ordinary way of dealing with his people in
whom he delights, is mercy. Though he did now threaten and
deal harshly with them, yet they might be abundantly convinced that it was hot his usual way to do so, nor a course
in which he took pleasure, if their case did not call for it.
See Mic. 7:18; Lam. 3:3.

11. That which God requires in his people is not so much
their profession and speaking, as their walking and conduct,
and that they study a constant course of uprightness and
sincerity, though they cannot attain to perfection. It is required that they walk uprightly.

12. As the upright walker will need the word much for
direction and encouragement, so to such the word speaks
only good, though they may read and apply it wrongly sometimes, because of their distempers and fears. They may
mistake when the word speaks against their corruptions,
which is without prejudice to their sincerity, and when the
word speaks hard things by which their further good is
promoted in the end; "do not my words do good to him who
walks uprightly?"

13. The word's saying of good is indeed a doing of good;
not only because comforting messages strengthen and revive
the heart, but also because of the certain performance of
what the word says. When it is said, it may be counted done:
"my words do good."

14. The goodness of God to his people may deeply convince and humble them, for by sin they provoke him to do
otherwise; therefore all this is set forth to be in God, that

their sin may be seen great when it causes such strange dealing.

> Ver. 8. Even of late my people have risen up as an enemy;
> you pull off the robe with the garment from those who
> pass by securely as men averse from war.

A third accusation is for their cruel robbery, by which also he sets forth the sad fruits of their contempt for the prophets and the true cause why God by their ministry handled them so roughly. The sum of the accusation is that they, whose fathers had been famous for valour in wars and for defending the country against a common enemy, had now of late become robbers of the innocent, and as cruel enemies took away both the upper and lower garment from those who were travelling peaceably, as minding no war; or did so deal with them as if they had taken them in war and sent them away stripped, as if they had been in a battle.

1. Contempt and oppression unto God's word and messengers makes men barbarous and inhuman, without all civility; and men following such courses cannot expect that the word should speak peace unto them. This is a fruit of their opposing the prophets, that they were given over to such cruelty; and this is the reason why hard things were prophesied.

2. The degeneration of men from former good ways, and the present evils of the time, are much to be observed and hammered upon by the servants of God; for this is the subject of his accusation, that even of late, or yesterday, they were thus degraded.

3. As declining professors are ordinarily plagued with singular profanity, so profession and privileges will serve to aggravate their guilt. Therefore, though only in name "the house of Jacob" (ver. 7), yet in the challenge the Lord gives them their titles: "my people have risen up." Since they desired to be esteemed so, he would make use of it to their disadvantage if they would not walk according to what they pretended to.

4. Oppression of others, and for men so to carry themselves toward friends as open and violent enemies do, is a practice not becoming in those who call themselves the people of God; for this is the challenge, "my people have risen up as an enemy."

> Ver. 9. The women of my people you have cast out from
> their pleasant houses; from their children you have
> taken away my glory forever.

He persists in his accusation, and gives a further instance
of their inhumanity in their carriage toward women and
children, whom wars ordinarily spare. They cast women violently out of their houses where they lived pleasantly; and
by bringing children to slavery and misery, they forever
deprived them of that dignity allowed them by God as his
people. Hence learn:

1. All the children of God will in divine providence meet
with their own share of trials, and should look for them; for
here women and children are not exempted more than men.

2. Though the church and its members may deserve afflictions at the Lord's hand, yet these same afflictions will
endear them to him, at least insofar as to be a ground of
challenge against instruments, that they have meddled with
such. Therefore whatever these afflicted ones were otherwise, yet in their trouble and in the challenge of oppressors
they are "the women of my people."

3. God, the preserver of men, has a special regard to the
weaker sex and tenderer years of persons, and will aggravate
injuries done unto them.

4. Pleasures and tender usage are not to be looked upon
as abiding things by those who enjoy them; but considering
them as transient, they ought to look for changes when the
Lord shall be pleased to call them to it, as we are taught
by the experience of these tender women, cast out of their
pleasant houses.

5. There is a special glory allowed by God unto his church,
by which she may be separated from all people; and the Lord
will maintain her in this against all who would deprive her
of it. This is signified by that external glory and privileges
conferred on Israel; and he now challenges oppressors for
depriving their children of them by putting them in a posi-
tion not beseeming the free people of God. "From their
children you have taken away my glory." See Exod. 33:16.

6. Perseverance in an ill way does exceedingly aggravate
the sinfulness of it. "You have taken away glory forever,"
that is, without quitting that wicked way or ceasing to rob.

7. It may also be interpreted that by making children
bondmen they aimed to deprive them of their glory perpetually; and so though the children might be relieved from
bondage, yet their oppressors are reckoned with according

to their aim and the nature of the work. This teaches that whatever the Lord may do to moderate the afflictions unjustly inflicted by men, yet instruments must answer to God for all that the nature of their work tended to, and for all they intended in it, though restrained by his providence.

> Ver. 10. Arise, and depart, for this is not your rest; because it is polluted, it shall destroy you, even with a sore destruction.

The Lord's sentence and threatening for this wickedness is that as they had cast others out of their houses, so the Lord would banish them from the Holy Land, which was given to them as a rest, only on condition of covenant-keeping; and because they had polluted the land by sin, therefore it should violently cast them out.

1. It is incident to men, when they have committed great wickedness, yet to promise to themselves peace because of some external privileges; for this charge, "arise and depart," implies that notwithstanding their sin, they were not thinking of removing, because the land was "a rest."

2. Sin provokes God to turn upside-down great privileges, which are conferred upon a visible church on condition of obedience; yea, it provokes him to prove himself superior, for they hold all their enjoyments from him, and to deprive them of rest and quiet if they are resting in sin. Whereas the land of Canaan was given for a rest (Ps. 95:11), now the Lord summons them to remove, and threatens it should not be a rest because of their sin. "Arise and depart, for this is not your rest." See Numb. 14:34; 1 Sam. 2:31-36.

3. Men by sin do not only set themselves against God, but do pollute and defile all the creatures and mercies given them by God, by employing them to the dishonour of God; for the promised land is polluted by these sinners. See Lev. 18:25, 28. Man going in rebellion draws many creatures, abused by him, away with him.

4. Mercies are given that we might serve God with them, not that we might defile them; therefore it is just with God to take away whatever we dishonour him in or by. "This is not a rest, because it is polluted."

5. Abuse of God's mercies draws on sharpest judgments of any; "it (that is, the land) shall destroy you even with a sore destruction." This the land did, both in spewing them out as it did the Canaanites (Lev. 18:28), as loathing to bear or feed those who dishonour God, and in being the great cause

of their sore judgment, that they had polluted a land of promise, where God in his ordinances dwelt; and so it had been better, when God should reckon with them, that they had dwelt elsewhere.

> Ver. 11. If a man walking in the spirit of falsehood lies, saying, I will prophesy to you of wine and of strong drink, he shall even be the prophet of this people.

In the fourth place, they are accused because, though they opposed true prophets, yet they approved and delighted in false prophets, and those who pretended to receive inspirations, and prophets who would flatter them and promise prosperity to those who were continuing in sin.

1. The most profane in the visible church may yet desire some show of divine institutions and ordinances, and some sort of divine approbation to their way if they can have it; for the speech, "he shall even be a prophet to this people," imports that they would not willingly lack prophets, but would have them, provided they go their way. So, though they reject true prophets, yet they may have prophets, and may seem not to lack divine approbation. Men may be thus profane, though they may not come to the height of rejecting all ordinances, nor declaring openly that they care not for God's approbation.

2. It is no new thing to see men pretending to receive the Spirit of God, and revelations and lights from him, who are only deceivers, if not deceived also, and sent as a plague to a sinful people; for there are those who "walk in the spirit" (that is, pretend to receive inspiration as prophets), and yet all this is but falsehood, and their doctrine is a lie.

3. There will never be false prophets and clawbacks lacking, to humour and soothe up a declining people; there shall be those who "prophesy of wine and strong drink."

4. As it is a great snare and judgment to a people, to find any shelter against naked truth, and prophets against prophets, so these false prophets are discouragements to the true messengers of God, for they flatter those whom faithful messengers threaten. It is the people's comfort that they have prophets to oppose those whom they reject (ver. 9). See Jer. 18:18. And it is a great cause why Micah's threatenings take no effect, that they in the meantime prophesy of wine and strong drink. Such was Micaiah's trial when he had to do with Ahab (1 Kings 22:12-14).

5. Those who pretend to any eminence in God's house or service, without his call or approbation, are ordinarily branded with badges of his displeasure; for these who "walk in the Spirit," or pretend to revelation, are plagued either with delusion or impudence (as they ordinarily are who abuse light most,) in that they dare "prophesy of wine and strong drink" to a rebellious people.

6. Though the Lord may for a time forbear gross sinners, yea, and plague them with prosperity also, yet it is false doctrine to preach peace and prosperity to a profane people, as if God approved of them when he gives them prosperity, or as if any prosperity they got were not ripening them for sorer judgments. As these false prophets lied in lacking a revelation and commission to deliver such doctrine, when on the contrary God was threatening the people, so it is still a lie to prophesy in these terms, and to prophesy "of wine and strong drink" to such a people.

7. It is a woeful condition when all that the visible church is set upon is pleasure and prosperity, and all that they have to do with prophets is to make them glad with hopes of it. He is not their choice who speaks to them of their sin and God's grace, but they who prophesy of wine; so a peole is in a desperate case when it delights only in such doctrine as may please their fancy, and will not admit of freedom in doctrine. Therefore it is a matter of challenge, and a cause of God's condemnation of them (calling them not "my people," but "this people"), that such a one shall be the prophet of this people, and not faithful Micah. See Isa. 30:10; Jer. 5:31.

> Ver. 12. I will surely assemble all of you, O Jacob; I will surely gather the remnant of Israel. I will put them together as the sheep of Bozrah, as the flock in the midst of their fold; they shall make great noise because of the multitude of men.
>
> 13. The breaker has come up before them; they have broken up, and have passed through the gate, and have gone out by it; and their King shall pass before them, and the Lord at their head.

In the close of the chapter, the Lord sweetens the former threatenings with promises of restitution of his Israel under Christ. In these are contained their recollection and gathering, that Christ as their shepherd shall gather them in one, shall feed, secure, and multiply them (ver. 12), that all impediments which might hinder their progress shall be taken out of their way, and that their march shall be stately and their conduct safe. Christ their King, who is the Lord, shall go before them as their general.

1. In the throng of greatest displeasure the truly godly are allowed comfort, that they may not be crushed with threatenings, of which they are most apprehensive because of their tenderness; in the midst of their threatenings Jacob and Israel get a promise. See Matt. 28:4, 5.

2. The children of God ought to study much the certainty of promises, that they may rely upon them without hesitation. "I will surely assemble, I will surely gather," says he; or "in assembling I will assemble," which imports his persistence in the work until he perfects it.

3. Spiritual restoration by Christ is ample matter of comfort to all believers in times of public calamities; for that is the substance of this promise held forth for their comfort. It was their comfort under the law to foresee it, and ought to be ours to enjoy it. See John 8:56; Luke 10:23, 24.

4. No vicissitude of providence has buried in oblivion the covenant made with Jacob and his seed; so the catholic church in all nations has a right to the spiritual promises made to Jacob and his seed. These to whom the promises are made are called Jacob and Israel, to show to the seed of Israel that he will assemble them, being mindful of his covenant, and will confirm all his elect, that by believing in Christ they are made his Israel and heirs to Israel's promises.

5. Christ the great shepherd will lack none of his chosen ones, however scattered, dispersed, and far from him; but will have them all gathered and brought in to the fold of his church. "I will surely assemble Jacob, all of you; I will surely gather the remnant of Israel," says the Lord to scattered Israel, and to his scattered elect through the world. See John 10:16.

6. Christ, having gathered his people as in one flock, will do the duty of a faithful shepherd, in feeding and securing them from dangers. "I will put them together as the sheep of Bozrah," a place in Edom or Moab, where there were many flocks and good pasture (1 Chron. 1:43, 44; Jer. 48:24; 2 Kings 3:4), "as the flock in the midst of their fold."

7. The Lord, who from remnants can make multitudes, will in his own time bless his church with increase and multiplication of converts, and hereby will make up the loss of their scatterings and sufferings. "The remnant shall

make a noise by reason of the multitude of men." See Isa. 49:20, 21.

8. Though there may be many difficulties in the ways of God which his people are to follow, yet a people waiting upon him shall find impediments removed; and they have nothing to do but go on until they dip their feet in Jordan's brink, and he will make it dry. "The breaker has come up before them; they have broken up and have passed through the gate, and have gone out by it." This alludes to the custom of armies, who usually send some before to prepare the way and break through strait passages, that the army may march without trouble. See Isa. 57:14; Isa. 62:10.

9. Christ's church does not lack a king to go out and in before her, to protect, defend, and guide her in her way, and as a general to fight her battles; for "their King shall pass before them, and the Lord at the head of them."

10. There is none to be acknowledged as having kingly power in and over the church except the Lord Jehovah; for "their King passing before them is Jehovah in the head of them"; that is, their general in the forefront of them, as the word is translated (2 Chron. 20:27). See Hosea 1:11; Isa. 52:12.

CHAPTER III

The prophet has until now faithfully revealed the sins of the body of this people, and denounced God's judgments because of sin. Now he comes more particularly to challenge the rulers both in church and state, especially in Judah, and to charge them for their sins. This he does:

1. Individually, in relation to their own particular punishments. The princes are threatened, because they ought to know right and wrong and walk accordingly, and yet they were most perverse and inhuman in oppression (ver. 1-3); therefore in their strait they shall not be owned by God (ver. 4). The false prophets, who deluded the people and preached to serve their own base ends (ver. 5), are threatened with such confusion as would make them ashamed of their trade (ver. 6,7), whereas he, a faithful man, should bear out in his duty (ver. 8).

2. Conjointly, in relation to the judgments which they have provoked by their sin to come upon the church of God. The rulers perverted justice (ver. 9) and built the holy city with

goods taken by oppression (ver. 10); and generally, both
rulers and teachers were corrupted with bribes and love
of gain, and yet they would presumptuously rely on God
(ver. 11); and therefore he threatens that for their sake
Zion should be laid desolate (ver. 12).

> Ver. 1. And I said, Hear, I pray you, O heads of Jacob, and
>   you princes of the house of Israel: is it not for you to
>   know judgment?

Here he challenges the rulers in peace and war, for
affected ignorance of the law of God; and he lays a reason
for lamenting their wickedness, in that it concerned them
to be better acquainted with the will of God in the matter of
justice and equity than others, and so they ought to be
exemplary in their knowledge and obedience (knowledge
including consequent affection and practice), whereas in
their practice they had proved themselves ignorant or
despisers of the law. We need not curiously inquire whether
by "Jacob" is meant the kingdom of Judah or of Israel, the
ten tribes; for at least the latter part of the threatenings in
this chapter is especially directed against Judah (Jer. 26:18);
but by these names we are generally to understand the people
who had come forth of Jacob, otherwise called Israel.

1. When a land in general is guilty of defection, rulers
in church and state have their own eminent guilt in it. This
is imported in the prophet's scope: having reproved the whole
body of the people, he now comes to challenge the rulers
in a special manner; "hear, O house of Jacob."

2. Faithful ministers ought not only to inveigh against sin
in general, or common sins only, but in particular ought to
reprehend the sins of every rank, even of rulers; for so
does Micah's practice teach.

3. Men in greatest eminence are bound to hear God speaking by his messengers, and to receive the messages sent
unto them, for they are under the law as well as others.
"Hear, O heads of Jacob, and you princes of the house of
Israel."

4. As rulers especially are unwilling to be brought to an
account for their ways by the ministry of the word, so ministers are bound to omit no discretion and tender insinuation
consistent with their fidelity and zeal against sin, which may
be instrumental to make the word effective and not to be
stumbled at. This does Micah's way of entreaty teach; "hear,
I pray you," which imports both the rulers' averseness to

hear him, and his tender condescension that they may hear.

5. Whatever may be the success of a faithful minister in the discharge of his duty, yet his faithfulness and diligence will be matter of peace to him when the conscience reflects upon it. Here Micah gives a comfortable account of his ministry; "I said, Hear."

6. Besides the general obligation lying upon all men, especially within the visible church, to know and obey the will of God, it is especially incumbent to rulers and great ones among the Lord's people to do so; for they are enabled with advantages because of their education, means, encouragements, leisure, offices, etc., and therefore obliged to know more than others, and to put their knowledge in practice, that they may be examples to others. "O heads of Jacob, and princes of Israel, is it not for you to know judgment?"

7. It is a good evidence that a man delights to know and obey the revealed will of God in all things, when he is careful in the matter of his particular station to walk by that rule. Therefore Micah puts them to trial in the matter of "knowing judgment," or justice and equity, which belonged to them in their particular station, as being judges to the people.

8. Whatever men may oppose to the challenges of ministers in the matter of affected ignorance or willful neglect of known duties, yet these excuses will not satisfy their own consciences when they are seriously put to it. Therefore the prophet asks them a question which they could not deny: "Is it not for you to know judgment?"

> Ver. 2. You who hate the good and love the evil, who pluck off their skin from them, and their flesh from off their bones.
>
> 3. Who also eat the flesh of my people, and flay their skin from off them, and they break their bones and chop them in pieces, as for the pot, and as flesh within the caldron.

In opposition to what they ought to be, he sets forth their contrary disposition and practice, that they were abhorrers of what was good and lovers of evil. And further, they cruelly oppressed and undid the Lord's people, by taking away the very means of their subsistence and livelihood, as if they had flayed their skin from off them, eaten their flesh, and broken their bones to boil them for meat, as butchers and cooks do with beasts for man's food. Hence learn:

1. The Lord does not reckon that men know anything, when the truth being known is not affected nor any endeavours used to put it into practice. They did not "know judgment"; and why? Because they "hate the good and love the evil."

2. The Lord notes chiefly the disposition and affection of men's hearts toward good or evil. It is a desperate condition when not only practice is out of course, but affection also is alienated from God and inclined to evil; "you who hate the good and love the evil."

3. Whatever oppressors may pretend to be the cause of their cruelty toward their inferiors, as that they stood in need, yet the Lord sees their malice to flow from their perverse and corrupt affections.

4. Greatest perversity is usually found in those who ought to, and may, and yet will not make use of such means as might promote piety and justice. This perversity is in the "heads of Jacob," who had means and occasions to incite them to do otherwise.

5. Oppression is inhuman butchery in God's account, and murder in a degree far above simple slaughter; the oppressed pine for want, and the oppressors (as barbarians or wild beasts) eat that which is the very life and flesh of the poor. They "pluck off their skin from them, and their flesh from off their bones, and eat the flesh of my people."

6. Though magistrates and great men think themselves to be above law, yet they have no power to oppress a people (especially God's people) and deal with them as they list, but they must be accountable to God for their conduct toward them; and though the oppressed or others dare not challenge them for their injurious dealing, yet there is a God who will lay it to their charge; for they are here challenged by God for oppressing his people.

> Ver. 4. Then they shall cry unto the Lord, but he will not hear them; he will even hide his face from them at that time, as they have behaved themselves ill in their doings.

Now follows their particular sentence and judgment by way of retaliation. As they, oppressing the poor, had a deaf ear to their cries, so they should meet judgment without mercy or compassion, and should not be recognised nor answered by God, though out of their trouble they should seek unto him.

1. The greatest of men, and they who most wickedly forget God, shall at one time or other be sensible of God's majesty,

and their errand shall come in his way; for so does this threatening import, that they shall be put to seek God whom otherwise they did not regard: "then they shall cry."

2. Natural men may make some show of seeking God in trouble, not in faith or in love, but out of sense of trouble. "Then," that is, when the common calamities formerly threatened, or their own particular corrections for their sin are lying on, "then shall they cry."

3. It is righteous with God not to own this crying of the wicked in their trouble, because of their former wickedness and present unsoundness, and particularly that he may recompence them for not hearkening to the cry of the poor whom they oppressed. "They shall cry unto the Lord, but he will not hear them."

4. It is extreme misery to be totally deserted by God in trouble, and to lack his favour and sense of reconciliation, which might support them in any extremity; for it is here the extremity of misery that in their trouble "he will hide his face from them at that time."

5. God, by not owning a man in trouble, would have wickedness seen and lamented as the cause of it (though he may seem also to do this at times to try the faith of his children); for so does this reason import: "as they have behaved themselves in all their doings."

> Ver. 5. Thus saith the Lord concerning the prophets who make my people err, who bite with their teeth and cry, Peace; and he who puts not into their mouths, they even prepare war against him.

In the next place, he accuses the false prophets, who by false doctrine deceived the people. By preaching peace, they did in effect destroy people's souls with delusion (as if these dogs had devoured the Lord's sheep with their teeth), or, they flattered the people in sin, that they might get somewhat to eat and devour their substance. If they were not satisfied and humoured, according to their own desire, they became bitter enemies, and denounced judgments, though they formerly flattered them.

1. False teachers are not the least among the sad companions of a declining time; nor will the Lord forget to reckon with them. Here the Lord has such to deal with: "thus says the Lord (not one prophet envying another) concerning the prophets." See Lam. 2:14.

2. An unfaithful ministry is a most effectual means to prevail with people, and carry them out of the way of God; for "the prophets make my people err." See how far they prevail above any other means (1 Kings 22:20-22).

3. As it is a great sin against God to seduce and mislead a people in whom he has interest, so the negligence and treachery of pastors endears the Lord's people much more to him, and calls for his special care. See Ezek. 13:23.

4. It is a great cruelty and murder to proclaim peace to a sinful and impenitent people; "they bite with their teeth and cry peace"; their very cry of peace is cruel biting and devouring of souls (Ezek. 22:25).

5. It is a mercenary and hireling disposition in pastors, to seek themselves or their goods as the chief and only scope of their calling. "They bite with their teeth, and cry, Peace"; that is, they flatter the people so that they may get occasion to eat them up and live upon them (Ezek. 13:18, 19), or they preached for their own advantage, seeking the things of the people and not the people themselves (2 Cor. 12:14).

6. It is also unbecoming in the faithful messengers of God, to accommodate the discharge of their ministry as may best promote their own ends, and to threaten or countenance, bless or curse, according as they get or miss their own gain. Such is the practice of false prophets. While they have somewhat to bite with their teeth, they cry, Peace; "and he who puts not into their mouths (or, 'he who gives not according to their mouths,' that is, as much as they desire or seek) they even prepare war against him" and become his mortal enemy.

7. Men who are covetous and given to filthy lucre, can hardly be faithful in a ministerial calling, to divide the word aright; this is taught by the example of the false prophets, who looked not to the mind of God in discharge of their office, but to what might best suit with their own ends, and framed their doctrine accordingly.

> Ver. 6. Therefore night shall be unto you, that you shall not have a vision; and it shall be dark unto you, that you shall not divine; and the sun shall go down over the prophets, and the day shall be dark over them.
>
> 7. Then shall the seers be ashamed, and the diviners confounded; yea, they shall all cover their lips, for there is no answer from God.

The Lord's sentence against these false prophets is that they shall have no visions or divinations from God; not that they had ever had any from him, but that the dark night of trouble and calamity should come on, and the sun of their prosperity and delights should go down (as the same form of speech is used, Jer. 15:9), they shall thereby be so overwhelmed and confounded that they shall not dare any more to feign false prophecies, or pretend to receive revelations, as they formerly did. This is amplified (ver. 7) from its effects: these who gave themselves out to be seers and diviners, when it shall appear by events that they never had any vision from God, and that (being confounded by trouble) they dare not speak so boldly as they did, they shall be despised of all, shall think shame of themselves, and shall cover their lip in sign of grief and confusion (Lev. 13:45).

1. God will have false teachers seen in their own colours, and will decipher them to the world; so does this threatening teach.

2. Events will prove that peace preached to a backsliding and impenitent people is no vision from God; for the Lord threatens that by sending "night and darkness" of trouble, contrary to their doctrine, he shall depose the false prophets and make it manifest that they had no vision from him. See Jer. 28:5-9.

3. However deluded and presumptuous men may be in the day of their prosperity and sunshine, yet trouble will confound their presumption and dry up their delusion; for when it is "night and dark, and their sun goes down, and their day is dark," then "they shall not have a vision nor divine."

4. False teachers and unfaithful men in God's house shall in due time be plagued with confusion, contempt, and ignominy, and shall be made to think shame of themselves and their way; for "then the seers shall be ashamed, and the diviners confounded." See Zechariah 13:4; Malachi 2:8, 9.

> Ver. 8. But truly I am full of power by the Spirit of the Lord, and of judgment, and of might, to declare unto Jacob his transgression, and to Israel his sin.

While Micah is denouncing judgments against false prophets, in opposition to their unfaithfulness in their calling through disloyalty and fear, he sets forth himself as furnished with gifts and endowments requisite for the faithful discharge of his office, though he had few or none to second him in carrying hard tidings, and great ones of all ranks against him. By this he clears himself that he was not a false prophet, and that he should not be confounded nor be forced to be ashamed of himself or of his office, as they should do.

1. It is in no way contrary to true humility for a man to assert his own calling and endowments from God, when otherwise he and his message are ready to be brought into contempt by the humours of men; for so does Micah's example teach, for he vindicates himself from any contempt which false prophets and their followers might cast upon him.

2. A man's clear testimony in his conscience, of his calling, fidelity, and equippage by God to discharge his calling, will prove comforting when the Lord is about to reckon with those who run without his calling. Thus Micah, after the threatenings against false teachers, comforts himself: "but truly I am full of power."

3. Though Micah had some extraordinary qualifications, yet from this we may gather several characteristics of a faithful minister, every one of which may be a lesson to teach ministers what to seek. (a) Though the Lord may bless the mean gifts of those who are honest, yet neither are ministers to be empty vessels, nor filled with ostentation, but with a large measure of real qualifications: "I am full," he says. (b) Their endowments must be not only such as are acquired by the use of ordinary means and helps of literature, and much less ought their own spirits to bear sway here; but they should seek the Spirit of the Lord to sanctify their spirits and abilities, and furnish them in their dependence upon him. Says he, "I am full by the Spirit of the Lord"; he had it extraordinarily as a prophet, and ministers ought to have it in an ordinary way. They ought to have not only the spirit of their calling, but the Spirit of sanctification also, as their duty, and for their souls' good.

3. As ministers need not only endowments of matter, but such life and zeal in publishing the word, as becomes the oracles of God; so where the Spirit of the Lord is present, there will be efficacy, life, and zeal accompanying the doctrine; for he says, "I am full of power by the Spirit of the Lord."

4. A faithful minister ought also to be endowed with sufficient knowledge to speak according to the word, and not to falsify the mind of God through ignorance, and to speak it seasonably with prudence; and with fidelity and straightness he should tell the whole mind of God according to equity and truth, without partiality or regard to one or another; this the word "judgment" imports.

5. Ministers also stand in need of fortitude and courage, to speak out boldly what is the mind of God, and constantly

to adhere to it, without fear of any or without being blown over with the wind of flattery. This a faithful minister must expect from God only: "I am full of might by the Spirit of the Lord."

6. A faithful minister looks upon all his endowments, as not given to be laid up and contract rust beside him, or for himself only; but that he ought to improve them for God and his people, in his place and station; "I am full," says he, "to declare unto Jacob," and to empty out that goodness for their profit and good.

7. It is an evidence of a faithful and able minister to be much in opposition to sin, and freely to charge it home, and to "declare transgression and sin" to the sinner, and not to be deceived or blinded with fair titles or shows, but to discern and reprove sin even in Jacob and Israel.

> Ver. 9. Hear this, I pray you, you heads of the house of Jacob, and princes of the house of Israel, you who abhor judgment and pervert all equity.
>
> 10. They build up Zion with blood and Jerusalem with iniquity.
>
> 11. The heads thereof judge for reward, and the priests thereof teach for hire, and the prophets thereof divine for money; yet they will lean upon the Lord and say, Is not the Lord among us? No evil can come upon us.

In the second part of the chapter, Micah gives a proof of what he had said of his own fidelity in speaking to all sorts of rulers, civil and ecclesiastical, ordinary and extra-ordinary, conjointly. He sets before them their sin, and how they procured Zion's ruin; he accuses the rulers in state that they, who ought to have been patrons of justice, did abhor and pervert it (ver. 9); that instead of adorning the holy city with justice and judgment, their care was set upon stately buildings, and they gathered means for that end by cruel oppression (ver. 10). And generally he accuses all of them that justice was perverted through bribery and covetousness, and that their churchmen were mercenary, and made their calling subservient to their gain; and yet all of them were carnally confident and presumptuous of God's favour and presence among them, and of exemptions from judgment (ver. 11). Hence learn:

1. Persons in eminence, especially those who are accus-tomed to sin, are usually deaf to what the Lord says, and

therefore must be called to hear, as they are called again after the former call (ver. 1).

2. The messengers of the Lord must not give over, when their message is not received; but they must cry until they get either an audience or have delivered their souls; for Micah repeats, "hear, I pray you."

3. It is the duty of faithful ministers in reproving the faults of rulers, to give evidence that they do not despise their authority when they reprove their faults, and not to be lacking in any respectful manner that is due unto them. Therefore Micah gives them their titles and again entreats: "hear, I pray you, you heads of the house of Jacob and princes of the house of Israel." The princes of Judah to whom this was spoken are called rulers in Jacob and Israel (Jer. 26:18), not only because the house of David still had a right to govern all Israel (and therefore such a title seems to be given to Jehoshaphat, 2 Chron. 21:2), or because their behaviour was more like Israel than Judah (and therefore it is given to Ahaz, 2 Chron. 28:1-8), or because there was no more left of all Jacob's race after the captivity of the ten tribes except Judah to govern; but because they were rulers of a people who came of the stock of Jacob the son of Isaac, otherwise called Israel.

4. The Lord's quarrel against men is not so much for sins of ignorance and infirmity, as for those which flow from a perverse disposition, going wrong because they love to do so, and because they hate what is right; therefore they are again challenged, that they "abhor judgment and pervert all equity."

5. The Lord will admit of no fair pretences to palliate any sinful deed. It is no excuse that they "build Zion," if it is done "by blood and iniquity," or with goods taken by bloody oppression from the poor; but these pretences defile more that which they endeavour to cleanse, and it is a matter of sadder iniquity that they should build the holy city by such means: "they build up Zion with blood, and Jerusalem with iniquity."

6. Those are unsurely built houses and estates, against which God is angry for the manner of their raising; it is a quarrel against them and their house, that they build it with blood and iniquity. See Hab. 2:12.

7. However the Lord may allow lawful maintenance to those who are publicly employed in church or state, yet to receive hire or gifts so as to judge partially, is gross iniquity. "The heads thereof judge for reward." See Exod. 18:21.

8. When bribes are received by men in office, either in church or state, it is an evidence that they will not do their duty faithfully; for "judging for reward, teaching for hire, and divining for money," is all one with false judgment and erroneous teaching and divination; for he is true who said, "a gift blinds the wise, and perverts the words of the righteous" (Exod. 23:8; Deut. 16:19).

9. Presumption will feed up men with delusion under very gross sins and swiftly approaching judgment; for "yet they will lean upon the Lord."

10. External privileges of the church and external reformation of worship are ordinarily turned by secure sinners into a snare or plague to themselves, making them dream of God's favour and of peace, when wrath is upon them and trouble at hand. Such a snare was God's presence in his temple, and Hezekiah's reformation, to these profane rulers. "Is not the Lord among us?"

11. External privileges will not exempt profane sinners from deserved judgments, nor will external reformation hold it off, but rather ripen the faster for it; as to say, "Is not the Lord among us? no evil can come upon us," as long as they had not repented indeed (Jer. 26:18, 19).

12. God will approve of no faith but that which is fruitful, and which stirs up men to purify and cleanse their heart and way. They are here challenged, for when they have done all the former iniquities, and are going on in them, "yet they will lean upon the Lord," or pretend to have true faith, by which a man casts himself and all his burdens upon God, "and say, Is not the Lord among us?"

> Ver. 12. Therefore for your sake Zion shall be plowed as a field; and Jerusalem shall become heaps, and the mountain of the house shall be as the high places of the forest.

Now follows the Lord's sentence subjoined to this accusation. He threatens that for their sins the stately buildings of the holy city should be made desolate heaps; and the ground it was situated upon, especially the kingly dwelling, should come to be plowed as a common field, and the mount Moriah, upon which the temple stood, should become wild and desolate, as a forest, and filled with shrubs and bushes. See Micah 1:6.

1. No place or visible church has any privilege which sin will not make desolate; for no place had such promises as

Zion, Jerusalem, and the mountain of the house, and yet they were to be "plowed as a field, and become heaps."

2. The servants of God must be bold and faithful, not only in speaking against the sins of the rulers, but even against a church having great privileges, when she is found in transgression; for this passage is recorded as a proof of Micah's fidelity. See Jer. 26:18.

3. It is our duty to look upon sin and to be affected with it, not only as procuring chastisements upon ourselves, but especially as having a hand in bringing calamities on the church and kingdom in which we live. This he tells them: "For your sake Zion shall become heaps, and the mountain of the house shall be as the high places of the forest."

4. Universal defection of a land, especially of rulers and teachers, will bring on speedy desolation unless by repentance it is prevented (as the execution of this threatening was, in Hezekiah's days, Jer. 26:18, 19). "For your sake Zion shall be plowed as a field," says he to the corrupt rulers and teachers, because their corruption had a chief hand in procuring this ruin, and would involve the people in the same defection, to hasten the judgment.

5. Judgments on a backsliding church are most severe and sharp, though there be moderation in them to the elect; for no less is here threatened than utter destruction, "being plowed as a field, becoming heaps, and being as the high places of the forest"; so great a sin is the contempt of mercy offered to a church.

6. As for this part of their calamity, that the ground upon which the holy city and temple stood was to be "plowed as a field"; though when it was first denounced in Hezekiah's days, it was delayed by their repentance (Jer. 26:19), and though we do not find that it was accomplished at the first destruction of the temple, yet common history informs us that after the second destruction of the temple it was performed by the Romans, who after their custom plowed up the very ground upon which the temple stood, as a sign of perpetual desolation.

So infallibly certain is the word of God that after so long a span of time it will take effect. Though after repentance it had been delayed, yea, and after they had passed through many troubles and had been delivered, and so might think they had escaped the sentence, yet upon new sin and provocation, that sentence is still standing against them, and at last it takes effect.

CHAPTER IV

In this chapter (which agrees in part with Isa. 2), the Lord comforts the godly against the calamities which were foretold (Micah 3:12) by setting forth the glorious blessings of Christ's kingdom, or of the church of Jews and Gentiles under the Messiah. The chapter describes the glorious excellence and increase of the church (ver. 1, 2), her peace and tranquillity under the government of Christ (ver. 3, 4), her zeal and constancy in religion (ver. 5), and her delivery from former misery, such as **Israel was** to be under (ver. 6, 7) In the second part of the **chapter,** he makes a more comforting and particular application of the promises, by showing that the kingdom, as of old, should begin with them (ver. 8), and by showing his mind concerning their troubles (ver. 9, 10) and concerning the enterprises of their enemies (ver. 11-13).

> Ver. 1. But in the last days it shall come to pass that the mountain of the house of the Lord shall be established in the top of the mountains; and it shall be exalted above the hills, and people shall flow unto it.
>
> 2. And many nations shall come and say, Come and let us go up to the mountain of the Lord, and to the house of the God of Jacob, and he will teach us his ways, and we will walk in his paths; for the law shall go forth from Zion, and the word of the Lord from Jerusalem.

The first promise for comfort of the godly contains the excellence of the church, and the accession of many nations unto it. It has two branches.

I. Though the church of the Jews was to be in great misery for sin, yet in the days of the Messiah it should come to pass that the church (called by the name of old Zion, or "the mountain of the house," as best known to the Jews), and the church of Israel, as eminent and chief among the rest, should be exalted and glorious above every society that is excellent in the world; as if the mountain upon which the temple stood were made higher than any hill, or set upon the top of them. Hence learn:

1. As the Spirit of God is a Spirit of unity, and does not differ from himself in his manifestations to his servants, so it is a comforting thing when the messengers of God

concur and unite in bearing testimony to any truth in the church. So it was with Isaiah and Micah, who as contemporaries preach the same things (Isa. 2).

2. God no sooner afflicts his people than mercies, to make up their losses, come to his mind; and the church's afflictions are never to be studied without taking up also the promises made to her; for immediately upon the back of the former threatening (3:12) this promise comes forth, to testify his affection and to enable her to look upon the other.

3. The church's happiness and felicity is much in gracious promises, and she looks forward to their performance; "it shall come to pass," says the Lord. This was especially true under the law in comparison to the days of the gospel; and yet even under the kingdom of Christ, her happiness will not be complete until eternity shall come, and she is to live on in hope of that.

4. The chief and great glory of the church was reserved for the days of the gospel, and for the manifestation of Christ in the flesh. Though knowing and enjoying the Messiah by faith, the church in that day was kept under a pedagogy of the ceremonial law and the shadows of good things to come. Only "in the last days" will it "come to pass." See Luke 10:23, 24; Heb. 11:40; 1 Pet. 1:10-12.

5. The days of the gospel are the last days, in which all things foretold by the prophets will be accomplished, and we are daily to expect eternity and the close of time. The time between the first and second coming of Christ is called the "last days," or the evening of the world. See Heb. 1:2; 1 Pet. 1:20.

6. The true church of Christ is firm and impregnable, and elevated above the world; it is "the mountain of the house of the Lord." A mountain is strong and fixed, and is elevated above other things.

7. The church of Christ, though base in outward appearance (as the little hill Moriah, on which the temple stood) shall yet be, and is, truly excellent and glorious above all worldly estates and kingdoms, and above all idols. "The mountain of the house shall be established on the top of the mountains, and exalted above the hills"; that is, above potentates (which are compared to mountains, Jer. 51:25), and above idols, which are worshipped on hills or high places, and which are generally above all that is eminent in the world. This is accomplished partly when the church is made to rise upon the ruins of kingdoms and idols which oppose her (Isa. 60:12) and partly when kings bring their

glory to her (Isa. 60:10, 11), and it will be fulfilled yet more when Antichrist shall fall and all Israel shall be saved. Their eminences are but as hills to set her up higher. Chiefly, however, this is accomplished by God's presence in her (Ps. 68:15, 16).

8. The excellence and glory which God puts upon his church is not a transient or vanishing thing; but however she may be tossed, and dust cast upon her, yet her excellency will remain; for she is not only "exalted," but "established" in this eminence.

II. The second branch of this promise is the increase and spreading of the church (which is both an effect and an instance of her spiritual glory and eminence), for people of all nations (Isa. 2:2) shall embrace the gospel and join themselves unto the true church. Their fervour in coming is held forth in their mutual encouragements and upstirrings to come unto the church, for direction in ordering their journey. As all this has already been verified, so it will be yet more accomplished when the fullness of the Gentiles, being converted, shall profess their communion in the Christian religion with converted Israel, and shall receive from them a perfect directory for God's service, and shall join in faith and worship with them, when God shall remember his covenant and prove himself to be the God of Jacob.

1. It is the glory of the kingdom of Christ that it is universal. He shall prevail with his enemies to become subjects and acknowledge the church to be the princess of societies; and he shall persuade even whole nations under the gospel to become his church and a part of his kingdom; for "people shall flow unto it, and many nations shall come." The church shall not be confined within the bounds of Judea or of one nation only, nor shall only part of a nation join, but the whole nation.

2. Under the gospel the distinction and prerogatives of nations are taken away, and all have access unto the church. Some of all sorts will come, for "many people and many nations shall flow and come," as well as the Jews. See Col. 3:11.

3. If the glory and privileges of the church of Christ were ·well seen, they would make people not only come, but flow with zeal and fervour and in great numbers to her; the word "flowing" teaches us that they shall come as abundantly and with as much fervour as rivers running downward. See Jer. 31:12. Yea, a sight of this would make kings desire to partake of the portion of Christ's poor (Ps. 72:10-14).

4. In a time of conversion, especially of nations to the gospel and to Christ, there will be a willing and cheerful people; for so it is said here. "Many nations shall come and say, Come"; see Ps. 110:3.

5. Our willingness to come to Christ in his church ought to be evidenced by stirring up one another to come to him; for "they shall say, Come, and let us go up."

6. A converted people do yet stand in much need of mutual edification and stirring up of one another in their stations; so much does the practice of these converts teach us.

7. True mutual edification consists not in mutual exhortations only, but especially in practice, in walking as may edify and excite others. "Come and let us go"; they who are going themselves can rightly exhort others. See Zech. 8:21.

8. True converts must be drawn upward in their aim, affections, and practice from the earth; and though there be seeds of good and willingness in them, yet they will find the way of godliness a strait and steep path to their nature. Therefore their course is compared to ascending a mountain.

9. Those who draw near to God and join themselves to him in his church, ought to lay hold upon the covenant in which he has engaged himself to be gracious to all who seek him; they "go up to the house of the God of Jacob," the house of him who has entered into a covenant with Jacob's posterity, and with the Israel of the spirit.

10. That which is most eminent in a true convert, and which is first gained in one whose heart is touched, is their affectionate willingness to obey God. "We will walk in his paths," they say; their affection is won, and then they are ready to receive instruction. See Rom. 7:22.

11. Affection toward God is not enough for a people to render their way approved, but they must have knowledge of the will of God also, to direct their path; "he will teach us, and we will walk," they say.

12. Every true convert is made sensible of his natural ignorance and proneness to error, and becomes willing to receive instruction. "He will teach us of his ways." They account it a mercy to be taught, though his doctrine is not what they like or desire; it is his will, and that is enough.

13. Though the Lord has appointed a teaching ministry in his church, which his people should and will acknowledge, yet every believer is taught of God. First, they do not hang their faith on men's authority, but exalt God alone as the infallible teacher and lawgiver in his church; and they try

what men say, to see if it is agreeable to his mind. Second, they feel God in and by his appointed means, teaching truth effectually and persuasively to their hearts. See 1 Thess. 2:13.

14. As all knowledge of divine things ought not to rest in contemplations, but should stir up to practice, so men of much literal knowledge may be more profane in their conversation than others; but those who are taught of God, and acknowledge his authority in the means of instruction, and feel the efficacy of his Spirit conveying what is taught to their hearts, their knowledge will resolve in practice. It is the Lord's prerogative to convince the conscience and to subdue and stir up inclinations to practice what is taught. "He will teach us, and we will walk in his paths."

Unto this promise the prophet subjoins a reason why nations should seek to join with the church, viz. because the doctrine of salvation should go forth from the Jews among all nations, to stir them up to seek the Lord; and this light shall shine forth in the church in all ages to invite nations to come and seek teaching. Hence learn:

1. The glory of the church of the New Testament does not consist in idle ceremonies, but in the profession and holding forth of true doctrine, according to the word, which is the badge and mark of the true church. "The law (or 'the doctrine,' as the word in the original bears) shall go forth from Zion, and the word of the Lord from Jerusalem," that it may shine in all the church of the Gentiles; and this is a part of the eminence of the mountain of the Lord's house.

2. The Lord has made it clear that the doctrine of salvation, in the days of the Messiah, was not to be treasured up among the Jews only, as of old (Ps. 147:19), but to spread throughout the world; for "the law shall go forth from Zion."

3. The doctrine of the gospel is the same in substance with what was in the church of the Jews, though clothed with new circumstantials. Therefore it is called a law, alluding to the old name; but it comes not from Sinai, clothed with dark shadows and fearful terrors, but from Zion, adorned with clearness and seasoned with sweetness.

4. As the word of God published in his church is the instrument of true conversion, so it is likewise the means by which Christ enlarges his kingdom, and will prevail in the world to persuade nations to join themselves to him in his church. Therefore this is given as a reason for the enlargement of the church; "the law shall go forth from Zion."

Ver. 3. And he shall judge among many people, and rebuke strong nations afar off; and they shall beat their
swords into plowshares, and their spears into pruninghooks. Nation shall not lift up a sword against nation,
neither shall they learn war any more.

4. But they shall sit every man under his vine, and
under his fig tree, and none shall make them afraid;
for the mouth of the Lord of hosts has spoken it.

The next promise contains her peace and tranquillity (setting out yet more the church's glory) under Christ's government. God in his Son Christ, by his gospel, shall have and
exercise a spiritual jurisdiction and kingdom in the world,
and subdue them to his obedience; and he shall govern them
so as to procure peace and tranquillity to the church, that the
converted may serve God quietly in their particular stations,
and become useful to each other. Their condition is expressed
in terms taken from the usual practice of peaceful times,
in which men out of war turn their weapons of offence into
weapons of husbandry and utility, and in which men go about
those callings, and abide in the fields without fear of danger.
See 1 Kings 4:25.

1. Christ, coming with his gospel, is to reign as a king
and have authority over those who receive him; "he shall
judge among many people."

2. Christ's kingdom is universal; his church is spread
over all the world, and he has power over all for her good.
This is a truth to be frequently studied, that he may have
his glory, and that every particular church and believer may
be comforted in such a head, and in hope of the enlargement
of his dominion, when by apostasy or persecution it is confined to narrow bounds. Therefore it is again promised that
"he shall judge among many people, and rebuke strong nations
afar off," i.e. far off from Judea; all people, far and near.

3. The Lord may deal very terribly with those whom he
purposes to do much good unto. He may convince, rebuke,
and afflict them for sin, that he may drive them to his mercy;
for that is a part of his work in gathering a kingdom, to
judge and rebuke.

4. Though the Lord does not make use of weapons of war
in gathering his church, but only his word with its reproofs
and terrors, yet that will suffice to subdue them to him, for
nothing in the creature is able to stand out against the Lord
when he convinces and rebukes for sin. If he "rebukes many

nations," they will feel his reproof and "beat their swords into plowshares," and will come under his government.

5. This promise of great tranquility and peace is not to be understood as if the Lord condemned Christians for making wars; for the magistrate, bearing the sword of justice, is the ordinance of God (Rom. 13). Nor are we to understand by this that the church is always to enjoy peace and tranquillity; for Christ refutes that himself (Matt. 10:34). Nor does the godly's spiritual peace in all troubles exhaust the full scope of this promise. But the scope is to teach us:

(a) The gospel has saving effect upon men when it daunts and subdues their corruptions, and makes them tractable and pliable to the will of God, and makes them peaceably study to serve God in their stations and to be useful to each other. When the strong nations are rebuked, they beat their swords into plowshares and their spears into pruninghooks, which are useful to themselves and others.

(b) This taming of men's corruptions by the gospel will appear farther in that saints and converted ones will live at peace, insofar as they are renewed (otherwise saints may be corrupted as well as other men, and bring forth of the fruits of the flesh, anger, malice, envy, etc.). And there shall not be such an enmity between believing Jews and Gentiles as there was before the partition was taken down, for "nation shall not lift up sword against nation, neither shall they learn war any more."

(c) Whatever troubles the church may meet from enemies, yet she shall give no cause nor occasion for them, though the corruption of the enemy may take occasion to raise troubles because of their profession of the gospel. The converted shall be peaceable men, and "beat their swords into plowshares."

(d) In spite of all the power and imagination of enemies, the church of God shall have even outward peace and tranquillity, so far as is needful and subservient to their spiritual good; otherwise, when it proves harmful, it is better to lack it, as the church has many times found in experience. And as the Lord has often given tastes of this to his church, so it will be more fully accomplished when the fullness of the Gentiles and all Israel shall be turned to the Lord; then "they shall sit every man under his vine and under his figtree, and none shall make them afraid."

6. The fidelity of God who promises, is sufficient to assure our hearts of the performance of greatest things, for

he is omnipotent and has all things under his power and at
his command. Therefore this promise, which might seem
improbable because of the great desolation which was threatened to come, is sealed with this: "for the mouth of the
Lord of hosts has spoken it."

> Ver. 5. For all people will walk every one in the name of
> his god, and we will walk in the name of the Lord our
> God for ever and ever.

In the parallel place (Isa. 2:5), instead of what is here,
we read an exhortation to the Jews. Since the church under
the Messiah was to be glorious, they should faithfully cleave
to God and true religion in all their calamities, until these
days should come; and since the Gentiles were thus to flow
in unto Christ, they should not fall away, but be provoked
to jealousy, and come in to partake. And indeed the hope of
the church of God is so great and sure that it may well
encourage men to be honest under any disadvantage; and
though this exhortation was not heeded at the first conversion
of the Gentiles, yet the day will come when it shall be
effectually upon them (Rom. 11:25, 26).

But Micah seems to hold forth further the aim of the converts, both Jews and Gentiles under the gospel, to renounce
all heresies and sects, and to adhere constantly and zealously to God and to the profession of the Christian religion,
exciting themselves unto this by the example of idolaters,
who were steadfast in their irreligious courses. And this is
a third evidence of the glory of the church, and a ground of
encouragement to the godly, that instead of the manifold
apostasies and pollutions with the ways of pagans which had
formerly appeared in the church of the Jews, the church of
God (especially converted Israel) should then prove constant
in their religion.

1. Constancy in adhering to the true religion is the great
glory of a church, and an encouragement to the godly, to
whom backslidings are a sad affliction.

2. The Christian profession and religion consists in walking in the name of the Lord, that is, in professing and practicing according to the revealed rule, which is "his name,"
not seeking to be wise above what is written and going about
these things in our own strength (1 Sam. 17:45; Ps. 118:11).
We shall be furnished with encouragement from him, for
his name (Isa. 2:5) is the light (i.e. of direction and consolation) of the Lord.

3. Those who would walk in these paths, and adhere to them, ought to make certain their interest in God by covenant, and ought to be filled with much affection toward their covenant God. "We will walk in the name of the Lord our God."

4. To perform our duty rightly, we need also frequently renewed resolutions, and other motives, to set us on edge. Here they gather arguments from idol-servers, and put on resolutions: "all people will walk, and we will walk in the name of the Lord."

5. Eternal resolutions, or resolutions of constant perseverance, are fit and becoming in so high a duty as walking in God's name; "we will walk," they say, and "walk forever and ever." This is a way in which there is no cause of weariness; its benefit is but in its prime, yea and will appear yet more fully when time and its contentments are ending.

6. Even in the days of the gospel, there are still many who are so blindfolded and deluded as not to see the glory of Christ's kingdom, but will pertinaciously follow their idols; for "all people," that is, many, "will walk in the name of their god."

7. The Lord's people should (and by grace will) be so far from being shaken or drawn away by the multitude of men who forsake the true God, that the faithfulness of idolaters should give occasion to the seekers of God to put on their own resolutions of more exactness and faithfulness. Their blind zeal toward that which is no god, may teach us our duty toward the true God. See Jer. 2:10, 11.

> Ver. 6. In that day, says the Lord, I will assemble her who halts, and I will gather her who is driven out, and her whom I have afflicted.
>
> 7. And I will make her who halted, a remnant; and her who was cast far off, a strong nation. And the Lord shall reign over them in mount Zion from henceforth, even for ever.

The fourth encouragement evidences yet further the glory of the church from a consideration of her former misery by affliction for sin, which he would now make up; and of such he will constitute his church and kingdom, over which he will reign forever and ever. And though this promise is of general truth, pointing out what base and contemptible matter he will gather his church of, yet it has a special application to the presently afflicted (and yet more to be afflicted) church of Israel, whom he comforts against all her afflictions and impediments, which might cut off all hope of her restoration, by promising to gather them under the gospel and make them a great nation, and that Christ in his spiritual government shall constantly rule over them in their own land after their conversion. Hence learn:

1. The Lord's afflicting of his church endears her in a special way to his affection, and makes it certain that she shall not be behind when mercies are dealt; for he says, "I will assemble and gather her whom I have afflicted." See Jer. 31:20.

2. Great afflictions are no impediments to the church's restitution, when its time comes and when omnipotence is employed about it, and when he in love remembers them in their low estate; for those who are so crushed with trouble that they are "halt," "afflicted," "driven out," and "cast far off," he can and will assemble and gather them, and make a remnant and strong nation of them. That is, he will preserve a remnant and keep them from total ruin in trouble, and will at last restore and multiply them.

3. The glory of a church restored, and the height of their felicity, is to have the Lord reigning and acknowledged as a king in all his prerogatives among them. Therefore it is added to their restitution, "the Lord shall reign over them in mount Zion."

4. The church's King is not subject to mortality, nor may he be put from his kingdom and leave them exposed to hazard, but "the Lord shall reign over them (and so protect them) from henceforth, even forever"; which also imports that he will forever have subjects to reign over.

> Ver. 8. And you, O tower of the flock, the stronghold of the daughter of Zion, unto you it shall come, even the first dominion; the kingdom shall come to the daughter of Jerusalem.

Here the Lord makes a more particular application of his comforting promises unto the church of the Jews. Though the promise is of universal truth in a spiritual sense, as applied to the catholic church, the Jerusalem which is from above, yet the following verses show that it is to be understood especially of the church of the Jews, whom he here calls the "tower of the flock," or Edar (Gen. 35:21), conceived to be a place near or in Jerusalem, and in particular that part which was later called the sheep gate; and "the stronghold of the daughter of Zion," or Ophel (2 Chron. 27:3; Neh. 3:26). The first encouragement given to them for the comfort of the godly, is that not only the kingdom of Christ should begin with them (as the New Testament history shows), but that under Christ they should be restored to their former dignity, resembling that which they had enjoyed of old under David and Solomon, before their ruin and calamity in Micah's time.

1. In gathering the universal church, the Lord has a special regard to the Jews his brethren; this appears in the special allowance given them in the promises concerning the kingdom of Christ. As the Lord has given them the first offer, the apostle concludes that much mercy shall yet be manifested unto them (Rom. 11:25, 26).

2. The church of God is the receptacle and fold of all his true sheep, in which they gather themselves under his government, and are environed with strength for safety. This is signified by these names which are given to Zion, "tower of the flock" and "stronghold."

3. The Lord's own application of spiritual comforts is especially needful for his afflicted people. Therefore the Lord counts it not enough to propound ample promises in general to the church, which might answer all their cases and which they were bound to be applying; but he holds it also necessary to apply these to the present church in her need.

4. The glory of Christ's kingdom is as great, and greater spiritually, than ever the glory of David or Solomon's reign was outwardly, and all the felicity of Israel under both are but shadows of that substance. Therefore it is called "the first dominion," not because it is the dominion first offered to the Jews, but because it is a dominion like the first flourishing times of Israel.

5. Christ, to fulfill the truth of God, made the first offer of his kingdom and gospel to the Jews; and in due time he will bring them under his dominion and spiritual government, and will restore them to their former dignity, thereby uniting under him all Israel, the seed of David, as they were before the schism made by Jeroboam. And he will adorn them eminently with the spiritual excellencies and privileges of his kingdom, if not also appearing gloriously for them in outward things as well; for he says, "unto thee shall the first dominion come; the kingdom shall come to the daughter of Jerusalem."

Ver. 9. Now why do you cry aloud? Is there no king in you?
Has your counsellor perished? For pangs have taken
you as a woman in travail.

10. Be in pain, and labour to bring forth, O daughter
of Zion, like a woman in travail; for now you shall go
forth out of the city, and you shall dwell in the field,
and you shall go even to Babylon. There shall you be
delivered; there the Lord shall redeem you from the
hand of your enemies.

The next encouragement given to the church of the Jews
is by showing his mind concerning the troubles that were
shortly to ensue. That he may more effectually comfort her,
he very pathetically propounds her trouble, as if she were
now under it. He shows that in outward appearance she had
cause of bitter sorrow, for her king and counsellors were
about to perish in that calamity, and she was to be driven
from the city and temple, which were to be destroyed, there
to sojourn a space in the fields until the rest of the captivity
were gathered, and then to be carried captive to Babylon;
yet in all this, upon better consideration she might find she
had no cause for fainting, but ought rather resolutely to
provide for and courageously to bear that trouble, since
God would be a King and Counsellor to her; and in Babylon,
where she might have expected least hope, she would find
deliverance. And so he declares his mind in this, that by
trouble she is going on toward deliverance. Hence learn:

1. The troubles of the church may prove very sharp and
bitter, as the pangs of a woman in travail.

2. Though the church of God in her trouble seem to have
reason for excessive sorrow and bitter discouragement,
really it is not so, but she has still some reason of encouragement, and ought to set about it. Therefore whatever her
troubles were, yet he says, "why do you cry out aloud?" as
if he had said, There is no reason for such excess of anxiety
and sorrow.

The reasons for this principal doctrine held forth in the
text are themselves so many doctrines, all of them teaching
and concluding that she ought not to give way to discouragement.

(a) Everything which the people of God lack in trouble,
which might be helpful or comforting to them, will be made
up in God. Though her king and counsellors were useless
and enemies to her safety, and were afterward cut off for
their sins; and though she might be emptied of all created

comforts and helps, yet the Lord will not have her to think that she lacked a king while he lived and reigned to preserve her in trouble, and in due time to reestablish his kingdom in her. This is taught by this sharp question: "Is there no king in you? Has your counsellor perished?"

(b) As the Lord often sees fit not to remove but to continue and increase a people's trouble, so the people of God in such cases ought to arm themselves with resolution for such lots, rather than by discouragement to make their own cross heavy, which is all they can do. This we are taught in that, though reproving their cries (ver. 9), yet he says, "be in pain"; which not only imports assurance to them that the trouble was to come, nor yet only a concession that it is no marvel that they should have pain and sorrow, but a command also to set themselves to bear it, as they are commanded to build houses in Babylon (Jer. 29:4-6) and to make their captivity as comfortable as lawfully they may.

(c) The right pondering of the fruit which the Lord brings out of the troubles of his people may help to crush discouragements under them. "Labour to bring forth like a woman in travail." He sets her out in her trouble, as travailing in birth of some mercy to make her forget her sorrow, which she should mind much and press after. See John 16:21, 22.

(d) The Lord's tender affection towards his people, especially under trouble, may much mollify their bitterness; therefore she is here called "the daughter of Zion," which is a name of tenderness. Having a place in his heart will make an affliction to be no affliction, or very tolerable.

(e) Every step of the people of God in affliction is a step towards deliverance; and the utmost degree of affliction is the door next to deliverance. Thus the scope and drift of this place teaches. The church, going out of the city and dwelling in the field, was going toward deliverance; and even when she went to Babylon, where in outward appearance she might have lost hope, yet there she will be delivered, and she is nearer a deliverance there than in the holy city. These things, rightly studied, may take away much seeming ground of discouragement under trouble.

3. The Lord is to be eyed as undertaker for the performance of improbable promises, which may cause all difficulties to vanish. Therefore after that promise, "there shall you be delivered," it is subjoined that "the Lord shall redeem you from the hand of your enemies." When he undertakes, it will be easy to raise a Cyrus and make him do it.

4. The Lord promises not only to deliver but to redeem them as well. This teaches:

(a) The Lord will show his kinship with, and interest in, his afflicted people, by appearing for them; for it was the duty of the nearest in kin to redeem, and the word in the original intimates as much.

(b) Since they had by sin sold themselves into captivity (Isa. 50:1), Christ by the price to be paid to justice for the elect among them, should procure their deliverance also, and of the visible church for their sake. All temporal deliverances to the children of God flow from that eternal redemption from sin, and as an appendix to the New Covenant, and the visible church receives deliverance for the sake of the elect among them.

(c) For enemies, who had captured them; as they had sold themselves to them for nought, so they should be actually redeemed to liberty without any price paid to their unjust possessors, but only with strokes (Isa. 52:3).

> Ver. 11. Now also many nations are gathered against you, who say, Let her be defiled, and let our eye look upon Zion.

For further confirmation of his mind concerning her afflictions, he sets forth, in the last place, his great and holy design concerning the enterprises of her many enemies, who in her ensuing calamity, and after her return from captivity, and after her return to Christ, should be gathered against her, as also against the church of Christ in all ages.

First he holds forth what is their purpose, so that his purpose, which overturns theirs, may be seen to be more glorious. Their purpose is to deal with her not as a privileged place, but to pollute her, as a profane place, with blood and other abominations, and to take her ornaments from her, and to put her from her dignity, that they might feed their eyes with such a sight.

1. The true church has the most enemies of any society; for "many nations are gathered."

2. It is useful for the church to note what enemies intend, and what our troubles would seem to threaten, so that we may see more of God in delivering; for this purpose the consideration of the enemy's end is contrasted with the consideration of the purpose of God. See Ps. 124.

3. As the wicked see no privilege the church of God has, why she should not be dealt with as other profane societies,

so the greatest bitterness the people of God have in their affliction is that thereby not only they, but their privileges, are trampled underfoot by enemies; for it is the sad sight they get of enemies' designs, when they hear them say, "Let her be defiled." See Isa. 10:9-11; Lam. 2:15.

4. There are many so wicked as to account the church's calamity a pleasant spectacle, and sweet sight to feed their eyes upon; for there are those who say, "Let our eye look upon Zion," which is an evidence of a desperately wicked condition.

> Ver. 12. But they do not know the thoughts of the Lord, neither understand they his counsel; for he shall gather them as the sheaves into the floor.
>
> 13. Arise and thresh, O daughter of Zion; for I will make your horn iron, and I will make your hoofs brass; and you shall beat in pieces many people. And I will consecrate their gain unto the Lord, and their substance to the Lord of the whole earth.

Now follows the Lord's purpose concerning their enterprise, which is incomprehensible and unsearchable by enemies, and quite contrary to their intentions. The Lord intends, by their gathering together, to ripen them for vengeance, as sheaves are gathered that they may be threshed; and he encourages the church in the execution of this, promising to enable them and give them a complete victory, which should be ascribed to him. Hence learn:

1. Enemies are not permitted to run at random in their ways, but the Lord has an effectual and wise providence overruling in all their designs; for in all of them he has "thoughts and counsel," and therefore we are not to heed their boastings, but to look to him who sets bounds to them and sits at the helm of providence.

2. The Lord's holy purposes of good to his people and wrath to his enemies, may be so conveyed in deep wisdom and so contrary to carnal reason and probability, that they will not be seen by any natural eye, nor by the enemies themselves, who are given up to run blindfolded upon their own ruin. "They know not the thoughts of the Lord, neither understand his counsel." See Ps. 92:6, 7.

3. In one and the same action, God may have an holy work of his providence, and wicked men in their wicked intents and sinful courses may be carried on without an eye to his revealed will, which is the rule of duty, nor to his providence,

but merely to their own ends; and he may make use of this same work of theirs to overreach them and bring about his purposes; for in this enterprise they gather themselves for a sinful end (ver. 11), and God gathers them as sheaves for a holy purpose. See Isa. 10:5-7.

4. The Lord's end in letting enemies loose upon the church, besides her trial from them, is to ripen and fit them for judgment; for "he shall gather them as the sheaves unto the floor," that is, to be trampled under foot, as corn is by the beasts that tread it out. Those whom the Lord abhors are let loose in opposition to his people, and they are ripened for destruction thereby. Their cup is thus filled to the brim, whereas otherwise it might be long in filling; and secret enemies thereby reveal themselves, and thus are brought to the floor for threshing. See Jer. 51:33.

5. Christ's church is not to look at what she has in herself, to oppose the enemies which assault her and to bring about the' mercies intended for her; but at what he will make for her, and how she shall be enabled to oppose and overcome all enemies. And in faith of this, she ought cheerfully to set to her duty. "Arise," says he, as to one sleeping or discouraged. "I will make your horn iron," to push, "and your hoof brass," to thresh according to their custom. See Deut. 25:4. Upon these terms the weakest may say, I am strong.

6. The church's victory over her enemies will in due time be made complete, and in due time Israel and the church of God shall have many enemies under their feet, either as ruined, or as true subjects, or as tributaries. This is imported in the text: not only shall she tread them with her hoofs and beat them in pieces, but their gain shall be consecrated or devoted. Thus is celebrated a complete victory given to Israel (Josh. 6:17, 19).

7. The glory of all the victories of the church, and of the benefits obtained thereby, ought to be given to God only; for so much also does the consecrating of their gain to the Lord import. As Jericho was offered to the Lord, and as it was a sin in Achan to take of the consecrated things of the Lord for himself, so it is a sin in the church to exalt herself, and not. the Lord only, in and by these successes.

8. The Lord only must be the undertaker to get himself the glory of all his wonderful dealing for his people, and make them forthcoming to his praise; and he will also crush and suppress whatever among his people would come between him and his glorious design. "I will consecrate their gain," says the Lord.

9. The Lord, by his vengeance upon the church's enemies, will have himself manifested and known to the world; and by his gracious dealing for his church and his blessing upon her endeavours, he will have himself acknowledged through the earth, and will have the kingdoms of the earth as his; for so much does the title, "the Lord of the whole earth," teach. He is so indeed, and by these victories he shall be known as such throughout the whole world (Ps. 9:16; Ps. 59: 13); and at last he shall have his dominion acknowledged and submitted unto more generally throughout the earth.

CHAPTER V

In this chapter the destruction of Jerusalem and overturning of the kingdom are foretold (ver. 1). The people of God are comforted with the promises of the birth of Christ, under whom they should be restored (ver. 2, 3) and of his government in relation to his people's tranquility (ver. 4-9), his purging his church from carnal confidences (ver. 10, 11) and idolatrous courses (ver. 12-14), so that he alone may be seen to do for them (ver. 14, 15).

> Ver. 1. Now gather yourself in troops, O daugher of troops. He has laid siege against us; they shall smite the judge of Israel with a rod upon the cheek.

Here is foretold the destruction of Jerusalem by the Chaldeans, and the ignominious and base usage of their kings and judges (2 Kings 25:7, 18-21) as a forerunner of the taking away of the sceptre from Judah, to make way for Christ's birth (Gen. 49:10). This began to be accomplished in the Babylonian captivity, in that none of the tribe of Judah swayed the kingly sceptre after that time. The prophet foretells all this by way of defiance from the church to their enemies to do their utmost endeavours; for though Jerusalem were taken and their rulers so abused, yet they had a king to come out of despised Bethlehem (ver. 2).

1. Christ's ordinary harbingers and forerunners, when he is to come with mercies to his church, are afflictions; for this destruction is prefixed to the promise of Christ's birth and kingdom. Afflictions are God's means to purge out and cut off many whom he will not make partakers of those mercies, to invite others to repentance for sin obstructing those mercies, to endear them to his heart, and to make them

capable of those consolations which in their prosperity they would readily despise.

2. Jesus of Nazareth is the true promised Messiah, who was to be raised to rule his people Israel, when their judges and rulers were ignominiously entreated and put down from their authority. He was held forth in the promise for the church's comfort, when this desolation began in their captivity, and he was actually exhibited when it was being completed. Their kingdom had then been reduced by the Romans to a province; and Herod, an Idumean, was made king, and the power of their courts restrained, shortly before and during the time of his ministry; and shortly after his ascension, their city and temple were utterly overthrown. So much does this verse, compared with ver. 2 and the accomplisment in the New Testament, teach us.

3. The church of God, rightly pondering her advantages in him, may in him give a defiance to enemies' utmost malice, seeing they can do no hurt but what he will make up with advantage, nor can they hinder any of his gracious purposes toward his people. Thus this challenge to the Chaldeans: "gather yourself in troops."

4. Oppression backed with authority and great power does not diminish the heinousness thereof before the Lord; for though the Chaldeans had ordered armies marching and acting at the command of authority, and though they would esteem what they subdued to be lawful conquest (Isa. 49:24), yet the Lord calls them a "daughter of troops" (or, as the word signifies, 'band of robbers') to signify that their great conquests were but great oppressions.

5. Whatever good the Lord brings out of the afflictions of his church, yet she may expect to be distressed with them in the mean time; for "he has laid siege against us," the people shall say, importing that all the land should be subdued, the city besieged, and the inhabitants thereof made to acknowledge their felt distress.

6. The contempt and injury done to authority and magistrates, under whom a people may be kept from confusion and the church protected, is a special ingredient in the affliction of the visible church, for they name it as a part of the affliction: "they shall smite the judge of Israel." So also Jeremiah laments the stroke made upon Zedekiah (Lam. 4:20).

7. Princes and men in authority, when wicked, dishonour God more than others by reason of their greatness, and it is their eminence which often makes them so much stand out

against God; and the Lord in his righteousness makes contempt to be their punishment. They are smitten with a rod
on the cheek, which is a contemptible stroke (Lam. 3:30).
See Job 12:21; Ps. 107:40.

> Ver. 2. But you, Bethlehem Ephratah, though you be little
> among the thousands of Judah, yet out of you shall he
> come forth unto me, who is to be ruler in Israel; whose
> goings forth have been from of old, from everlasting.

Now follows the consolation of the godly from a promise
of Christ to be the ruler in Israel. His birth as a man is
foretold to be in Bethlehem-Ephratah, the city of David
(whose heir he was) in the tribe of Judah (Judg. 17:7),
called Ephratah (Gen. 35:19; Gen. 48:7) to distinguish it
from another Bethlehem in the tribe of Zebulun (Josh.
19:10, 15). By this means it is likewise foretold that this
city, though base in comparison to others, should become
great and famous indeed. And lest any should look upon this
ruler as only man, it is also declared that he is the Son of
God, whose generation is eternal.

1. Christ's incarnation and manifestation of himself is the
true church's comfort in all her troubles; his birth is subjoined to the desolation mentioned in ver. 1, as the salve for
that sore.

2. Mercies manifested to any place or person, ought to
be noted and marked, that they may be thankfully acknowledged and use made of them. The speech is directed to the
city, that they may consider their high privilege: "and you,
Bethlehem-Ephratah."

3. Christ ordinarily uses and honours most such things
as are least considerable in outward appearance. He will not
be born in Jerusalem, but in Bethlehem-Ephratah, which is
"little among the thousands of Judah," that is, a small city
and governed by lowly rulers. The speech relates to the
division of the people by thousands under the government
of their rulers (1 Chron. 12:20). And therefore in Matt. 2:6,
instead of thousands, the princes are named who governed
them. See 1 Chron. 12:14.

4. By enjoying Christ, or having relation to him, smallest
and basest things become great. Thus is the text read in
considering the event: "you are not the least"; and the Hebrew
text here may be read as a question, and as including a
denial: "are you little?" No indeed, though you seem to be
so, "for out of you shall come forth a ruler in Israel."

5. The Lord in his providence sometimes brings about the performance of his promises in a strange and wonderful manner, as may be seen in the accomplishing of this promise (Luke 2:1). Joseph and Mary lived in Nazareth all the time after the conception of Christ, and thought little of a removal; but they are charged by the emperor's edict to go up to Bethlehem, so that the word of the Lord might not fail, and that the prediction concerning the Messiah might be fulfilled in the person of Jesus Christ.

6. Christ is Ruler and King in his church; he will be acknowledged to have dominion, and will perform the duties incumbent to a faithful ruler.

7. Christ in his mediatory office is a king acting for God the Father; and the Lord specially allows of him, and will maintain and defend him and his kingdom. He shall "come forth unto me," says the Lord. See Ps. 2:6.

8. Christ the mediator is not only to be considered as man, but the same Christ born in Bethlehem in the fullness of time is also true God, begotten of the Father from all eternity; he is God and man in one person. For "he who comes forth of Bethlehem-Ephratah" (the same person, though not according to the same nature) is "he whose goings forth have been of old, from everlasting," or 'from the days of eternity,' as the original has it.

9. Christ's eternal generation as God is superexcellent and incomprehensible. Therefore it is called "goings forth" in the plural number, to show its excellence, for in it all excellence, and infinitely more than we can comprehend, is summed up. And here both his eternal generation and eternal designation to the office of mediator may be imported.

> Ver. 3. Therefore he will give them up, until the time that she who travailed has brought forth; then the remnant of his brethren shall return unto the children of Israel.

The threatening and promise in the former verses are conjoined, and the way of bringing about this mercy is further explained; to wit, that he would give up that church into the hands of her enemies, to be vexed as a woman in travail until Christ should be born of that nation, or of a virgin among them; and then all his scattered brethren should be returned and be joined in one body with the church of Israel. This was accomplished in part when the Gentiles were engrafted in the olive, and shall be accomplished yet more when the salvation of Israel, after their long rejection, shall be a resurrection of them from the dead, and the fullness of the Gentiles shall come in unto Christ and join with them. The church of the Jews had indeed a birth after her pain, at her deliverance from Babylon, but that was only a forerunner of a more joyful bringing forth of Christ, the author of her spiritual deliverance. Until that time she was, for the most part, under the power of strangers, and did not at all recover her former dignity which she enjoyed before the Captivity, and therefore she is said to be "given up" until that time.

1. The church needed great troubles to prepare her for Christ and his spiritual kingdom. Though all their troubles will not exhaust his treasure, yet it is needful by afflictions to make them sensible of sin, to fit them for him; and it was needful to take away from the church of the Jews their carnal doting on the ark, the temple, and their other privileges, that they might seek after the spiritual things of his kingdom. "Therefore," he says, "he will give them up," or reject them, "until the time."

2. The great ground of confidence for the church, for not perishing in her troubles, is that she is to bring forth Christ. "He will give them up until the time that she who travailed has brought forth." This imports not only that their sorrows should end in joy, as the pain of a woman in travail when she brings forth, but further, because she is to bring forth, she shall not perish, but her sorrows shall have an end. This was the promise that might assure Ahaz, that the church of the Jews could not perish, since Christ was not yet born in her (Isa. 7:14); and it is yet a ground of assurance that Christ's catholic church shall not cease in the world, because she has Christ mystical to bring forth.

3. Christ is a true brother and kinsman to all his people, and makes them to be brethren among themselves; for they are "the remnant of his brethren."

4. Though no effects of Christ's special love may appear toward a man so long as he is unconverted, yet he has a relation toward his elect, and loves them from all eternity; for "the remnant of his brethren" are the elect Gentiles, then unconverted, who are his brethren in respect to his eternal love in election, and to his purpose to make them brethren by conversion, and so to give them actual right to the privilege. This purpose of good toward them was in his heart from all eternity.

5. All Christ's elect brethren shall be converted and brought in to him; "the remnant of his brethren shall return."

6. All the Gentiles have right to the covenant and salvation by fleeing to Christ, and in him to be made heirs to the spiritual promises made to Israel, and to be engrafted in that stock where they were; and the full fruit of Christ's incarnation is not answered until Israel also is brought in, and both they and the Gentiles are joined in one body. This promise, "the remnant of his brethren shall return unto (or 'together with') the children of Israel," imports both that the Gentiles are brought in unto the stock of the Israelite church, and that the children of Israel shall be brought in, to whom and with whom the Gentiles shall return.

7. That which is propounded as matter of comfort in a promise may be much mistaken and stumbled at when it is seen in performance. Here it is a comfortable promise to the church of the Jews, that the remnant shall return to the children of Israel, and be one sheepfold; and yet when it began to be performed, they repined for a long time. But in its full accomplishment they shall look upon it with rejoicing.

> Ver. 4. And he shall stand and feed in the strength of the Lord, in the majesty of the name of the Lord his God, and they shall abide; for now shall he be great unto the ends of the earth.

In the next place the government of Christ, formerly hinted at, is more largely described, for the comfort of the church and particularly of Israel. Here it is held forth under the similitude of a faithful shepherd feeding his flock, in which he shall show such care and stability, such invincible power and majesty in his providence, doctrine, and miracles, according to the covenant of redemption, that his church shall be established and his name famous, and his kingdom increased by the conversion of the Gentiles throughout the earth.

1. Christ is a careful and watchful shepherd and overseer of his church and the souls of his people, and will bear out in his charge; "he shall stand," importing both vigilance (Ps. 121:4) and stability, that his government shall endure forever.

2. God will feed his people with wholesome food, not allowing them to starve, and will rule and direct them in their ways. These two are to be conjoined by us; if we expect his feeding, we must submit to his government, for the word in the original imports both. He shall both feed and rule.

3. Christ has all-sufficiency of endowments for discharging his duty to his flock, and these shall gloriously shine forth in the performance thereof. "He shall feed in the strength of the Lord, and in the majesty of the name of the Lord"; that is, he shall have divine omnipotence to carry him through, and the fullness of the Godhead shall dwell in him bodily, gloriously manifesting itself in drawing, caring for, and maintaining his flock against all opposition. See John 10:28, 29; Ps. 89:19.

4. Though Christ as God has power and majesty equally with the Father, yet as Mediator he is also furnished for his calling by virtue of the covenant of redemption passed between the Father and him, concerning the redemption and salvation of the elect. In this covenant the Father undertakes to fill him with all endowments necessary for his office and to give him success; and he undertakes to be faithful in attaining that end, which accordingly he performs; for it is "in the strength and name of the Lord" that he feeds, with whom he is in covenant, and whose servant he is in this work.

5. By Christ's care and providence, his flock and people shall be established and protected, and shall persevere and be out of danger of perishing. "He shall feed or rule, and they shall abide."

6. Christ's care for his church, if it were well seen, would make him famous and precious, as an ointment poured out, to invite others to come under his yoke. It is his prerogative to have a universal government and kingdom over Jews and Gentiles throughout the earth, which he will still prosecute until he obtains all that is in his charter. He will, as the text imports, "be great to the ends of the earth." See Zech. 8:23.

7. The conversion of souls to Christ, and bringing them under his yoke, tends to set forth his greatness; and the conversion of many sets out his greatness the more, for he draws all these, cares for them, and makes them to depend upon his fullness and flow. And it should be the care of all who are converted, in their expressions and carriage to commend and set him forth as great and superexcellent. Therefore the enlargement of his kingdom is described from this effect: "he shall be great to the ends of the earth."

8. Whatever is promised in the word is as certain to faith as if it were already performed, and ought to be looked on as coming speedily. The Lord's choosing of times and seasons for performing his promise is no delay in a believer's eyes, and no impediment unto his faith to feed upon it as present;

thus it is said, "now shall he be great." God's keeping his appointed time is great assurance to the believer (Isa. 60:22), and the promise, apprehended by faith, gives the thing promised a present subsistence to his use and comfort.

> Ver. 5. And this man shall be the peace when the Assyrian shall come into our land; and when he shall tread in our palaces, then shall we raise against him seven shepherds and eight principal men.
>
> 6. And they shall waste the land of Assyria with the sword, and the land of Nimrod in the entrances thereof; thus he shall deliver us from the Assyrian when he comes into our land, and when he treads within our borders.

Now follow some special fruits of Christ's governing his church, such as peace and means sufficient not only to oppose disturbers (as the Assyrians were to Israel of old), but also to attack them also, and thus they shall be delivered. Though this promise, spiritually considered, belongs to the whole church, and literally also, as far as is for her good, yet it seems to have a special relation to the church of Israel, when they shall be converted and restored to their land.

1. Christ is the only author and maintainer of the church's peace; for "this man (or 'this one', implying a demonstration of him to others as one notable) shall be the peace." He appeases God's anger toward us, and in him only do we have true peace among ourselves; for lukewarmness breeds divisions, and he it is who makes peace in his church's borders and creates a cloud over her.

2. The church will not lack enemies of her peace, and those who will study to disturb it, and such may seem at times to prevail; for "the Assyrians shall come into our land, and tread in our palaces." She must resolve to have a peace with continual battles.

3. The church has her peace secured in Christ in the midst of trouble, and through him will have means sufficient to oppose her enemies and maintain her peace; for "he shall be the peace when the Assyrian shall come," and there are "seven shepherds and eight principal men" to raise against him, or a sufficient number of leaders (seven being a number of perfection, and eight yet more) with armies to oppose him.

4. It is a great blessing upon a land when the Lord furnishes them with able men for government and rule in all

exigencies. That is Israel's mercy, to have such to employ, and they are the means of their peace and safety. "We shall raise (or call and send out) shepherds and principal men"; their princes are called shepherds, as related to the people, a flock.

5. The enemies of the church oppose her always to their own great disadvantage in the end; for the church shall not only defend themselves, but "they shall waste the land of Assyria with the sword, and the land of Nimrod in the entrances thereof," or their borders, or "with their own swords." Babylon is here called "the land of Nimrod" because he founded their kingdom (Gen. 10:9-11) and was a great oppressor, as his successors were.

6. The inconveniences which the church sustains by her troubles do not prove so great as they may seem to be; for though "he treads in our palaces," ver. 5, yet it is but "treading within our land and borders" (ver. 6).

7. As the church is sure to be delivered from her enemies, so the glory of all her enterprises and victories is to be ascribed to Christ only, whatever be the part of instruments in bringing them about. Therefore though they raise up shepherds and principal men (ver. 5) yet "he shall deliver us" (ver. 6).

> Ver. 7. And the remnant of Jacob shall be in the midst of many people, as a dew from the Lord, as the showers upon the grass that tarries not for man, nor waits for the sons of men.

The similitude of dew leads us to a twofold interpretation of this passage. 1. The Lord's blessing of the rest given to the church by these deliverances, shall make her to multiply and flourish marvelously, as the dew and rain falls down in great abundance, suddenly and unexpectedly, without human industry; and thus the similitude is used (2 Sam. 17:12; Ps. 110:3). 2. The church of Israel shall not only flourish themselves, but shall be instruments of the flourishing and increase of the church among the nations, as the Lord is the principal refresher and fructifier of his church, and therefore his operations are compared to dew and rain (Hos. 14:5; Ps. 72:6). So they shall be instrumentally dew and rain to many nations; that is, they shall be furnished with the Spirit from above, and with refreshing doctrine, and shall water them therewith as dew and rain water the ground, and so they shall conquer them to the kingdom of Christ, and shall be instruments of their fruitfulness and blessings to them.

Both these interpretations agree in holding forth the miraculous increase of the church, either Israel herself or the Gentiles also by her means, as another fruit of the government of Christ over them; both may be safely taken in here. From the first interpretation, learn:

1. Afflictions may make many sad and sore breaches on a church before they recover from them; now they are brought low, and are "the remnant of Jacob."

2. The Lord can easily, when he pleases, restore his broken people and make them increase as admirably and incredibly as their decay was singular, and will do so when they return to him; for "the remnant shall be as a dew."

3. The Lord's singular dispensations toward his afflicted people will make them admirable and remarkable to all people, and above them; for "they shall be as dew in the midst of many people," which imports that they should be conspicuous and exalted above all the people. See Deut. 33:29.

4. Rest and deliverance from troubles is a blessing to the church when it is followed with fruitfulness and increase of the church; for so this promise is subjoined to the former verses as a completion. See Acts 9:31.

From the second interpretation, learn:

1. The church of God is a blessing to the world, if they forsake not their own mercy; partly she is a means of bringing blessings on every place where she gets shelter and protection, and partly she is a means of men's conversion, begetting still more and more to Christ; for there is a promise here, "she shall be in the midst of many people as dew." See Isa. 19:24.

2. The greatest good that can be done unto the world is to be a means of their conversion and of bringing down spiritual blessings upon them; for it is said that the church shall be unto them as dew and rain, which are choicest blessings.

3. All the spiritual happiness of a people, and the efficacy of the means bringing it about, is of God and from above; for it is as "the dew and showers which tarry not for men, nor wait for the sons of men," that is, which do not depend upon human industry. See 1 Cor. 3:6.

4. The means of conversion, especially the word preached and accompanied with the power of the Spirit (which God has placed in his church) are as dew and showers, for four reasons. (a) Dew is the presage of a fair day; so these means

flow from the favour of God toward the elect, and are an evidence thereof. (b) Dew and small rain are but small things, and yet have great effects; so it is also with the word (Rom. 1:16; 1 Cor. 1:21). (c) Dew and rain cannot be hindered by men; neither does the power of the word depend upon men's consent. (d) Dew and rain make fruitful; so is every true convert made fruitful by the word and Spirit.

5. A converted person or people, joining themselves to the true church, come under a sweet yoke and under the drop of many blessings; for so does the similitude also teach. As their conversion is by this dew, so being converted, they shall constantly enjoy it, and their fleece shall be wet with this dew when other places are dry.

6. Israel, when converted to Christ, shall be the means of blessings, and of much conversion to the Lord among the Gentiles; for it is "the remnant of Judah" which "shall be in the midst of many people as dew."

> Ver. 8. And the remnant of Jacob shall be among the Gentiles in the midst of many people as a lion among the beasts of the forest, as a young lion among the flocks of sheep; who, if he goes through, both treads down and tears in pieces, and none can deliver.
>
> 9. Your hand shall be lifted up upon your adversaries, and all your enemies shall be cut off.

Another fruit of the government of Christ over Israel, and a fruit of their deliverance, is that all their neighbouring enemies who are not brought in shall fall under their dread, as a lion is dreadful to other wild beasts; he tears his prey, and none dare interpose. This, spoken of the church in borrowed terms (ver. 8), is spoken again plainly (ver. 9) for her greater encouragement; she is assured that she shall be above all her enemies, and that they shall be so far crushed that they shall not dare to profess their enmity.

1. The church, in her most thriving times, will not lack enemies, nor will she be as dew and a savour of life to all. She shall yet have "adversaries" and "enemies."

2. There is as great a difference between the church of God, when he is pleased to arm her with his strength, and all her enemies (however potent) as between a lion and other beasts or weak sheep, whom he easily and without resistance destroys.

3. The Lord requires that his church's heart be settled in the confidence of his giving her victory over her enemies

in due time, though it is hard to get it believed. This repetition of the promise (ver. 9) teaches both the difficulty of believing it, and his will notwithstanding that she should be established in her belief.

4. The church of God should expect no less than that in due time even all her enemies shall be cut off, and so she may be assured of complete victory; and converted Israel shall get a special proof of this within time, in being above her enemies and seeing their enmity against her crushed. "Your hand shall be lifted up upon all your adversaries, and all your enemies shall be cut off."

> Ver. 10. And it shall come to pass in that day, says the Lord, that I will cut off your horses out of the midst of you, and I will destroy your chariots.
>
> 11. And I will cut off the cities of your land, and throw down all your strong holds.
>
> 12. And I will cut off witchcraft out of your hand, and you shall have no more soothsayers.
>
> 13. Your graven images also I will cut off, and your standing images out of the midst of you; and you shall no more worship the work of your hands.
>
> 14. And I will pluck up your groves out of the midst of you; so will I destroy your cities.
>
> 15. And I will execute vengeance in anger, and fury upon the heathen, such as they have not heard.

A further fruit of Christ's government is the purging of his church from the evils by which they were corrupted of old, showing the condition in which he will put them, to fit them for these deliverances and victories. He foretells:

(a) The taking away of all their human confidences, such as horses, chariots, cities, and strongholds, in which they confided of old, and despised his threatenings.

(b) The cutting off of devilish arts and idolatrous confidences, such as witchcraft, divinations, idols and groves for worship, which were much used in Israel of old. These were all to be destroyed and purged away by judgments to come upon Israel and Judah, shortly after this prophecy; and in the time of the restitution, it is promised here that Israel shall be a people stripped of all confidences, that they may depend upon God and be a people worshipping the true God in a pure way. And when they are put in that condition, he promises remarkable victories over the heathen, their enemies. Hence learn:

1. Christ will have nothing seen in his church's protection and deliverance but himself only, and he will not use anything which might seem to obscure his glory in doing all. Therefore whatever might seem to challenge any of his glory must in that day be cut off. See Judg. 7:2; Zeph. 3:12, 13.

2. Human helps, confided in, prove a great hindrance of deliverance. Therefore cities, horses, etc., will be cut off; not only in judgments, but even in "that day" of restitution, they will be laid by as impediments.

3. Confidence in outward things is idolatry. Therefore here their cities, horses, chariots (i.e. that which they depended on) are ranked with withcrafts and idols.

4. It is rare to see a people enjoy outward things that may seem to promise anything to them, and yet not confide in them. Their cities, chariots, etc., must be cut off, for they can hardly enjoy them and trust in God as they should.

5. When the Lord is pleased to deprive his people of probable means of help, and when he calls them to depend upon him, it is a pledge of his appearing in an eminent way for them. When their cities are cut off (ver. 10, 11), he will destroy their enemies, as the latter part of ver. 14 ought to be read, as agreeing with the original and also fitting the scope best in this place.

6. In the church of God there is hazard of falling into grossest evils, for even here there may be witchcrafts or magic, by which men who lack the fear of God enter into an express or implicit league with the devil, for attaining such ends as their discontentment, impatience, envy, malice, or curiosity propound unto them. There may also be soothsayers, or divinations, by which men not content to know their duty, nor with what God has revealed of future events, do take sinful and damnable courses, and put other things in God's place to foretell what they desire. There may also be images and the work of men's hands set up in God's place, as the object of worship, and "groves" or shady places, in which they pretended to worship God, or indeed worshipped their idols after their own imagination. There are no evil courses into which the church of God, no matter how reformed, may not fall.

7. These devilish courses and corruptions in worship do hinder the Lord's appearance for his people; they must be "cut off," so that he may do for them.

8. The cutting off of idolatry and wicked courses is a work of the Lord's own hand; it is he who often destroys them by

sore plagues, and it is he only who can banish these things out of men's hearts. "I," says the Lord, "I will cut off witch-crafts out of your hand; I will cut off your graven images."

9. There can be no blessed delivery from trouble without a complete and thorough reform of religion endeavoured, and a destroying of the very monuments of idolatry. Not only shall they not worship any more the work of their hands, but their images and groves shall be cut off and plucked up, and so he will destroy their enemies.

10. The Lord will appear for his church in a singular and wonderful manner, and plague their enemies with unusual judgments, after he is reconciled with them and has brought them to walk in his ways. After all this is done, "I will execute vengeance and fury upon the heathen, such as they have not heard," says the Lord.

CHAPTER VI

In this chapter the Lord again, after these many promises, stirs up the prophet to plead his controversy, and expostulates with his ungrateful people (ver. 1-3), showing forth his kindness toward them (ver. 4, 5) and comparing the duty which they offered to him (ver. 6, 7) with what they ought to have done (ver. 8). Since they did not obey this, he gives an alarm of the rods and punishments coming upon them (ver. 9); then he more particularly sets forth and proves their transgressions of their duty, in sins against the second table (ver. 10-12), for which he gives out sentence against them (ver. 13-15) and for their idolatry against the first table (ver. 16).

> Ver. 1. Hear now what the Lord says: arise, contend before the mountains, and let the hills hear your voice.
>
> 2. Hear, O mountains, the Lord's controversy, and the strong foundations of the earth; for the Lord has a controversy with his people, and will plead with Israel.

The prophet propounds in general the Lord's controversy, given him in commission to plead publicly, as it were in view of all the creatures, from the high mountains to the low channels or foundations of the earth. This procedure, formerly used (1:2), teaches us:

1. Sin causes a controversy between God and the sinner; "the Lord has a controversy."

2. This controversy is so much the sadder, for it breaks out not between God and strangers, but between him and his church, with whom he dealt friendly, and who professed friendship and subjection to him, and therefore he will deal worse with their offences. "The Lord has a controversy with his people, and he will plead with Israel."

3. The Lord is zealous to have the controversy discussed and himself cleared. Since the prophet's zeal was short of his own forwardness to plead this cause, he cries, "Arise, contend!" And further, "he will plead with Israel"; that is, not only will he have his quarrel shown, but he will have it clearly demonstrated that he gave no cause for the discord, and therefore he will justly punish, as the following purpose shows.

4. Even insensible creatures are, so to speak, more fit to be spoken to than an obdurate people, and will bear witness against them. Besides the reasons mentioned in 1:2, the prophet now adds that "the mountains and strong foundations of the earth" will be called in this proceeding. They still keep their obedient subjection to their Creator, and tremble when he threatens, whereas Israel was stupid. Further, these had been shaken and revealed for the good of Israel (Ps. 18:15, Ps. 114:3, 4), and therefore they might bear witness against their ingratitude.

5. A backsliding people are for the most part dull of hearing, and plaged with obstinacy, and therefore cannot be aware of their danger. Therefore the dispute is repeated again, and they are called to hear: "hear now what the Lord says."

6. The reproofs of the messengers of God are not to be slighted, but to be noted as the Lord's controversy; for by contending, Micah will cause the Lord's controversy to be heard.

> Ver. 3 O my people, what have I done to you, and wherein have I wearied you? Testify against me.

Now follows the pleading of the controversy. God first appears and challenges them for their ungrateful departing from him and his obedience, which he proves by purging himself of any wrong done to them, and showing them that they had nothing to say against his dealings with them, and nothing to lay to his charge as a reason for forsaking him. The Lord charges their consciences that, as he had called the mountains to witness against them, so they should

declare if they had any injury against him to complain of,
and should bring out anything they had to say, to clear themselves of that crime of ingratitude. Hence learn:

1. It is the Lord's love to his people which makes him
challenge them for forsaking them; and this should make
the challenge affect their hearts, and will aggravate their
guilt if it does not. So much does this title, "O my people,"
teach us.

2. By her backsliding, the church of God raises an evil
report upon God, as if he did not deal well with his people,
and as if he were not fit to serve. Such do his questions,
"what have I done unto you? Wherein have I wearied you?"
imply; their backsliding said in effect that he had done them
injury and wearied them with rigorous service.

3. Though our corruptions snuff and weary us in God's
service (as Mal. 1:13), yet there can be no true cause shown
why any should choose to forsake God. Yea rather, all should
cleave unto him, since his commands are not grievous, his
yoke easy, his trials not above measure, his punishments
not above deserving, and a Mediator ready to undertake for
his people in all exigencies. Therefore the Lord will have
it disputed, and will have the consciences of backsliders
to clear him: "wherein have I wearied you? Testify against
me!" See Jer. 2:5, 31.

4. To forsake the Lord without cause is great ingratitude;
for this is the scope of the challenge, that they could say
nothing against him and yet turned away from him, and are
therefore guilty of the crime of ingratitude.

> Ver. 4. I brought you up out of the land of Egypt, and
> redeemed you out of the house of servants, and I sent
> before you Moses, Aaron, and Miriam.

A further proof of his challenge for their ingratitude is
taken from his mercies toward them. By this he further
vindicates himself and proves that they were so far from
having any harsh usage to lay to his charge, that on the contrary he had manifested many rare and singular favours
toward them, which aggravated their fault. He proves this
charge by several instances. The first instance is his re-
deeming them from Egypt, when Egypt dealt most strictly
with them and made them bondmen (though the Egyptians
themselves ought rather to have been slaves, as coming of
cursed Canaan, Gen. 9:25). A second instance is taken from
his conducting them through the wilderness, giving to them

a well settled government and faithful governors: Moses, to give laws from God's mouth and to conduct the people; Aaron to be priest; and Miriam their sister to instruct the women in that extraordinary time (Exod. 15:20).

1. Mercies received only aggravate the defection of a people. See 1 Sam. 15:17-35.

2. Our deliverance from bondage, spiritual or temporal, inward or outward, is given that we may serve the Lord, and ought to be an eternal bond upon the delivered to be for God; therefore their being brought of the land of Egypt is brought to remembrance, though past and done long ago, as yet obligating them to his service. "I brought them up out of the land of Egypt."

3. The Lord's conducting and guiding of his people in this world, under a sweet and orderly government, and honest governors in church and state, working to advance God's honour and the good of a people, is a singular and obliging mercy, though the people enjoying it be in a wilderness; for it aggravates their ingratitude that he sent these three servants before them.

> Ver. 5. O my people, remember now what Balak king of Moab consulted, and what Balaam the son of Beor answered him from Shittim unto Gilgal, that you may know the righteousness of the Lord.

A third instance of mercy is taken from a particular instance of his goodness in the wilderness, turning Balak's intended curse into a blessing and causing Balaam (against his own inclination) to bless the people and to publish God's good-will toward them. See Numb. 22:5; Numb. 23:7; Numb. 24:1-24; Deut. 23:4, 5. This instance is yet further enlarged, that when Balaam had counselled Balak to tempt Israel to whoredom and adultery at Shittim, so that God's anger might be aroused against them (Rev. 2:14; Numb. 25:1), yet the Lord spared them and justly brought Balaam to a violent death (Josh. 13:22; Numb. 31:8). He gave them victories over Og and Sihon (Numb. 21:21-35); he brought them to the promised land, and renewed in Gilgal the covenant of circumcision and the Passover (Josh. 4:19; Josh. 5:2). By all this they might be effectually convinced of God's fidelity in keeping promise and covenant in all things.

1. Forgetfulness of mercies is the cause why they take so little effect and produce such small fruit. Therefore Micah calls, "remember now."

2. In assuring his people that he takes pleasure in their prosperity, the Lord is pleased to descend so far to our capacity as to express himself as a man whose heart is warmed at the remembrance of past familiarity and who would have it renewed. Therefore after rehearsing this benefit, he repeats again, "O my people," as if his affection were kindled and revived by the rehearsal. See Jer. 2:2. Much more should it so work upon us.

3. The Lord has the power of cursing and blessing in his own hand, however men may be disposed, and he may turn intended curses against his people into blessings. He can, when he will, protect them from the fraud as well as the violence of enemies, yea, and make their very enemies befriend them, as we are taught by the history of Balak and Balaam here mentioned.

4. The Lord's people's hearts ought to be engaged much unto him for his delivering mercies, his goodness in striving with his people's wickedness, his keeping covenant when their sins deserve that it should be broken, and his just judgments upon their violent and fraudulent enemies. Therefore they should remember what had passed "from Shittim to Gilgal."

5. There are standing monuments and experiences in the church, which may abundantly satisfy them of the Lord's truth, mercy, and steadfastness in goodwill toward them, to encourage them in walking in his way and that they might clear and acquit the Lord in his dealings. All these passages are rehearsed "that you may know the righteousness of the Lord," or the manifold proofs of his fidelity in keeping promise.

> Ver. 6. Wherewith shall I come before the Lord, and bow myself before the high God? Shall I come before him with burnt offerings, with calves of a year old?
>
> 7. Will the Lord be pleased with thousands of rams, or with ten thousands of rivers of oil? Shall I give my firstborn for my transgression, the fruit of my body for the sin of my soul?

Having reproved their ingratitude, the prophet now challenges their hypocritical formality. Having cleared the Lord and shown what he had done, the prophet brings in their contrary actions in making great offers of service and duty to God, in which they manifest not only their empty formality and affected ignorance, but their malicious hypocrisy as well.

Whereas the prophet spoke sharply against them, they complain that they are most willing to appease God's anger and to offer him all kinds of service, if it would please him; and yet he would not be pleased, but his prophets still cry out against them. Hence learn:

1. The right way of worshipping God and of appeasing his anger, has been an old controversy, and the truth has been found by few, though clearly revealed. "Wherewith shall I come before the Lord (or, 'prevent the face of the Lord,' i.e. the breaking forth of his anger)?" they say, as desiring yet to learn.

2. Whatever convictions of sin men may attain to, or whatever necessity they may see of being brought back to God by these convictions (both of which may be revealed here by their professions), yet corrupt men do heal these wounds slightly, placing all their confidence in external performances of ceremonies or religious duties, and neither fleeing to Christ nor regarding the substantial duties of faith, repentance, and new obedience. "Shall I come before him with burnt offerings?" is all their concern.

3. Men may have fair and broad professions, and pretend much reverence to God, when all the while their deeds prove to be nothing; for they pretend to "bow before the high God," and yet give him no more but a ceremony.

4. Corrupt and unrenewed men would rather be at any pains, yea, even what is impossible or sinfully cruel, than follow God's way in fleeing to Christ, leaving their own unrighteousness and studying mortification of sin. So we are taught by their offer of "thousands of rams and ten thousand rivers of oil," which could not be had in all the world, and their "first-born" to be slain in sacrifices for sin, as idolaters do. All this they would undertake, rather than the killing of one lust.

5. External performances of religion prove ofttimes a great snare to wicked men who use them, and a great obstruction to the ministry of the word reproving sin; for this was their defence cast in the prophet's teeth, that they were very observant of the ceremonial law, and were ready to do more of that kind, and therefore how could God be angry at them?

Ver. 8. He has shown you, O man, what is good; and what does the Lord require of you, but to do justly, and to love mercy, and to walk humbly with your God?

In opposition to their way, the Lord sets down the true way of pleasing him, and of their duty, containing the duties of justice and mercy, unto which they stood obliged and which hypocrites ordinarily neglect, and their duty of keeping communion with God in humble and sober walking before him in the exercise of religion. All these must be done as a fruit of faith, fleeing to God through Christ in the covenant, whereby he becomes our God. Hence learn:

1. Though men may be ignorant or contentious, the way of pleasing God is clearly revealed in his word; for in answer to their questions he replies, "he has shown you, O man."

2. The Lord's commands are not rigid, or severe and unreasonable, as hypocrites would allege, but are gentle and desirable. What the Lord has shown is "what is good."

3. The Lord requires, especially of men professing piety, that they make conscience of justice and equity in their dealings with one another, that thus they may prove the sincerity of their religion and may adorn it. The Lord "requires to do justly."

4. Besides the duties which we owe to our neighbours in justice, there are other duties which we are also bound to perform in humanity, or by the bond of Christianity and charity. These are here called "mercy," and though no human law can teach them, yet "the Lord requires" them, and conscience and Christianity call for them.

5. Though love is required in performing every commanded duty, yet for performance of mercy it is especially requisite, for it binds the duty upon us, and it must season the duty when it is being done. The Lord requires us "to love mercy."

6. No duties can ever be acceptably performed by an unrenewed person, or one who has not fled to God by faith, to be reconciled with him through Christ, so that his duties may be performed as fruits of faith and so that strength may come from God daily to enable him to perform them. God must be theirs by covenant, "your God."

7. A man who is reconciled to God by faith ought not only to be diligent in performing duties of the second table, but ought to join therewith a study of keeping communion with God in the exercises of true piety. By both of these, conjoined and flowing from faith, he may prove himself to be somewhat more than either a moral civilian or an hypocrite, and may not provoke God to punish his neglect of communion with himself by allowing him to fall into some sin against the second table. Thus it is required "to walk with your God."

8. In relation to God, humility and sobriety are required in the performance of duties either of the first or second table. There is no conceit of righteousness or merit to be allowed in what we do, but when we have done all, we are required to come humbly, to find grace by virtue of a free covenant. We are to debase ourselves when we are before God in religious worship; we are in all sobriety and humility to receive commands, take on employments, and go about them with an humble dependence on him for constant supply of wisdom and ability. "Walk humbly with your God."

9. The people of God are to study constancy in their way, and especially in humility, and for this end the bond of communion with God and interest in him is to be kept fast and daily to be made use of. "Walk humbly with thy God."

> Ver. 9. The Lord's voice cries in the city, and the man of wisdom shall see thy name; hear the rod, and who has appointed it.

This verse contains a general sentence given out against this people, and a preface to the following special accusations and sentences. The sum is that since they made no conscience of this duty, though clearly revealed (ver. 8), therefore the Lord by his prophets gives warning of another teacher to be sent unto them, to wit, his rods and judgments, which they are commanded to hear, since they will not hear his servants, and to consider the author of them; and in addition he declares that only the true fearers of God, who are indeed the wise ones, will take notice of God manifesting himself, either in the admonition or in the rod.

1. Slighting of clearly revealed and commanded duties will bring a rod upon a person or people.

2. The Lord does not come stealthily in judgment upon his people, but in great mercy forewarns them of their danger, if they would make use of it. "The Lord's voice cries," to give the alarm.

3. The testimonies of the Lord's servants against sin, and their warnings of wrath to come in their public ministry, is the Lord's own warning to the rebellious; "the Lord's voice" is his voice in the mouth of his messengers.

4. Cities and eminent places have greatest occasions and encouragements to serve God; so when they come short, their guilt is great, and they share deepest in the cup of afflictions. Therefore "the Lord's voice cries in the city," that is, in Jerusalem, Samaria, and other cities of the land;

as the prophets had preached most in these cities, so they are warned especially, as those upon whom the rod will light most sadly when it comes.

5. We ought to be sensible of afflictions sent upon us, as God's messengers sent with a message to us; and the Lord will cause the most stubborn to feel his hand in them. This word, "hear the rod," is not only an exhortation to be sensible of the rod when it comes, but a prediction that, though they would not hear the prophets, yet they would both hear and feel this messenger. See Jer. 1:15, 16.

6. We ought not only to be sensible of the pain of the rod when it comes, but ought also and chiefly to look to the hand of God in it, and to what he would teach by it. "Hear the rod, and who has appointed it."

7. It is an evidence of the fear of God to take warning of a rod's coming, or to get God's mind in the rod seen, and to be affected with it and obey it; and only fearers of God get this use of it. "The man of wisdom shall see thy name," that is, take up thy authority in these warnings from the word, and discern what thou dost manifest of thy mind by the rod.

8. They alone are wise, who fear God and who learn to make use of his word and providences toward them; for he who fears God is called "the man of wisdom," or 'substantial wisdom,' as the word signifies; all other wisdoms are but empty and vain.

> Ver. 10. Are there yet the treasures of wickedness in the house of the wicked, and the scant measure that is abominable?
>
> 11. Shall I count them pure with the wicked balances, and with the bag of deceitful weights?
>
> 12. For the rich men thereof are full of violence, and the inhabitants thereof have spoken lies, and their tongue is deceitful in their mouth.

To help them understand his purpose in the rod, the Lord enters upon a more special accusation of them for the sins which procure it. Here he sets before them their violation of justice and mercy, and charges that by wicked means they had gathered great treasure, which proved them to be wicked when they thus enriched themselves. The means by which they made this purchase (or at least endeavoured it) and for which they are challenged, are: (a) Scant measures, lean in themselves and starving the buyers. (b) Inexcusable deceit in the matter of weights and balances, bringing in more gain to them than was right. (c) Cruel violence against the poor. (d) Fraud and circumventing one another, which was universal among them. All these accusations the Lord refers to themselves, to bear witness of the truth of them; he asks their conscience if the Lord could justly acquit them, notwithstanding their professions by external sacrificing, and whether he should not rather abhor, condemn, and plague them.

1. The Lord abhors those sins especially which are committed after many admonitions, and by those who profess much piety. "Are there yet the treasures of wickedness?" says he, and after so many admonitions and threatenings of the rod, and notwithstanding your great profession.

2. It is a great sign of unsoundness when those who are eminent in practicing external duties of the first table can without scruple commit wickedness against the second; for, says he, "are there yet (after the great offerings and sacrifices) treasures of wickedness?"

3. Excessive love unto, and desire after, riches, which drives men to use unlawful means of purchase, is a sure mark of wickedness, let the purchaser pretend what he will; and it is a sure mark of God's displeasure, though in his providence he may permit such to prosper. They are "treasures of wickedness in the houses of the wicked," and for this the Lord pleads against them.

4. Deceitfulness in balances and measures is a sinful means of purchasing riches, and a clear instance of injustice, which is abominable in the sight of God.

5. Even ourselves, seriously considering our case, may not only see the truth of what the word challenges, but may easily judge that God will not pass by approved gross guiltiness, nor justify the doers, whatever mask of profession they cover it with. Therefore the Lord appeals to themselves, both for the truth of the fact ("are there yet treasures?") and for the sin of it ("shall I count them pure with wicked balances?").

7. Though men study to blind or silence their own consciences, so that they may sin without molestation, yet in the day of God's controversy it will be men's foremost adversary, and will plead God's quarrel most thoroughly. Therefore he leaves this challenge at the door of their own conscience, as that which in due time would speak out an answer to that question: "shall I count them pure?"

8. It is a great sign of wickedness in any person to employ the power God has given them above others, for wicked ends. "For the rich men thereof (that is, of the city, ver. 9, or of the land) are full of violence"; because they are rich, therefore they are violent.

9. Violent oppression and deceitful circumvention are equivalent sins in God's estimation; both tend to one end, i.e. to gather further riches through wronging others; and both flow from the same fountain, being only fitted for diverse times and according to the diverse conditions of the wicked. If they are powerful, they are violent; and if not, they supply that defect by deceit. Therefore they are joined together: "the rich men are full of violence, and the inhabitants have spoken lies."

> Ver. 13. Therefore also will I make you sick in smiting you, in making you desolate because of your sins.

Lest by sparing these hypocrites, they might think he was such a one as themselves, therefore he gives out sentence and threatens them, explaining what the rod was. He threatens that by striking them and making them desolate, he will make them sick; that is, not of bodily sickness (which is a judgment of itself, Lev. 26:16), but that as they had made others faint by oppression, so he would crush them by judgments, and make them as weak as a sick man.

1. Sin will lay a land desolate, and leave a people helpless and friendless, and without comfort against crosses; so much do these words hold forth.

2. Sin is most of all to be looked unto in our desolations and afflictions, as having a greater hand therein than the power of our enemies. Therefore he mentions sin alone as the cause of their desolation: "because of your sins."

3. Judgments for sin will not only affect the afflicted man, but will be ready to make him faint and succumb; for, says he, "I will make you sick in smiting you." Those whose hearts are effeminate with love to sin (Ezek. 16:30) will prove feeble in bearing the punishment of sin (Ezek. 22:14).

> Ver. 14. You shall eat, but not be satisfied; and your casting down shall be in your midst; and you shall take hold, but shall not deliver, and that which you deliver I will give up to the sword.
>
> 15. You shall sow, but you shall not reap; you shall tread the olives, but you shall not anoint yourself with oil and sweet wine, and shall not drink wine.

Now follows a particular enumeration of those judgments by which he would make them sick and desolate.

The first stroke is famine, flowing not from scarcity of provision but from the Lord's withdrawing of a blessing (Lev. 26:26; Hos. 4:10). Hence learn:

1. Threatenings given out of old against sin stand still in force against the same sins in all generations; for the threatenings of the law of Moses are declared to be in force in Micah's days.

2. God has so immediate a hand in feeding men by the creatures that when he withdraws his blessing, the creatures, though given in ever so great an abundance, will not feed; for "you shall eat and not be satisfied."

3. It is just with God to let those who provoke him in gathering together outward things, know how far they wrong themselves while they dote on the creature, forgetting the Creator. Therefore against those who provoked him by gathering of wealth, he threatens that all of it should not so much as keep them from starving.

The second stroke is their "casting down in your midst"; that is, they shall be exhausted in their own land, and with internal evils, though they were secure from foreign enemies and from captivity by them. This teaches that as internal troubles are a sore judgment and sharp punishment for sin, so the Lord can reach a person or people in the midst of all their contentments, and can abase them as low by his secret curse as by any outward enemy. "Your downfall shall be in your midst."

The third stroke is that there shall be no possibility of exemption from his plagues, when they shall try all means to preserve what is precious to them, as wives, children, or treasures. It shall be to no purpose, for what escapes at one time shall be cut off at another. Hence learn:

1. Human endeavours will not exempt men from divine judgments pursuing them for sin: "you shall take hold," in order to hold fast or pull out of danger, "but you shall not deliver."

2. When wicked and impenitent sinners are preserved from one stroke, it is only that they may be reserved for a greater; "what you deliver, I will give up to the sword."

The fourth stroke is that they shall be deprived of their comforts; the land shall be given as a prey to their enemies, who should devour their provision. As they had bereft others of the fruit of their labours, so should the enemy, or other instruments of God's wrath, deal with them: they should not reap, much less eat, of what they had sowed; they should not, as in times of joy, anoint themselves with the oil they had trodden out, nor drink of their own wine. See the like punishment threatened in Deut. 28:38, 39; Amos 5:11; Zeph. 1:11, 13, and the contrary promises, Isa. 62:8, 9; Amos 9:13, 14.

1. Sin provokes the Lord (though he is longsuffering and slow to execute) to make man's endeavours for his own subsistence to be in vain; and he will give proof of this when the cup of iniquity is full. "You shall sow, but you shall not reap."

2. The Lord contrives the way of his judgments in such deep wisdom that they may give the sorest dash to the wicked, and may repay their sin. Therefore, as they by oppression and deceit reaped where they had not sowed, so now he will make them sow and not reap; yea, he lets them not only sow but tread the olives and sweet wine, that having employed their pains and having been filled with much expectation, their disappointment may be the greater.

> Ver. 16. For the statutes of Omri are kept, and all the works of the house of Ahab; and you walk in their counsels, that I should make you a desolation, and the inhabitants thereof an hissing; therefore you shall bear the reproach of my people.

Here we have another cause of God's rod, and a further accusation for their idolatry, which, being set up by Omri and Ahab his son (1 Kings 16:25-33), was followed by the people of Israel, and of Judah also, because of the affinity that was between the two kings at that time (2 Kings 8:18). For this sin, whatever pretences they held out, the Lord threatens them further with extreme desolation.

1. Idolatry and corruption of true religion and the worship of God is the great cause of God's controversy with his visible church; "for the statutes of Omri are kept."

2. The authors and promoters of idolatry in the visible church are marked and observed by the Lord, as were Omri and Ahab.

3. No injunctions of rulers or concurrence of public authority can make idolatry lawful nor justify those who walk in such ways; for this is the Lord's controversy, "the statutes of Omri are kept, and all the works of the house of Ahab."

4. No example of multitudes, nor shows of prudence, can justify idolatry or perversion of truth. "The works of the house of Ahab are kept, and you (both Judah and Israel) walk

in their counsels." They thought it a prudent way, by conformity with the heathen, to keep peace with them and be free of the scorn of the wise of the world, because of their singular religion. But all this does not excuse.

5. Whatever outward advantage men expect by corrupting religion, yet the nature of their work tends to the opposite end, and draws on all those evils which they by sinning hope to escape. Whatever pretences they had, yet he says, "You walk in their counsels, that I should make you a desolation, and your inhabitants an hissing." It exposed them both to spoil and reproach, which they sought to shun.

6. Idolatry is a land-destroying sin, and it makes a people extremely desolate and contemptible; so much also does this threatening teach, for there are sadder things threatened than for their sins against the second table. "I will make you a desolation, and your inhabitants an hissing."

7. As the Lord's people have their peculiar privileges, so also their peculiar reproach, or punishment proportionate to their profaning of that great privilege (Ezek. 36:20, 23); and this sin, in those who boast themselves to be the people of God, is singularly great. "Therefore," he says, "you shall bear the reproach of my people."

CHAPTER VII

In this chapter Micah, in the name of all the godly, laments the paucity of good men and the universal corruption of all ranks, as a presage of approaching ruin (ver. 1-4). He mourns further that no relations could tie men to faithfulness (ver. 5, 6), and yet comforts himself and the godly in God (ver. 7) by the expectation and hope of a satisfactory deliverance (ver. 8-10), by God's promise of restoring them after some trouble (ver. 11-13), by his promise to hear the prayers of the godly in behalf of the church (ver. 14, 15), to the astonishment of all her enemies (ver. 16, 17). He concludes all with exaltation of the infinite mercy, bounty, and fidelity of God (ver. 18-20).

> Ver. 1. Woe is me, for I am as when they have gathered the summer fruits, as the grape-gleanings of the vintage. There is no cluster to cut; my soul desired the first ripe fruit.

The prophet laments the paucity of good men, who were desired by him as earnestly as a traveller would desire fruits by the way, and as precious in his eyes as the first ripe fruits are to men (Isa. 28:4; Hos. 9:10). Yet they were as rare as fruits after the gathering of the vintage; that is, there were only some few gleanings left (as Isa. 17:6) to bemoan with him this decay, and in whose name he now laments.

1. The truly godly are very precious and useful in the visible church, as being not only refreshing to other godly men, but as instruments and means of bringing down blessings, by dealing with God in prayer and by standing in the breach. Therefore Micah says, "my soul desired the first ripe fruits," so precious were they in his eyes.

2. The truly godly may be reduced to a very small number in the visible church, when many who appeared to be such make defection, and many of these who are indeed such are taken away by death. "I am as when they have gathered the summer fruits, and as the grape-gleanings of the vintage," says he.

3. The wane and decay of godly men is much to be lamented by the visible church, and by those who are left behind, especially by faithful ministers. "Woe is me," says the prophet; not only because it is sad to zealous ministers when they see not the fruit of their labours, but because in such a time all the godly are deprived of sweet fellowship, and by this decay are forewarned of judgments to come. See Ps. 12:1; Isa. 57:1.

> Ver. 2. The good man has perished out of the earth, and there is none upright among men. They all lie in wait for blood; they hunt every man his brother with a net.

He explains in proper terms what was figuratively set down in the former verse: instead of justice and humanity among men, cruelty and deceit abounded.

1. When corruption has once begun among a people, it will soon become universal, if the Lord does not prevent; there are sins of a time, which few have zeal to oppose or guard against. "The good man perishes; they all lie in wait; every man hunts his brother," says the prophet.

2. Those only are truly merciful to others who have themselves obtained mercy of the Lord; and from the sense of this they are merciful toward others. The word rendered "the good man" signifies such a one as is, so to say, "mercified" by God, and therefore actively merciful to others.

3. When mercifulness departs from among men, then also uprightness, or doing what justice and strict obligation require, will not stay; the Lord plagues the casting off of the one with the removal of the other. Therefore these are linked together: "the good man has perished, and there is none upright."

4. The defection of members of the visible church is ordinarily plagued of God by giving them up to be most grossly wicked; for "they all lie in wait for blood," to oppress or murder; "they hunt every man, even his brother, with a net." They are most intent and subtle in undermining and oppressing, and they seek to entrap their closest friends, as hunters pursue wild beasts and birds.

> Ver. 3. That they may do evil with both hands earnestly; the prince asks, and the judge asks for a reward; and the great man utters his mischievous desire; so they wrap it up.

For further confirmation of this universal defection, he instances it in several ranks.

The first instance is in the person of great ones, who are bent on evil; princes and judges avow bribery, and they (whose requests are commands) ask for gifts and expose justice to sale. And so those others in the land, who are great and can give money, do not fear to communicate counsels with the judge, to defraud and oppress the poor; and the judge and the rich man conspire to perfect what they have agreed upon.

1. Great men are ordinarily first and most eminent in public and general defections; therefore they are here first spoken to.

2. The Lord especially marks and abhors men's eager disposition to do evil, though he is tender toward those who slip through temptation and infirmity. He says, "that they may do evil with both hands earnestly, the prince asks," etc.

3. Though it is a sin in judges to receive bribes privately, yet the sin is much aggravated if it is publicly avowed. "The prince asks, and the judge asks for a reward."

4. Sins are most dangerous when they appear veiled under the name of virtue, or committed under the false pretence of equity; for so it was in this time of defection. Bribery went under the name of reward, or retribution for their service and favour shown.

5. It is a great iniquity when men in authority do not bear down great wicked men, but give them their encouragement to do wrong, and let them accomplish their will by reason of their greatness and wealth; for so it is complained in this time of defection. "The great man utters his mischievous desire"; he dares to utter it even to the judge for concurrence, and gets it put in execution on the poor. It is a usual sin also, in declining times, for great men to play to others' hands so as to strengthen themselves and one another in evil courses; for so it was in this time. "They wrap up," or "they twist up," a similitude taken from cords twisted together to make them strong, signifying the conspiracy of the judge and great man, that the one may get his bribe and the other may get his prey of the poor.

> Ver. 4. The best of them is as a briar; the most upright is sharper than a thorn-hedge. The day of your watchmen and your visitation comes; now shall be their perplexity.

A second instance of this defection is in the persons of those, especially great ones, who seemed to be better than others. The best and most straight of them were both harmful and catching, as thorns are. To this he adds a threatening, showing that it portended the near approaching of the judgments foretold by the prophets. As they had formerly entangled others with their thorny, gripping covetousness, and strengthened themselves as twisted cords in their wicked ways, so now they themselves should be so perplexed that they should not know where to turn.

1. In times of defection there may be some ready to shelter themselves under this pretext, that they are not so evil nor so unjust as others. Therefore a word must be directed in particular to "the best and most upright," to let them see the vanity of that pretext.

2. No goodness or uprightness in men is sufficient to cover their declining after the sins of the time. Therefore the prophet speaks out even against the best and most upright.

3. Even men who seem to be better than others are in hazard of being drawn away with the evils of the time; so they were in Micah's day, with covetousness and oppression, which were the sins of that time. "The best of them is a briar."

4. It is an evident symptom of a declining time when men become covetous, oppressors, catching, and dangerous to meddle with. Therefore decliners are here observed to be "briars, and sharper than a thorn-hedge." Covetousness is the ordinary evil into which backsliders fall, and the ordinary forerunner of judgments; for then the world becomes an idol, and so is fitted for God'.s stroke.

5. Though the Lord may bear long with the filthy, their being filthy still is a sign of speedily approaching ruin. When those who have a show of goodness are either wicked under that mask, or cast it off and run to the same excess with others, and when the best of men follow the sins of the time, so that the disease becomes universal, then "the day of the watchmen comes now."

6. It adds much to the weight of a rod, that the Lord has forewarned sinners of their danger, and yet they have not taken warning. Therefore their affliction is called "the day of your watchmen," not a day of vengeance upon their false prophets and wicked governors, but the day which the true prophets had foretold as coming unless they repented.

7. The Lord, in the dispensation of his providence toward men, has a special regard to his own word carried by his servants, that its truth and certainty may be seen. Therefore also is their stroke called "the day of your watchmen," that they might take notice that what his servants spoke was certain.

8. God's ministers ought carefully to study the condition of his people, and labour to stand in God's counsel, that they may understand his mind concerning the church, and faithfully give warning thereof. Therefore they are called "watchmen," a name borrowed from the practice of sentinels and sentries in armies or cities.

9. Though men in their wicked ways dream that they should not be accountable unto any, yet the Lord will take inspection of their ways, and will call them to account for them; "your visitation comes."

10. The Lord will so pursue guiltiness with affliction, that the guilty man shall be entangled and have no way to escape the rod; and guiltiness in a time of need will reduce men to such straits and perplexities, such anxieties and pressures of mind, that they shall not know where to turn. Therefore, says he, "now shall be their perplexity" or "entangling," whereas to the righteous there arises, even in darkness, light of clearness and comfort.

> Ver. 5. Trust not in a friend; put no confidence in a guide.
> Keep the doors of your mouth from her who lies in your
> bosom.
>
> 6. For the son dishonours the father, the daughter
> rises up against her mother, the daughter-in-law against
> her mother-in-law; a man's enemies are the men of his
> own house.

A third instance of this defection in all ranks and conditions of men is held forth in the unfaithfulness and inhumanity that was among them. Neither friends (whom men in a way entrust themselves unto, to be guided by them, Ps. 55:14) nor yet wives are to be trusted in; yea, those whom the strictest bonds of nature, affinity, or subjection would tie to be friendly do prove most treacherous.

1. Lack of natural affection, and men's turning monstrous in their dispositions and behaviour, is the usual companion and symptom of a declining time; for he says, "the son dishonours the father, and the daughter rises up against her mother," and so violate the bonds of nature; "the daughter-in-law against her mother-in-law," and make void the bonds of affinity; "a man's enemies are the men of his own house," for no bond of subjection will tie inferiors. This evil temper is foretold to be in the perilous latter times (2 Tim. 3:2, 3).

2. There is no sure hold to be had in any man, no matter how strictly he be bound, if he is declining from God and has not a tender conscience standing in awe of God; for in this declining time, friends, guides, wives, sons, daughters, or servants, are not to be trusted in. He who is false in his duty to God will prove true to none.

3. In times of defection and backsliding, the godly ought out of love to believe all things (1 Cor. 13:7) and not easily to take prejudice; and they are themselves to walk warily and prudently. The prophet says, "trust not, put no confidence, keep the doors of your mouth"; especially none is to be looked to for help, or trusted in, but God alone.

> Ver. 7. Therefore I will look unto the Lord; I will wait
> for the God of my salvation; my God will hear me.

Now follows the consolation of the godly who lament this defection, and who were to be involved in these common miseries and calamities. The prophet, by his example, directs them to encourage themselves in God, and look unto and wait for him, in hope of acceptance and deliverance.

1. The Lord makes use of troublesome and declining times to drive his people the more to their duty and charge; for "therefore," says he, "I will look unto the Lord."

2. There is in God sufficient matter of encouragement to counter-balance any difficulty or discouragement that his people meet with in the world; for in expectation of this they in such a time "look unto the Lord," as an all-sufficient remedy to keep them from being carried away with a declining time, and from discouragement in a sad time.

3. In declining and sad times, the people of God ought to be most earnest in dealing with him, depending on him and expecting his help; for the word signifies that, like a watchman upon a tower, the prophet will intently observe and watch, and "look unto the Lord," for help from him. See Ps. 5:3. Lukewarm dealing with God, though it may please fools in a calm day, yet will not bear out in a time of public defection.

4. In the reeling and turning upside-down of things here below, the people of God are not so much to look to these uncertainties, as unto the immutability of God in what he is to his people; for such is also implied in Micah's looking to the Lord.

5. With our faith and ardency in expecting God's help, patient waiting is also to be conjoined, by keeping his way, notwithstanding difficulties or delays of deliverance, and resolving to have faith exercised before it gets the victory; therefore he resolves also to wait for God.

6. In all the waiting of the people of God there is still hope and confidence, though it may not always be seen to the waiter; for the same word in the original signifies both waiting and hoping.

7. It is the Lord only who can save and deliver; and as he is the only Saviour of his church by virtue of the covenant of grace made with her in Christ, so will he save all who will implore him only in their straits, and will have all their salvation from him and in him, according to the covenant. This is implied by that word, "the God of my salvation," which is made the ground of his waiting.

8. We ought to encourage ourselves to deal with God by acting faith, that we shall be accepted. "I will look and wait," he says, and that because "my God will hear me."

9. God is bound by covenant to hear the lawful and needy desires of his people in due time. "My God will hear me."

10. God's hearing of our prayers, or our confidence that he will hear them, is sufficient encouragement in hardest

times; for such is the prophet's encouragement here. "My God will hear me." A man who gets access unto God, and knows he will speed in heaven, may defy the world, having such an heavenly means and source of strength.

> Ver. 8. Rejoice not against me, O my enemy; when I fall, I shall rise; when I sit in darkness, the Lord shall be a light unto me.

The prophet proceeds to hold out more special grounds of consolation and encouragement. The first of these is that the church has ground and hope of a satisfactory deliverance; and in this verse the prophet, speaking in her person, tells her how to manage this hope and comfort, in reference to her enemies. Having such ground of hope, he says, she should resolutely profess her hope before them, and scorn their insolent mockery and resolutely endure it, until the Lord by actual deliverance should put them to silence.

1. The church of God may for sin be deprived of the possession of her dignities, and be cast into a perplexed, desolate condition, lacking both comfort and judgment to know what to do; for she may "fall" and "sit in darkness."

2. The people of God, when in trouble, will not lack enemies to reproach and insult over them, to embitter their calamity. Here they have an enemy rejoicing against them.

3. It is no strange thing to see the church brought very low, and yet to be raised up again. Her fall is not her ruin, and her eclipses will not always continue. Therefore she may expect to arise after her fall, and to have light in her darkness: "when I fall, I shall arise; when I sit in darkness, the Lord shall be a light." The fall of her enemies has no such comfort.

4. The Lord is all-sufficient to give unto his people comfort in trouble, and an issue and fruit from it. Therefore the believing church seeks no other ground for her faith except this: "the Lord shall be a light unto me," for it was he who had undertaken, and who by manifesting his own presence could create comfort and issue in the midst of troubles.

5. When the church's privileges and grounds of hope are rightly seen, enemies will not be found to have such cause of boasting, because of her troubles, as they suppose; nor need she be concerned with their insulting, but may profess her spite for both it and them, in hope of his help. Therefore

she says, "Rejoice not against me, O my enemy," as if to say, you do not have such reasons as you dream of.

6. Though enemies, with present advantage against the church, will not give over their insolent reproaching, which she must endure in hope, yet the Lord by delivering her will put them to silence, and let them see that their joy was groundless. "Rejoice not against me; when I fall, I shall arise."

> Ver. 9. I will bear the indignation of the Lord, because I have sinned against him, until he plead my cause and execute judgment for me; he will bring me forth to the light, and I shall behold his righteousness.

The church is yet further directed how to manage this her hope of comfort, in relation to her guilt, which might seem to stand in the way of it. It might be objected that she could not expect that God would be her light, since she by sin had provoked him to anger; but she answers that in submissively stooping and accepting in these troubles the punishment of her iniquity at his hand, she did expect that in due time the Lord, whom she had provoked to afflict her, would plead her cause against her enemies who unjustly oppressed her, and plague them, and would restore her to her ancient glory, and would in public view give her to enjoy the effects of his bounty and fidelity. Hence learn:

1. The Lord may have fatherly indignation against his people for their sins, and may testify the same by inflicting outward calamities, and yet not reject their persons. Thus the godly's trouble is here called "the indignation of the Lord," though men were instruments. See 2 Chron. 19:2-4.

2. It is the duty of the godly, when God is angry and chastises, to be sensible of their sin which procures the same, to stoop humbly under his afflicting hand, and to bear it patiently and submissively, accepting the punishment of their iniquity. Says she, "I will bear the indignation of the Lord, because I have sinned against him."

3. A sense of sin and its great demerits will make men submissive and stoop patiently under the rod, when otherwise they would repine more. For this is the reason of her bearing the rod, "because I have sinned." This is the reason why men get so many rods dipped in their own guilt, because they do not bear patiently the rod of chastening. There is no cross so humbling as a sinful cross. See Lam. 1:18.

4. True patience and submission to God in affliction, ought to prescribe no term-day unto itself, but to refer all to his will. "I will hear until he pleads."

5. Those who humble themselves before God, and patiently stoop under a procured affliction, may expect that God will take their part against all the instruments who had a hand in their trouble, and will clear their righteous cause against those who sought only their own ends in afflicting them. Their hope and patience ought to be seasoned with this hope: "he will plead my cause," says she, though she "bears his indignation." See Isa. 47:6; Zech. 1:15.

6. The Lord will not only clear his people's right against their oppressors by pronouncing sentence in their favour in his word, but will accordingly put his sentence in execution. So Micah expounds his pleading: "he will execute judgment for me."

7. When the Lord has by affliction humbled his people for sin, and exercised their patience and faith, he will restore unto them their former privileges, and will as it were in public view make manifest that they were his. Therefore he says, "he will bring me forth to the light," not only to comfort but publicly to own and honour me, "and I shall behold," or enjoy to my satisfaction, "his righteousness," or the effects of his fidelity in keeping covenant, notwithstanding this seeming interruption.

> Ver. 10. Then she who is my enemy shall see it, and shame shall cover her who said to me, Where is the Lord your God? My eyes shall behold her; now shall she be trodden down, as the mire of the streets.

This hope for deliverance is further commended from its effect upon the church's enemies, to her satisfaction. She is here directed to profess her hope that her enemies, who mocked her faith, should be confounded at the sight of her deliverance, and be ignominiously cut off, to her great joy and satisfaction.

1. God sees it fitting sometimes to make his people's happiness conspicuous to the world, yea, even to their enemies, that it may make them of a sore heart; for "then she who is my enemy shall see it," i.e. her deliverance. See Rev. 3:9; Ps. 110:1.

2. Faith in God, and adhering to the true religion, has been an old object of derision to the church's enemies when

she was in trouble; "they said unto me, where is the Lord your God?"

3. Scorning of faith and piety, whatever disadvantage seem to follow them, shall result in the scorner's shame and confusion, by seeing God do for his people what they expected from him. "My enemy shall see it, and shame shall cover her"; she shall be utterly confounded with it.

4. When the Lord has tried his people, then the cup is put to the head of the wicked, and the enemies of the church and the mockers of her confidence shall be destroyed as contemptible things; for "now shall they be trodden down as the mire of the streets."

5. It will be a comforting sight to the people of God, to see God's justice against their enemies, and his good-will toward them cleared and made manifest after long trials. Says she, "my eyes shall behold her," though otherwise to take pleasure in the calamities of others, though enemies, is not lawful (Prov. 24:17), further than in that God is hereby glorified in the execution of his justice and his fidelity in keeping covenant with his people. See Ps. 58:10, 11.

> Ver. 11. In the day that your walls are to be built, in that day shall the decree be far removed.
>
> 12. In that day also he shall come even to you from Assyria, and from the fortified cities, and from the fortress even to the river, and from sea to sea, and from mountain to mountain.

A second ground of encouragement and comfort is held forth in God's promise to his church, confirming her formerly professed hope. He assures her of restitution and of deliverance from the yoke of strange authority, and from their cruel decrees, by which they had been scattered among the Gentiles, oppressed by tyrants, and the work of God obstructed among them, as when the building of the Temple was discharged (Ezra 4:5, 6, 21-24). And the prophet assures them further of the enlargement of the church of Israel, not only by their return from all the places where they had been scattered and detained (Isa. 27:12, 13), but also by the conversion of many nations, who should join themselves to the church, from Assyria, and from Egypt, and from all the quarters of the world. This decree may also, without wronging the text, be safely understood of the doctrine of the gospel (called a decree in Ps. 2:7) which after the restoration of the Jews should be sent through the world for promoting this promised enlargement; by the gospel both Jews and Gentiles should be gathered to the church, as by the decree of Cyrus the Jews were set at liberty to return to their country from all places where they were scattered.

1. The church, endeavouring to comfort herself with hope in God in her troubles, will abundantly be confirmed therein by God; for after her profession of hope (ver. 8-10) the Lord confirms it here by a promise. See Ps. 27:14.

2. The church may procure by her sins that the Lord should lay her desolate, exposed to the fury of enemies, without all government, protection, or apparent being, and he may for a time in justice so deal with her; for her walls were to be built, and therefore were ruined at that time, not only as a vineyard with the hedge pulled down, but as a city totally desolate.

3. The Lord will in due time restore and make up the ruins of his destroyed church and people; for "your walls are to be built."

4. God's time is patiently to be waited upon for restoring his church. There is a day for doing it, which he will keep, and no sooner.

5. It is one of the church's great trials to lie under the power of oppressing tyrants and strangers, who by their decrees and injunctions, executed with rigour, do labour to ruin her, and bear down the work of God; but when he has wrought his work upon the church by such a trial, the Lord will deliver them also from that yoke, and set them at liberty to serve him and to enjoy tranquillity without such interruptions; for "in that day the decree shall be far removed." This the Jews had some taste of, at their return from Babylon and at some times thereafter, but it shall be fully accomplished at their turning to the Lord, when there shall be no more decrees of captivity to follow.

6. All sorts of persons of all nations have free access into the church under the gospel, and the Lord has undertaken to make them come; for "in that day also he shall come even to you from Assyria, and from the fortified city, and from the fortress even to the river, and from sea to sea, and from mountain to mountain"; that is, generally from all quarters of the world, by sea and by land, which seems to be expressed with relation to the situation of Israel, the borders of which, according to God's charter, were from toward Egypt to the river Euphrates, and that which they ordinarily possessed was bounded by the east or Dead Sea, the west or Great

(Mediterranean) Sea, and by the mountains Lebanon and Hor on the north, and other mountains in the wilderness toward the south. See Exod. 23:31; Numb. 34; Josh. 1:4.

7. In the church of the gospel, the Lord has determined that the church of Israel or of the Jews shall be very eminent, not only as being the mother church of old, from which the gospel came to all nations to join with her, but as being yet to be made so conspicuous that she will invite many nations to come in unto Christ, and to be a means of their conversion. In relation to both these times, it is said to the church of the Jews, "in that day he shall come even to you," alluding to the proselytes coming up to Jerusalem of old.

8. The privileges and advantages of the church of God, when rightly seen, may and will prevail even with her greatest enemies, and with those who have their own good accommodations, to lay down their enmity, and renounce all, and come and share with her; for "he shall come from Assyria," her most inveterate enemy, "and from the fortified cities, and from the fortress," by which Egypt seems to be signified. Egypt was well fortified by nature and art, and the Hebrew word here is related with the Hebrew name of Egypt, and Assyria and Egypt are ordinarily joined in such promises (Isa. 19:23-25).

9. The Lord's means for gathering and enlarging his church is the preaching of the gospel, by which he leads all captive unto the obedience of Christ. This we are taught by the other interpretation of the decree. "The decree (i.e. the gospel of Christ) shall be far removed," and "he shall come." The gospel may be called a decree, as containing God's eternal purpose and ordinance concerning the salvation of sinners; and it "shall be removed," that is, published in his name to the world, for sinners to lay hold upon.

10. The spread of the gospel throughout the world, notwithstanding all impediments and opposition, is a work in which the hand and power of God is to be seen for what is already done, and to be rested upon for what is to be accomplished; for it is he only who can undertake so that "the decree shall be far removed."

> Ver. 13. Notwithstanding the land shall be desolate, because of those who dwell therein, for the fruit of their doings.

Lest the people should flatter themselves in their sins, a caution is subjoined to enable them rightly to understand the promise. Before the performance, a desolation must be made because of their sins; this was first accomplished by Nebuchadnezzar, and again by the Romans.

1. The promises of God ought to be warily heeded, and rightly understood and applied, that secure sinners may not suck poison from them. Therefore a caution is given to be taken along with the promise; "notwithstanding, the land shall be desolate."

2. God may carry thoughts of love to his people, hidden in his heart for a long time, and may let out much trouble on them whom he loves and purposes to manifest love unto. "Notwithstanding" his purpose, ver. 12, yet "the land shall be desolate." See Jer. 29:10, 11.

3. The reason of the Lord's striking a people toward whom he has a purpose of love, is their sin. Because of sin he will plague their contentments, lay their habitation desolate, and make them taste of the bitterness of their way in departing from him, so that they may be humbled and fitted for his mercy, and that he may cut off wicked generations and raise up others to enjoy his mercies; for "the land shall be desolate, because of them that dwell therein, for the fruit of their doings."

> Ver. 14. Feed your people with your rod, the flock of your heritage, which dwell solitarily in the wood in the midst of Carmel; let them feed in Bashan and Gilead, as in the days of old.
>
> 15. According to the days of your coming out of the land of Egypt, I will show unto him marvellous things.

A third ground of encouragement is held forth, in an answer to the prophet's prayer. Upon mention of the ensuing desolation, he turns himself to God, or to Christ the great Shepherd, requesting that he would care for his scattered and desolate people, in whom he had so much interest, and would at last bring them to enjoy the former sweet fruits of his government, and feed them as flocks were fed in the fruitful pastures of Bashan and Gilead (Numb. 32:1; Deut. 32:14). To this prayer an answer is returned, in a promise that they shall get a deliverance no less famous and miraculous than when they were delivered of old from Egypt. This promise is spoken to Israel (and to the church as well) not only because she was abundantly satisfied with the first deliverance, and therefore it is spoken to her to stir her up to believe the other, but also to show the Lord's constancy in doing her good in the latter; as if to say, before her face and behind her back, he is the same.

1. A sense of judgments imminent or incumbent, calls for much prayer and dealing with God; for such use does the prophet make of the threatened desolation.

2. The church of Christ in her trouble especially, is in a solitary condition and full of hazard, being disconsolate, exposed to want and danger, unless he have a care for her. "They dwell solitary in the wood, in the midst of Carmel"; they are like a .solitary flock in woods and mountains; and though Carmel signifies a fruitful place, and was so in the land of Canaan (Isa. 33:9; Isa. 35:2; 2 Kings 19:23), yet it is here taken in with the woods, to show that their most fruitful places in exile should look like a wilderness to them; or because it was an open field and mountain, and consequently not safe; though others join that rather with the latter part of the verse, and make it read, "let them feed in the midst of Carmel, in Bashan," etc., as in Jer. 50:19.

3. Christ is the church's only Shepherd; to his care she is entrusted, and he will have a special care for her in trouble. To him does the prophet pray: "feed thy people who dwell solitarily."

4. Christ not only feeds his people, but exercises a jurisdiction over them, by which he keeps them in subjection to him, drives them to their food, and expels noxious humours, which may hinder their feeding and thriving; and he also, by his power, protects those whom he thus feeds and governs. All these things are desirable, and all are to be prayed from him: "feed thy people with thy rod." See Ps. 23:4.

5. Christ has many relations to and interests in his church, which are not broken off by any trouble, to endear her to his affection and care; and these may encourage faith to go to him in need. Therefore he says, "feed thy people, the flock of thy heritage, who dwell solitarily." Notwithstanding their desolate condition, they are his peculiar portion, in which he has not a temporary, but an eternal right, as men have to their heritage in all generations; and accordingly he will care for and possess them, and this charter and privilege stands fast to the church of the Jews here prayed for, and will be manifested after all their dispersions.

6. Christ has ample substance to bestow upon his people, and has all fullness for faith to lay hold upon in prayer, for the supply of every need. He can make them "feed in Bashan and Gilead," which were very fruitful pastures for flocks;

though in relation to Israel this may be understood more particularly of restoring them to their own fruitful land, to enjoy it in its full extent, even to Bashan and Gilead, which lay far off beyond Jordan. See Jer. 50:19.

7. The church of God has rich experiences of his former goodness, encouraging her in present straits, and faith ought to make use of these past blessings; says he, "let them feed as in the days of old."

8. Christ will not deny the needy and lawful desires of his people, particularly those which flow from public mindedness and which are put up for the church; but he will take charge of his people, to give them a blessed issue; for the request is here granted.

9. Christ is omnipotent and will do wonders, if need require, in behalf of his people. He takes pleasure to convey the expressions of his love to them, and to bring about their deliverance to their own and others' admiration; for "I will show him," or make him to enjoy, "marvelous things."

10. As Christ's manifestation of himself in former times for his people does engage him to do yet more for them, so he will make good whatever they have reason from former experience to expect; for, "according to the days of your coming out of Egypt I will show him marvelous things." Faith is made to feed not only upon the great acts he did, but also upon his way of doing them, his passing over their iniquities, their murmurings and unbelief, his reducing them to straits before he appeared for them, his working by small, unlikely, and contrary means, etc.

11. The Lord stands engaged to his ancient people, to give them a deliverance from their troubles and bondage, as great and wonderful as that from Egypt was; for this is expressly promised. And though this is spiritually accomplished, and daily being accomplished in the spiritual deliverances of the Israel of God, yet this promise is made chiefly to the church of Israel, in relation to their desolations; and though some pledge of this was given at their return from Babylon, yet then it came short among other things of the deliverance from Egypt, in that it was not national, even of the Jews; and therefore it seems to have relation to the time of the restitution and saving of all Israel, which will be so great a mercy that it will in a way obscure their former mercies. See Jer. 16:14, 15.

Ver. 16. The nations shall see, and be confounded at all their might; they shall lay their hand upon their mouth; their ears shall be deaf.

17. They shall lick the dust like a serpent; they shall move out of their holes like worms of the earth; they shall be afraid of the Lord our God, and shall fear because of thee.

A fourth ground of encouragement, and a result of the former, is taken from the effects which all this shall have among enemies. Seeing all this mighty power of God appearing for the church, they shall be astonished and made deaf with the fame of God's acts, and dumb that they dare not speak, as formerly, proud things; and the terror of God's majesty appearing in and for his church, shall so seize upon them as to make them submit with all fear and subjection to God and his church, stooping as low as serpents and creeping things. See Ps. 72:9; Isa. 49:23. All this does not necessarily infer their true conversion, but only that they shall yield external obedience and pretend friendship to secure themselves.

1. The deliverance of the church of God is brought about in such a way that natural men could never have expected it; therefore "the nations shall see and be confounded."

2. The Lord sees it fitting at times, not only to be kind to his people, but to give public demonstrations of his good will toward them, in such a measure as may astonish all beholders. "The nations shall see and be confounded; they shall lay their hand upon their mouth." See Ps. 126:2.

3. The church's privileges and strength, when well seen, will be terrible to enemies in their greatest power; for "they shall be confounded at all their (that is, the church's) might," or "for all their might," that is, all the power the Assyrians thought they had shall not keep them from confusion, but they shall be astonished so much the more that it has proved vain.

4. Men without God, and not walking in his way, are easily confounded when the Lord turns his hand against them, and begins to work for his people; for they, though no doubt insolent and proud before, "shall lay their hand upon their mouth."

5. God's wonderful works of providence for his people, and against their enemies, do ordinarily produce but vanishing and empty fruits, in the world and among enemies,

as perhaps to confound and astonish them, as if they were
dumb and deaf, when what God has done for his people is
mentioned. "They shall be confounded, they shall lay their
hand on their mouth, their ears shall be deaf." Or, if they
work any more, it is but pretended subjection, and friendship out of fear. "They shall lick the dust like a serpent,
they shall move out of their holes; they shall be afraid."
A hard piece of work are men's hearts to work upon,
especially when once engaged in enmity against God and
his people, and hard, if not impossible, is it for any work
to work savingly where the word has no place, and where
men's misery and God's mercy are not revealed unto them.

6. It is a great proof of God's power, and matter of encouragement to the church, to see their enemies brought so
low as to yield obedience, though but feigned, and to pretend
friendship, as is usual in the time of the church's prosperity; for this is an encouragement, that "they shall lick
the dust like a serpent." We are to be sensible and wary of
the falsehood of some who pretend to serve Christ and to
be friends to his church, as to adore the power of God, making them to stoop so far as to lie, as Ps. 66:3 says in the
original.

7. All the glory of bringing down the Lord's enemies and
making them to stoop, is to be ascribed only to God; the
church is so terrible and mighty only because of God's interest in her and presence with her. "They shall be afraid
of the Lord our God, and fear because of thee." The latter
part of this text may either be understood of God, the sweetness of the encouragement making them turn the speech to
him by way of warm and hearty acknowledgement, or of the
church made dreadful because God makes manifest that he
is hers by covenant.

> Ver. 18. Who is a God like unto thee, who pardons iniq-
> uity and passes by the transgression of the remnant
> of his heritage? He retains not his anger for ever,
> because he delights in mercy.

In considering all these encouragements, the prophet in
the church's name concludes all with a commendation and
praise of God, as singular in his mercy (ver. 19) and in his
fidelity (ver. 20). He begins with God's mercy, and sets it
out in a speech full of various affections, sometimes directed to God by way of praise, sometimes spoken of God
for the church's own encouragement, sometimes spoken with

particular application to themselves, sometimes with relation to all the people of God, to set forth the public mindedness of all who have obtained mercy. He instances this singular mercy of God in the matter of pardoning sins, which is propounded in this verse and further cleared from two expressions, setting forth more of the riches of this benefit, and of the security and comfort which may be had by it.

1. Mercies received from God, ought to commend and endear him to our hearts; therefore after rehearsing these mercies, the prophet begins to commend the giver.

2. The Lord, rightly seen and considered in himself and his dispensations, will be found peerless and matchless, as one in whom we may boast over all idols, whose ways alone are best to be followed, who will do singular things for his people, and make them singular, and consequently who ought to be singular in their affection. "Who is a God like unto thee?" says he.

3. God's matchlessness appears to his people, and affects their hearts, not so much in acts of his power absolutely considered (though they ought to be sensible of these also) as in his acts of grace, and his being great in Christ, pardoning sin. Yea, when great things are done or promised to them, they marvel not so much at these, as that his mercy should come over their transgressions, to make way for these great things. Therefore they declare that there is no God like him, "who pardons iniquity," and when they hear of all the former encouragements, they admire this above them all, that their sin had not stood in the way of these mercies. The godly are sensible of the desert of sin, and of their inability to satisfy justice for it, an therefore pardon is sweet above all to them.

4. Outward mercies, though ever so great and full, will never yield true satisfaction unless they are joined to reconciliation with God and pardon of sin. So much are we taught here; all the former encouragements refresh, when they may also admire and rejoice in God, "who pardons iniquity."

5. By a free pardon, God will for his Christ's sake lift off and take away the burden of the guilt of sin, though ever so great, from his wearied people who flee to him for refuge; and so he eases them of it, and gives them ground of quietness in their conscience. So much does the word rendered "pardoning" import in the original, and it is extended even to "iniquity and transgression"; and this is the only way to get true ease and deliverance from sin.

6. The self-condemned sinner, in looking for pardon from God, ought to look upon him as singular, and not measure his condescension or mercy by their thoughts, or by any other mould; but they should expect that as he is matchless, so is his mercy, pity, and love; for the question, "who is a God like unto thee, who pardons iniquity?" does teach us so much; and this is to be taken along with every expression of pardon, that he is matchless, for he does that and does it matchlessly.

The first expression, clearing this benefit yet further, is, "and passes by the transgression of the remnant of his heritage." Here pardon is expounded to be a passing over, or, so to say, a seeing and yet not seeing of his people's faults; and it is further declared to whom this benefit belongs. Hence learn:

1. So great and many are sinful man's provocations, and so great is his inability either to be rid of them or to satisfy God for them, that there is no way of reconciliation between God and him except by the Lord's quitting the plea and passing over his faults, not calling him to any strict account for them; and this he does to those who see their own faults much, and flee to him through Christ; for "he passes by," or over, "transgression." See Isa. 57:17, 18; Gen. 8:21; Ps. 130:3, 4.

2. These advantages are not to be expected by all, but by the Lord's own, who are "his heritage." This imports on their part, that they abide with God as a constant portion, intending to be his heritage, which is a qualification required in those who come for quieting of conscience from particular guilt; and further, it imports on God's part that whatever just displeasure he conceived against them, yet at the last he will be reconciled with "his heritage." They are also called "the remnant," which is another argument why he pardons, i.e. that being already consumed in part for sin, they would be utterly destroyed if mercy did not end the controversy.

3. Those whom God pardons are expressed under the name of "the remnant of his heritage," or a remnant of Israel after trouble; partly because this benefit is reserved for them also, and spoken of here with special relationship to them, and will be very greatly set upon them after their restitution. But further, though reprobates may also be spared and reserved in public calamities, yet the comparison holds: (a) In that the elect and pardoned ones are the fewer in

number, as a remnant in comparison to the bulk, who are cut off. (b) In that a remnant left from trouble ought in their behaviour to resemble much the godly and elect in sobriety (Isa. 38:15), in needy dependence (Zeph. 3:12), in mourning for sin (Ezek. 7:16), in holy walking (Zeph. 3:13), etc.

The second expression is, "he retains not his anger, because he delights in mercy." His great mercy and his taking pleasure in it, in pardoning sin, is amplified and commended from his putting off his just displeasure against sin and the sinner. Hence learn:

1. The Lord will put on just anger against the sins of his people, and may possibly not pass them over at all times, but may testify his displeasure by effects against them, though he will yet pardon them; for it is here supposed that he may have anger, and let it out for a time.

2. When the Lord is provoked and testifies his displeasure, he is not unwilling to be reconciled; for "he retains not his anger," or, as the word signifies, holds it not with a strong hand, but seeks when he is angry that we should stand in the gap and entreat him to pass from it.

3. It highly commends God, and is matter of great consolation to us, that his anger against his people is not everlasting; that "he retains not his anger forever" is a mercy to us, though it may endure for a long tract of time.

4. God's mercy is the only reason why he does not pursue his controversies against his people with eternal wrath, and this is clearly to be seen and acknowledged by all who are so graciously dealt with. They do so here: "he retains not his anger forever, because he delights in mercy."

5. Though God, blessed over all, may delight in himself and his attributes, and in the manifestation of them in the world, yet after the manner of men, he is said to "delight in mercy," for that attribute is most manifested in the world. It is shown in his bounty to all (Ps. 33:5), in his not taking pleasure in the death of the wicked, even of reprobates (Ezek. 18:32), though for the manifestation of his justice he wills it; and to his own people, justice is his strange act (Isa. 28:21) and mercy his ordinary way of dealing; and all the mercy he shows them, he does not do it grudgingly (Jer. 32:41), nor does he delight to be at odds with them, but always to have them refreshed in his love. Therefore his mercy ends many a plea, that it may make way and burst through clouds to manifest itself.

> Ver. 19. He will turn again, he will have compassion upon
> us; he will subdue our iniquities, and thou wilt cast all
> their sins into the depths of the sea.

This great privilege is yet insisted on, and further commended and developed in several expressions. The first is, "he will turn again; he will have compassion upon us." It is declared that the pardon of sin and the removal of its effects flow from the tender mercy of God; and this pardon is commended: (a) From its effect, that God in mercy will turn to his pardoned people with compassion, and (b) from God's constancy herein, that after compassion has been formerly shown and abused, he will yet again have compassion, as the Hebrew way of speech is often taken and translated. Hence learn:

1. Many of our conceptions and expressions will not be able to reveal or utter the great goodness of God in pardoning sin, nor the great mercy a self-condemned sinner sees in it, nor the great benefit he reaps by it. Therefore are expressions so multiplied about it.

2. Though it is a sweet sign of a pardoned man, that he thinks highly of his pardon and of God as a pardoner, and loves God because he will forgive his own people, yet it adds much to the assurance and comfort of this benefit when every self-condemned sinner lays hold on this benefit and applies it to himself, which should be endeavoured and may be attained; for here the church comes to the application, and says, "he will have compassion upon us."

3. God is provoked by his people's sins to turn away from them, and to seem to neglect them, their prayers, and their conditions. Thus they pray him to "turn again" unto them.

4. Upon the Lord's pardoning of sin, not only is anger taken away (as v. 18), but reconciliation and the shining of his favourable countenance will follow in due time; for "he will turn again, and have compassion."

5. Though favours formerly received and abused by us may be a great impediment to our faith in expecting favour, when we need it again, yet the Lord in mercy will again and again be kind to his people. "He will again have compassion." See Judg. 10:11-14, 16.

6. Although the guilty child of God, having abused former mercies, and lying in his own sin and misery, is an unworthy and contemptible object, and has nothing with which to commend himself to God, yet God will in pity condescend to look

upon him, and bring an argument from his very misery to help him. "He will have compassion upon us," they say.

7. The Lord is so far from rejecting his people for their unworthiness and miserable condition, that he will keep them in such a needy condition that they need compassion. The church need not expect to be freed altogether of the badges of her misery, unless she would banish his tender compassions out of the world.

8. The Lord's needy and distressed people will get a place in his tender affections until they are helped, and compassion shall carve out their supply and issue; for so much also does his compassion teach us.

Another expression clearing this benefit is, "he will subdue our iniquities." This may be taken up either as a further explication of the way of pardon, that God overcomes the great provocation of sin which stands in the way of his mercy, or else as an effect of pardon, that God not only pardons the guilt, but mortifies the power of sin in his people.

1. The Lord pardons sin in none but those whom he makes sensible of the great provocation of sin, and makes them to see it as an army, standing in mercy's way, to be subdued; for so do they express the way of pardon.

2. God's mercy is all-sufficient to overcome all provocations, and to overcome the ill-deserving of sin; for "he will subdue iniquity." See Cant. 2:8; Rom. 5:20.

3. Whoever gets pardon of sin, they also fall in love with and see the need of mortification of sin. This the second interpretation of "subduing" teaches. The pardoned church accounts God singular, because "he will subdue iniquity."

4. Mortification of sin is to be wrought by God, and expected from him; otherwise our endeavours will not prevail. But even though our endeavours of mortification do not prevail, yet our case is not hopeless, for "he will subdue our iniquities."

The last expression, "thou wilt cast all their sins into the depths of the sea," contains a further effect of pardon, that sins once pardoned shall not be remembered nor laid to their charge again. This is held out in a borrowed speech taken from among men; for a thing is without possibility of being recovered by men when it is cast into the bottom of the sea, and that where it is deepest. Hence learn:

1. Though a pardoned sinner, when he commits new sins, or is not humble, tender, and thankful under the sense of pardon, may have former sins brought to remembrance, to be matter of humiliation and stirring up to repentance; and though an hour of temptation may shake loose all evidences of pardon; yet when sin is once pardoned, the remission stands never to be repeated (only new confirmations are still to be sought after), nor will the pardoned sin come in account against the pardoned man before God again. See Isa. 38:17; Ps. 103:12; Jer. 31:34.

2. God's mercy is so infinite that multitudes of sin in the self-judging sinner will not hide his full and free pardon, nor need they obstruct the peaceable effects thereof in the conscience of the pardoned man. This fountains stands open daily for the justified man to flee unto with all his faults as they are committed, with renewing of his faith and repentance. Thus the promise is written large: "thou wilt cast all their sins into the depths of the sea."

3. As the sense of the pardon of sin, and freedom from the apprehension of God's keeping it in remembrance, is a warm and refreshing condition, so it should be much entertained by frequent looking to God by faith and praise about it. Therefore the speech is again directed to God: "thou wilt cast their sins."

> Ver. 20. Thou wilt perform the truth to Jacob, and the mercy to Abraham, which thou hast sworn unto our fathers, from the days of old.

In the next place, God is commended as singular in his gracious fidelity, keeping the covenant made with their forefathers.

1. The privileges of the church are made theirs by contract and sworn covenant, and are certain; the word speaks of "truth and mercies sworn."

2. The Lord is to be seen and commended as incomparable in fidelity and promise keeping, notwithstanding all impediments in his way, and all our apprehensions of him to the contrary; it is to be repeated: "who is a God like thee, that will perform the truth which thou hast spoken?"

3. The sum of God's covenant with his church is "mercy," in respect of the fountain from which all his bounty flows, and in respect of our ill deservings, which we should daily see, and "truth," in respect that the freedom of mercy in

promising diminishes nothing of the certainty of performance. As mercy opens the door, truth keeps it open. Hence
it is that these two are so frequently conjoined in the expectations and desires of saints. See Ps. 57:3; Ps. 61:7.

4. The covenant of mercy is the church's first and irrevocable privilege; for it is "sworn of old," and so the law,
which came after, cannot disannul it (Gal. 3:17).

5. As the spiritual blessings of the covenant belong only
to true believers, who may reckon Abraham and Jacob,
with whom the covenant was made, as their fathers by faith;
so even the natural posterity of Jacob and Abraham have a
peculiar interest in that covenant made with their fathers,
not broken off by any interruption or desolation, but to be
still coming forth for them. The covenant promises their
being called as a nation to be his church and people, if not
also their being given the promised land in heritage; for so
do they reckon, while they are threatened with ensuing desolation. "Thou wilt perform the truth to Jacob, and the mercy
to Abraham, which thou hast sworn." For this cause the
apostle reckons that God's purposes toward them are among
the "gifts which are without repentance" (Rom. 11:29), never
to be recalled and made utterly void, no more than his dealing with his elect in the matter of their calling and glor-
ification.

6. It is the duty of the godly, when they are called to
trouble, to confirm their faith in the hope of issue, according
to God's promise, and to be comforted and rest satisfied
therewith, accounting it sweet to have hope of future mercy
sure, although it were ever so long in coming, and the way
to it ever so rough; for so the godly, hearing of this future
desolation, close all, believing and resting satisfied with
this: "thou wilt perform the truth to Jacob, and the mercy to
Abraham," for the accomplishment of which every godly man
should pray. Even so, Lord Jesus, come quickly. Amen and
amen.

NAHUM

THE ARGUMENT

The Lord had suspended the execution of the judgments denounced by Jonah against Nineveh, the chief city of the Assyrian Empire, upon their repentance. They did again return to their vomit, and added unto all their other sins, the oppression of the people of God, by capturing the ten tribes and overruning Judah. Therefore the Lord, for the comfort of his people thus afflicted, raises up Nahum, to set forth at large the ruin of that monarchy, especially of the chief city, Nineveh. Whether he prophesied in Hezekiah's days, or afterward, is not certain; yet certainly the oppression of Judah recorded in 2 Kings 18 and 19 is pointed at by him. For the comfort of God's people, setting forth a description of God in his justice, power, and mercy, suitable to the present purpose, he foretells the ruin of the state of Assyria by the Medes and Chaldeans, with the comfort and advantage redounding to the church thereby (chap. 1), and the destruction of the chief city, with the preparations against it and its taking (chap. 2), which is further amplified and confirmed by setting forth their provocations, the example of other places, and the fruitlessness of all their endeavours to defend themselves (chap. 3).

CHAPTER I

This chapter, after the inscription (ver. 1) contains:

1. A description of God in his justice and power against his enemies (ver. 2-6) and mercy toward his people (ver. 7).

2. An application of this description to the present purpose. (a) The Assyrians are threatened with violent and total destruction (ver. 8) notwithstanding their insolent presumption in thinking to be able to wrong the church or defend themselves (ver. 9), or their formidable union and their prosperity, which God would use to bring on their stroke (ver. 10). (b) The cause of all this is declared to be their injurious dealing against God and his people (ver. 11), for which they are again threatened, so that he may comfort his church with deliverance from their oppressions (ver. 12, 13). (c) To confirm this sentence yet more, Assyria, or the royal family, is again threatened with utter rooting out

(ver. 14), the news of which should produce comfort to the church, as she would have liberty thereby to enjoy and go about the ordinances (ver. 15).

Ver. 1. The burden of Nineveh. The book of the vision of Nahum the Elkothite.

The inscription holds forth: (a) The penman of this prophecy, described from his name and the place of his birth, of both which we read no more elsewhere. (b) The nature of the message, containing hard tidings against the chief city of the Assyrian Empire (called Nineveh, or 'the habitation of Ninus,') under which the Empire itself is to be understood. (c) The authority and certainty of this message, in that he had it by vision. Hence learn:

1. Even enemies to the church are under the dominion of God's providence and liable to his rebukes and corrections; for he has a "burden" against Nineveh.

2. There is nothing to be expected from God to impenitent sinners, or those who seem to repent but do not continue in that exercise, except hard tidings; for Nineveh, forgetting to continue in the repentance which they began at Jonah's preaching, get now from the Lord a burden.

3. Judgments denounced by God against the wicked for sin, are insupportable and crushing, such as the creature cannot stand under; therefore they are called a "burden."

4. Wrath denounced against impenitent sinners is infallible and certain, whatever may appear to those who judge by appearance; for this "burden" is "the book of the vision," containing what God had certainly revealed to his servant and commanded him to publish in his name and authority.

5. As Nahum saw this by vision, so let those who would see the ruin of flourishing enemies study to be near God, and to get it delivered from the word.

Ver. 2. God is jealous, and the Lord revenges; the Lord revenges and is furious, the Lord will take vengeance on his adversaries, and he reserves wrath for his enemies.

The justice of God in taking vengeance on his enemies is described both from the cause moving him to it, which is his jealousy or tender feeling of the injuries done to his honour and his dear people, and from the severity and certainty thereof, though suspended for a time. Hence learn:

1. As the Lord is jealous of his people's affections towards him (Exod. 20:5), so he is jealous and cannot endure the wrong done to his honour by those who hurt his people, who are dear unto him.

2. This jealousy and affection of God will in due time break out in just revenge against his and the church's enemies, recompencing the wrongs they do, which his people cannot take course with; "God is jealous, and the Lord revenges."

3. Vengeance executed by God, jealous for his people whom he loves, flows from great displeasure and is most severe; for "the Lord revenges" all injuries, "and is furious." The Hebrew word imports great fury, as to say (with reverence to him who speaks so to our capacity) that he is transported with it.

4. The justice and severity of God against wicked men should be seriously studied, both by enemies to deter them from doing evil, and by his oppressed people for their comfort. This repetition, "God is jealous, and the Lord revenges; the Lord revenges and is furious; the Lord will take vengeance," imports that there should be many thoughts of it.

5. The Lord owns his people's quarrel, and declares himself a party against their enemies; for they are "his adversaries and his enemies."

6. That wrath which the Lord's word denounces against the wicked, and which their wickedness calls aloud for, and yet is kept off, is only reserved for a more fit time, to be poured forth in greater measure. "He reserves wrath for his enemies." The original has it only "reserves," without any addition, which shows how inexpressible that anger is, which God treasures up to be poured out together.

> Ver. 3. The Lord is slow to anger, and great in power, and will not at all acquit the wicked; the Lord has his way in the whirlwind and in the storm, and the clouds are the dust of his feet.

This justice of God taking vengeance on enemies is further described from the way of its manifestation, which is slowly but certainly. The Lord's forbearance does not come because he purposes to forgive, nor because he lacks power; this may appear from his majesty and state, when he appears environed with whirlwinds and tempests raised by his power (as Ps. 18:8-11), and the airy clouds being as dust raised by his stately progress, as armies raise dust in their march. And this is one part of the description of his power in executing this just vengeance. Hence learn:

1. Even toward enemies, the Lord is long-suffering and slow to execute his anger: that their destruction may be seen to be of themselves; that in his holy providence they may stumble more upon his indulgence and fill up their heasure; and that his church's faith and patience may be tried. Therefore he says, "the Lord is slow to anger."

2. When the Lord spares his enemies, it is not because he is unable to meet with them; nor ought we to judge, because of any outward appearances, that they are invincible; for however unlikely the destruction of enemies may be in the eyes of men, yet the Lord, who is "slow to anger," is also "great in power."

3. As the Lord is able to reach his enemies when he pleases, so his forbearing of them is no evidence that they shall be exempted altogether; but he will undoubtedly give proof of his power in dealing with them as their way deserves; for "the Lord is great in power, and will not at all acquit the wicked." He will punish them, lest his sparing them altogether should give ground to think that he held them innocent, or absolved them as guiltless, as the word signifies.

4. The Lord is able, by his power, speedily to bring greatest things to pass, and can when he pleases overturn, confound, and darken all things which appeared to be stable, well ordered, and clear. This is taught in that he has his way in the whirlwind, storm, and clouds. These suddenly confound what they surprise, and clouds and storms darken the face of a clear sky; and God's way in these points at their suddenness (Prov. 10:25; Isa. 19:1).

5. Even when the Lord manifests himself in his great glory, he does but (so to speak) obscure himself because of our infirmity, which cannot comprehend his glory in its brightness; for so much does his manifesting of himself in dark storms, or tempests, and thick, lowering clouds, teach. See Ps. 97:2.

6. God's dispensations, even when they are most dreadful and terrible in effects, may yet be deep and unsearchable, and his purpose and counsel in them hard to discern; for so much further are we taught by his way in "whirlwinds," "storms," and "clouds," which all darken.

> Ver. 4. He rebukes the sea, and makes it dry, and
> dries up all the rivers; Bashan languishes, and Carmel,
> and the flower of Lebanon languishes.
>
> 5. The mountains quake at him, and the hills melt,
> and the earth is burnt at his presence; yea, the world,
> and all who dwell therein.

This power of God is yet further described from its effects, that he can in his anger dry up seas and rivers, as of old appeared at the Red Sea and Jordan; he can blast the beauty of fertile and pleasant trees, such as "Lebanon" for trees, "Bashan" for pasture, and "Carmel" for corn; he can make the stable hills to quake and melt like wax or snow, and the earth to burn up with drought, or as Sodom was destroyed; yea, and can dissolve all the creatures, and make the habitable world to feel the effects of his power. Hence learn:

1. The power of God is much to be studied by all those who oppose him, and by those who expect help from him in trouble; therefore this ample description of his power is here recorded.

2. Whatever men boast of themselves, yet it is no small task to give God the glory of omnipotence, and fix faith upon him as one who is able to do whatever he pleases; for this commendation of his power is no vain repetition, but imports that neither do enemies fear it, nor his people trust in it, as they ought.

3. The Lord gives such ample proofs of his power in his works of providence upon the creatures in heaven and earth, that we may be clearly confirmed in our faith in his omnipotence; and they are to be studied that we may be confirmed. This is held forth in what he does daily in the air in "storms" and "clouds" (ver. 3), and in what he can so upon seas, rivers, hills, etc., of which he has given us ample proof as recorded in scripture.

4. All the creatures are subject to the power of God, to be disposed of, and their ordinary course to be overturned, at his pleasure; "he makes seas and rivers dry," makes fruits to wither, hills and earth to melt and burn, and the world to be turned upside down.

> Ver. 6. Who can stand before his indignation, and who can
> abide in the fierceness of his anger? His fury is poured
> out like fire, and the rocks are thrown down by him.

From the former evidences of God's power upon the creatures, the prophet infers the inability of any to stand or endure when an angry God calls them before his tribunal; his anger, being attended with invincible power, would as a fire burn up all before it without mercy, and overturn hard rocks, as at Christ's death and as recorded in 1 Kings 19:11.

1. The Lord's indignation against sin should be looked upon as attended with divine omnipotence, able to make the creature feel it sadly; for so does this verse, dependent upon the former, teach. See Ps. 90:11.

2. No attribute in God, however dreadful, is formidable to any but to the man who provokes him to anger, and continues therein without repentance. Therefore his dreadful power is held forth as a ground of this conclusion: "who can stand before his indignation, and who can abide in the fierceness of his anger?"

3. It is but mad presumption in wicked men to think to avoid God's judgment seat, or to keep their feet when he is angry; for God will draw them to his tribunal, and will rebuke and condemn them, and cast them out of his presence, and destroy them in his fierce displeasure. "Who can stand before his indignation?"

4. When God's anger is rightly considered, when the effects thereof upon the creatures are seen, and when man becomes well acquainted with his own weakness, he will easily see the folly of standing out against God; for "his fury is poured out like fire" upon combustible matter, such as man is before him, "and the rocks are thrown down by him"; how much more weak man?

> Ver. 7. The Lord is good, a strong hold in the day of trouble; and he knows those who trust in him.

Now follows a description of God in his mercy, that he is good and meek, a defence in trouble, and an approver of and carer for those who are his people and trust in him. And as the former description of his justice and power was verified upon the Assyrians, so this has relation to the behaviour and success of Hezekiah and Judah, who trusted in God (2 Kings 18:5; 2 Chron. 32:8) and were protected and delivered.

1. The people of God ought to flee out of themselves and renounce all human helps and confidences, making God their only refuge against sin and trouble; for so does the word rendered "trusting" import. "They trust in him."

2. The Lord in his greatest majesty and terribleness, is still good and favourable to those who trust in him; for after the description of his power and justice, it is subjoined, "the Lord is good." See Matt. 28:4, 5.

3. The people of God ought to resolve for times of trouble and strait, which yet do not prejudice the goodness of God toward them, for they are sent to do them good and for their advantage. "The Lord is good," and yet there will be a "day of trouble."

4. The power of God which is employed against enemies is forthcoming for the people in their need; for thereby he is a "strong hold," or strength.

5. The Lord's goodness, his protection and defence, are best known and discerned in times of difficulty; for "the Lord is good, a stronghold in the day of trouble." His people's lack of difficulties would take away the sense of what he is to them and for them (Ps. 31:7).

6. The Lord not only knows, as omniscient, but approves and delights in those who lean to him and give him the glory of his attributes, by believing; for "he knows those who trust in him."

> Ver. 8. But with an overrunning flood he will make an utter end of the place thereof, and darkness shall pursue his enemies.

The prophet proceeds to apply this description of God to the present purpose, and in opposition to his goodness his severity against the Assyrians is held forth, comprehending the sum of all the threatening, that the city or empire shall be so suddenly and violently overthrown, as if a deluge had swept it away, and that any who escape that storm shall be pursued and cut off with judgments.

1. The people of God ought to learn to esteem highly of their safety in him, by considering the woeful case of those who are without him; therefore this calamity is set in opposition to their safety, that they may stand as it were upon the bridge of this deluge, and see the wicked perish, and may rejoice in him who has become their salvation. "The Lord is good, but with an overrunning flood he will make an utter end."

2. The judgments of an angry God are as irresistible, and make as great havoc of persons or places, as an inundation or deluge breaking in upon a land. "With an overrunning flood he will make an utter end of its place," i.e. of Nineveh,

or the Assyrian Empire; it should be so destroyed and swept away that the place where the city stood should bear no monument thereof, nor should there be any face of the empire. This form of speech frequently points out total extirpation (Ps. 37:10; Dan. 2:35; Rev. 12:8).

3. There is no possibility for man to shun the righteous judgments of the Lord; nor can exemption in horridest calamities secure a sinner from other plagues. Though they escape the deluge, or think to flee, yet "darkness shall pursue his enemies."

4. The portion of God's enemies is to be cut off and sent out of the world in affliction, ignominy and terror, and afterward to be sent to the pit; for so much does darkness import. See Job 10:21, 22; Jer. 13:16; Matt. 8:12. "Darkness shall pursue his enemies," and where he pursues he will overtake.

> Ver. 9. What do you imagine against the Lord? He will make an utter end; affliction shall not rise up the second time.

This sentence is confirmed in that their enterprises against the church would be so far from taking effect, and their projects to uphold themselves and their monarchy should stand in so little stead, that he should totally ruin and cut them off, so that there should be nothing left for a second stroke to hit upon.

1. It is a presumptuous and vain course for men to plot and enterprise evil against the church of God, for this is to oppose themselves against God, and it will draw speedy destruction upon themselves from him, which will mar their projects. "What do you imagine against the Lord? He will make a bitter end," says he to the Assyrian plotting the church's destruction.

2. All human endeavours to keep off judgments will prove vain when God is a party and about to punish for sin. This also are we to understand in this place by "imagining against the Lord," which he scorns, and judges as foolish thoughts, to think to be delivered thereby. "What do you imagine against the Lord?" See Prov. 21:30.

3. Though the Lord spares wicked states when his own church is often troubled, yet when their cup is full, he will once for all repay them with total ruin. For "he will make an utter end; affliction shall not rise up the second time."

Ver. 10. For while they are folded together as thorns, and while they are drunken together as drunkards, they shall be devoured as stubble fully dry.

A further confirmation of this sentence, and of the certainty and completeness of their calamity, is held forth in a three-fold similitude: (a) Of thorns folded together, which while one cannot separate, he casts into the fire, and so all easily burn, (b) Of drunken men, who are easily overcome and slain. (c) Of stubble fully dry, which easily takes fire.

By all these they are taught the vanity of all they had to oppose against God's stroke. Whereas they confided in their numbers, union, and terribleness (signified by thorns folded together, and pricking on all sides), yet the Lord proclaims that they should indeed prove a fit bundle for the fire, and should be perplexed in their own counsels, that they may run to destruction. And whereas they confided in their pleasures, they should be infatuated by them, and prove as drunken men, ready to hurt themselves, and fit to be slain by others; and their sunshine of prosperity should but dry them as fuel for the fire.

1. God can make use of things which men conceive to be their advantages, to procure their ruin and to blast all of them. God can turn the union and terribleness, in which the Assyrians confided, into perplexity and total destruction, as "thorns folded together" are fit to be cast into the fire.

2. Abused pleasures and prosperity ripen the abusers, and fit them for judgment; their hearts, being effeminate therewith, cannot stand out against any blast of trouble; and trouble comes from God unexpectedly upon such, while they are taken with the noise of their delights. "While they are drunken as drunkards," who have not their wits about them, "they shall be devoured."

3. There is as little ability in sinful man to stand out against the just vengeance of God, as in dry stubble to resist the fire, that it should not kindle and burn in it. Though they are "folded together," and "drunken" with pleasure, yet that shall not so much make them endure trouble as thorns do the fire; but yet more, "they shall be devoured as stubble fully dry."

Ver. 11. There has come one out of you, who imagines evil against the Lord, a wicked counsellor.

Now follows the Lord's controversy and cause of this calamity, which was the injuries done by Sennacherib (and other kings before), who purposed and plotted the ruin of the church, and who by his servant Rabshakeh uttered blasphemy against God, and counselled his people to quit their confidence and yield to him. See 2 Kings chap. 18; 2 Chron. chap. 32; Isa. chap. 36. This verse makes it clear that the threatenings in this chapter are not chiefly directed against Sennacherib and his army (though it may sometimes be hinted at as a presage of great ruin), but against the Assyrian Empire, for Sennacherib is "one come out of you"; that is, out of Assyria or Nineveh, who are here threatened.

1. Injuries done to God's people bring most speedy and total ruin upon any state; for such was the quarrel here, "imagining evil against the Lord."

2. Wicked governors and rulers draw on speedy calamities upon those they rule over and lead in wrong courses; Assyria and Nineveh are to be cut off, because "there has come one out of you, who imagines evil against the Lord."

3. When the Lord's people are wronged, he will appear in the quarrel, and avenge the injury as done to himself; for his people are under his protection, and the design of the plot tends to deprive him of a people and a throne in the church. Therefore all their enterprises are expounded to be "imagining evil against the Lord." See Zech. 2:8.

4. The Lord observes and will severely punish the wicked projects and machinations of enemies, whatever effect he in his providence permits them to have; for it is laid to their charge that "there has come one out of you, who imagines evil against the Lord, a wicked counsellor," although he is not allowed to execute all his purpose. See Ps. 21:11.

5. It is a wicked imagination in men which leads them to blaspheme God, in denying his power and providence, and mocking his people's confidence in him, or to think that to be the way to prosper. And it is a wicked counsel to persuade God's people to renounce their confidence and renounce the way of his worship, that it may be well with them. God will not allow the authors of all this to go unpunished, for thus did Sennacherib and Rabshakeh "imagine evil against the Lord," and prove "a wicked counsellor," as the sacred history relates; and for this Assyria is threatened.

6. It is the character of one indeed desperate, to enter the lists against God, by plotting against his glory and people; for he is "a wicked counsellor" or "a counsellor of Belial," that is, not only one who has cast off all yokes and

awe of God, and fallen upon such devilish plots, but one who
will never do well, as the word signifies.

> Ver. 12. Thus says the Lord: Though they be quiet, and
> likewise many, yet thus shall they be cut down when he
> shall pass through. Though I have afflicted you, I will
> afflict you no more.
> 13. For now will I break his yoke from off you, and
> will burst your bonds in sunder.

Upon the back of this challenge they are again threatened
with destruction, notwithstanding their quiet and secure condition, or their confidence in their great multitudes; and
this sentence is further amplified from God's end in it, which
is to comfort his church in Judah, which had been afflicted
by the Assyrians. He promises that she should no more be
smitten with that rod, but that by the destruction of Assyria
she should be delivered from that slavery and bondage under
which she had been held by them.

1. As prosperity makes a people usually fat and rank, so
does their waxing gross call for strokes. Being "quiet,"
they became "likewise many," and therefore "they shall be
cut down" or "shorn." When the prophet says, "thus shall they
be cut down or shorn," he has either, in delivering this
message, used some gesture representing the way of cutting
down or mowing; or else he alludes to the signification of the
word "cutting down," which is used of cutting down rank
grass, wool, or hair, by sharpened instruments, so signifying
the cutting short of their flourishing and luxuriant condition.
The word translated "thus" may be rendered "likewise," as
it is immediately before, and so it imports that as they had
tasted of peace and multiplication, so they should also find
"cutting down"; or it may be rendered "certainly," as it is
frequently used in scripture.

2. Nothing the creature can enjoy is able to hold off God's
stroke, nor needs he at any time to ruin his enemies, but
can do it with one sudden stroke. "Though they be quiet,"
free of trouble and secure in their fortifications, "yet shall
they be cut down," and that will happen "when he shall pass
through," or with a sudden stroke, alluding to the stroke on
Sennacherib's army.

3. The repetition of the sentence teaches how hard a thing
it is to get threatened judgments believed in prosperity.
Therefore the Lord again undertakes it, whatever they had
to oppose, and teaches that it is useful for the church to

look on injuries done to her as a sufficient quarrel to bring judgments on her persecutors; for therefore after that challenge (ver. 11), the sentence is again repeated.

4. The Lord would have his church observing the kindness shown to her, and the benefits that redound to her by his judgments on the world; therefore he directs the speech to her, that she may observe it. "Though I have afflicted you, I will afflict you no more."

5. The Lord claims himself to be the afflicter of his people, whatever and whoever may be the instruments; and he would be seen by them to be so. Therefore he says, "I have afflicted you." See Isa. 10:5-7.

6. Though the church will never get an end to her afflictions until eternity comes, when God shall wipe all tears from her eyes, yet she ought to acknowledge the Lord's great mercy in cutting off her present enemies, and giving a breathing time; for so must this promise, "I will afflict you no more," be understood in this place, with relation to the present enemy, that the church should be free of their trouble and enjoy a little rest.

7. The Lord's former sharp dealing ought to be no obstacle to our faith in expecting good things; for he can easily, when he will, change his dealing. "Though I have afflicted you," says he, "I will afflict you no more."

8. As the Lord sees it fitting at times to humble his church by bringing her into bondage, so he easily can and in due time will set her at freedom. Therefore he says, "now will I break his yoke from off you, and will burst your bond in sunder."

> Ver. 14. And the Lord has given a commandment concerning you, that no more shall your name be sown. Out of the house of your gods will I cut off the graven image and the molten image; I will make your grave, for you are vile.

It is true that Sennacherib's glory was stained by the discomfort received in Judah (Isa. 37:36), and he was shortly after killed in the house of his gods (Isa. 37:38), by which that temple was polluted from being the habitation of their idols, since the king was slain and perhaps buried there; yet this cannot exhaust this full threatening, since his son reigned in his stead (Isa. 37:38), and so his name was yet sown. Therefore the threatening is to be looked on as reaching the whole empire of Assyria, the final and irreparable ruin of which is pointed out in various ways. (a) By having no more of their name sown, whereby we are to understand that their very memory should be quite cut off, and the dreadful report which had gone before them would be forgotten by other nations. And so their cutting down (ver. 12) should differ from the cutting down of grass or other things, for they grow up again after they are cut down, and of corn, which is yearly sown after being cut down. (b) By the destruction of their idols and supposed sacred things, which is another sign of total ruin of an idolatrous land. (c) By burying them, and putting them off the face of the earth, as being vile and stinking above ground, which seems to have begun after that overthrow of their army in Judah. Hence learn:

1. Such is the presumption of wicked men, and the heartless dissidence of God's people, that God's sentence against his enemies is hardly received and credited. This frequent repetition shows that this truth is not easily inculcated.

2. It is sufficient ground of assurance for the coming to pass of greatest things, that the Lord has determined they should be; for this is given as a sure ground of Assyria's ruin, that "the Lord has given a commandment concerning you," or purposed their destruction, his purpose concluding as effectually the concurring of all means to bring it about, as if they were especially commanded.

3. The Lord does justly root out the memory of persons or states who make it their only work to get a name on earth, and to be eminent and terrible; for such as Assyria's doom. "No more shall your name be sown."

4. The threatening of the destruction of idols, as a sign of total ruin, should put us in mind of the Lord's great controversy against idolatry and idols; for he will ruin their worshippers to ruin them. Further, if the cutting off of their idols was a sign of utter destruction, how much more ought it to be grievous unto us, beyond any of our other losses, when our God in his honour and house is wronged! And how sad a presage is it of a sad stroke, when God does not spare his own interests in a land. All of this we may gather from this sentence, "out of the house of your gods will I cut off the graven image and the molten image."

5. By affronts put upon the greatest and most formidable nations by his providence, God can make them contemptible, not only before him by their vices, but in the view of all the world, and so that he may cut them off from the face of the earth, as unworthy and unfit to live upon it.

Ver. 15. Behold, upon the mountains the feet of him that brings good tidings, who publishes peace. O Judah, keep your solemn feasts, perform your vows; for the wicked shall no more pass through you; he is utterly cut off.

A passage like this, Isa. 52:7, is applied unto the gospel (Rom. 10:15), since Christ, promised in the gospel, is the foundation of all the church's deliverances, and these glad tidings and deliverances are but shadows of the glad tidings of the gospel and of the salvation therein held forth; yet the proper drift of this passage is to show the effects which the destruction of the Assyrians should produce in the church of Judah, who hearing these tidings proclaimed openly, as upon the mountains, should rejoice in them as glad tidings and tidings of peace; and she should, without disturbance, keep her solemnities and praise God, for the enemies who disquieted and interrupted her are now cut off. They had a notable proof of all this when Sennacherib's army, which made havoc of Judah and shut up Jerusalem, was overthrown. Hence learn:

1. The Lord will refresh his church, which has received the glad tidings of salvation, with glad tidings of his appearing and doing for her in difficulties; for there are "glad tidings" and "peace," published openly "upon the mountains."

2. The report of the Lord's doing for his people ought to be seriously considered by them, and they should be affected therewith. "Behold upon the mountains," says he.

3. It is the church's sorest affliction to be deprived of the free use of the ordinances of God, and the enjoyment of them is her greatest mercy; for such is implied in the command now to keep "your solemn feasts" (which before she could not) as the great mercy in her deliverance.

4. The lack of public ordinances and the solemnities of worship, is a bitter trial, though it may fare well with the people of God in their private exercises of religion and in their inward condition; such is imported in that Judah may now keep her public "solemn feasts."

5. Our esteem of and respect unto the ordinances of God must be evidenced by our eagerness in going about them (especially after we have been deprived of them for a time) and by our endeavoured thankfulness to God for enjoying them. This speech, "O Judah, keep your solemn feasts," is a stirring up to alacrity, and the command, "perform your vows," imports a sensible obligation of thankfulness unto God for the restoration of the ordinances.

6. The Lord will cut off the sons of Belial, who molest his people in the free use of his ordinances, though they be ever so powerful. Such is assured of the Assyrians: "for the wicked (or Belial) shall pass no more through you; he is utterly cut off." And this sentence stands still in force, to be executed in due time upon those who trace the Assyrians' footsteps and imitate their sins.

CHAPTER II

This chapter contains a lively description of the destruction of Nineveh. In it are set forth their preparations for the siege, which they might in reason now expect (ver. 1-5), the taking of the city (ver. 6), the captivity of the queen (ver. 7), the flight of the inhabitants as defenders (ver. 8), the sacking of the city, and the terror, confusion, and sorrow which shall be among all (ver. 9, 10). All this is amplified from the cause of the stroke, and the insulting of those who see or hear of their ruin (ver. 11, 12), and is expressly declared by the Lord to be his act, punishing her sin (ver. 13).

> Ver. 1. He who dashes in pieces has come up before your face; keep the munition, watch the way, make your loins strong, fortify your power mightily.

The preparations against Nineveh are set down in general, that the Medes, and Nebuchadnezzar, and the Chaldeans, who crush all they set upon, are to assault her also; and she shall not be able to resist, though she use all means for defence. And therefore the enemy is spoken of, as if he were already in sight of the city, and she is exhorted by way of derision to prepare herself, by keeping her walls, sending out her scouts to observe the enemy's approach, and by encouraging and strengthening herself in every way she could.

1. The Lord can make a nation formidable, as long as he has service for them, and yet make them feeble when their own cup is filled. The enemies, because of former successes, appear to the Assyrians as "he who dashes in pieces," or "the hammer" (Jer. 50:23), and yet they were afterwards brought down.

2. When God sends a prospering enemy against a wicked people, it is so that it may contribute and add to that terror of God with which he will confound them in their trouble.

Therefore the enemies are named here, "he who dashes in pieces," to strike Nineveh with terror.

3. Though secure sinners put the evil day far off, yet those who know the mind of God may see it as present, and sinners themselves will at last find it so. Therefore the prophet says, "he has come up before your face," because he saw it so from God, and they should find it so.

4. Wicked men are not soon sensible of the hand of God against them, but may think to bear out against the trouble which is sent to destroy them; for so does Nineveh prepare, as if she would stand it out.

5. The most prudent and courageous preparations of men are but matter of derision, when God has a quarrel; and they will prove but fools who trust in them. These exhortations, "keep the munition, watch the way," etc., are spoken by way of holy derision, showing that the utmost of their endeavours should not avail them.

> Ver. 2. For the Lord has turned away the excellence of Jacob, as the excellency of Israel; for the emptiers have emptied them out and marred their vine branches.

A reason is given, why Nineveh might expect that the Lord would now come against her, though before she had been prosperous by his permission. The Lord had by the Assyrians, as his scourge, chastised Judah (for such seems to be imported by "Jacob," as distinguished from "Israel"), as well as the ten tribes, and overturned and trodden underfoot their proud glorying in their excellencies; for the one had been depopulated by them, and the other deformed by the taking and sacking of their towns and villages, which were as branches sprung out of Jerusalem, the mother city; and therefore he would not spare Nineveh, but it was now time to take course with them, and to cast the rod into the fire.

1. The Lord has a special quarrel with the pride of his people, which rises from considering their excellencies or privileges, and he will have it stained; for "the Lord has turned away the excellency of Jacob, and the excellency of Israel," and so spares it in none; and the same word (signifying both excellency and pride) shows that as privileges and conceit often go together, so the Lord abhors such conceit most of all.

2. No less often will serve to stain pride and bring down a people's conceit than almost total destruction; for in

turning away their excellency, "the emptiers have emptied them out, and marred their vine branches."

3. The Lord so much abhors the pride of his people that he will even tolerate blasphemous enemies, until they have been instrumental in bringing it down. Therefore Nineveh is allowed to stand until by them "the Lord has turned away the excellency of Jacob." See Isa. chap. 10, 11, 12.

4. When the church is humbled, and her vain glory laid low before the Lord, he will then take order with those who have been instruments of her affliction; therefore this is a reason of the enemies' coming against Nineveh: "the Lord has turned away the excellency of Jacob." The church's sins, unmortified by the rod, are the safeguard of their enemies, and the reason why they are so long preserved.

> Ver. 3. The shield of his mighty men is made red; the valiant men are in scarlet. The chariots shall be with flaming torches in the day of his preparation, and the fir trees shall be terribly shaken.
>
> 4. The chariots shall rage in the streets; they shall jostle one against another in the broad ways; they shall seem like torches, they shall run like the lightnings.
>
> 5. He shall recount his worthies; they shall stumble in their work; they shall make haste to the wall thereof, and the defence thereof shall be prepared.

The army of the Chaldeans, and their preparation and actions against Nineveh, are yet more particularly described. (a) The armour and clothing, chiefly of their leaders, were red and bloody coloured, to terrify others, and to hide their own wounds and blood so that the sight thereof might not encourage the enemy nor make themselves to faint. (b) Their chariots, both in preparations and assaults, for speed and number, and because of the fierce disposition of those who manage them, should rage, jostle, and march nimbly as torches and lightnings, the iron of their wheels striking fire on the streets. (c) Their lances, which were so many as if a wood of fir trees were divided among them, should be shaken and managed, to the terror of the Assyrians. (d) The Chaldean king shall encourage his leaders and call them by their names, and they shall stumble for haste to be at the wall to assault it, and shall set up defences under which they might fight with less hazard.

1. Learn to adore the infinite providence of God, who gives by his prophet an exact and particular account of

every circumstance in this action, as if it were already done, intimating that his purposes, effectual providence, and foreknowledge, condescend even to particular circumstances of actions.

2. This large description of their clothes, garments, activity, etc., teaches how terrible are those who are employed to execute the Lord's vengeance and controversy, how strong they are who are on his side, and how formidable to those whom he is to destroy.

3. If natural men, for their own ends of ambition and vain glory, may be made so resolute as to run swiftly on hazards and to care nothing for death or wounds, as is here declared, how much more ought the Lord's people to be resolute and courageous in resisting unto blood, striving against sin, and in acting for God in their places and stations.

4. The practice of these men in "preparing the defence" under which they might fight, teaches that it is no true valour, even in nature's eyes, nor warrantable, to run so desperately upon hazards as to neglect any lawful means of self-defence.

> Ver. 6. The gates of the rivers shall be opened, and the palace shall be dissolved.

Now follows the way of taking the city, by the inundation of the river Tigris, on which it stood. Because the wall was thus broken down, way was made for the enemy to enter as at gates, and the stately buildings or royal palace would be carried away by the flood, or dissolved and destroyed by the enemies. Tigris is here called "rivers," either by way of excellence, i.e. above many rivers, or because it grew then as big as many rivers. Hence learn:

1. The Lord will so make use of men's courage in doing his work, that his own immediate hand and judgment may be seen; for he will have the river made great by his hand, to make way for the enemy's entry and victory, so that it might be seen not to be their hand only. "The gates of the rivers shall be opened."

2. The Lord's immediate hand is seen in prevailing against his enemies, where they think themselves most secure; for so way was made to enter Nineveh by the river, where it seemed most impregnable, and where it seems their palace was built: "the gates of the rivers shall be opened."

3. Divine vengeance can strike kings and wicked rulers, not only with judgments abroad, on armies or subjects, but

can pursue them to their very palaces and pull them down upon their heads; for "the palace shall be dissolved."

> Ver. 7. And Huzzah shall be led away captive; she shall
> be brought up, and her maids shall lead her, as with
> the voice of doves, tabering upon their breasts.

To omit the various interpretations of this verse, I conceive it most clear to expound it of the queen (or generally, of the great ladies) who lived before quietly and delicately, in an established or settled condition, as the word "huzzah" signifies; she shall now be found out, and pulled away to go into captivity, accompanied with her maids, who have been with her in pleasure and shall now condole with her and lament her misery and theirs. And this is the first effect of the taking of the city. Hence learn:

1. The most delicate and weak, and those who have not been accustomed to hardships, may look for a change when they provoke God, no matter how stable their prosperity seems to be; for "Huzzah shall be led away captive," or "discovered," and spoiled and made bare, as the word also signifies, and it may be she was handled so. See Deut. 28: 56, 57; Lam. 4:5.

2. As giving of oneself to delicacy may contribute to embitter afflictions, so those who have been companions in pleasure may contribute to set an edge upon one's grief. So much are we taught by the example of this mournful company, brought out of pleasure to misery; and "her maids leading her, tabering on their breasts" for sorrow, do help to set before her the bitterness of her condition.

3. It is an addition to common calamities, that the afflicted must smother their grief and dare not vent it openly, for fear of further injuries from enemies. Therefore, though women usually express their sorrows most violently, yet "her maids lead her as with the voice of doves," which is a secret groaning and bemoaning, not daring to do it openly.

> Ver. 8. But Nineveh is of old like a pool of water; yet they
> shall flee away. Stand, stand, shall they cry, but none
> shall look back.

Another effect of the taking of Nineveh is the flight of the inhabitants and defenders, which is amplified from her former condition. Though she had always been populous, rich, and at ease, not stirred with commotions, as a pond of standing water abounding with fish, yet at the enemy's entry she should be troubled and forsaken, and no entreaty should make men remain within her.

1. God's former sparing of a people, or their quiet prosperity, or numbers of men, will prove no shelter against God's judgments when their cup is full; for "Nineveh is of old like a pool of water, yet they shall flee away."

2. No encouragements will hearten a people pursued of God, and effeminate with security and ease, when their day of trouble comes; for "stand, stand, shall they cry," to those who had lived in her as in a pond, "but none shall look back."

3. The great ill-deserving of sin may be seen in the great changes it brings upon most flourishing places; so in Nineveh of old, like a pool of water, there is not one now to take her part, or abide.

> Ver. 9. Take the spoil of silver, take the spoil of gold; for there is no end of the store, and glory out of all the pleasant furniture.

Another effect of the taking of the city is the spoiling by the soldiers, unto which (as exceeding great for treasures and precious furnitures, and that which the Ninevites gloried much in) the Lord invites them by his prophet.

1. Riches, jewels, and pleasant furniture, are so far from delivering in a day of wrath, that they are a bait and invitation to enemies, to set courageously upon the enjoiners. Such is imported by the Lord's speech. "Take the spoil, for there is no end of the store"; the hope of spoil made the enemies bold.

2. God justly allows to be spoiled of their riches and treasures those who are endless and immoderate in purchasing, and place their glory in such things.

3. Though instruments may unjustly deprive wicked men of their gloried riches, yet it is done in the Lord's righteous judgment; he allows it to be done, though he does not approve the way of men's doing of it; and he will in due time take order with them for their conduct. Though the enemies did spoil Nineveh for their own ends, yet the Lord's invitation, "take the spoil," shows that it was righteous with him that it should be given up.

> Ver. 10. She is empty and void, and waste, and the heart melts, and the knees smite together, and much pain is in all loins, and the faces of them all gather blackness.

The sad case of this taken city is further held forth, that it should be made empty and desolate, and the inhabitants thereof should be utterly discouraged. The inward, feeble, and desperate condition of their minds, through trouble and fear of death, are expressed by usual signs in their body, such as the trembling of the knees (Dan. 5:6), pain in the loins, expressing the sorrow of a woman in travail (Isa. 13:8; Jer. 30:6) and blackness in the face, which is a sign of a fatal condition, reaching to the heart (Joel 2:6).

1. The Lord can (and will, because of sin) make most populous and flourishing places utterly desolate. Nineveh, that great city, "is empty, and void, and waste."

2. Guilt, and the lack of reconciliation with God, will make men prove great cowards in a day of trouble, either in bearing what they are under, or in looking to what they may expect; for all these signs of discouragement do teach how heartless their case was, and how little man is able to bear out, when he has to do with a God dealing in justice.

> Ver. 11. Where is the dwelling of the lions, and the feeding place of the young lions, where the lion, even the old lion walked, and the lions whelp, and none made them afraid?
>
> 12. The lion tore in pieces enough for his whelps, and strangled for his lionness, and filled his holes with prey and his dens with ravine.

The greatness of this desolation, as also the cause procuring it, are insinuated in the insults of all who see or hear it, wondering what had become of Nineveh, which had been a safe place of abode for magnanimous oppressors, both princes and people, who as lions had oppressed all others so that they might enrich themselves and their families, and had brought their purchase there; but now Nineveh is abolished, and no more conspicuous as formerly.

1. Oppression proves men to be brutish, and turns their palaces and cities into lions' dens, and makes their wealth abomination. For here these oppressors are called "lions" and "young lions," and their city or houses "holes" and "dens," and their purchase "prey" and "ravine," which they "tore" and "strangled."

2. The judgment of the Lord will so follow oppressions that the place of oppressors, where they bring that which they have purchased by oppression, shall not be found, though

it seemed ever so impregnable. "Where is the dwelling of the lions, and the feeding place of the young lions?"

3. As the ruin of great oppressors will be matter of admiration to those who looked upon their secure condition, so it will in time be matter of derision to those who have suffered by them, or abhor their way; and they glorify God in his justice; for this question may be expounded of the admiration of some and the insulting of others. See Isa. 14:10-12; Ps. 52:6, 7; Ps. 58:10, 11.

4. A faithless and irreligious care of a family and of posterity, to have them great, is a great snare and inducement to draw men to be oppressors. "The lion tore in pieces for his whelps, and strangled for his lionness."

> Ver. 13. Behold, I am against you, says the Lord of hosts; and I will burn her chariots in the smoke, and the sword shall devour the young lions, and I will cut off your prey from the earth, and the voice of your messengers shall no more be heard.

The Lord here expressly owns the stroke, threatening to cut off with fire and sword their means of defence and of oppression. He declares his quarrel to be with their oppression and taking of prey, and he threatens to take away what they had so gotten and to hinder them from oppressing any more, and that their messengers or ambassadors sent to proclaim war against nations or govern provinces (and especially their blasphemous messengers, such as Sennacherib and Rabshakeh, 2 Kings 1:19), should be made to cease from their insolencies, and not to be any more heard of.

1. The Lord's having a quarrel against a people or person will produce remarkable effects, for "behold, I am against you, says the Lord."

2. The Lord has all-sufficiency of power and means to bring down any enemy, and to effect what he will; for he is "the Lord of hosts," who has all creatures at his command, who can make invincible armies from the weakest of creatures, and at whose command nothing will send forth all things.

3. God can easily, and will openly, to the terror of others, cut off the warlike preparations and confidences of wicked men; for, "I will burn her chariots in the smoke." This may import that he will overthrow them by small means, as if a smoke from a fire recently kindled should burn chariots,

or else that he will overthrow them as in a fire, whose smoke should be seen afar off.

4. God will cut off the race of oppressors who continue in their sins, by some remarkable judgment; for "the sword shall devour the young lions, and I will cut off your prey."

5. It is a mark of wicked men never to give up sin until the Lord in judgment renders them unable to commit it. Not until "the sword shall devour" is "their prey cut off from the earth."

6. Oppression of the church, joined with insolent blasphemy against the Lord, is a quarrel which he will never put away until he has destroyed all the impenitent authors of it, and rendered them unable to commit the same again. For he says, "the voice of your messengers shall no more be heard." Though God did cut off Sennacherib and his army, who were the immediate actors, yet his hand is stretched out still, until it also reaches Nineveh, from which they came.

CHAPTER III

For the encouragement of the church of God, Nahum repeats and confirms again in this chapter the certain and total ruin of Nineveh, and also that he may remove all doubts out of the minds of any who could hardly believe that so ancient and powerful a kingdom could be destroyed. Nineveh, because of her cruel oppression, is threatened with the terrible preparations of her enemies, who shall come against her, and with great slaughter (ver. 1-3); and she is again threatened, for her enslaving of all nations, with extreme contempt which shall be poured upon her (ver. 4-7). This sentence is amplified and confirmed by the example of other places (ver. 8-11), and by showing the vanity of all which she confided in for safety, as strongholds, citizens, hired soldiers, officers and nobles (ver. 12-18), and at her irreparable ruin all nations oppressed by her should rejoice (ver. 19).

> Ver. 1. Woe to the bloody city; it is all full of lies and robbery; the prey departs not.

Nineveh is here accused for cruelty, oppression, and deceit, in which she was incessant and threatened with woe, or all miseries to come upon her. Hence learn:

1. The Lord has a special controversy against a people given to cruelty and bloodshed. "Woe unto the bloody city," that is, the city which raised itself by blood and cruel practices, which yet continue in them toward other nations and among themselves, as is usual for those who are too full, to be very insolent.

2. Dissimulation, which flows from a covetous disposition and a desire to oppress, is hateful unto the Lord, as well as open violence, for he can see robbery under false dealing. Therefore lies and robberies are yoked together: "it is full of lies and robbery"; that is, these evils have overspread all.

3. Their oppression, and the woe denounced against it, are frequently repeated. This teaches that whatever men, who judge by outward appearances, or the people of God in the hour of temptation, may think, yet the Lord exceedingly hates oppression and oppressors. Let them thrive as they will, they are yet in a woeful condition. "Woe to the city that is full of robbery."

4. The Lord notices and especially hates perseverance in wicked courses. Woe is denounced also because "the prey departs not"; that is, after so long a span of time, in which they have continued in this sin, and notwithstanding their abundance, yet they will not give up their oppression; for no measure of worldly wealth will satisfy the appetite of those who transgress the limits prescribed by God. See 1 Tim. 6:8-10.

> Ver. 2. The noise of a whip, and the noise of the rattling of the wheels, and of the prancing horses and of the jumping chariots.
> 3. The horseman lifts up both the bright sword and the glittering spear, and there is a multitude of slain and a great number of carcases; and there is no end of their corpses; they stumble upon their corpses.

The sentence is enlarged, and the woe explained to consist of two parts. The first is the terrible preparations of the Chaldeans against them, which he sets out in detail, as if they were then entering the city, the noises of their chariot wheels and horses' feet sounding in the ears of the Ninevites, and the weapons of the horsemen dazzling their eyes. Second, they are threatened with execution and slaughter by these enemies, which should be so great that the dead corpses lying in the way should hinder men from walking in the streets, or from fleeing.

1. To be under a woe from the Lord speaks most bitter judgment; for the woe of ver. 1 is expounded to cover so great and terrible a slaughter. This implies that whoever is under the Lord's curse will meet with a like or worse judgment, though it may not be so visible to a carnal eye.

2. The judgments of God sent forth in wrath upon his incorrigible enemies, will be terrible and dreadful unto them, and the very approach will be a kind of death unto them before they are slain. Therefore he threatens them with the sounding noise and dazzling sight of enemies, and their preparation and approaches, as that which would prove dreadful to Nineveh.

3. Those who delight in blood and cruelty shall be recompenced by the Lord to the full, in their own coin; in Nineveh, given to blood (ver. 1), "there is a multitude of slain and a great number of carcases."

4. The judgments to come upon the enemies of the church are to be regarded as already being inflicted, that they may be comforted in the Lord's judgment for them, and that they may not be tempted with beholding the present prosperity of enemies. Therefore also every circumstance of this ruin is marked, as if it were happening, and the Ninevites are represented as dead corpses by the prophet.

> Ver. 4. Because of the multitude of the whoredoms of the well-favoured harlot, the mistress of witchcrafts, who sells nations through her whoredoms and families through her witchcraft.

Another branch of the Lord's accusation and quarrel against Nineveh is that by her subtle courses (resembling witchcrafts) she defrauded the wealth of other nations and brought them to slavery, using them for her own advantage. As harlots by their beauty and artifices ensnare their paramours and bring them and their wealth under their power, so Nineveh made use of her greatness and power, together with her policies, to allure nations to submit unto her, as if it had been for their own good. In this sense Tyre's merchandising is called harlotry (Isa. 23:15, 17).

However, I would not exclude another interpretation also. As idolatry (which is frequently called whoredom) and devilish arts were frequent among these eastern people (Isa. 2:6; Isa. 47:13), so Nineveh made use of these arts to carry on her designs of greatness, and enticed others to embrace her idolatry, so that they might be united the more firmly unto her for her own advantage, as in 2 Kings 16:10.

1. Though men often glory much in their wit and skill in increasing their greatness and outwitting others, yet before the Lord such ways are the ground of a controversy, and are nothing less than whoredoms and witchcrafts.

2. Men are naturally immoderate and excessive in their desire and hunting after greatness; for they are compared to harlots, those who commit "multitude of whoredoms" and are never satisfied in their lust.

3. Worldly and political states and people are to be looked on in their dealings with others, as seeking their own interests only, whatever they pretend to the contrary; for though Nineveh held out her beautiful condition to other nations (as a harlot to her paramours) to invite them as it were to their own benefit in being under the protection of so mighty a state, yet her real intentions were thereby to dispose of them to her own use, as slaves which are bought and sold. "The well-favoured harlot, the mistress of witchcrafts, sells nations through her whoredoms and families through her witchcrafts."

4. Wicked men are given to abuse all favours and good things conferred upon them by God, and to make them subservient to their lusts and designs. As harlots prostitute their beauty to allure men to filthiness, that they may reap gain, so did Nineveh make use of her greatness to allure others to join with her, to her own advantage and their disadvantage. "The well favoured harlot sells nations through her whoredoms."

5. Men who are given to their lusts and worldly designs make no scruple of unlawful means to attain their ends. Nineveh was "the mistress of witchcrafts," that is, of wicked policies and deceits, or (according to the other interpretation) of devilish arts, so that she might be great and "sell families through her witchcrafts."

6. Wicked men make no account even of that religion which they profess, except insofar as it may be subservient to their worldly ends; for "Nineveh sells nations through her whoredoms." That is, according to the second interpretation, she pressed her idolatry upon others in order to secure them to her, as conceiving religion to be the surest bond of union, to tie them to subjection that she might reap benefit by them.

Ver. 5. Behold, I am against you, says the Lord of hosts, and I will reveal your skirts upon your face, and I will show the nations your nakedness, and the kingdoms your shame.

6. And I will cast abominable filth upon you, and make you vile, and will set you as a gazing-stock.

7. And it shall come to pass that all they who look upon you shall flee from you, and say, Nineveh is laid waste; who will bemoan her? Where shall I seek comforters for you?

The Lord professes himself Nineveh's enemy.

(a) He first threatens her, in opposition to her former beauty, with ignominy and deprivation of her excellencies and ornaments, that she may be loathsome and contemptible to all, as if an harlot were stripped and her clothes cast back over her head, that her nakedness may be exposed to mockery in view of men, as profane soldiers do with captive women. See Isa. 47:2, 3; Jer. 13:22.

(b) He threatens to put yet more affronts upon her beauty, by granting her enemies victory over her, and power to tread her down, as if women in their pomp were all befouled with dung, and so made loathsome.

(c) He threatens that by this means she should be made a public spectacle, and the matter of horror and detestation to all beholders, for there will be none to comfort her. Hence learn:

1. God's being an adversary to the wicked is neither soon seen by them, nor if seen is the sadness of such a condition easily laid to heart; therefore it is again inculcated, "behold, I am against you, says the Lord of hosts," though it had been told before (2:13).

2. Abuse of mercies will in the end resolve in the abuser's misery; for beautiful Nineveh, who played the harlot with it, shall have "her skirts revealed, and abominable filth" cast upon her; and she, with whom the nations committed fornication, is made the object of people's detestation.

3. People in their greatest pomp and glory, do but flee with borrowed wings, and are in such a condition that God can easily strip them of what they gloried in, and set them as contemptible objects; for Nineveh has "shame and nakedness" which he will "show to nations and kingdoms," when he strips her of her borrowed glory.

4. As wicked men cannot enjoy honour and greatness in the world, without abusing it, so the Lord is provoked thereby

to plague the abusers with ignominy; for "I will cast abominable filth upon you, and make you vile," says he to glorious Nineveh.

5. The Lord will make those who have publicly sinned without repentance to become public spectacles of his justice and severity, to the terror and astonishment of the beholders; for "I will set you as a gazing stock, and it shall come to pass that all who look upon you shall flee from you."

6. It is righteous with God to smite his enemies so heavily that the stroke shall surpass the cure of any consolations from friends, and the terror thereof so overwhelm them that they cannot and dare not appear to bemoan and comfort them; and it is righteous also that those who have oppressed without pity, should have none to condole with them in their justly procured and inflicted corrections. All this is imported in this threatening: "all who look upon you shall flee from you, and say, Nineveh is laid waste, who will bemoan her?" No sorrow should express her stroke, nor any consolations prove sufficient; her friends should not be able through terror to appear for her, and she should be abhorred and detested in all her miseries.

> Ver. 8. Are you better than populous No, that was situated among the rivers, who had the waters round about her, whose rampart was the sea, and her wall was from the sea?
>
> 9. Ethiopia and Egypt were her strength, and it was infinite; Put and Lubim were your helpers.
>
> 10. Yet she was carried away; she went into captivity; her young children also were dashed in pieces at the top of all the streets, and they cast lots for her honourable men, and all her great men were bound in chains.
>
> 11. You also shall be drunken; you shall be hidden; you also shall seek strength because of the enemy.

To confirm what had been said, and to crush all presumptuous thoughts in Nineveh, as if she could be able to stand it out, he sets before the example of No, or Thebes, a great city in or near Egypt (Jer. 46:25; Ezek. 30:15). And in this example:

(a) He rehearses the flourishing condition of that city. It was populous, or "nourishing"; that is, a great market town, nourishing the country about it. It was strong by situation, being built among the channels of the Nile, and environed with strong ramparts, the sea also enclosing it on

divers parts; it was also strong by great and many confederates, such as Ethiopians (or Arabians, who are frequently named Cush in scripture), Egyptians, and other
people of Africa. The speech is directed to No, as insulting
over her vain confidence in these, to the terror of Nineveh.

(b) He repeats their stroke. That city had been made
desolate, her people being carried captive, her young children dashed in pieces, her honourable men divided among
the soldiers as prey, and carried away as slaves. As for
the time of this desolation, and the persons by whom it was
acted, it is needless for us further to inquire, since the
Spirit of God puts it out of controversy that it was done before
the ruin of Nineveh.

(c) This example is applied to Nineveh. It is shown that
since she had no more advantages than the other had, it was
but folly to think herself invincible; and she is assured that
no matter how potent she be, yet she shall be drunk with the
wine of God's wrath; and that notwithstanding her former
splendor, she should be made to hide herself in shame and
fear, and become obscure, as if she had not been; and that
notwithstanding her own strength, she should be forced to
seek help from abroad, or to supplicate her enemies for pity.
Hence learn:

1. The Lord has given abundant proof that there is no
power nor probable means of defence able to stand out
against him when he prosecutes a controversy. This instance
is added to teach that no means whatever can stand before
him.

2. Men are still ready to be presumptuous and confident
of their own standing, whatever they see done to others.
Therefore this example is produced and applied, that her
conceit may thereby be crushed. "Are you better than populous No?"

3. Men have nothing to boast of as sufficient to preserve
them from ruin, but others have had the same or better,
and have yet fainted. Therefore all the circumstances of
ruined No's strength are pointed out, to show that she might
well have compared to Nineveh in anything that would have
seemed to be a defence.

4. The Lord's mind concerning sin and impenitent sinners
is the same in all ages, and he will so declare himself by
his judgments. As No was carried away for her sins, so is
Nineveh threatened because of her provocations. "You also
shall be drunken."

5. The wicked may not only expect to be deprived of counsel and prudence in straits, as drunken men are, but to drink of it until they are drunken. "You also shall be drunken." See Jer. 25:15, 27.

6. The Lord can, and because of sin will, bury in obscurity the greatest of nations, as if they had never been, and make those who made great show of glory and courage to seek holes to hide themselves in. For he says, "you shall be hid."

7. Unto those who are pursued by the justice of the Lord, their enemies are made terrible, and all their strength and preparations are not sufficient to secure them from fear or to keep them from being brought into awe of their enemies. Whatever Nineveh had to oppose, yet "you also shall seek strength, because of the enemy."

> Ver. 12. All your strongholds shall be like fig trees with the first ripe figs; if they be shaken, they shall even fall into the mouth of the eater.

For further confirmation of this sentence, the Lord propounds all the vain confidences of Nineveh and the Assyrians, and declares that they should not be able to deliver them from his hand. Her first vain confidence is her strongholds, which he threatens shall be as easily taken by the enemy as ripe figs, which fall from the fig tree when it is shaken into the shaker's mouth. That is to say, they shall be rendered up at the first assault. Hence learn:

1. Men in a wicked way are ready to delude themselves with many vain thoughts of safety. Therefore all this pains is taken to refute the vain imaginations of Nineveh.

2. Strongholds are too weak fortifications to hold out during God's controversy against sin. As the sins of the owners ripen them for ruin, and as they are much desired by enemies, so will they be easily taken. So much does this similitude teach us.

> Ver. 13. Behold, your people in your midst are women; the gates of your land shall be set wide open unto your enemies; the fire shall devour your bars.

Her second vain confidence is her formerly valiant men, concerning whom the Lord declares that though they were enclosed in fortified cities and strongholds (which may make cowards stout), and in their own cities and country, which they sought resolutely to defend, yet they should prove timorous and faint-hearted like women, and so should yield up what they ought to defend. See Jer. 50:37; Jer. 51:30.

1. Men will prove stout no longer than the Lord is with them in mercy, or by them is doing some work in the earth; for the lion-like Assyrians (2:11) have now become feeble. "Behold," says he, "your people are women."

2. No outward encouragement or consideration will put courage into those whom God has made faint.

A third vain confidence, the vanity of which depends upon the former, is their frontier garrisons. No doubt observing that others had been destroyed by themselves through improvidence in that way, they had fortified these garrisons as the gates of their land, and as bars to hinder the enemy's progress into the country. Concerning these the Lord threatens that through the cowardice of their soldiers they should be set open to the enemy, as if fire had burnt them up. This teaches that no political courses of men, learning wisdom from the folly of others, or fortifying themselves where others through weakness have been overcome, is sufficient to secure a people from God's vengeance. "The gates of your land shall be set wide open to your enemies; the fire shall devour your bars."

> Ver. 14. Draw the waters for the siege; fortify your strongholds; go into clay, and tread the mortar; make strong the brick kiln.
>
> 15. There shall the fire devour you; the sword shall cut you off. It shall eat you up like the canker worm. Make yourself many as the canker-worm; make yourself many as the locusts.
>
> 16. You have multiplied your merchants above the stars of heaven; the canker-worm spoils and steals away.

The vanity of all the former confidences is yet further held forth in a holy mocking of all their preparations, which should not avail. Though they should use ever so much diligence to defend their cities, and for that end should draw water and diligently repair their strongholds with brick (under which are to be comprehended other things necessary for enduring a siege), yet in their greatest strength the sword should destroy them, and the judgment of God should consume them like fire, and like the canker-worm, which eats all green fruit. And though both the king and the city of Nineveh (for the original seems to direct the speech to

both) should multiply armies both of their own people, who
were for the most part merchants, and of their confederates
who traded with them, and that in as great numbers as if
they were swarms of locusts or canker-worms, or as the
stars of heaven, yet thereby they should not be delivered.
And because the canker-worm spoils all, there is nothing to
eat, and then he flees away; so their soldiers, confederates,
and their own merchants should desert them, when there
should be no commodity to be had by them, and should waste
and take from them, but do them no good. Hence learn:

1. The Lord's power is so far above man's that he will,
so to speak, defy man to avert his judgments by his endeavours. Here he bids Nineveh to do her best. "Draw the waters
for the siege, and make yourself as many as the canker-
worm."

2. Presumption may continue with carnal men, even until
their ruin. Nineveh is preparing for the siege, and gathering men when she is to be destroyed; not that it is unlawful
to use lawful means to prevent destruction when it is threatened, but her sin was to confide in these means, without
looking to God or his controversy.

3. Strokes from the Lord may readily light upon men where
they think themselves most secure; "there," that is, in your
strongholds, manned and fortified by you, "there shall the
fire devour you; the sword shall cut you off."

4. Wrath from the Lord is a sore party to deal with, as
destroying totally and without mercy; for the wrath of God
against Assyria, executed by the Chaldeans, "devours as
fire, and eats up like the canker-worm."

5. Multitudes of men will not avail nor help in the day of
the Lord's vengeance; yea, such helpers may hurt when God
is angry. Though she make herself many, and multiply her
merchants above the stars of heaven, yet "the canker-worm
spoils and flees away," and so do they.

6. As men usually respect one another and public interests, not sincerely, but for their own ends, so they desert
what they seemed to seek when the wheel of prosperity
turns about. "Their merchants, as the canker-worms, do
spoil," and when there is nothing left to spoil or reap benefit by, then they "steal away."

Ver. 17. The crowned are as the locusts, and your captains
as the great grasshoppers, which camp in the hedges
in the cold day; but when the sun arises, they flee away,
and their place is not known where they are.

18. Your shepherds slumber, O king of Assyria; your
nobles shall dwell in the dust; your people are scattered
upon the mountains, and no man gathers them.

A fourth vain confidence is their great men, their counsellors and valorous commanders, concerning whom the
Lord threatens that some of them were only for eating,
and were idle, effeminate wasters, as locusts and grasshoppers are; and since they had made a shelter of Assyria
for their own advantage, whenever a storm appears they
shall be terrified, but seeing some sunshine of a deliverance, and of living without Assyria's favour, they shall
quite desert them and run away. This seems to be spoken
of their tributary kings and princes, or hired officers. He
threatens also that others of them (i.e. their own counsellors,
princes, and commanders) should become stupid, base, and
careless, and destitute of counsel as men in a slumber, and
that they should not prove active for defence of the country
and city, but dwell or lie still (as the original has it) in their
strongholds, as if they were sick. So Jer. 51:30. Further, by
this means even the king (to whom the speech is directed)
should be undone, and the people exposed to all hazards, as
sheep scattered upon the mountains without a shepherd.

1. The greatness of men, though often confided in, can
contribute nothing for standing out against the judgments
of him who is higher than the highest; for this also is declared to be a vain confidence, and therefore it ought not
to weaken the church's faith in expecting vengeance on the
wicked.

2. Men debase their own greatness when because of it
they take liberty to drown themselves in sensual delights and
to give themselves to effeminate idleness. For such were
these, "crowned as the locusts, and captains as the great
grasshoppers."

3. It is incident even to great men, whatever they pretend
of generosity, to make themselves and their own commodity
the scope and drift of all their actions, and so to walk as
may lead to that end. For he says, "your crowned (as well
as merchants, ver. 16) are as the locusts, and your captains
as the great grasshoppers, which camp in the hedges in the
cold day; but when the sun arises they flee away, and their
place is not known where they are."

4. It is an iniquity and great baseness, and a plague on
rulers, to be stupid, sluggish, selfish, and careful only of
their own defence and safety, when public hazards are

imminent or incumbent. Such was their judgment here: "your shepherds slumber, your nobles dwell or lie still."

5. Those who have most eminently abused days of prosperity shall be made to feel most adversity, though ever so great. This threatening is directed to the king, as he who should feel it most. "Your shepherds slumber, O king of Assyria."

6. Evil rulers are sent of the Lord as a plague and presage of ruin to come upon a sinful people; for when "shepherds slumber," then "people are scattered upon the mountains, and no man gathers them." See Isa. 3:4, 5; Isa. 19: 13, 14.

> Ver. 19. There is no healing of your bruise; your wound is grievous. All who hear your clamour shall clap the hands over you, for upon whom has not your wickedness passed continually?

The judgment is here summed up, and declared to be an irreparable stroke, a wound not to be bound up nor drawn together, nor wrinkled as wounds do when they begin to heal. And as it should not be healed, so it should be very painful and grievous; and there should be none to comfort them under all this, but all ready, when they hear of it, to clap their hands with joy and to insult over them, because for a long time they had been wicked oppressors of all round about them.

1. As the Lord's chastisement of his people ends always in mercy, so his last and final word to the wicked is wrath. This message closes with a denunciation of judgment, without hope of recovery or comfort under it.

2. It is matter of great comfort in trouble, to have hope of a blessed issue in due time; for this may be gathered from Assyria's misery, that strokes are without all comfort when "there is no healing of your bruise."

3. It is also a great mercy in troubles, to get an easy way of bearing them and breathing under them; but to the wicked it is not so. Their wounds are daily ripped up afresh: "your wound is grievous (or painful)."

4. It may make afflictions easier when the afflicted have sympathisers to bemoan and condole with them in their troubles; for it heightens Assyria's misery yet more that "all who hear your clamour shall clap their hands."

5. The world shall in due time be refreshed and comforted with seeing or hearing of the ruin of oppressors. "They shall clap their hands over you, those upon whom your wickedness has passed."

6. Cruelty and oppression shall be rewarded in its own coin, by cutting off the authors thereof, without pity from any. So much is imported in the reason of the world's insulting and joy: "for upon whom has not your wickedness passed continually?"

HABAKKUK

THE ARGUMENT

It cannot be certainly determined at what time this prophet lived and exercised his function -- whether under Manasseh, in whose reign iniquity had come to a great height, or at the same time that Jeremiah began to prophesy; yet certain it is that he lived toward the latter end of God's patience with the Jews, and before the last destruction by the Chaldeans. A part of this, if not the whole, seems to be inflicted in the days of those to whom he preached, as appears from 1:5.

The prophecy is held forth partly by way of doctrine or prediction (chap. 1, 2) and partly by way of meditation or prayer (chap. 3). It may be summed up as a dialogue between the Lord and his servant, in which the prophet, complaining of the iniquity of the times, and being forewarned of the destruction and captivity of the Jews by the Chaldeans, does again plead with God about the prospering of such a wicked people as the Chaldeans (chap. 1); and waiting for an answer, he is commanded to stir up the godly to live by faith, and to take heed of apostasy in the time of their captivity, expecting the ruin of the Chaldeans their oppressors (chap. 2); in which answer the prophet acquiesces, submitting unto the Lord's will, and praying and believing that God would preserve and at length deliver his work, his church, and his elect (chap. 3). All these exercises the prophet publishes and leaves on record, for terrifying the wicked and inviting them to repentance, and for encouraging the godly under the sad calamities that were approaching.

CHAPTER I

In this chapter, after the inscription (ver. 1):

1. The prophet complains to God of the iniquity of the times, and that no course was taken to correct or suppress the desperate wickedness of that people, notwithstanding either his former complaints (ver. 2) or the vexation of his or the godly's souls by it (ver. 3), or the fearful abuse of God's indulgence (ver. 4).

2. The Lord, in answer to this complaint, shows to the church by the prophet, the admirable, incredible, and

speedy judgments that were to come upon them (ver. 5), by the Chaldeans, whose dispositions, equipment, and actions, together with the ill use they should make of their success, is held forth (ver. 6-11).

3. The prophet, receiving this answer, establishes himself in the faith of the preservation of the church and the godly in the midst of this destruction (ver. 12), and expostulates with God concerning his holy providence, in permitting so wicked a people as the Chaldeans to prevail against the church, though sinful (ver. 13), considering both their unjust and violent conquest (ver. 14, 15) and their sinful abuse of it (ver. 15, 16), which therefore he thinks improper (ver. 17).

Ver. 1. The burden which Habakkuk the prophet did see.

This verse holds forth the subject matter of this prophecy, which is chiefly grievous threatenings, first against the Jews and then against the Chaldeans. The penman and divine authority of this scripture are also given; he was not only a prophet by office, but had this doctrine by vision and special illumination. Hence learn:

1. In making use of any portion of holy scripture, we ought to begin at the study of its divine authority, so that we may come to it with more reverence, confidence, and more of that spirit which indited it. Therefore it is prefixed that the penman of this scripture was a "prophet," and that he "saw" it in vision.

2. The study of the divine authority of scripture may hide and take our minds off looking to or stumbling at the weakness or meanness of the instruments which carried it. The Spirit of God thinks it a needless work for those who take up this doctrine as a divine vision, to inquire much about the penman, and therefore expresses only his name and office, "Habakkuk the prophet." See 1 Cor. 15:11.

3. The doctrine of divine vengeance against sin and sinners, rightly considered, will be found sad and insupportable; therefore though all divine doctrine may be called a "burden," as it is in Prov. 30:1 in the original (because of the weight it ought to have upon our spirits, whether to obey directions, Rev. 2:24, 25, or how to walk answerably under comforts), yet in the ordinary scripture-phrase, and by the prophet here, the name is applied to threatenings. He calls this doctrine "the burden": (a) As being sent from a God burdened with the wickedness of sinners (Isa. 1:4; Amos 2:13); (b) As being a grief and burden to the messengers to

carry such tidings; (c) As being burdensome to the secure, to hear their sinful ways contradicted and reproved (Jer. 23:33); (d) As being sad to the penitent when they lay it to heart; (e) As portending sad ruin, though men account them but wind (Jer. 5:13); and (f) finally, it ought to be a burden that God, who delights to speak in other terms to his church, should be provoked to write only bitter things.

4. Though vengeance on impenitent sinners, being long forborne, may seem incredible, yet it is most certain and clear that it is coming. Therefore no matter how secure people bless themselves, yet the prophet not only hears but "sees" their "burden," as if it were present; and though the extraordinary gift of prophecy has ceased, yet every godly man may be as certain from the word of judgments on impenitent sinners, as if they saw them with their eyes.

> Ver. 2. O Lord, how long shall I cry, and thou wilt not hear; even cry out unto thee of violence, and thou wilt not save?

The prophet in his own and the godly's name, begins an expostulation with God. Though the generality of the Jews were generally wicked, as he instances in several iniquities, especially against the second table, yet the Lord in his patience bore with them, and took no course to vindicate his own glory or to abate this deluge of sin one way or other. This complaint he amplifies and aggravates from other considerations, the first of which is in this verse. He had taken much pains on this people to no purpose, but their injustice swelled up and broke out in open violence, and he had been forced for a long time to cry to God against them; but neither was his prayer regarded, nor the oppressed saved from violence, which he thinks strange.

We are not to understand this as if the prophet were quarreling with God, or cruel to this people, toward whom he evidences so much tenderness afterward; but having long dealt with that people, and with God by prayer for some success in his ministry, and yet finding iniquity to abound, to the dishonour of God and the oppression of the godly, he (not out of any hatred against them, but out of zeal to God's honour, hatred of sin, and pity toward the oppressed) complains that there was no redress of this.

1. The duties of the second table are a touchstone by which to try the sincerity of those who profess true religion and are within the visible church; and when professors once

declare their unsoundness that way, they may readily come to a very great height in it. Here they had come to the extremity of "violence" and combustions among themselves.

2. The ready way to make men's endeavours in their callings effectual, especially those who are employed in dealing with souls, is to be much with God in prayer. Therefore the prophet, who had spent much time in vain, is put to "cry" to God about it. Cries to God are our best weapons against sin.

3. The iniquity of a visible church may come to such a height that those who would stand in the gap may be ready to submit if God should send judgments, if not indeed to cry for judgment upon them; for the prophet is so put to it, with their sin in dishonouring God and oppressing the godly, that he "cries" that God would, one way or another, stop the course of their iniquity. See Numb. 16:15.

4. Zeal for God and his honour, and hatred against sin, ought to oversway our respects to any creature whatever; for it is from this principle that the prophet cries to God against this people, who were otherwise dear to him.

5. The truly godly, and especially those who are called to carry the Lord's name unto his people, are to set their minds not to have a smooth and easy life, but to wrestle under much humbling, toil, and vexation; for such was the prophet's lot here, and the godly's, in whose name he complains.

6. So unsearchable are the Lord's counsels, that he may see fit to delay the answer of desires which are put up from much zeal to his glory, and compassion toward the godly oppressed, against sinful men and their courses; for the prophet here has cried, and cried so long that he is about to quarrel and question with God about it, and yet the Lord did not hear nor save.

7. The patience of God toward his sinful church and people does far surpass the patience of the best of men; for when the prophet is weary and about to fall into impatience because of God's long-suffering, yet the Lord was not weary to wait upon them.

Ver. 3. Why dost thou show me iniquity, and cause me to behold grievance? For spoiling and violence are before me, and there are those who raise up strife and contention.

A second amplification of this complaint (which clears more the ground of his crying, ver. 2, and sets out more of their sin) is in their wickedness, in vexing and grieving one another and the godly among them, and their violent spoiling of one another, together with their lawsuits and contentions (or strife against the messengers of God who reproved them, as was usual, Jer. 15:10; Hos. 4:4). All these were not only public and open in the view of the godly and the prophet, wherever they went, but were a great grief and vexation unto them; their hearts were overcharged when they saw such wickedness, and God taking no order with it.

1. When once men shake off the fear of God, it is righteous with him to give them up to break all bonds of love, humanity, and civil society among men; for these godless men are given up to "iniquity, grievance, spoiling and violence." Thus the Lord shows how unfixed men are in all things, if they hold not fast the root of his fear.

2. It may be the lot of the Lord's most faithful servants to see sad sights of wickedness among the people committed to their charge, instead of comfortable fruits of their ministry. After his pains taken, this prophet sees only "iniquity and grievance," and everywhere "spoiling and violence are before him," these sins being so impudently committed that the actors cared not who saw them. See Isa. 49:14.

3. Though it is the duty of the Lord's people and faithful servants, not to carve out what shall be their own lot and success in the world, yet they ought to keep themselves unspotted, and to be seriously affected and vexed with the iniquities of the times; for the prophet says, "why dost thou show me iniquity, and cause me to behold grievance?" not so much quarreling with God's providence toward him as testifying his own and the godly's vexation with seeing these things. See Ezek. 9:4; 2 Pet. 2:7, 8. To be vexed with the evils of the time is a way to keep ourselves from falling into them, and a ground of hope that God will appear, as the prophet's reasoning imports.

4. Though the godly may be called to contend and strive both for God and for their own rights, yet it is a mark of an unsanctified spirit to delight in the fires of contention, and either to beget or entertain them needlessly or unjustly. This was one of the vexing evils of the time; "there are those who raise up strife and contention."

> Ver. 4. Therefore the law is slacked, and judgment never
> goes forth; for the wicked compasses the righteous
> about; therefore wrong judgment proceeds.

A third aggravation of his complaint (holding out yet more
of the iniquity of the time) is taken from the consequences
of God's indulgence toward that people. They were emboldened by it to sin, and grew the worse for being spared.
When the prophets preached, and men rebelled, and yet
God spared them, they hereby took occasion to scorn the law
and word of God as a dead thing, having no vigour or authority, and so ran into all mad courses, insomuch that no justice
was to be found; for if there were any who respected equity
or right, they were so overpowered with the multitude of
wicked men that they dared not appear, nor could they effect
anything, and so justice was necessarily wrested.

1. It should be the endeavour of the godly to have their
zeal against sin clean, and arising upon justifiable grounds;
for here the prophet shows that his zeal against the iniquity
of the times did not flow from any prejudice he sustained
thereby, but from the overturning of all religion and justice
that appeared in it.

2. The Lord's forbearance and longsuffering often prove
a snare to wicked men, hardening them in their evil course;
for because of God's indulgence, "therefore the law is
slacked, and judgment never goes forth."

3. It is not the enjoyment of the word of God or ordinances,
but their having authority and vigour in our hearts and practices, that will prove us blessed in enjoying them. This people
had the law, but it was their quarrel that it was slacked or
dead in its authority. "The law is slacked"; the similitude is
taken from the faint or lifeless pulse of a dying man.

4. Contempt of the authority of the word opens the door
to all wickedness, and justice will go to ruin among men,
where religion has no place; for these two are conjoined.
"The law is slacked, and judgment never goes forth."

5. It is a great height of a land's guiltiness when judges
and courts of justice become corrupt. That is the height of
their impiety, and the evidence of a dispersed law, that
"judgment never goes forth."

6. Times of general defection prove ordinarily times of
great trial to the godly and righteous; not only are their
souls vexed and they supplanted in their righteous cause,
but they dare hardly appear against the stream of injustice;
or if they do appear, they cannot perform anything that is

right; for when "the wicked encompasses the righteous, therefore wrong judgment proceeds."

> Ver. 5. Behold among the heathen, and regard, and wonder miraculously; for I will work a work in your days, which you will not believe, though it be told you.

From now until ver. 12, we have the Lord's answer to the prophet's remonstrance, containing a prophecy of the destruction of the Jews by the Chaldeans, which is here described generally from several properties. (a) It should be a singular and wonderful destruction, insomuch that if any of the heathen should consider it, it would breed amazement in them (Deut. 28:37; Deut. 29:25; 1 Kings 9:8); or if the Jews should consider any stroke inflicted on the heathen, they would be amazed that their own stroke was sadder (as Dan. 9:12). (b) It should be incredible to themselves, who dreamed of ease, and yet be true. (c) It should be speedy, and come to pass even in the time of those to whom this was preached.

1. When men harden themselves in their evil ways because of God's forbearance, and when the word has no authority among them, then the Lord will speak in another language by his rod; for because of their contempt of the word (ver. 4) the Lord will "work a work," that is, will send judgments which he will own and in which he will be seen.

2. The Lord's longsuffering and patience toward impenitent sinners will not always last, but when their iniquity has come to a height, it will also end in sad judgments. Therefore although the Lord's patience had out-wearied the prophet's patience, yet now "I will work a work in your days," says the Lord.

3. As abuse of mercy offered to the church deserves sadder judgments than the sin of the heathen, who have not had such an offer (Matt. 11:22, 24), so it is an addition to the church's calamity when the heathen and enemies, who have been witnesses to God's working for her, shall become spectators of the hand of God against her. Both these are held forth in the preface, "Behold among the heathen, and regard and wonder marvelously; for I will work a work."

4. It is usual that when judgment comes upon an impenitent people, they do not attain to any right use of it, but are surprised with admiration and astonishment under it; for such is prophesied even of the Jews, that they shall "behold and regard, and wonder marvellously" at their own calamity, and yet go no further.

5. This stupid disposition flows from a former contempt of God's word, which has so stupefied the conscience that judgments cannot pierce; so it will prove fruitless. And moreover, it portends the further ruin of those who continue in it. The apostle, citing this place (Acts 13:41) makes clear that those who wonder are "despisers," as is also clear from ver. 4, and that they "wonder and perish," or "vanish." That is, as their admiration and astonishment usually vanishes and comes to nothing, without any fruit, so such a disposition portends ruin, and such a stroke will so undo a people that they are not able to endure and bear out under both the stroke and the fearful astonishment accompanying it.

6. As the Lord's judgments upon the church may be far beyond the expectation of the heathen and her very enemies (Lam. 4:12), so it is just with God that those who dote on their privileges and scorn the word, should meet with unexpected and incredible judgments; for so he says to the profane Jews. "I will work a work which you shall not believe, though it be told you."

7. Divine indignation against sin is more terrible, and will appear more sad when it is inflicted, than secure sinners ordinarily imagine. This is intimated in that this work will be above belief; "you will not believe, though it be told you." See Ps. 90:11.

8. The contempt of the gospel, and the rejection of Christ offered to lost man, is the height of iniquity, and draws on all the judgments which at any time have been threatened against any sin. Therefore the apostle (Acts 13:41) denounces the same judgment, here threatened for contempt of the law and sins against the second table, to come upon the Jews who opposed the gospel and rejected the Messiah.

> Ver. 6. For lo, I raise up the Chaldeans, that bitter and hasty nation, which shall march through the breadth of the land, to possess the dwelling-places that are not theirs.

The prophet subjoins a particular description of this calamity, in describing the instruments of it, the Chaldeans under Nebuchadnezzar their king, whose disposition, equipment, and proceedings are exactly set down to confirm the truth of the prediction. This may set forth the justice of God in repaying the Jews in their own coin, may be terrible to the stout-hearted among them, and may confirm the hope of the godly in a deliverance from the way of the Chaldeans.

This description is contained in several particulars, the first of which is that they are a nation of bitter, cruel, fierce, and active temper, and will therefore, to satisfy their ambitious covetousness, speedily and without fear overspread the land of Judea, not only to overrun it, but to make a conquest for themselves.

1. When God has a controversy against a people, he will not lack instruments by whom he may prosecute it; for he can bring the Chaldeans from afar, though they were already satiated with victory and conquest, and needed not otherwise to have minded so remote a corner as Judah.

2. Instruments of vengeance upon the church should be looked upon as employed by God, and therefore the church's eyes should be more on God than upon them. The Lord says, "Lo, I raise up the Chaldeans."

3. It is usual for the Lord to give up troublers and oppressors of the world, to meddle also with his church, that it may hasten their ruin, however sinful the church may be. Therefore the church is to be chastised by the Chaldeans, who were "the hammer of the whole earth" (Jer. 50:23), that this might hasten the filling of their cup.

4. The Lord can make holy use even of the sins of creatures, employed for executing his judgment; for "he raises up the Chaldeans, that bitter and hasty nation," and makes use of this their temper, without any imputation to his holiness.

5. When the Lord arms any instruments with vengeance against a sinful people, they will not lack dispositions and success for attaining this end; for if God raises up the Chaldeans against the church, they are not only "bitter and fierce," but a "hasty" or "active" nation, and will "march through the breadth of the land" without opposition and fear; and they will not only overcome, but will carry all before them, that they may "possess the dwellings that are not theirs" without molestation.

6. The Lord in executing vengeance does righteously proportion men's sins and his judgments, and pay transgressors in their own coin. Therefore the Jews, who had been cruel, now meet with bitter adversaries, and they who had used "spoiling and violence" toward others (ver. 2) are now overrun and cast out of their own possessions. The same also may be read in the following purpose.

7. Though men account it purchase good enough, when they are able by power to overturn others and sit down in their room, yet the Lord does not so reckon; but he puts a

difference between men's power or possession and their right. Although the Chaldeans conquered Judah, yet in the Lord's account "they possess the dwelling places that are not theirs."

> Ver. 7. They are terrible and dreadful; their judgment
> and dignity shall proceed of themselves.

The Chaldeans employed in this work are yet further described. Being armed with divine vengeance, emboldened with former victories, and exercising the same cruelty, they should fill the land with terror and dread, which they should also tyranically improve, and be their own carvers in all matters of advantage and honour. They should stand to no law, either of nature or of nations, in their dealing with a terrified and subdued people, but should solely follow their own will armed with power.

1. Divine indignation pursuing sinners will take away their heart and courage in a strait, and make their enemies terrible to them; for so are the Chaldeans to the sinful Jews, "terrible and dreadful."

2. When a people do not stand in awe of God speaking in his word to them, he righteously sends judgments upon them, which will cause their hearts to faint; for the Chaldeans are "terrible and dreadful" to those wicked Jews, who slighted the law and God Almighty speaking in it (ver. 4).

3. It is a great height of impiety before the Lord, when besides the unlawfulness of a war in general, and many particular acts of injustice in the heat of hostility, a conqueror even in cold blood has no respect to right and wrong; whereas the fear of God should be a law to men, though they had ever so much power. Therefore it is the Chaldeans' sin that "their judgment and dignity shall proceed of themselves."

4. It is righteous with God to punish corruption in judges, and perverting of justice and willful stubbornness in sin, with unjust oppression from enemies, and to send a conqueror's sword to give laws to those who have perverted justice; for because "the law is slacked and judgment never goes forth" (ver. 4), therefore he sends the Chaldeans, whose "judgment and dignity shall proceed of themselves."

> Ver. 8. Their horses also are swifter than the leopards,
> and are more fierce than the ravening wolves; and
> their horsemen shall spread themselves, and their

horsemen shall come from far; they shall fly as the
eagle that hastes to eat.

It is thirdly declared in this description that the Chaldeans
shall not lack means by which to prosecute their designs and
enterprises. An instance of this is their horses, who are
swifter than fierce leopards, and more fierce or sharp to go
where they are employed and to tread down opposition, than
wolves who are hungry through fasting all the day, and
therefore run furiously to their prey at night. Thus their
fierce riders may easily and quickly be in every part of
the land; and though the Chaldeans are far off, yet their
swift horses shall speedily bring them to Judea, and bring
them as swiftly upon their desired prey as an eagle flies to
the carcass. See Jer. 4:13; Jer. 48:40.

1. The Lord's hand should be noticed, in furnishing the
enemies of his sinful people with all necessities for carrying on their enterprises. Therefore are the number and
swiftness of the Chaldeans' horses, to carry them on so
long a journey and make such speedy execution, recorded.
"Their horses also are swifter than the leopards."

2. The fierceness of divine anger against sin may be
read in the celerity and activity of the instruments which
execute it. Therefore the Chaldeans are described as speedily
"spreading themselves" in all places, as "coming from far,
and flying as the eagle" to get prey; as if divine displeasure
furnished them with wings, and could forbear no longer.

3. It is vain for impenitent sinners to lean upon any
apparent ground of security or confidence, when God arises
to plead with them; for "their horsemen come from far;
they spread themselves, and fly as the eagle that hastes to
eat," showing that distance of place between the enemy and
them, or having their goods and themselves out of the way,
should not avail them.

Ver. 9. They shall come all for violence; their faces shall
sup up as the east wind, and they shall gather the captivity as the sand.

It is fourthly declared that the enemy shall be so confident that they shall not much mind fighting in this expedition,
but only to spoil and prey on a base people, in which they
shall not be disappointed; for their very coming and presence shall overwhelm and blast all, like an east wind, which

was violent in these countries (Isa. 27:8; Jonah 4:8), and they shall not only destroy people's substance, but shall lead innumerable people into captivity.

1. As it is righteous with God to repay violence with violence, so it is a very great sin to engage in war, by which men and countries are destroyed, without a just quarrel, but merely for the satisfaction of men's lusts. Therefore "they all come for violence," in God's righteousness, to punish the oppressing Jews; and yet they sinned in their own way, as minding only to run them down and satiate themselves.

2. The Lord sees fit sometimes to wink at the sins of evil men, and let them have success in their evil cause, when he has his church to punish by them. Therefore though the Chaldeans were both insatiable and presumptuous, in that "they come all for violence," yet it succeeds with them. "Their faces," or presence, "sup up as the east wind," raising a tempest and carrying all before it; and "they gather captivity as the sand."

3. The Lord's justice is to be seen and adored in the ignominious strokes which he inflicts upon his incorrigible people; for so does this stroke by the Chaldeans import, that they should come against Judah, not as a people to be fought with, but preyed upon; and that at their coming or face, they should destroy all and gather captives, possibly more than themselves; so base are God's people when he deserts them for their sin, though invincible while he is with them.

4. It may be the lot of the Lord's church not only to suffer the calamities and desolation of war, but to lose her liberty, which she so much abused, and to be carried into captivity and bondage; for the Chaldeans' faces "shall sup up as the east wind, and they shall gather captivity as the sand." See Deut. 28:47, 48.

5. The consideration of the cruelty of men, and of the calamities that attend war and conquests, ought to invite sinners not to provoke God to give them up thereunto; ought to terrify those who do not fear the threatening of the word; and ought to point out unto those who are under such a lot, the bitterness of departing from God. For these ends are the Chaldeans' cruel deportments recorded, both for the use of the Jews, while they yet continued in their present condition, and with reference to their case when the threatening should be accomplished.

> Ver. 10. And they shall scoff at the kings, and the princes
> shall be a scorn unto them; they shall deride every
> stronghold, for they shall heap dust and take it.

It is yet further declared that no opposition shall hinder them from effecting what the Lord had threatened should be done by them. They shall slight and despise all the power, authority, and opposition of the Jewish kings and princes, or any of their confederates; and having conquered them, they shall use them ignominiously (as was accomplished, 2 Kings 25:7, 19-21); and they shall easily take in their strongholds by raising up mounts against them. In the original, this is spoken in the singular, of the Chaldeans, pointing at their king, who was chief and head in this enterprise.

1. All opposition against God, when he pursues for sin, will prove vain, be it kings, princes, or strongholds.

2. It is not an easy thing to put men from their carnal confidences, that they may humble themselves before the Lord. All these things were opposed by the Jews to the threatenings, to keep themselves from being frightened; and all these does the Lord declare to be empty, that they may stoop.

3. It is just with the Lord to expose the greatest of men to contempt and ignominious usage, when they provoke him and do not employ their power and authority for him; for the Chaldeans, in executing God's controversy, "scoff at the kings, and the princes shall be a scorn to them."

4. Forts and strongholds, in which men often place their confidence, will prove only matter of derision to the instruments of God's vengeance; for "they shall deride every stronghold." And no matter how men boast of these, yet they are easily reached; for an enemy can "heap up dust," which lies under his feet, and by that means take it.

> Ver. 11. Then his mind shall change, and he shall pass
> over and offend, imputing this his power unto his God.

The Lord subjoins all this as a ground of encouragement and hope to the godly. The Chaldeans, and especially their king, would make a sinful use of all their victories, and of this among the rest, that he shall be so drunk with success that his swelling thoughts of himself shall increase, and in his arrogance he shall pass all bounds of modesty and humanity, which formerly he might seem to have. And he shall increase the power of his idols, and take the glory from

God who employed him as his scourge. All this might assure the godly that such a power could not stand long. Some instances of this carriage we may read in Dan. 4:30; Dan. 5:4.

1. Prosperity is no less a trial, to bring out what is in men's hearts, and no less difficult to bear, than adversity is; for here adversity tried the Jews, and prosperity brought out more of the Chaldeans' naughtiness. Thus also was Hezekiah tried (2 Chron. 32:31).

2. Though many are employed in making wars and conquests, yet there are but few who reap any great benefits by all their toil. The most part of the conquerors as well as most of the conquered were but slaves to promote the ambitious designs of a few, and furnish fuel to their lusts. Notwithstanding the great armies of the Chaldeans, all this swelling (which they accounted the fruit of their victories) is enjoyed chiefly by their king. "His mind changes, he shall pass over," etc.

4. It is a judgment for men, following a false religion, to prosper in their opposition to the truth; and it is a further judgment when men are not led to repentance by God's liberal dealing with them, but are given up to advance a false religion as they prosper. For this was a plague on the Chaldeans, that being idolaters and yet prospering against the people of the true God, they go on, and he "offends, imputing this his power unto his god."

5. It is one of the difficult tasks of man's life, and one which will never be cleared without the sure word, to read the language of divine providence without mistaking, and to gather favourable dispensations rightly, to see aright what bestows them, and upon what ground; to see what good things in men are encouraged by providence, what evil is reproved; and to observe whether the good success men have is because of any good in their way, or any evil that is in their opponents. In this judgment the Chaldeans fail, for the Lord employed them and punished Judah by them, not because they were right, but because of Judah's sin; yet they applaud themselves as if they had prospered because of their idolatry, and impute all this power to their idols.

6. Though it is not the duty or disposition of the truly godly to take pleasure in the sin of any, yet it furnishes ground of confidence to them that God will own their quarrel in due time, when they see their enemies abusing their prosperity; they will gather that insolence and arrogance shall not escape unpunished, that nothing shall be a stable

conquest which is either withheld or consecrated to idols
and a false religion, to the dishonour of the true God. To
this end, and to clear this truth, the Lord subjoins their
sinful carriage here to their great success in the former
verses.

> Ver. 12. Art thou not from everlasting, O Lord my God,
> my holy one? We shall not die. O Lord, thou hast or-
> dained them for judgment, and, O mighty God, thou hast
> established them for correction.

Now follows, to the end of the chapter, the prophet's exercise about this answer, and his reply to it. In this verse,
in a speech directed to God, he confirms his own and the
godly's faith in their being preserved from destruction in
the calamity. This is not to be understood only of the preservation of the godly from eternal destruction, whatever
becomes of them outwardly, nor yet of the particular preservation of any particular person, wicked or godly, further
than may have a particular promise for it, as Baruch and
Ebed-melech had; nor is it strictly to be applied by every
particular visible church, as if it might not be destroyed by
judgments. Though the Lord may bring many judgments on
a church before he gives her a bill of divorce and causes
her to cease to be a church, yet the sad experiences of the
churches in Asia and elsewhere do refute that. But the
meaning is that as the Lord had resolved to keep a church
continually in the world, and as there had been a particular·
promise to the church of the Jews of their enjoying that
privilege of being the only people of God until the Messiah
should come out of them, the prophet upon that general
ground and principle, and upon that particular promise,
gathers that the church should not be totally extinguished
nor cut off by her captivity in Babylon. And he yet further
confirms this confidence from God's covenant with them,
from his eternal immutability and his holiness, and from
his purpose, power, and providence in appointing the Chaldeans to punish and correct, but not to destroy the church.
  1. Judgments threatened or inflicted may speak sadder
things to the apprehension of the godly than God really intends by them; for such is insinuated, that to die, or to be
dissolved irreparably, was presented to their mind in this
stroke.
  2. As the Lord was pleased to continue a church of the
Jews under the law in the midst of all their calamities, so

he will never lack a church and people in the world, however
he may correct. And he may inflict many judgments on a
visible church, and yet not cast her off; and he will be good
everlastingly to the souls of his people, though he toss their
bodies and their minds in the world. But all this should be
accounted as a great mercy in time of captivity and sad
dispensations, for all is held forth by way of glory in the
prophet's speech: "we shall not die."

3. Believers, having God's promise, may humbly crave
their own answer according to it; and when they come to
God in prayer, they may by faith tell him what they look for
and will get; therefore the prophet says to God, "O Lord,
we shall not die."

4. It is a characteristic of the truly godly man that in
times of common calamity he is public minded; and his care,
prayer and confidence are taken up about the church and
the godly, and not his own case only. Therefore the prophet
says, "we" shall not die; i.e. the church and a seed of God in
it shall not perish.

5. Interest in God by virtue of the covenant made in a
redeemer, speaks comforting things in saddest times; for
the prophet gathers his confidence from this: "O Lord my
God."

6. Those who are in covenant with God, and have promises
made unto them, will be notably confirmed in the faith of
them by taking up the nature, properties, and way of God,
the covenanting party and promise maker. Thus does the
prophet confirm his faith, that his God is Jehovah, able to
give a being to things promised; that he is "from everlasting," and eternal, and so is immutable in his purposes,
and will eternally have a people to be his spouse and subjects, as is gathered from the same attributes (Ps. 102:27,
28).

Or the prophet may reason that he is (as the words will
also read) "from of old the Lord my God," or the church's
God, by a covenant of grace, even before the law (Gal. 3:17).
He had proved so to that day, and therefore the law will not
disannul that covenant to those who renounce their own righteousness and flee to God through Christ in the covenant; and
the Lord in his future dispensations would prove himself to
be like himself of old.

Lastly, he confirms his faith from God's holiness, that
he is "my holy one", without all spot of impurity; and therefore as he disapproves sin and punishes it in his people, so
he will not spare it in enemies; far less will he make any

imputation on his holiness, by falsifying his covenant and promise made to the church and elect in it (Ps. 60:6; Ps. 85:35). In sum, "they who know his name will trust in him" (Ps. 9:10).

7. As faith must not expect to go on without much opposition within, so it is the duty of a believer not to succumb or give it over at every apprehension or temptation, but to set himself against it and shame himself from it by venting it to God. Note the way the prophet expresses his confidence: "art thou not from everlasting?" This does not import his total hesitation or questioning of this, but rather that as God's dispensations ministered occasion to his weakness to apprehend death, so also when he would fasten faith on God, sense did question his attributes; and his heart rises against this, and he shames his own unbelief by venting this question to God, holding forth the absurdity of sense's doubts and apprehensions. As these apprehensions would take away the believer's comfort by making him question promises, so also they would make him turn atheist and deny unto God the glory of his attributes; and he shows that the way of curing such distempers is to lay them out to God, although faith could do no more than question the truth of what sense said.

8. God is sovereign Lord in all calamities, and sets bounds and limits to them, which (whatever either the power of enemies or greatness of trouble inflicted by them seems to threaten) shall not be transgressed. Therefore the prophet reckons that the Chaldeans, being sent out "for judgment," to punish the church, yet might not harm those who keep within bounds of fatherly correction and reproof; or that they might plague and punish the rebellious, and correct but not destroy the godly and church. The Chaldeans were "ordained or established," or solidly founded and supported for that work only, by the Lord, who is mighty in power, or "a rock" (as the word is), unalterable in his purposes, therefore they should not be permitted to go beyond his commission and purpose, but they should do his work and pleasure, not their own. "We shall not die, O Lord, but thou hast ordained them for judgment; and, O mighty God, thou hast established them for correction."

> Ver. 13. Thou art of purer eyes than to behold evil, and canst not look on iniquity; why then dost thou look on those who deal treacherously, and holdest thy tongue when the wicked devours the man that is more righteous than he?

The prophet had confirmed his faith in the preservation of the church. Now he subjoins an expostulation that, as the Lord is so pure and holy that he cannot so much as look upon any sin in which men approve themselves, and for pardoning and purging of which a Mediator is not sought unto, far less could he view gross iniquity and unjust grievance of others, without indignation and anger. Yet he seemed to take no notice, but tolerated the Chaldeans in their treachery and violence against the church, who, though sinful, were more righteous than their persecutors; should he rather punish the church than them? In his complaint there is not only an expression of the godly's weakness and wrestlings under such dispensations, but their faith also is insinuated, that as God in his holy indignation at sin had not spared the church, so he would not long wink at the Chaldeans' iniquities, but would punish them in due time, and deliver his church. The practice of the Chaldeans upon which he bases the expostulation, is gathered from the former prediction (ver. 6, 7).

1. Such is the weakness and instability of the spirits of the Lord's people, and so various the occasions of exercising their graces, that they meet with few dispensations at which their hearts are not ready to quarrel. The prophet had formerly complained out of zeal that God took no course with the sins of his people; and getting an answer, he is yet not satisfied, but his compassion finds new matter of exercise and complaint.

2. The clearest-sighted saints may be so bemisted as not to be able to reconcile God's dispensations with his nature and attributes, but be ready to apprehend a contradiction between them. The prophet cannot well reconcile God's holiness with his tolerating the Chaldeans.

3. We are so weak and selfish that when providence works not according to our mind and apprehensions, we are ready to succumb under temptations of atheism, and to question providence; for the prophet sees God as "looking on" and holding his tongue, as a spectator only, when he tolerated the Chaldeans.

4. It is the duty and will be the care of all the godly to justify God, and to clear him from any imputation, though their weakness cannot see through all the deep mysteries of his providence about his church and her enemies; and for that end they should prevent the language of misbelief and temptation with something of faith. Therefore the prophet, in the midst of dark mists, begins with this as an unalterable

ground, whatever his heart may say: "God is of purer eyes than to behold evil, and cannot look upon iniquity." See Jer. 12:1.

5. The only best way to refute temptations and dispel mists is not to debate dark cases within our own hearts, overcharged with weakness and fears, but to vent the matter and our case to God, and seek his resolution upon it; for so does the prophet, lying under this temptation. "Why dost thou look upon those who deal treacherously?"

6. The Lord has just indignation against, and will in due time punish, the gross iniquities of men outside the church; yet considering the many aggravations of less sins within the church, and considering God's jealousy over his people and his care to have them reclaimed from every evil course, it is no wonder to see the church's sins (though less in their own nature) punished, when more gross sins outside the church escape for a time unpunished. The prophet's complaint, that God "holds his tongue when the wicked devours the man that is more righteous than he," imports that God does so, and God's doing of it proves it to be a righteous act, no matter how we may quarrel.

7. The Lord makes use of wicked instruments to punish his people, that in the foulness of the rod he may reveal the vileness of their sin. Thus the Jews are "devoured by the wicked," and by men viler than themselves. See Ezek. 7:24.

8. Treachery is a great aggravation of and addition unto oppression, when the oppressor by his practices belies his general profession or particular pretences in a quarrel, or does otherwise than in reason might be expected, considering either his obligations or any provocations given, or injuries done to him. Therefore it is the prophet's complaint that they "deal treacherously and devour." Though the scripture does not speak particularly of the Chaldeans' treachery, yet it is here asserted that there had been such, and therefore the prophet laments that they should be permitted to prosper.

9. Though God is righteous in punishing his church by wicked instruments, yet the holiness of God compared with their wickedness gives ground of hope that he will at last reckon with them. This expostulation imports this truth, that the holiness of God would not always fit with this, but in the end would right it (Ps. 50:21).

Ver. 14. And thou makest men as the fishes of the sea, as the creeping things that have no ruler over them.

Ver. 15. They take up all of them with the angle; they
catch them in their net, and gather them in their drag;
therefore they rejoice and are glad.

16. Therefore they sacrifice unto their net, and burn
incense unto their drag; because by them their portion
is fat, and their meat plenteous.

The prophet proves his expostulation concerning the enemies' wickedness from two grounds. The first is their
unjust and violent conquest and oppression. By their oppression men were treated as irrational creatures, such
as fishes, where the greater devour the lesser, or as
creeping things lacking rulers, who run one over another,
and are trodden down by every foot. Yea further, men
should be like fishes, not only devouring one another, but
exposed as a prey to everyone who can first catch them.
As fishes are easily taken, and (when nets and drags are
used) in great numbers, so men and multitudes of people
and nations should without difficulty be preyed upon by
oppressors; and as nets and drags promiscuously draw all
to land, so oppressors should get liberty promiscuously to
overrun nations good and bad, the church as well as others,
those who never wronged the oppressors as well as they
who injured them most. The prophet cannot see how all this
is consistent with the holy providence of God, and therefore
lays it before him to clear and consider. Hence learn:

1. Temptations are very ready to grow upon our hand;
and the more we think upon them, the more ground we may
seem to have to subscribe to them. Therefore as fast as
they are suggested to us, we should tell them to God, as the
prophet does here with his fertile invention in expostulating
and complaining.

2. Men are so naughty by nature that, if the Lord would
let loose the reins of a restraining providence and give
them up to themselves, the world would become monstrous;
for so does the prophet teach. Men would be "as the fishes
of the sea, as the creeping things which have no ruler over
them."

3. It is an evidence of monstrous and brutish wickedness
when men acknowledge no rule of right and wrong except
power, and employ all the power they have for usurpation
upon others; for then indeed men "are as the fishes of the
sea, and they take up all of them with the angle; they catch
them in their net, and gather them in their drag."

4. Since men are exalted by God above the creatures, it is a great abuse when their lot from others debases them from that dignity, i.e. that the oppressing Chaldeans should live in the world like monstrous beasts and fishes, depraving the image of God after which they are made, and observing no shadow of equity; and that the oppressed should be used, not as rational creatures after the same image, but as "fishes taken up with the angle."

5. Though we be unsatisfied with dispensations, yet it is our safest way, and a step to blessing, to keep God's providence about them still in our eye. Thus does the prophet better his former thoughts of God's looking and holding his tongue, for he says, "thou (for the speech is still directed to God) makest men as the fishes of the sea."

6. It well beseems the Lord's providence to restrain brutish violence, to see to right and wrong in the world, and to protect the weak and poor from the strong and mighty, or give a redress when they are injured by them; for the prophet's reasoning imports that it would beseem God not to make men as fishes of the sea, and so he proved in due time.

The second ground of the prophet's expostulation (showing yet further the Chaldeans' wickedness) is taken from their abusing of their success, and that the Lord should permit them not only to do wickedly in their purchasing, but yet more wickedly in their boasting and insulting because of their victories, and in their glorying in their own wisdom and strength, as if by them they had conquered the world and made themselves feasts and a good life.

1. Evil purchase is not ordinarily well used, but the purchasers are given up to insolence, conceit of themselves, and luxury, which are the usual plague and snare of prosperity. "Therefore (that is, since they speed in oppression) they rejoice and are glad; therefore they sacrifice unto their net and burn incense unto their drag, because by them their portion is fat."

2. Dispensations are then saddest to the godly, when they seem to minister occasion to men to deprive God of his honour, and to exalt any other thing or way besides him, as the author of their felicity; for this affects the prophet, that "they sacrificed to their net and drag; because by them (as they judge) their portion is fat."

3. When men have troubled themselves and the world also, to make themselves great, the result of all will be but a

poor addition to their felicity, and that which may be as
well lacked as enjoyed. All that the Chaldeans reap is that
"they rejoice and are glad that their portion is fat and their
meat plenteous"; that is, they have good cheer and a merry
life. Yet they who lack such abundance live as well as they,
and they who are mean may have as much joy and contentment.

4. God will not tolerate, but in due time will punish, men's
insolence and glory in their unlawfully purchased pleasures;
for the prophet's expostulation on this ground, which at last
gets a satisfactory answer, teaches as much.

> Ver. 17. Shall they therefore empty their net, and not
> spare continually to slay the nations?

Upon all these grounds the prophet concludes and infers
that although the Chaldeans had gone long and far on, yet
the Lord would bring their violent courses to an end, and
would not allow them to empty their net, that they might
spread it for new purchase; nor would he so much as permit them to enjoy their desired end in their oppressions (as
if a fisher should not empty his net when he had taken his
fish), and all this because of their bloody cruelty toward all
the nations under their power, in prosecuting their ends. This
he propounds by way of question, to testify his indignation
and zeal against its being otherwise.

1. God's people may meet with and apprehend many things
in his dispensations, which will be matter of much vexation
and provoke much indignation in them; for such do these
questions teach.

2. Oppression and bloody cruelty, joined with insolence,
shall come to an end in due time; and oppressors shall never
reach their utmost end and design, but be miserably disappointed when their hopes are most bent; for this question
includes a denial, and imports that because of what he has
charged against them in the former expostulation, "therefore they shall not empty their net," and shall not be allowed
"continually to slay the nations."

CHAPTER II

In this chapter we have the Lord's answer to the prophet's
expostulation, showing that after he has exercised the godly's
faith and patience in adhering to the word, and tried and

revealed hypocrites and hypocrisy, he would severely punish the Chaldeans for their manifold sins. And so in the
chapter, the prophet, waiting for an answer to his expostulation (ver. 1) is admonished to publish the vision which he
was to receive conspicuously and clearly (ver. 2), and that
because it was not speedily to be accomplished, but would
not disappoint them in the end (ver. 3). By this delay the
Lord would try the faith or unsoundness of that people, or
any of them (ver. 4). In obedience to the command, the prophet publishes the sore judgments that were to come on the
Chaldeans for their luxury and ambition, making them insatiable (ver. 5-8), for their covetousness and aim to be
perpetually great (ver. 9-11), for their cruel and bloody
purchase (ver. 12-14), for their luxury, to which they consecrated their success, or their carnal policy by which they
carried on their enterprises (ver. 15-17), and for their
idolatry in which they had hardened themselves because of
their success, and unto which also they consecrated their
unjust conquests (ver. 18-20).

> Ver. 1. I will stand upon my watch, and set me upon the
> tower, and will watch to see what he will say unto me,
> and what I shall answer when I am reproved.

The prophet had vented his grief and plunged himself in
temptations and confusions; but now he begins to recollect
himself. As a watchman attends eagerly on his watch-
tower, to get news of any danger for the good of the city, so
he (a watchman to the church by office) resolves by meditation and prayer to wait for a vision in answer to his
expostulation. By this also he might be able to quiet his own
reasonings and to satisfy the people, who were ready to quarrel at those hard tidings concerning their ruin, and who did
reprove him in the manner which he expresses in his expostulation.

1. It is our safest way in times of temptation and perplexity, not to lie down under discouragement, but to recollect ourselves and fix our eyes on God, who only can
clear our minds and quiet our spirits. Therefore the
prophet, after his deep plunge in temptation, "sets himself"
to look to God and get some "answer," or "reproof" (as the
original will bear), so that his mind may be settled.

2. It is by the word that the Lord clears dark cases, and
would have his people answer their temptations and silence
their reasonings; and a temptation caused by the prosperity

of wicked men is a knot that can only be loosed by God speaking in his word. The prophet "watches to see what he will say to him," or "in him," by way of vision; and every believer should seek to the law and testimony for this end. See Ps. 73:16, 17.

3. Meditation, earnest prayer, and withdrawing our minds from things visible and elevating them toward God, are the means in which God reveals himself and his mind from his word to his people in dark times. This was the watch-tower upon which the prophet expected his vision, and upon which saints may expect God's secrets revealed from his scriptures. This lifts us up above the mists in which things below are often covered to our sense, and will help to lead us safe through the delusions which are frequent at such times.

4. Faithful ministers ought to acquit themselves like watchmen in a city or army, to be awake when others sleep, to be watching with God and over the people, seeking after faithful instructions which they may communicate, seeking to be filled from heaven with light and life, that they may pour it out upon his people; and all this especially in hard times, for this the prophet professes to be his practice. "I will stand upon my watch, and set me upon the tower, and will watch to see what he will say and what I shall answer."

5. As the word of the Lord, for most part, gets but evil entertainment in hard times, and as sharp messages meet with hot disputers against their equity, so people's dispositions at such a time will give faithful messengers much to do, and many errands to God. The prophet (besides his own arguings within himself) was beset with reprovers, arguers or quarrelers at these messages, which puts him the more earnestly to "stand and watch, to see," says he, "what I shall answer when I am reproved."

6. Though the Lord's people may have their own debates and faintings between God and them, yet it is their part to smother these as much as they can, and to bring up a good report of God and his way to others; for though the prophet afterwards records the expostulation which he had with God (chap. 1), yet it appears that in the meantime he carried himself before that murmuring people on God's behalf, and that they were arguing and contending with him, and he was "reproved" by them.

Ver. 2. And the Lord answered me and said, Write the vision, and make it plain upon tablets, that he may run who reads it.

The Lord answers his servant attending on him, by giving him a vision, which is afterward revealed (ver. 5); and this vision he is commanded to publish clearly, and make it plain to everyone's capacity, and to affix copies thereof on the gates of the temple or other public places (as is reported to have been their custom) and in such legible characters and plain terms that everyone might without difficulty read and understand it.

1. Though it may seem to be in vain for souls plunged in perplexities to pluck up their loins, and eye and wait on God, yet the experience of the saints proves it to be an enriching trade; for "the Lord answered me," says the prophet, who had waited for an answer from him in his perplexity.

2. It is the will of God that what light or ground of encouragement is given to any in a sad time shall be forthcoming for the good of others; for the prophet is commanded to "write the vision" for the use of the church, which (though it was his duty because of his particular office) may be a pattern for everyone so to act within their station.

3. It is the church's great advantage that in her hard lots she has the mind of God in his word, whereby she may expound his dealing with her, her duty in every case, and what she may expect concerning herself, her troubles, and her troublers; for there is a "vision" here, which the prophet is to "write" for her use.

4. The Lord has seen fit in his deep wisdom and rich love, and for preventing all occasion of delusion, forgery, or misrepresentation, and for helping our forgetfulness and perpetuating his truth in the world, not only to deliver his mind to his church by word of mouth, by himself or by his prophets, but to leave it on record in writing with her. On this she may build her faith as certainly as if God were speaking to her by word, from day to day. Therefore the prophet is commanded to "write the vision," on which the godly were to rest their faith in a hard time.

5. The approved way of publishing God's word is not when it is adorned with wisdom or excellency of words, but when it is delivered in simplicity and plainness, condescending to the capacity of the meanest; for the Lord says, "make it plain upon tablets, that he may run who reads it."

6. The word of God is deposited with the church, not to be read and made use of by some sort of persons only, but indifferently by all the members of the church, and accordingly it is fitted to the capacity of all; for this written vision is not to be hidden up in a strange language and dark

expressions, but to be made "plain upon tablets, that he who runs may read it."

> Ver. 3. For the vision is yet for an appointed time, but at the end it shall speak and not lie. Though it tarry, wait for it, because it will surely come, it will not tarry.

The Lord subjoins a reason to this command (which is also a premonition to the godly, concerning the subsequent message), i.e. that the performance of his decreed vengeance, revealed in this vision, had a prefixed period during which it could not be accomplished, but after which it should certainly come to pass; and therefore the godly were to look much to the clearly revealed vision, and laying aside all fervour and haste, they should patiently wait for the accomplishment, which should be seasonable and timely, however their sense might judge the contrary.

1. As the mercies promised to the church, so also the timing of them is in God's hand. We are not to expect that the performance of comforting promises or threatened vengeance against enemies will be always ready at our call, but must wait the time of the Lord, who has his own seasons for afflicting, trying, and delivering; for "the vision is yet for an appointed time," says the Lord.

2. The Lord's delaying to appear diminishes nothing of the certainty of performance of what he has promised the church or threatened against her enemies; for "the vision has an appointed time," and an end prefixed, so that the exercise will not be perpetual; and at this time "it shall speak," i.e. by performance. Though we undervalue other expressions of it, yet then it shall "speak" to our satisfaction, "and not lie" nor disappoint us, whatever fears we have to the contrary.

3. Such is our weakness, haste, and distrust, that when the Lord delays to perform promises, or what he has foretold in his word, we are ready to think that he denies to do it at all. This is to contradict the scripture's verdict, here published to remove such apprehensions. "Though it tarry, it will surely come."

4. When we do not simply doubt of the certain performance of God's word, yet we must not expect to have sense subscribing to all which faith apprehends concerning God's method in performing; but faith will often see cause to speak in contradictory terms to sense's verdict. "Though it will tarry, it will not tarry," says he. Sense will soon weary and

say the performance tarries, when the Lord does not satisfy its hasty desires; but faith will consider: (a) God's love and wisdom, his holy purposes in filling the cup of the enemies and bringing good to his people out of every delay; (b) Our duty and the exercise of graces we are called to when he delays; (c) That his performances come never out of date, but that still when he comes he makes up all, as if he had come the first hour; and (d) That there is strength enough in God to carry through till deliverance comes (Isa. 40:29-31)-- faith, I say, considering all these, will say, "it will not tarry," but will come in a seasonable and best time.

5. The faith of God's certain and seasonable coming to help his people will enable them patiently to wait for him, without limiting him and without taking a wrong way, for his blessing will be worth waiting for in his own way. The Lord says, "though it tarry, wait for it, because it will surely come, it will not tarry."

6. In a time when the Lord suspends the performance of his word, ministers are so much the more to inculcate and cry up the sure word, neither eating it in because of delays nor speaking according to probabilities; and likewise it is the duty of the godly in such a time to be much engaged in studying the scriptures, to fill their hearts with promises, that they may commend them and be supported by them; for the vision's being "for an appointed time" is a reason why the prophet is commanded to "write the vision and make it plain" (ver. 2).

7. It is a sweet help to make us lean to the word when we study to see Christ in it, somewhat of him held forth and promised in it, and he in whom the promises are yea and amen, engaged for the performance of it. Therefore the apostle, instead of the vision, holds forth Christ, the substance of the thing promised and the party engaged for performance. "He who shall come will come" (Heb. 10:37); this makes this particular promise concerning the Chaldeans applicable to all the difficulties of the church, because Christ is all-sufficient for every need.

> Ver. 4. Behold, his soul, which is lifted up, is not upright in him; but the just shall live by his faith.

The Lord clears his purpose and end in delaying to perform and fulfill the vision, which is to try and reveal who are the lofty and unsound, and who the truly righteous; and so he admonishes all of their hazard in that time of exercise, and informs the truly godly how they may subsist and hold out. Hence learn:

1. Times of God's exercising his church by not appearing for her, are times of severe trial and discovery of unsoundness or hypocrisy; for so does the Lord teach us, that "the lifted up soul and the just" shall both appear in their own true colours, when "the vision is yet for an appointed time."

2. The matter of men's behaviour in a time of trial and temptation is of great importance, and much notice is taken of it by God, as tending much either to his honour or dishonour, and to the promoting of our own peace or disquiet; therefore a "behold" is prefixed to this doctrine.

3. Affliction and trial ought to be an humbling exercise; yet without God's blessing and meeting with corruption, it will reveal and bring forth much pride and high towers of imaginations swelling against God's sovereignty, complaining that he should dispose of us at his pleasure, censuring his way of proceeding with us, conceiving of wisdom and power to secure ourselves better than by waiting on God, etc.; for in this affliction there will be some whose souls are "lifted up."

4. As a proud, murmuring and conceited disposition under trouble reveals men's unsoundness, so it will not long wait on God, but will make apostasy, either from a general profession of being his followers, or from keeping his way, to the use of sinful means. Because of this the Lord does and will testify that he abhors such decliners; for "his soul, which is lifted up, is not upright in him." The apostle, in citing this text (Heb. 10:38) explains that the proud soul will "draw back," and that God's "soul will have no pleasure in him."

5. Though that trial will narrowly sift and reveal the naughtiness of many, yet there are still some who find grace to subsist and get through in hardest times; for in opposition to the former, the Lord subjoins, "but the just shall live."

6. The way of the godly in patient waiting on God in hard times is not a senseless stupidity, hardening themselves in sorrow, but an exercising, feeling, and living way; nor is it a poor and sorry shift, but a comfortable means of subsistence; for "the just shall live"; he shall have a lively exercise and a life of it.

7. Before a man can attain to a comfortable way of bearing trouble and waiting on God in hard times, he must first

make sure of his personal reconciliation and righteousness before God, which will be only when by faith he lays hold on Christ's righteousness offered in the gospel. He must first be "just," and that "by faith," and then he "shall live by faith" in trouble, as it is expounded (Rom. 1:17; Gal. 3:11).

8. The man who is just and righteous by faith in Christ shall not only live a life of grace by dwelling constantly under the shadow of imputed righteousness (by which he is hid from death and wrath), and by drawing life and virtue out of Christ to quicken his heart and to enable him to perform every good word and work; but also his faith will carry him through the snares of prosperity, and through hardest dispensations, without apostasy or fainting. The righteous man does not walk by present sense, but by faith takes up God as his Father in Christ; he studies all the promises made to saints in every condition, and magnifies the truth of them; he sees God his Father to be the carver of all his and the church's lots, and that every condition is useful, and has a blessing in it to the godly, and that waiting on God is the sure path to a blessed issue; and he finds now and then God's presence sensibly with his spirit. While the godly man is thus exercised, he cannot but have a good life, and be hidden from the blasts of temptations, with which others are assailed and blown over. "The just shall live by faith"; his faith shall afford him a life in hardest times and provide for him in wildernesses.

9. Many may be believing in Christ and so born again, though they cannot yet discern faith in themselves; yet those who expect righteousness through faith in Christ, and by faith to be thus supported in evil times, should study the reality and sincerity of their faith, that it is not a notion or fancy, but real, and such as they have a sure hold of. It is "by faith" that "the just shall live," a faith which he has made sure he has. And for this end we ought to study exactly the nature of faith, that neither the presumptuously secure nor the fainting soul may mistake their own case.

> Ver. 5. Yea also, because he transgresses by wine, he is a proud man; neither does he keep at home; who enlarges his desire as hell, and is as death, and cannot be satisfied, but gathers unto him all nations and heaps upon him all people.

Now, to the end of the chapter, follows the vision itself, concerning the destruction which was to come upon the

Chaldeans, propounded for the most part in general description of God's vengeance upon gross and impenitent sinners, such as the Chaldeans were. The Lord threatens wrath and sad judgments to come upon them for their gross abominations, such as ambition, covetousness, oppression, sensuality, carnal policy, and idolatry. He lays out this controversy in several branches, sometimes repeating the same things in substance and amplifying them from several considerations, to the end that there may be a more distinct and clear sight of the sinfulness of their sin, of the vanity of the pretences they founded their courses on, and of the equity of God's judgments subjoined to every branch.

The first branch of the controversy is that the Chaldeans, especially their king, being given to sensuality and ambition, or drunk with pride and ambition as with wine, was insatiable in his conquests, like death and hell, or the grave (of which see Prov. 30:15, 16; Isa. 5:14); and, not being content with his own portion, did labour to add one kingdom after another to his dominions. Hence learn:

1. As the godly's honest wrestling through an evil time by faith is an evidence that God will reckon with their oppressors, so the Lord's reproving and punishing the apostasy of any within the church may assure men that he will not spare wicked enemies. For this is subjoined to what was said (ver. 4) with a "yea, also" or "how much more," importing that when he made the just to live by faith, he would also reckon with the Chaldeans; and if he revealed and made bare the puffed up soul, how much more the Chaldeans. See Jer. 25:29; 1 Pet. 4:17, 18.

2. The most part of unrenewed great men's actions and enterprises are consecrated to the service of their vile lusts; for "because he transgresses by wine, and is proud, he keeps not at home." His great enterprises are undertaken to satisfy sensuality and ambition.

3. Men once enslaved to the service of their lusts do become brutish, and in a manner renounce their very reason; for so may the words also be read. "The proud man transgresses as through wine"; he is drunk with ambition as with wine, which deprives men of the use of sense and reason.

4. It is a sin flowing from ambition, and a violence offered to nature (which is content with little), when men cannot acquiesce in their lot and portion assigned them by God, especially when it is so full, but do by all means hunt after more. It was the Chaldean king's sin and ambition, that having a kingdom, yet he "keeps not at home."

5. It is the Lord's judgment upon ambitious men that the more they go beyond bounds to satisfy their lusts, the more they become insatiable; the more they drink, the more they are thirsty. Such a one "enlarges his desire as hell, and is as death, and cannot be satisfied, but gathers unto him all nations, and heaps to him all people."

> Ver. 6. Shall not all these take up a parable against him, and a taunting proverb against him, and say, Woe to him that increases that which is not his; how long? and to him who lades himself with thick clay.

The Lord threatens that because of these their sins, his judgments should make them contemptible and matter of derision. Even those whom they had oppressed should insult over them and mock them, and declare them accursed in their unlawful conquests (which, though they had groaned under them, could not long remain) and in their overcharging and burdening themselves with the dross of this world.

1. Even the consciences of wicked men, if they were awake or allowed to speak, would give out doom and sentence upon them, and subscribe to the righteousness of God's judgments; for here he appeals to themselves, "shall not all these take up a parable?" So also ver. 7.

2. When men sinfully endeavour to satisfy their pride and ambition, it is righteous with God to make them most contemptible and ignominious; for the proud man (ver. 5) meets with "a parable and taunting proverb," or becomes an object of public derision.

3. Though the oppressed and subdued may seem to be far behind with conquerors and oppressors, yet the Lord will in due time clear that there is but little cause for such an apprehension. Greatest oppressors will meet with their own stroke, in which the lowest may insult over them, and they shall be rather the object of pity than of envy; for "all these (i.e. the nations subdued by him, ver. 5, and those who were sorest smitten) shall take up a parable against him, and a taunting proverb against him, and say, Woe unto him." See Isa. 14:4-12.

4. As unjust conquest gives a man no right to his purchase, so it brings on God's curse, and at last makes the purchaser an object of derision. "Woe" here may be taken both as an insulting expression and a declaration of a curse upon him. "Woe to him (or 'woe he,' by way of triumphing

over him and laughing at him) who increases that which is
not his."

5. Though the oppressed ordinarily groan under the oppressor, amazed at God's patience toward him, yet it may
be concluded that oppression shall not continue as long as
either the oppressed or oppressor might expect, and that
disappointment of the oppressor's hopes of continuance
shall be matter of derision. All this is imported in that
part of the proverb, "how long?"

6. Though oppressors promise to themselves much ease,
contentment, pleasure, and happiness in their great enjoyments, yet they are miserably disappointed; for riches are
in themselves but base, and great abundance of them beyond
what is needful is to the ambitious a burden and cause of
vexation, drawing down the soul from God, and entangling
and polluting it; and this may point out the misery of those
who hunt so much after these things. "Woe to him who lades
himself with thick clay," that is, base riches, which do but
burden, pollute, and entangle him.

> Ver. 7. Shall they not rise up suddenly, those who shall
> bite you? and those awake who shall vex you? And you
> shall be for booty unto them.
>
> 8. Because you have spoiled many nations, all the
> remnant of the people shall spoil you; because of men's
> blood, and for the violence of the land, of the city, and
> all who dwell therein.

The Lord yet declares his mind concerning these sins,
and threatens yet further that he will pay them as they had
served others. As the Chaldeans had ranged up and down the
world like ravenous beasts, so he would suddenly raise up
the Medes and Persians, who at present were little noticed,
to trouble, devour, and prey upon them (ver. 7). And as they
had robbed and spoiled many nations, so he would stir up
the remnant of the nations (either those who had been reserved from their fury, or the remainder of the nations
which they had ruined, who should join with their enemies)
to prey on them. In all this the righteousness of God would
appear, in requiting them for their bloodshed and the great
desolation they brought on cities and countries wherever
they came, and the havoc made of the inhabitants, and especially for what they had done to Jerusalem, Judea, and
the Jews (ver. 8).

1. The Lord's judgments on impenitent sinners come un-expectedly, and when they least imagine, and often by instru-ments little thought of until God raises them up and employs them. "They shall rise up suddenly and awake," to bite and vex. They may seem to be asleep and sit very quiet, and yet shall do this work, being employed of God.

2. Oppressors will be made in due time disciples at their own school, and be made to feel themselves what sad strokes they had inflicted on others, and will be dealt with as they had dealt with others. These preying beasts shall be "bitten and vexed," or brought into inextricable difficulties; and they who "spoiled many nations shall be for booty" and be spoiled.

3. Though oppressors prove invincible as long as God permits them to execute his vengeance, yet when their day comes they shall be as feeble as any; for the Chaldeans, who before had no more to do than come and gather spoil, are now themselves for booty to their enemies, who spoil them as easily as they had spoiled others.

4. Though oppressors dream that they have under their feet all who could harm them, so that none dare open the mouth or move the wing or peep, yet the Lord has a scourge ready when he pleases, to avenge himself upon them; for "all the remnant of the people shall spoil you," says the Lord. He has either nations hidden from their fury, whom they think not worth their anger, or the very remnants of spoiled nations, who if he employ them will do their turn.

5. When the Lord announces or executes his judgments on bloody oppressors, it is useful to study much his contro-versy against them, that we may gather his judgments aright, may adore the righteousness of God, and may learn from their example to abhor all violent and bloody courses, especially against God's people, which he so severely pun-ishes. Therefore he subjoins that all this is "because of men's blood, for the violence of the land, of the city, and of all who dwell therein," which is to be understood with special relation to Judah.

> Ver. 9. Woe to him who covets an evil covetousness to his house, that he may set his nest on high, that he may be delivered from the power of evil.

The second branch of God's controversy (held forth in general terms) is that out of a desire to build stately palaces (as the Chaldean did, Dan. 4:29, 30) or to the end that they might establish themselves and their prosperity in perpetual greatness and wealth, and be exempted from the common miseries of mankind, they are extremely and sinfully covetous, for which the Lord pronounces them accursed.

1. The certainty of God's judgments on particular sinners and enemies may be read from general denunciations against such sins, for it is agreeable to the rule of justice that all who do such things should be so punished. Therefore the Lord accuses and threatens the Chaldeans in a general sentence, "woe to him who covets," that it may appear how agreeable to justice his sentence against them is, and that every sinner in after-times may put in his own name, as if he were the man pointed at.

2. It is a plague on wicked men when they are given up to imagine that their prosperous condition shall never change, but that they shall be able to secure it for them and theirs forever. This is the prospering wicked man's thought, which brings him to woe, that he will "set his nest on high," as birds do to secure themselves and their young ones, and will "be delivered from the power of evil." See Ps. 49:11.

3. Men's vain imaginations and their apprehension of that which will never be, and in which all others have failed, often proves a great snare to engage them in courses which otherwise they might see to be not only sinful, but needless and foolish. Because the worldly man thinks that he can secure uncertain riches to him and his, and can guard against any emergent evils to which men are condemned for sin, therefore "he covets an evil covetousness, that he may set his nest on high," and uses any means which he thinks will make his lie prove a truth.

4. Though men may lawfully, yea and should in duty endeavour the good of their posterity, even in external things, and though they may study to prevent inconveniences which may confront them, yet this endeavour proves sinful when it either arises from or tends to greediness and covetousness, or ensnares men by drawing them to use sinful means. "Woe to him who covets an evil covetousness," though it were even for "his house," or "that he may set his nest on high."

5. Let it be enough to deter men from courses, that the word declares them to be sinful and a curse to follow them; for so does the word import here, that it is "an evil covetousness," and "woe is to him who covets it"; therefore men should be far from it.

Ver. 10. You have consulted shame to your house, by cutting off many people, and have sinned against your soul.
11. For the stone shall cry out of the wall, and the beam out of the timber shall answer it.

The Lord expounds his own pronounced woe, and threatens that these their projects should tend to the ignominy of their family; for it is just that they should be so dealt with, for they ruin so many to build up themselves, and sell their souls to make up their outward estate (ver. 10); and though there should be none who dared complain of them, yet the very materials of their buildings should witness against them, that they were acquired by robbery, and should in a sort of music (heard by God's justice) cry for vengeance (ver. 11). Hence learn:

1. Though covetous oppressors often carry themselves in great state, as the only honourable of the earth, yet their way is in itself shameful, and will end in ignominy. "You have counselled shame to your house."

2. Men who prosecute their designs by unlawful means readily fall into the snare which they would most gladly escape; for the Chaldean, seeking to set his house on high, not only covets "evil to his house," (ver. 9), but even brings "shame," which he seeks to avoid, to it.

3. There needs no more to pull down the family of the oppressor than his way of making it great. His very building, his nest is a plague to it, and enough to make it totter; for thereby he "consults shame" to it. He could do no more if he bent his wits to ruin it.

4. The projects of men who lean to their own wit for gaining their ends, and neglect piety or waiting on God for counsel, will prove shameful and sinful. Men who lean to their own wits will find that their most serious consultations will leave them in the mire; "you have consulted shame to your house," says the Lord.

5. It is a high degree of impiety and a clear presage of ruin, when a man in managing his affairs casts off all his love to his neighbours, and not only minds himself only, but thinks nothing of others, and does not hesitate to rise upon their ruin or to cut them off, though ever so many, if he think it may tend to his advantage. "You have consulted shame to your house by cutting off many people."

6. As men for the most part neglect their souls when they are mad upon their worldly designs, so it is a dangerous case when it is so, and it will prove a poor bargain in

the end, when men have gained ever so much and yet "have sinned against their soul," which the Lord here not only uses as a challenge but declares it as a judgment on the Chaldean.

7. Sin and guilt will pursue and find out the sinner, and will of itself call for vengeance, though all the world should be silent and not challenge him; for "the stone will cry out of the wall, and the beam out of the timber shall answer it."

> Ver. 12. Woe to him who builds a town with blood, and
> establishes a city by iniquity.

The third branch of the controversy points chiefly at the way of their prosecuting their covetous and ambitious ends, which was (as one sin usually comes not alone, but draws other sins with it) by oppression, cutting off of people, and other unjust ways. This course the Lord pronounces to be accursed, though they gilded it over with pretences of public good, or pretended that thereby they endeavoured to protect and settle their civil state.

1. The Lord looks much unto the dispositions of men, by the means which they use in pursuing an end, whether the means be right or wrong in itself; for he charges them here that they carried on their work "with blood and by iniquity."

2. Pretence of public good and zeal to advance the state and government is one of the fig-leaves with which men think to cover their oppression and make it plausible; but in vain, for "woe to him who builds a town with blood, and establishes a city by iniquity."

3. Though all oppressions are not equally horrid in themselves, and though men readily account themselves good enough when they do not go to the length they might, or which others go to in that sin, yet the Lord will pursue with vengeance the fairest way of oppression men can take, as being sinful in itself, and sometimes being more cruel in its lingering way than the most violent oppression in hot blood. "Woe to him who establishes a city by iniquity," no matter what iniquity it be, as well as "to him who builds a city with blood."

> Ver. 13. Behold, is it not of the Lord of hosts, that the
> people shall labour in the very fire, and the people
> shall weary themselves for very vanity?

The Lord explains this woe, and declares that he should himself appear against them, in making all their endeavours to establish themselves (in which they employed many nations and had much toil, as in a fiery furnace, every head being made bald in their wars, Ezek. 29:18) to prove not only vain and to no purpose, but to tend also to their own prejudice. As one whose work is cast into the fire loses both his material and his labour, and endangers himself by following to get it rescued, so should they perish in their hunting after wealth, and with it. See the same threatening, Jer. 51:58.

1. When men take sinful ways to prosecute their designs, they may meet with much toil and vexation in their work, as an earnest of further judgment. "The people (that is, the Chaldeans and many instruments employed by them) labour and weary themselves."

2. The utmost of men's endeavours shall not promote nor perfect a work which God is against, nor uphold what he has a mind to overthrow; for though they "labour and weary themselves," yet it shall be "for very vanity," and to no purpose.

3. Those who seek by bloody oppression to exalt and es-' tablish themselves, shall not only lose their labour, but shall incur further damage by their attempt, and lose themselves, their work, and the materials which they had to begin their work upon; for the Chaldeans "shall labour in the very fire," which shall not only breed them toil and pain in labouring, but shall devour all their conquests, themselves, and the kingdom of Babel, which they had when they began their tyranny.

4. The Lord will so order his judgments upon violent oppressors that his hand shall be visibly and remarkably seen by all, to be the inflicter of them, and he shall prove himself omnipotent by frustrating men in their wicked purposes and consuming all their labours. "Behold, is it not of the Lord of hosts, that the people shall labour in the very fire?"

Ver. 14. For the earth shall be filled with the knowledge of the glory of the Lord, as the waters cover the sea.

The Lord subjoins a reason for this sentence, showing how he would be much seen in this judgment. Though he seemed to let his own name and glory be obscured when he allowed the Chaldeans to oppress the world and lead his people into captivity, yet in due time he would make his glory so conspicuous in their just destruction and in his powerful asserting of Judah's liberty, that the nations should be filled with the knowledge thereof, as the sea is full of water. And all this is a type and pledge of the glory to be revealed in Christ, and the knowledge of his name to be then communicated. Hence learn:

1. When oppressors prosper, and the Lord's people with the rest of the world are brought into bondage by them, the Lord's glory is engaged for his appearing against them in due time; for it is subjoined as a reason of the Chaldeans' evil success: "the earth shall be filled with the knowledge of the glory of the Lord."

2. The greatness of oppressors contributes to illustrate and set forth the glory of God in bringing them down, and therefore it is rather an argument why the Lord should destroy them than a hindrance to it; for when he does so, "the earth shall be filled with the knowledge of the glory of the Lord." See Ps. 9:16.

3. As God is most glorious in himself, so he will make his glory to shine in the deliverance of his people, though for a time he allows them to be in bondage; for in bringing back Judah at the ruin of Babylon, "the earth shall be filled with the knowledge of the glory of the Lord." See Ps. 126:2.

4. All the glorious manifestations of God against his enemies, and for his people of old, were but shadows of what he manifested and does manifest in and by Christ in the latter days; and any effects of these works which appeared among his people, or the Gentiles, were but a taste of what the glory of God, shining in Christ and made known to the world by the gospel, should produce among Jews and Gentiles. Therefore this prophecy is applied to the days of the gospel (Isa. 11:9), as getting then full accomplishment.

> Ver. 15. Woe unto him who gives his neighbour drink, who puts your bottle to him and makes him drunken also, that you may look on their nakedness.

The fourth branch of the controversy, if we take it properly, holds forth a denunciation of vengeance to come upon them for their beastly luxury and sensuality, usual in the Babylonish court; and that not only in their own persons, but that they drew one another to drunkenness, so that they might mock at their infirmities, which they could not hide in their nakedness (as did Noah, Gen. 9:21, 22), or that they might abuse one another in an unnatural way through their drunkenness. And so it teaches:

1. When men abuse their prosperity to luxury, it is an evidence of a curse upon them and it; so it was with the Chaldeans. "Woe to him who gives his neighbour drink," as having no other end for his oppression of the world than thus to abuse himself and others.

2. Sin has come to a great neight, and is near a curse, when men entice and draw others to the same excess of riot with themselves. "Woe to him who puts your bottle to him, and makes him drunken also."

3. It is a beastly disposition to take pleasure in making men abuse themselves by drink, for a woe is denounced against it. Nor is it a mark of any true kindness, as the profane reckon, but is done "that they may look on their nakedness" and bring it out to open view.

4. Intemperance is an usher to let in any other vice. When a man is drunk, revealing or "looking on nakedness" will not be accounted shameful, nor unnatural filthiness an abomination.

But the words may also be taken figuratively, and so the scope is to tax them for their endeavours, by public practices and false promises, to engage their neighbours in their undertakings. As they were drunk with ambition themselves, so they filled their neighbours with the same principles and drunken hopes of sharing in their victories; though indeed they intended nothing else than, if any inconvenience should befall their confederates, to despise them, or to be ready themselves, upon occasion, to bring them into slavery and make them base. Thus does the whore make the world drunk with the wine of her idolatrous cup (Rev. 17), and thus did Nineveh entice the world with her whoredom and witchcrafts (Nahum 3:4). This interpretation teaches:

1. Great men in the world are ordinarily so infatuated with their hopes and projects that like drunken men they reel, and cannot be sober nor ruled by sound principles. The Chaldeans are thus drunken, and they "make their neighbours drunken also," as well as themselves.

2. Carnal policy and interest is the greatest steersman of human affairs among men, and it frequently brings a curse upon those who use it. "Woe to him who thus gives his neighbour drink."

3. No true kindness can be expected from men who walk politically, and who upon interests of state pretend whatever they will. All that they do to others is done so "that they may look on their nakedness."

> Ver. 16. You are filled with shame for glory; drink also, and let your foreskin be uncovered. The cup of the Lord's right hand shall be turned to you, and shameful spewing shall be on your glory.

Whatever way we expound the challenge, the Lord's judgment is very equitable, that all these courses should tend rather to their ignominy than to their honor. As they had been butlers to draw others to sensuality, and to intoxicate and allure them to join their oppressions of the church and the world, so the Lord would bring about the cup of his wrath to them, and make them drink of it to satiety, whereby they should be as contemptible as when a drunken man is lying naked, and with his uncircumcised foreskin (which was an abomination to the Jews) uncovered, or when he is polluting all his bravery or stately house with his filthy vanity.

1. The sinful courses which men follow to advance their greatness would appear most ignominious to a clear discerner, and will at last be seen to be so, to the conviction of all; for "you are filled with shame for glory," says the Lord.

2. The measuring of all afflictions and judgments is in God's hand, so that none can add to them or diminish from them, nor get them shifted when God lays them on. Therefore they are called a "cup," which is a set measure, and "the cup of the Lord's right hand," which is irresistibly powerful. See Jer. 25:15-18.

3. The Lord will at last bring the storm of vengeance upon the head of wicked men, who were instruments to execute it upon others. As they drink last of the cup, and therefore are nearer the dregs, and since they were often outside the church (as the uncircumcised) and so without God, their stroke shall be more eminently ignominious than any others; for when "the cup of the Lord's right hand is turned to them (after others have drunk of it, Jer. 25:26), then they shall drink, and their foreskins shall be uncovered, and shameful spewing shall be on their glory."

> Ver. 17. For the violence of Lebanon shall cover you, and the spoil of beasts which made them afraid, because of

men's blood, and for the violence of the land, of the city, and of all who dwell therein.

To clear the equity of all these judgments, the Lord subjoins and recapitulates his controversy, threatening that the Chaldeans shall be overwhelmed for the violence done to the land of Israel, bordering upon Lebanon, or the Temple made of the wood of Lebanon; yea, and for the very destruction of that forest, and for spoiling and frightening the beasts there as they came through, and cut down the timber for the siege of Jerusalem; and for their beastly and bloody violence upon the inhabitants of every city and country where they came, especially in Judea.

Or it may be thus interpreted: as in the forest of Lebanon beasts are hunted, frightened, or destroyed, so should they be pursued and ruined because of their horrid cruelty and violence, and so it is the same in substance with ver. 7, 8.

1. It is necessary that we study over and over again the Lord's controversy with impenitent sinners, that we may adore his equity in punishing, and tremble at his severity in so much insisting to punish for sin; for therefore are their sins repeated and the threatenings renewed.

2. Those who, like brute beasts, trouble and vex all the creatures, and make havoc of all wherever they come, and do especially oppress the people of God, those may expect to be dealt with accordingly. Without repentance they shall be irrecoverably destroyed; for so do these words, taking in both expositions, teach us: they shall be "covered" or overwhelmed with the calamity, for their violence against the creatures and the church (see Isa. 14:6-8), and for their violence they shall be hunted and pursued as wild beasts (whom they resembled in actions) are pursued by hunters.

> Ver. 18. What profits the graven image, that its maker has graven it; the molten image, and a teacher of lies, that the maker of his work trusts in it, to make dumb idols?

The last part of the controversy (held forth also in general terms) is their idolatry, and particularly their making of idols and images to represent what they acknowledged as a deity, and to be worshipped in that religious state. The vanity of this he proves from idols' unprofitableness and inability to teach anything of God; for though their makers take much pains on them, and when they have done, trust in them and set them up above men in God's place, yet they have no authority so to do.

1. Few of those who receive greatest things of this world from God acknowledge him for them, but rather follow idols to his dishonour, and in defiance of him. So did the Chaldeans do, as is imported here; and so do the most part of Adam's posterity.

2. In a time when idolaters prevail, and the true church is brought to bondage by them, it is necessary to study well the vanity of idolatry, and to set it out to the world, to the end that neither may the wicked dream of being exempted from vengeance by their idols, nor may the godly stumble at the prosperity of those who follow them; for to these ends does the doctrine of the vanity of idols tend.

3. Besides fearful idolatry committed in the world by men's taking for their god that which is no god (of which charge none can be free who perform religious worship, due to God only, to any creature whatever), the world is also guilty of idolatries by making idols or images, for representing an invisible God or object of their worship, be what it will, and by worshipping them in that religious state and relation. This is what is expressly reproved in the Chaldeans here, that they not only accounted that to be their god which was no god, but that they had "graven images" and "molten images"; not that they acknowledged these to be their gods, but they were represented by them, and their gods were to be worshipped in and through these images. This challenge is expressed in general terms, so that all may be reproved who make use of such devices in religious worship, be the ultimate and last object of their worship what it will.

4. Whatever conceit men may have of images, as useful in many ways for exciting them and keeping them in remembrance of a deity, yet upon narrow search it will be found that they are unprofitable, if not pernicious, as everything in worship proves which is not instituted by God; for he puts it to any unbiased conscience to tell, "what profits the graven image?"

5. The origin and authors of images prove the vanity of putting them in any religious state; since it has a maker among men, "what does it profit?" It cannot be God (Hos. 8:6), and though its maker gave it a being and has graven it curiously, yet he has no authority to command it to be worshipped, nor can such an author make it bless the worshippers. And it is "folly" in the maker "to trust therein";

yea, it sufficiently disgraces any point of religion, that it is of man's making or devising.

6. Though men commend images as books for the ignorant, by which they may be helped to take up a deity, yet they can teach or represent nothing of God as he is revealed in his word, and do imprint false and carnal conceptions of a deity; for "the molten image is a teacher of lies."

7. Though those who use images to represent a deity, do imagine that they do not rest upon the representation but ascend by it to the thing represented, yet here their heart deceives them. Whatever they pretend in their thoughts, yet practically they honour them as their god, and whatever they pretend to offer to God in and by them is expounded by God as offered really unto them; for "the maker of his work," though he might have made any other thing of the materials, "trusts therein."

8. Those who worship graven images do proclaim their own brutishness, and that they are as great blocks as these which they adore, when they exalt that which is below themselves to be above themselves and in God's place; for what a brutishness it is in man, endued with sense and reason, "to make himself dumb idols," which have no sense at all.

> Ver. 19. Woe to him who says to the wood, Awake; to the dumb stone, Arise, it shall teach. Behold, it is laid over with gold and silver, and there is no breath at all in the midst of it.

Upon what has been said, the Lord denounces a woe upon those who implore idols for help or direction. However curiously they are formed, yet their vile matter remains still the same; nor can the artificer's skill put life into them to move themselves, far less to help others.

1. Image worshippers proclaim their own wretchedness, in that they are given up to a reprobate sense, void of discerning; and many sorrowful disappointments shall befall those who expect a remedy from them in hard cases; and in the end they shall be confounded by God, who will not give his praise of being an helper and director of the children of men, to graven images. "Woe unto him who says to the wood, Awake; to the dumb stone, Arise, it shall teach."

2. Though the vanity of worshipping idols and images be palpably gross, so that seriously to consider it is sufficient to refute it; yet such is man's stupidity, when he delights not to retain God in his knowledge, that he needs stirring up to

take notice of the error of his way. Though a little thought reveals that their idol is "wood and stone," and that "there is no breath in the midst of it," and consequently that it is vain to worship it, yet man must be called to "behold" this, and must have it often pointed out to him.

3. Outward pomp and splendor in the exercise of religion, though it be pleasant to natural hearers, is yet not the thing God looks to, but he observes how his own prescribed rule is followed, and what reality there is in such show. For he says, "their idol is laid over with gold and silver, and yet there is no breath at all in its midst."

> Ver. 20. But the Lord is in his holy temple; let all the earth keep silence before him.

In opposition to the vanity of idols, the true God is commended. He dwells in heaven, and manifests himself in the church by the signs of his presence, of his own appointing, and by prescribing rules of his own worship, whose authority and greatness is such that they make all the world give over their disputing for idols, and submit to his doctrine; and it may cause them to stand in awe to come in opposition to him, or to wrong his people when they are scattered among them.

1. The consideration of the vanity of idols and misery of idol worshippers, ought to commend the true God to his church, and set out their own happiness; for they have him not only reigning in heaven, but in the midst of them, and they know how to serve him acceptably according to his will. Therefore it is subjoined to what has been said, "but the Lord is in his holy temple."

2. The authority of the true God, and his presence among his people, if seriously thought upon, will call for much reverence, will silence all debates against his revealed will, and may terrify men from being in opposition to him or his people; for "the Lord is in his holy temple; let all the earth keep silence before him," where silence is the badge of their reverencing his majesty and authority. See Job 29:9.

CHAPTER III

The prophet has heard God's mind concerning both the church and the Chaldeans. In this chapter he expresses his exercise upon that which had been revealed to him, by a meditation or prayer, penned for the edification and direction of the church in the times they were to meet with (ver. 1). Out of his deep apprehension and fear of the approaching stroke, having prayed for preservation and moderation of severity in the captivity, till the time foretold for their deliverance should come (ver. 2), he gathers grounds of faith that there should be a deliverance from their future captivity, from the Lord's glorious manifestations of old for his people, in carrying them from Egypt through the wilderness, to the possession of the promised land, and settling and securing them in it (ver. 3-15). He then changes his style, and instead of praying he records his expectation that present fears will end in future confidence (ver. 16), and he glories in the hope of preservation and deliverance (ver. 17-19). In testimony of this, he commends his meditation to be sung with joy (ver. 19).

Ver. 1. A prayer of Habakkuk the prophet upon Sigionoth.

The inscription of this exercise holds forth the prophet's scope, which is to per a prayer to God with reference to the ensuing calamities, such a prayer (as the word signifies) as is made by a supplicant to a judge. Because it was penned in meter for the help of memory, therefore the tune is prescribed, "on Sigionoth." Though the clear signification of this be uncertain, yet that which is most likely is that the prayer was indited in a mixed meter, and was to be sung with variable tunes and instruments fitted accordingly.

1. When the Lord's people abuse their privileges, they may be put to plead for them before the Lord's tribunal by prayer, and be content to hold fast by faith to those things which sometimes they had full possession of. Habakkuk and the church are put to pray for their very being, and to deprecate the total ruin of God's work.

2. It is the duty of all in a time of imminent or incumbent judgments, to stir up themselves and others, in their stations, to get the spirit of prayer, so that being exercised in religious duties, they may be kept from declining or fainting, and may be preserved from the senseless stupidity which usually attends such times (Ezek. 24:23). Therefore the prophet by his example stirs up, and by this public form (prescribed by the spirit of God, and therefore lawful) directs the Jews how to employ themselves in their captivity.

3. The people of God are not to expect that their prayers will always be in one form under trouble; for as their exercise will be various, in fearing, believing, trembling,

rejoicing, etc., so their prayers may begin low, rise high, fall low, and rise high again. This may be gathered from the nature of the meter in which the prayer is penned, or the tune to which it was sung, called "Sigionoth," or "variable"; as of one wandering here and there, and not keeping one way. This appears further in the prayer itself, or the prophet's subsequent exercise, and such variety makes the comfort and melody of that spiritual exercise more sweet.

> Ver. 2. O Lord, I have heard thy speech, and was afraid;
> O Lord, revive thy work in the midst of the years; in
> the midst of the years make known; in wrath remember
> mercy.

This verse contains what is properly the prophet's prayer in this exercise. Being afraid of God's threatened and imminent judgment of the captivity (to which he submits without further contending), he prays that the Lord would not allow his church nor his work to come to nothing by their captivity, but that he would during that time keep in their life by undeserved tokens of his favour, until he should deliver; and notwithstanding their sins, which had procured wrath, that he would magnify his mercy toward them.

1. When judgments are threatened against the church, though she may believe the Lord's love in them, and that she is the Lord's whatever may come, yet threatened trouble ought to be an exercise unto her. It should make her humble herself under God's threatening hand, and tremble to deal with such a bitter cup. "O Lord," says he, "I have heard thy speech," to wit, concerning the captivity, "and was afraid." Both the majesty of the speaker and the matter of the speech frightened him.

2. Prayer to God is the kindly vent of all the fears of the godly, without which fear might readily crush them; and by it the thing feared is either removed, or blessed and made more easy and comfortable unto them. But prayer will not speak well in trouble where there is not some sense of God's word threatening, or of his hand striking at the root of it; for the prophet, being afraid, subjoins, "O Lord, revive," as the issue of his fear, and as being a suitable and fit time and disposition for prayer.

3. When the Lord has disclosed his purpose concerning his people's being in trouble, it is the duty of the godly to submit without contending, and to forbear it until God's prefixed time of deliverance shall come. The prophet

presupposes that the appointed "years" of the church's captivity were yet to come, and does not quarrel as formerly, but prays that the church may be helped and borne through that time. This is a way to make many a cross easy, which our quarreling makes insupportable. See Jer. 29:5, 6.

4. The people of God are sometimes left to lie under a long continued tract of trouble, so that they may be narrowly tried, and have much sorrow to repay with joy (Ps. 90:15); for this trouble did endure for "years," even seventy of them.

5. Besides the Lord's general relation to all his creatures, as his handiwork, he has a peculiar relation to his church and people. Their calling to be his people, and their building up and establishment in that privilege, is his own peculiar work, and among them his elect are made anew by him in a new work of redemption and regeneration, so that they become "new creatures," the work of his hands (Isa. 45:11), and in the midst of them also he has a work of his ordinances and kingdom, to be preserved and carried on. Therefore the church ought to acknowledge this relation, and to consider all she has as given by him, and to make his work the matter of her chief care in trouble; and this interest endears the Lord's people to him, and is a reason why he will not let them go to ruin and so lose all that he himself has done. Thus the prophet reasons, "revive thy work."

6. The Lord's people and work may by reason of long and sore captivity, and possible desertion accompanying it, be reduced to such extremities that all may seem to be in peril of ruin, and the faith of the godly in peril of giving over. There may be such low ebbs that the godly may be put to pray, "O Lord, revive," or "preserve alive."

7. The Lord both can and will preserve his work and people, who wait on him, from ruin, and that in the midst of extremities; and the Lord's doing this ought to be much esteemed. Therefore the prophet, resolving on captivity, makes it his suit which he has warrant and ground of hope to ask, and whose granting will be refreshing, though otherwise trouble be pressing: "O Lord, revive thy work in the midst of the years."

8. It is a very refreshing dispensation, and one which the people of God have warrant to look for, that the Lord will season and sweeten their times of trouble with some evidences of his favour, either in their bosoms or by some tokens for good in his providence. Therefore the prophet is directed to pray further, "in the midst of the years make

known," i.e. his former favour, by some manifestation. And he was answered in the Lord's raising up prophets to them in Babylon, and by raising up the head of their king about the middle of the years of their captivity (2 Kings 25:27-31) as a pledge of their future liberation, and by other favours bestowed upon them.

9. As the Lord's proceeding in wrath against his people would undo them, so the apprehension of God's just anger against them for their sins is a great hindrance to them in their prayers. Therefore the prophet, when he thinks of God's wrath, is made to cut off his prayer abruptly, that he may run and turn the wrath away. "Make known," says he, not saying what; "in wrath remember mercy."

10. Despite the Lord's just indignation against sin, he will not forget mercy nor deal in strict justice, without all moderation, to his afflicted people; and this may give warrant to all who are sensible of sin and wrath, to flee to his free favour, and to pray with the prophet, "in wrath remember mercy." And it further teaches all to magnify God when this prayer is answered in any way, and that God mixes a cup of wrath with any mercy or moderation.

> Ver. 3. God came from Teman, and the holy one from mount Paran. Selah. His glory covered the heavens, and the earth was full of his praise.
> 4. And his brightness was as the light; he had horns coming out of his hand, and there was the hiding of his power.

In order to strengthen his own and the godly's faith, in assurance of an answer to his prayer, the prophet gathers together several grounds upon which he expects it. These are taken from the manifestations of God in delivering his people from Egypt, in carrying them through the wilderness and settling them in the promised land; and he expects by faith that the Lord (being unchangeable, still the same, and the people still his) would repeat these in their future delivery. And so he lifts up his heart above all difficulties in the captivity, which might impede their restitution, as looking to what had been done as pledges of what God would do, before his word failed or his people perished.

God's glorious manifestations of old, among and for his people, are branched out in several particulars. The first (agreeing much with Deut. 33:2) is the Lord's manifestation of himself on mount Sinai, at the giving of the law, and on the hills adjacent in the desert. He marched before his people, as their confederate God, in glory and majesty, insomuch that the splendor filled heaven and earth, and was as bright as any light. And though rays like horns, which shined forth from his hands or sides when he appeared, did point out his power, yet they did so but darkly, as a veil cast over his glorious power, for his power is in itself so incomprehensible that the light could not be steadfastly looked upon by the infirm eyes of man.

1. It is a thriving way in prayer, not only to put up desires to God, but to gather arguments by which to confirm our own faith, which will make us cheerful in prayer, and quiet after we have done our duty. Therefore, though all this exercise is called "prayer" (ver. 1), yet after a short suit (ver. 2) the prophet makes his chief work a study of arguments for faith. See 1 John 5:14, 15.

2. The church is a storehouse of experience for a time of need. She has treasures of instances of what God has already done, ready to be repeated again in a new extremity. The prophet here repeats works done of old, which he looks upon as pledges of the like in this new perplexity.

3. God's glorious manifestations of himself in and for his church, ought to be joined with a consideration of his holiness; and his glory and splendor ought to set out his perfection in purity, that the church may fall in love with it and study conformity to it; for appearing thus, he is "God the holy one."

4. The Lord's glory among his people may shine brightly in a wilderness, which will not obscure it when he lets it out. All this glory shined in the barren deserts of Teman, or "the south," which is a part of Seir, or Edom (Obad. 9; Amos 1:12; Deut. 33:2; Judg. 5:4), and mount Paran, a place also near Seir (Gen. 14:6) where Ishmael lived (Gen. 21:21), and where Israel encamped shortly after they came from Sinai (Numb. 10:12; Numb. 12:16), and thus it is joined with the former (Deut. 33:2).

5. The glory of God, revealed to and for the church, is not to be looked upon in a transient way, but ought to be gravely and seriously considered, till our hearts are affected and warmed with it. Therefore "Selah" (used nowhere but in the Psalms and this chapter) is subjoined, to show the weight of this matter, and how our hearts should pause and dwell upon it until it grows upon our hands; yea, to show that a sight of him indeed will give our hearts such a set that they must stand and breathe a while.

6. As the excellence of all the creatures is from God, and daily sets out his glory, so when he is pleased to appear in any special manifestation, it obscures all other glory besides, and sets him out as alone praiseworthy; for in this progress "his glory covered the heavens, and the earth was full of his praise," in a singular way, besides what ordinarily appears of his glory in heavens and earth.

7. We ought to commend the infinite wisdom of God, and his tender respect to frail man, that he has chosen fit means and instruments of ministers and ordinances by which to make himself known, as we are able to bear; for immediate manifestations of him who dwells in light inaccessible would undo us, while we are in our mortal bodies. When he appeared, "his brightness was as the light," filling heaven and earth as if it had been all a sun. This was acknowledged by Israel, when they could not endure this glory nor hear God speak (Exod. 19:16; Exod. 20:18, 19), and by Elijah, in wrapping his face in his mantle when God appeared to him (1 Kings 19:13).

8. The Lord's most glorious manifestations of himself to mortal creatures are but as veils cast over his infinitely glorious essence and attributes, and (so to say) an obscuring of himself, that he may reveal himself to their capacity. Yea, it much commends the glory of God, and may help our faith, if we consider that the most glorious effects of his power are but a veil cast over his glorious omnipotence, for he can do far above what we ask or think. "He had horns coming out of his hands," or glorious manifestations of his power shining in these glorious rays with which he arrayed himself on every side, and yet "there was the hiding of his power."

9. The Lord took his church by the hand when she came out from the pots of Egypt, and entered with her in a covenant of marriage, in so glorious a state as testified his estimation of her, and what respect he would put upon her. This gives warrant to the church in all ages, to believe that the glorious Lord will not despise her in her low estate, but notwithstanding his great majesty and her baseness, he will appear for her, will deliver her out of trouble, will give her tokens of his favour, and will renew his covenant with her. Therefore the prophet by faith looks to all this as forthcoming for the church in her second captivity.

Ver. 5. Before him went the pestilence, and burning coals went forth at his feet.

The second branch of the description of God's glorious manifestation is taken from his attendants for executing his judgments. He had "the pestilence and burning coals" (that is, destroying lightnings, as Ps. 18:12, Ps. 78:48; or pestilence and burning diseases, as Deut. 32:24), which as lackeys ran before him and at his feet, wherever he went, ready to run at his command. Both the Egyptians, and themselves in the wilderness, had proof of this (Exod. 9:3, 23; Numb. 11:1; Numb. 16:46, and elsewhere). In naming these plagues, as most devouring, other plagues are not to be excluded, but understood.

1. The glory of the Lord shines, and is to be seen and adored, in his works of judgment as well as in other acts; for the prophet brings it in here, to set out his glory, that "before him went the pestilence."

2. It is a further manifestation of God's glory, and ought to be a ground of the church's faith, that he can (and will, when he pleases) find ways to plague enemies, though second causes and probable means fail. So does the prophet reckon, when he brings in "pestilence and burning coals," as ready to do that work.

3. It is a part of our duty in glorifying God, to acknowledge all afflictions to be his pages, ready to come and go at his command, so that our eyes may be most on him under them. So does the prophet set out his glory, in saying that these plagues "went before him and at his feet," attending on his progress.

4. Faith may safely gather, from judgments executed for sin of old, that judgment shall be executed for the same sins again committed; and may gather from judgments inflicted upon the church when she sins, that undoubtedly the sins of enemies will not be passed over. Therefore the prophet records what had been done on Egypt and themselves, as a certain pledge of Babel's ruin, that the church may be delivered.

> Ver. 6. He stood and measured the earth; he beheld and drove asunder the nations. The everlasting mountains were scattered, and the perpetual hills did bow; his ways are everlasting.

A third instance of his glory of old, appeared in his dividing the land of Canaan by Moses and Joshua, to the twelve tribes. He "stood and measured," that is, not only fixed their rest when they came there, after they had long wandered with the ark of his presence, but he also openly manifested himself to be a sovereign Lord and their God in doing it, and that he needed not any deliberation or time to do it. His glory also shined in putting them easily in possession of that land, scattering the nations with a look of his countenance in anger, by which he overthrew and subdued the inhabitants of that hilly country, whose possession had been ancient (as the hills which they possessed) and whose stable condition, like the hills also, did promise them perpetuity. But the Lord, who can remove fixed mountains, overthrew and subdued them. And no wonder; for his ways and purposes concerning his people (Deut. 32:8) were more ancient than their possession; and since God is eternal, and still the same, he will yet be forthcoming in the same need.

1. God, the sovereign king of all nations, who casts down and lifts up whom he pleases, will manifest himself in carving out even the outward lot of his people according to his covenant with them. This he proved "when he stood and measured the earth," or "the land," to his Israel, to whom he had promised it, and so made them hold it sure by the sure tenor of his free gift. And thus the prophet expects that the Lord will yet do the same.

2. It is a notable encouragement to faith, and sets out God's glory, to consider that what is most difficult in men's sight is yet most easy to God, when he puts his hand to it. He "stood" of old and designed a land; he but "beheld and drove asunder the nations"; and though their possession was nearly as ancient, and appeared as stable, as "the everlasting mountains and perpetual hills," yet even these "were scattered and did bow."

3. The Lord's eminent appearing in bringing about a mercy for his people, according to the tenor of the covenant, gives a ground of claim when it comes in hazard again, and is a pledge that God will assert and maintain his own glorious purchase, though for a time it seem to be plucked out of his hand. So would the prophet gather. The Lord, who had not only promised but gloriously put his people in possession of that land, would bring them back to it again in due time. And to this purpose Jehoshaphat also reasons (2 Chron. 20:11).

4. Though men's having a long and firm possession of what is the church's right may be a great trial of faith, yet the study of God's unchangeable nature and his eternal, irresistible purposes will strongly support faith. Therefore the prophet, in opposition to the Chaldeans' power and long possession (Isa. 49:24) holds forth God's eternal purposes

concerning the church; as of old they had overturned the Canaanites, so yet they would take place in all generations (Ps. 33:11). In both these respects "his ways are everlasting," as being more ancient and sure than the Canaanites' possession, and yet the same unchangeably, to overturn the Chaldeans.

> Ver. 7. I saw the tents of Cushan in affliction; and the curtains of the land of Midian did tremble.

A fourth instance of this glory shined in the terror which God's presence among his people put upon their enemies, and all round about, as instanced in Cushan and Midian, whose habitation was in tents and under curtains. This was accomplished partly when in Israel's march through the wilderness, all the Arabians (descended of Cush, as well as the Ethiopians on the other side of the Red Sea) and the Midianites, who lived thereabout, were affrighted, as not knowing on whom they would fall; and this fear also took hold on other nations (Exod. 15:14, 15; Numb. 22:3, 4; Josh. 2:9-11) and put them in great affliction and terror; and partly it was accomplished in the notable defeat of Cushan and Rishathaim, by Othniel (Judg. 3:8-10) and of the Midianites by Gideon (Judg. 7). All this the prophet looks back unto by faith, and sees the Lord ready to do the same again.

1. It serves to illustrate God's glory and strengthen the faith of his church in believing promises, to consider that God can reveal the vanity of creatures by making stout-hearted nations to tremble; that he can fight against men with his terror, and can reveal himself terrible in and for his church when she is in a wilderness and low state. This is a ray of his glory, and a ground of the prophet's faith, that "the tents of Cushan were in affliction (or 'under vanity,' which this terror revealed to be in them), and the curtains of the land of Midian did tremble."

2. It is a notable way to strengthen faith, when we consider how satisfactorily God at any time has made his word good, and when we fully study such grounds and props to our faith, until we come to a full assurance. The prophet says, "I saw the tents," etc.; that is, not only that the church (in whose name he speaks) at that time saw God clearly performing his word, and therefore they should not doubt in the new difficulty; but further, by this practice he teaches every believer to look back on what God has done, and study

it, till the sight of it affords ground of comfort in new troubles, and till they see cause to expect the same if need be.

> Ver. 8. Was the Lord displeased against the rivers? Was
> thy anger against the river? Was thy wrath against the
> sea, that thou didst ride upon thy horses and thy char-
> iots of salvation?
> 9. Thy bow was made quite naked according to the
> oaths of the tribes, even thy word. Selah. Thou didst
> cleave the earth with rivers.

A fifth instance of this glory shone forth in two very contrary effects, of dividing the Red Sea and Jordan to give
way to his people (Exod. 14; Josh. 3) and making hard rocks
to furnish water to quench their thirst (Exod. 17:6; Numb.
20:8, 11).

The first of these is amplified from God's great love and
fidelity appearing in it. Though he had no quarrel against
the seas and rivers, yet he would trouble them and march
through them in state, on his horses and chariots of the pil-
lar of cloud and fire (contrasted with Pharaoh's chariots
and horsemen) for the safety and protection of his people,
and did draw forth his weapons against his enemies, to
prove his fidelity and the truth of his word, frequently
repeated and confirmed by oath to the tribes of Israel.

The second is amplified from God's liberality in giving
them water in abundance, so that it clave the ground and cut
itself a channel, and followed them in rivers (Numb. 20:11;
Ps. 78:15, 16; 1 Cor. 10:4).

1. Variety of contrary trials and difficulties on the right
hand and on the left cannot exhaust the fullness of sufficiency
and love which is in God toward his people; if "seas and
rivers" trouble them, he can turn them into dry land and
make a way for them to pass through. If again lack of water
troubles them, he can make rocks furnish and afford it.

2. It is a point of spiritual wisdom to read and observe
God's mind and scope in his works, and what his thoughts
are toward the creatures he works upon or about, so that
none may mistake or stumble, and that his people may more
distinctly read his love to them. Therefore a question (which
implies a denial) is thrice asked, that none might be so foolish as to think that his dealing spoke any anger against these
creatures; it rather proclaimed his love to his people.

3. God's great anger against wicked men, sinfully troub-
ling his people, may appear from considering his dealing

with insensible creatures when in their ordinary course they stand in the way of his people's well-being. The prophet would have the church consider that if he divided seas and rivers, he may do the like again, if need be; and further, if the Lord did so make the sea and rivers to reel, though he had no quarrel against them, what will he do to those against whom he is justly angry?

4. God can easily appear in great majesty when his church is at a low ebb; and when he appears, anything will bring safety. In his church's greatest difficulty, he will get arms to reach his enemies a sad blow. The church's troubles may be proofs of love, and even in her lowest condition the Lord can plague his enemies; for at the Red Sea, the clouds were his horses and chariots of salvation, and there "his bow was made quite naked," or his power manifested to the Egyptians' overthrow. (In those countries they drew their bows out of cases, in which they were kept, when they went to battle.)

5. The people of God never look rightly upon his works unless thereby their hearts are warmed toward him; and the study of his working is one means appointed for stirring up our affection. Therefore both here and afterward, the prophet, who formerly spoke of God, is driven to speak to God of his own working. "Thou didst ride, thy bow was made naked."

6. The Lord stands bound to his people, and to every one of them, by his word confirmed by oath, to do for them what they need and what is for their good; for here is "the oath of the tribes (made to them by God), even thy word."

7. It is a notable confirmation to faith that in hardest times and greatest extremities, God will not swallow his word, but will make it good by performance. In this the prophet encourages himself, that at the Red Sea, where Pharaoh thought he had Israel enclosed, even there the Lord's "bow was made quite naked, according to the oaths of the tribes."

8. It is the duty of the godly, seriously to notice every accomplishment of God's word, that it may be matter of praise, and clearer ground of future confidence and relying upon his word. Therefore "Selah" is again subjoined to this passage.

9. God's people will not lack refreshment even in a wilderness, and that in abundance; and God will supply all their wants, though everything should promise the contrary. God

did cleave the earth with rivers, when there were nothing but flints in a dry wilderness to bring it out of.

> Ver. 10. The mountains saw thee, and they trembled; the overflowing of the water passed by; the deep uttered his voice, and lifted up his hands on high.

The prophet recounts the instance of God's appearing on mount Sinai, and the hills about, and the instance of his dividing the sea and Jordan. He amplifies both from a consideration of the great majesty of God appearing in them, which was such as made the hills to tremble by an earthquake (Exod. 19:18; Ps. 114:4-7), and the water, which ordinarily overflows all, ran out of his way. The depths, by making a noise, testified how much they were troubled at his presence, and by standing up on heaps on every side (Ps. 78:13; Josh. 3:16). They lifted their hands, as it were, to adore and testify their subjection to their Creator.

1. The majesty of God appearing for his people, and the truth and certainty of what he has promised to them, is confirmed by many proofs and witnesses, which we should take notice of, for confirmation of our faith; and for this end we should again and again study God's working, and every new sight will afford a new lesson and matter of encouragement. These confirmations grow upon the prophet's hand, and in this review of God's work he finds yet more in them to help his faith. God's work on mountains and waters concurs to prove the same point.

2. It is our duty to study and be affected with God's work, not only because it brings about our good, but chiefly because it sets forth and illustrates his majesty and glory. Therefore the prophet, in this review, observes as a chief consideration that "the mountains saw thee, and they trembled; the overflowing of the water passed by."

3. The brutishness of men who do not stand in awe of God, may be read from the trembling of mountains and seas, and their doing homage to him, when he puts them to it. And the vanity of all opposition to God's saving his people may be seen in what God did to any of these creatures when they stood in his way. This is manifest in that "the mountains saw him and trembled; the deep uttered his voice, and lifted up his hands on high."

> Ver. 11. The sun and moon stood still in their habitation;
> at the light of thy arrows they went, and at the shining
> of thy glittering spear.

The prophet also resumes that which had been spoken (ver. 1-6) of God's subduing Israel's enemies, and giving to them a peaceable possession of the land. He illustrates yet further the glory of God shining in this, from several instances.

The first of these is taken from God's making the sun and moon to serve his people in their wars, and contrary to their course, to stand still in heaven, and his ordering their motions so that they might give time and light to the church to employ their weapons, and so that they might attend and bear witness of God's fighting for his church with hailstones as arrows and spears (Josh. 10:1-13). These stones are called "bright and glittering" because of God's immediate hand in them, putting a splendor upon them, and because the sun shone upon the stones as they fell, making them to glitter. Hence learn:

1. Though the people of God seem to be low and base things in comparison to many glorious creatures which God has made and set above them; and although ordinarily they get only the common use of these creatures, with the rest of the world (Matt. 5:45); yet these singular dispensations prove that all the creatures are servants to the saints in a special way. The sun is a candle, to be lit or put out when God sees fit, as their affairs require, without any respect to the world besides; for the sun and moon "stood still" and "went" as God and his people had to do. This may teach the godly to read more special love in the ordinary use of these benefits than is revealed to others.

2. Enemies to the church may expect that the heaven and earth, and all the creatures, will be against them, and when means or second causes on earth cannot overtake them, yet heaven will reach them; for "the sun and the moon stood still" to behold and give light to the execution made upon them; and when Israel could not reach them in their flight, God overtakes them with "arrows" and a "glittering spear."

> Ver. 12. Thou didst march through the land in indignation; thou didst thresh the heathen in anger.

A second instance of God's glory in that work appeared in his speedy and sore destruction of the Canaanites, against whom he was highly offended, as being heathen and enemies to him and to his people. His chariots went speedily through them and trod them down, as corn is threshed out by the feet of beasts.

1. God's anger against wicked enemies (whether pagans or those whose behaviour toward his church is pagan-like) is a sore enemy, and will make great havoc of them; and it is a short cut of long work. Though the Canaanites were many and potent, yet he says, "Thou didst march through the land in indignation; thou didst thresh the people in anger."

2. God is alone the subduer of enemies to his people (though sometimes he may employ more instruments, sometimes fewer, or none at all), and he is to be seen in what is done and to be looked to for what is undone. "Thou didst march through the land," says the prophet, acknowledging what was past and expecting the like to come.

> Ver. 13. Thou wentest forth for the salvation of thy people, even for salvation with thine anointed; thou didst wound the head out of the house of the wicked, by revealing the foundation unto the neck. Selah.
> 14. Thou didst strike through with his staves the head of his villages; they came out as a whirlwind to scatter me; their rejoicing was as to devour the poor secretly.

He further instances the Lord's glory in this work and in several others (as in Egypt, under the judges, David, etc.). God's glory shone in these works:

(a) In his design, which was to bring salvation to his people by his anointed instruments, Moses, Joshua, David, etc., as types of Christ and of eternal salvation by him.

(b) In the remarkable judgments inflicted upon enemies. He destroyed the heads and rulers of those wicked societies, as was verified on Pharaoh and other kings (who troubled them after they had settled in the land); and he overthrew not only the kings of Canaan, but all the sovereignty and power which was in the land and which opposed Israel's possession. Yea further, he not only cut off the head of sovereignty in the persons of rulers, but also rooted them out in their subjects by overturning ignominiously their stable condition, as a house when it is rased from the top to the foundation, or when a man's body (which supports the head) is made bare from the heel (which is the foundation he stands on) to the neck; and by cutting off their sovereignty, not only in cities, but even in inferior villages, and their rulers. And this he did even by those same means which they employed against the church.

This was accomplished in the sad strokes that befell Egypt, with Pharaoh, especially at the Red Sea, and in the strokes that many times came upon the subjects of Israel's oppressors, and the invasions and conquests made of their territories under David and others; but especially was it accomplished in the entire conquest of Canaan, in which the people were not only subdued and put under the power of Israel, but the very root of the heathens' sovereignty over the land was rooted up by the utter extirpation of the inhabitants in cities and villages (except the Gibeonites, and those whom they sinfully spared), that Israel might possess their habitations.

(c) God's glory shone in these works, in frustrating the proud hopes of enemies; for the Lord thus destroyed them when they were both violent and confident of victory, and when they thought to overwhelm the weak church as with a tempest, and made it their delight by waste and cruelty to devour her.

Hence learn:

1. Unto the Lord's people, salvation is his purpose and will be the result of all his enterprises; for it is twice marked that "he went forth for the salvation of his people."

2. Christ is the ground of all salvation to his people, and every deliverance they get is a pledge of eternal salvation by him; for "he went forth for salvation with his anointed." These fitted instruments (whom the church will never lack in her need) were but types of Christ, and employed by him from whom all safety comes, and these deliverances were shadows of his saving to the uttermost those who come to God through him. And though the possession of Canaan was in a peculiar way typical, yet the godly in all times may look on temporal mercies as pledges of better things.

3. In wicked nations or combinations those who are chief in authority are ordinarily most eminent and instrumental in evil, and the Lord will break the combination by cutting them off, and no greatness nor eminence shall be able to avert it; for "he revealed the foundation to the neck, and struck through the heads of his villages."

4. In due time the Lord will do to his implacable enemies that which may afford matter of serious thoughts to themselves and others; and merciful dispensations of his are wisely to be considered. Therefore "Selah" is again subjoined to this purpose.

5. When the Lord has enemies great and small to root out, he needs no other means than their own weapons, or the very designs by which they think to thrive best and to ruin the church; for "thou didst strike through with his staves, the head of his villages." This was the result of Pharaoh's pursuing Israel at the Red Sea, of all the Canaanites' enterprises against them, and was more clearly verified on the Midianites (Judg. 7:22), on the enemies of Judah in Jehoshaphat's days (2 Ch 20:22, 23), and others.

6. As the church has long been exercised with violent, cruel, and insatiable enemies, and must still expect to meet with such, so the Lord will repay past and present enemies even when their hopes and earnestness to carry their designs are greatest. It was both a cause of their destruction and the time of it, when "they came out as a whirlwind to scatter me," says the prophet in the name of the church, or violently to overrun and destroy her, and when "their rejoicing was to devour the poor secretly," or "in secret and hidden places." That is, they took pleasure not only in overthrowing them, with great armies coming like a tempest upon them, but also in surprising them with sudden incursions, by which they were exhausted and had fled to secret holes for shelter and refuge. This well agrees with the condition of Israel under Midian (Judg. 6:2, 3), under the tyranny of the Philistines (1 Sam. chaps. 13, 14), and at other times, as at the Red Sea (Exod. 15:9, 10) and when the Canaanites made headway against them.

7. The church of God in all ages is one body and society, having interest in the same privileges and communion in the same faith; and the latter ages are heirs of the sufferings of the former and of the advantages to be reaped by them. Therefore Habakkuk says, in the name of the church, "they came out to scatter me," as if the church in his time, in the same individual persons, had been under the former trials, because they were heirs to any benefit or experience that might be gathered from them.

> Ver. 15. Thou didst walk through the sea with thy horses, through the heap of great waters.

The prophet closes all this with a second look at God's glorious marching, as a man of war, guarding his people, through the sea and deep waters gathered upon heaps. Hence learn:

1. Though in a time of ease we are ready to satisfy ourselves with a slender view of God's works, yet a time of trouble will put us to study them over and over again, to see what we can find in them for our relief; and though many times we find little in his works, yet when we study well we shall find that we never dwell enough on them, and that the oftener we study them the more we shall find in them. And in particular, extraordinary mercies should be much and often remembered. Such we are taught by the prophet's practice in looking over and again on this act, which was an extraordinary work.

2. It is worthy our second and serious thoughts, both to set out God's honour and to confirm our faith, to consider that God's people are so dear to him that he will turn the world upside down and change the course of nature, if need be, before they perish; and that he can make his people go safely, and like conquerors, through great afflictions and dangers. Such are we taught by the repeating of this act of God's power, in making seas a way and riding with his people through it, as if they had been guarded by an army.

> Ver. 16. When I heard, my belly trembled, my lips quivered at the voice. Rottenness entered into my bones, and I trembled in myself, that I might rest in the day of trouble; when he comes up unto the people, he will invade them with his troops.

The prophet, after this meditation concerning God's way of old, returns to his former course (ver. 2) about the ensuing captivity. Instead of praying, he from the former grounds confirms his own and the godly's faith against all the imaginable difficulties in it. First, he confirms himself and the godly against the affliction and humbling exercise, to which the denunciation of this trouble put him and the godly. It was a very heavy exercise, insomuch that his belly, or inward bowels (which the scripture sometimes puts for the heart, because of its secrecy, Prov. 20:27, and because of its affections, Isa. 16:11) did beat and shake for fear, which made his mouth and lips to quiver so that he could not speak. His body, even to his bones, was consumed with musing about it; yea, he "trembled in himself," as in a total distemper, so that nothing he could do was able to bear it down, or "in his place," so that through trembling he could neither sit nor stand, nor rest any place. Yet he reckons by faith that God, by this exercise, would make that sore day of trouble more easy when it came, and when God should send the Chaldeans against that rebellious people, to cut them off.

1. Much use of faith makes easy and comforting work of prayer; for so the prophet, after this meditation, carves out his own answer and glories therein.

2. The Lord, in his longsuffering, usually gives fair warning to his church before he strikes, if we would observe it from his word; and as he ordinarily strikes sorely when his church abuses his patience and puts him to it, so his word of threatening ought to be believed, and our faith in it ought to appear in our deep sense and trembling because of his rod shaken at us. Here is a voice of invading, or cutting in pieces with troops, sounding against the church before it was inflicted; and this the prophet "heard," and believing made him "tremble within himself" and "rottenness enter into his bones."

3. It is God's way with his people to humble them by trouble, and to lay them and their strength of every kind by, before they get a right way of bearing it; and it is their great valour to renounce their own ability, that they may lean on him. The prophet speaks of himself as one spent with the apprehension of the burden: "my belly trembled, my lips quivered at the voice; rottenness entered into my bones, and I trembled in myself."

4. The Lord never puts his people to any sore exercise or unusual trial without having a good purpose in it; and he will reveal that they are not behind with others, who sit idle when they are kept busy; for in all this exercise of the prophet, when others of the Jews were sleeping, the Lord aimed at "rest in a day of trouble," when others should be terrified with the invasion.

5. As the Lord sometimes begins at his own house with trouble, by which they are exempted from the dregs of the cup which the wicked drink out (Ps. 75:8; 1 Pet. 4:17; Ps. 94:12, 13), so the Lord's exercising and humbling of his people with the apprehension of approaching trouble is a presage and means of making it easy when it comes. Hereby they are prepared and not surprised, as sinners and hypocrites (Isa. 33:14); they see God's justice in his stroke, and submit without quarreling; they are made to deny themselves and seek strength in God. Yea, apprehension may conceive trouble to be more terrible than it will prove, and

disappointment will bring ease; therefore the prophet says, "I trembled in myself, that I might rest in the day of trouble."

> Ver. 17. Although the fig-tree shall not blossom, neither shall fruit be in the vines; the labour of the olive shall fail, and the fields shall yield no meat; the flock shall be cut off from the fold, and there shall be no herd in the stalls;
>
> 18. Yet I will rejoice in the Lord; I will joy in the God of my salvation.

The prophet by faith ascends yet higher, to grapple with the trouble itself; and though all creature-comforts and means of subsistence under trouble should fail (as if means of livelihood from trees, land or cattle were cut off from man, as in a general desolation by war), yet he undertakes to bear out and to rejoice in God for the hope of salvation and deliverance, by virtue of the covenant and the interest which the church has in him.

1. The calamities of war and captivity are very great and sore; and it is the Lord's way in the church's trouble to blast and lay aside all matter of confidence in anything beneath God, for this is no idle or impossible supposition; the church may expect that "the fig tree shall not blossom, neither shall fruit be in the vines."

2. Faith never gets right footing or exercise so long as the believer would set bounds and limits to trouble, that it may come here and no further; and does not see through and submit unto the worst that possibly may come. The prophet supposes that the very course of nature for man's preservation may fail, to the end he may cast himself wholly and cleanly upon God.

3. As the promised mercies of the church are surer than the very course of nature, so faith apprehending these promises will outlive the worst of storms without fainting; for "although the fig tree shall not blossom, yet I will rejoice in the Lord," says the prophet in the name of the church.

4. Faith in hard times gets sure footing when it considers that God, who is omnipotent and all-sufficient, lives whatever may come and go; and that it is usual for God to give deliverance according to the covenant, when all means fail; and for saints to get it in such a way, and at such a time, and not before. Indeed God has this as a title, by which he

is known in his church, and the prophet calls the Lord "the God of my salvation."

5. Faith is given in hard times, not only to bear the believer up, but also to furnish matter of joy and glory, which should be sought, for it honors God. It evidences that we get more in him than trouble can take from us; it is a means to make the trouble easy, by avoiding the extremity of discouragement to which it drives us, and a testimony that we expect good by trouble, and something that is out of the reach of it. Therefore the prophet resolves to "rejoice" and "joy" in the midst of his calamity.

> Ver. 19. The Lord God is my strength, and he will make my feet like hinds' feet, and he will make me to walk upon my high places. To the chief singer upon my stringed instruments.

The prophet by faith speaks out positively. He expects from God the matter of his joy, in reference both to subsistence during the time of the captivity and issue from it. He believes that God would be the church's strength when all means failed, that he would gather and bring them back after scattering, and make them nimble to overcome all difficulties in their way (as a hind skips over mountains and inaccessible places) till they come to possess their own country again, which was for the most part hilly, and to enjoy communion with God in the temple, which was situated upon the holy mountains (Ps. 87:1); and to avow his confidence and edify the church, he gives out this exercise to be publicly sung by the musicians of the temple and played upon "my stringed instruments," prescribed by him and therefore called his.

1. It is an extraordinary proof of love, and ought to be matter of joy to the afflicted church, when she is supported and kept from fainting under her trouble, though she has no more. Here the prophet joys in that he has strength. See 2 Cor. 12:8, 9.

2. When all props and grounds of encouragement on earth do fail, there is abundance of furniture to support God's people and make them subsist, do, or suffer, as he calls them; and this will be forthcoming for the self-denied who wait upon God. Thus does the self-denied prophet reckon: "the Lord is my strength." See Isa. 40:29-31.

3. The Lord's people are not utterly undone and past hope, even when they are brought into captivity out of their own

land and under the power of others; for the Lord can return their captivity, as the prophet here expects.

4. The promises of the Lord are so certain to be accomplished that every promise of a mercy is also an undertaking for the removal of every impediment which may stand in its way. "He will make my feet like hinds' feet," says the prophet, and carry me over all impediments, and "make me to walk upon my high places."

5. Though God's mercies may be often little thought of when they are enjoyed, yet the lack of them will reveal how rich they were, and will make the restitution of them sweet; and to the godly man, enjoyment of God in his ordinances is far above any lot besides. Therefore the prophet calls the land and mountain of the temple "my high places," to show that though it was a hilly land in comparison with pleasant Babel, yet it was his choice above all the world besides, and that it would be sweet to be restored to it again with liberty.

6. Though faith may often be conjoined with much fear, and the believer may afterward be ashamed if he utters anything of his confidence, yet what faith gathers from the word may be boldly avowed. So the prophet avows his exercise and makes it public: "to the chief singer."

7. When in a hard time faith apprehends God for strength and a blessed issue, it ought to be stirred up to praise in hope, in the midst of the trouble. Therefore the prophet directs this to be sung: "to the chief singer on my stringed instruments."

ZEPHANIAH

THE ARGUMENT

This prophet exercised his function in the days of Josiah, as appears from the inscription of the prophecy, and after the reformation begun by him, as may be gathered from 1:4, where the land is threatened for the remnant of Baal. Thus the prophet is in part a contemporary with Jeremiah, and among the last who prophesied before the captivity. His scope in a great part is to confirm and enlarge that sad sentence (2 Kings 23:26), by which, if possible, some might yet be called to repentance, and the impenitent rendered yet more inexcusable. Therefore, having to do with an obdurate people, who were not bettered by Jeremiah's doctrine nor by Josiah's example and endeavours, he begins with a denunciation of God's sore judgments, which were to come upon them for their sins (chap. 1). He exhorts them to repent, by a consideration of the judgments that were to be inflicted on the nations around them (chap. 2), and having given them up as incorrigible, he makes ample promises concerning his church under the gospel, for the comfort of the remnant who feared God (chap. 3).

CHAPTER I

In this chapter, after the inscription of the prophecy (ver. 1), we have a denunciation of the general desolation that was to come upon the land (ver. 2, 3) because of the gross iniquities that abounded among them (ver. 4-6). To press this sentence yet more home, (a) He sets before them the nearness of that bloody day (ver. 7), in which he would punish the dissolute court (ver. 8) and the instruments of oppression (ver. 9), and would give up the city to the Chaldeans (ver. 10), who would make their rich men and merchants to howl (ver. 11) and spoil epicures of their wealth (ver. 12, 13). (b) He sets forth that day in its terribleness, making the stoutest to cry (ver. 14), the wrath of God bringing men in distress without any comfort (ver. 15), affrighting them with the alarms and assaults of their enemies (ver. 16), leaving them void of any counsel in their greatest calamities (ver. 17) and destitute of all relief in which they trusted, for it would be suddenly consumed (ver. 18).

Ver. 1. The word of the Lord which came to Zephaniah, the son of Cushi, the son of Gedaliah, the son of Amariah, the son of Hizkiah, in the days of Josiah, the son of Amon, king of Judah.

The inscription holds forth: (a) The messenger employed in this service, who is described from several of his ancestors, who were either prophets themselves or men of note in their time; for such is generally true when the progenitors of the prophets are recorded. (b) His commission from God, and the authority of his doctrine, which he did not devise of his own head nor learn by ordinary means, but received it by immediate inspiration. (c) The time when he was employed. Hence learn:

1. Though the persons of men add nothing to a divine message, yet sometimes it pleases him to make choice of men of eminence, to show that it is the honour of the greatest to be his ambassadors to his people. Further, thereby he makes inexcusable those who despise his message because of the meanness of the messenger. Therefore he employs this prophet, Zephaniah the son of Cushi, the son of Gedaliah, whose parents in many generations had been of eminent note among that people, and consequently he himself was famous for his descent and pedigree.

2. Through long obduration in sin, people may sink to such a depth that no endeavours of pious rulers will bring them to repentance, by which they might prevent sad threatenings and judgments; for this word of sad denunciation is spoken "in the days of Josiah," a pious king and zealous reformer, but "the son of Amon," who by his corrupt ways, following his father Manasseh, had made that people incorrigible.

3. In a time of general and continued defection, the Lord's longsuffering is so great as to multiply messengers and warnings before he strikes, so that men may be reclaimed or made inexcusable; therefore this prophet was sent out with many others, about the time of approaching captivity. See 2 Chron. 36:15, 16.

4. As the divine authority of God's word is always to be studied and seen in messages in the mouth of his servants, so especially when the word speaks sad things, it is good to see God our party, and how little cause we have to fix on messengers or their humours as the cause of such unpleasing doctrine. Therefore, when the prophet brings out this

message, it is avowed and held out to be "the word of the Lord which came unto Zephaniah."

Ver. 2. I will utterly consume all things from off the land, says the Lord.
3. I will consume man and beast; I will consume the fowls of the heaven and the fishes of the sea, and the stumbling blocks with the wicked. And I will cut off man from off the land, says the Lord.

The Lord begins here as with a closed process which needs no more than to pronounce the sentence. Since this people had been abundantly warned and convinced by former prophets, he threatens them with a general desolation of the land, by the destruction and removal of all things in it: not only of men who had sinned, but also of the creatures which they had abused to satisfy their lusts. The beasts should be cut off and destroyed; yea, the very fowls should be driven away, and the fishes exhausted from their ponds, lakes or rivers, as is usual in countries infested with wars. By this judgment the Lord threatens to make short work with the sinner, and his abused riches, and his idolatry, which no reformation could purge from him. Hence learn:

1. The Lord's Spirit will not always strive with his sinful people, but will at last give out his sentence according to their ways; such does this abrupt beginning of threatening, without any previous dealing, import.

2. A public reformation, though ever so piously intended and zealously prosecuted by rulers, after much defection, will be so far from keeping off wrath, when the people are not cordial and thorough in the reformation, that on the contrary it may ripen a people faster for a stroke. Though Josiah was a pious and approved reformer, yet the people dissembled and dallied with God in the matter (Jer. 3:6), insomuch that after Josiah's death, within three months they went all wrong with the succeeding king (2 Kings 23:31, 32). Therefore the Lord gives them up as incorrigible, and begins, "I will utterly consume all things."

3. When men will not read the greatness and dreadfulness of divine displeasure against them in the greatness of their sin or in the threatenings of the word, it is righteous with God to write it in legible letters of extreme desolation. Here he threatens to do so with this incorrigible people, by utterly consuming all things from off the land, both man and beast.

4. Sinful man is a great burden to the creation, in his abusing of the creatures to fight against God with them and to provoke God against them, not for any fault of their own, but that he may punish man (for whose use they were created) by smiting them. Judah's sins make "all things utterly consumed from off the land," and bring strokes on "beasts, fowls of the heaven, and fishes of the sea," where by "sea" we may understand any gathering of waters, in ponds, rivers, or lakes; for in scripture the very laver in the temple is called a sea, because it contained much water (1 Kings 7:23). So also the lakes of Gennesaret and Tiberias (Matt. 8:24, 27; John 6:1). See Jer. 4:25; Jer. 12:4; Hos. 4:3.

5. As wicked men's prosperity proves the brokenness of their souls by their abuse of it, and hardening themselves in sin by it; and as idolatry will certainly end in the eternal ruin of the impenitent idolater; so these sins are often so rooted in the heart of sinners that there is no ceasing to sin until the sinner ceases to be. And in this case the Lord will not spare, since there is no remedy. Here, after reformation had tried them in vain, either as to removing their idols from them or making them to cease from abusing the creatures to sin (in which they are "stumbling blocks" as well as idols), God threatens to cut off "the stumbling blocks with the wicked," and so to put an end to their sin by destroying themselves.

6. In a time of general calamity on all the creatures, man ought to look at himself as the chief and only delinquent, and to see the controversy pursuing him. Therefore he is twice pointed at here: "I will consume man and beast," and again, "I will cut man off from the land, says the Lord."

> Ver. 4. I will also stretch out my hand upon Judah, and upon all the inhabitants of Jerusalem, and I will cut off the remnant of Baal from this place, and the name of the Chemarims with the priests;
>
> 5. And those who worship the host of heaven upon the housetops, and those who worship and swear by the Lord, and who swear by Malcham;
>
> 6. And those who are turned back from the Lord, and those who have not sought the Lord nor inquired for him.

The Lord proceeds to declare more particularly upon whom this sore desolation was to come, to wit, upon Judah, which was the head of those who were left after the captivity of the ten tribes, and particularly upon the chief city

Jerusalem. He clears up the causes of this sentence by pointing at the particular sorts of sinners whom he would cut off. These he instances in several kinds, especially against the first table of the law.

(a) Gross idolaters of all sorts, as those who notwithstanding Josiah's reformation still held up some remnant of Baal's worship. (Baal was an old idol of the Sidonians, whose worship was of old followed by Israel in the days of the judges, and was later brought into Israel by Jezebel, 1 Kings 16:31; and from there it came into Judah.) These the Lord threatens to cut off, together with the ministers of Baal, both Chemarims (who are mentioned also in 2 Kings 23:5; Hos. 10:5 in the original, and who seem to have been some inferior order of attendants on the idol, much resembling monks in Popery), and priests of a superior order. Also he threatens to cut off another sort of idolaters who imagined a deity in the stars and planets, and worshipped them on the tops of their houses (which were flat in those countries), intending to do them homage in their own view.

(b) Those who halted between God and idols, who made a profession of worshipping the true God (a part of whose worship is swearing by his name), or having sworn obedience to God in that covenant renewed by Josiah, did yet mix his worship with the service of idols, and particularly of Malcham, or Molech, the idol of the Ammonites (1 Kings 11:7).

(c) Apostates, who after they had made vows and covenant and had begun religion, had fallen back from God to idols.

(d) Atheists, who had no respect to God nor his worship, whether they followed idols or not.

Hence learn:

1. No former stroke inflicted on the church, and no privilege, will exempt impenitent sinners; but if they go on in their way, the last stroke will be sorest. Though Judah was now only left of all the children of Israel, and though Jerusalem had God dwelling in the midst of her, yet the Lord will plague "Judah and all the inhabitants of Jerusalem," and that not in an ordinary way, but he "will stretch out his hand upon them," which imports a stroke beyond ordinary (Exod. 3:20; Exod. 7:5; Deut. 4:34), even that which is mentioned here (ver. 2, 3).

2. When the Lord plagues a land, the controversy must be revealed by himself, lest we err in taking it up. Therefore when the Lord threatens to strike, he also makes known for what cause it is.

3. Though common calamities come indifferently upon all, and though the godly, who study to keep their garments, ought to be sensible in such a time and to renew their peace with God, yet it is a ground of comfort to them that the stroke is not principally for their sakes, nor the wrath pursuing them. Therefore the Lord mentions the gross sinners, who are his adversaries, that the godly (whatever their lot might be) might see their names out of that roll.

4. Men's hearts are naturally so besotted and addicted to idolatry that it is hard to get a thorough reformation of it, where once it has place. Moreover, God is so jealous of his glory that for the least transgression of this kind, he may justly destroy a land; for here, after Josiah's reformation, there is "the remnant of Baal, Chemarims and priests, and they who worship the host of heaven," for which he will consume all things that he may "cut them off."

5. It is too usual with men, when they see any excellence in the creatures or find any advantage by them, for their hearts to dote in them and to be drawn from God by them; for upon these grounds did they "worship the host of heaven upon the housetops," and many do yet dote on some creature or other, though that gross idolatry be not present.

6. The Lord cannot endure any halting in his matters, nor any mixing of true religion with creature-worship or idolatry; but he will make that a ground of controversy against a land, as well as grosser idolatry: "they who worship and who swear by the Lord, and who swear by Malcham," are here put in the roll to be cut off with "the remnant of Baal, and those who worship the host of heaven."

7. Oaths are a part of divine worship, in which there is ascribed to God the glory of omniscience and of power to avenge false swearers, and he is called upon for that effect; and therefore they are not to be lightly used, nor to confirm a falsehood; nor is this glory to be given to any creature, to swear by them; for "swearing by the Lord" is subjoined to "worshipping him," as a chief part of it.

8. Apostasy from professions and engagements is a land-destroying sin, and a great aggravation of sin, whatever the decliner turns to. So may these words be read: "they swear to the Lord," i.e. in renewing the covenant, and yet "swore by Malcham"; and clearly (ver. 6) "they who have turned back from the Lord" are put in the roll to be cut off.

9. It is usual in times of reformation, where different ways of religion are jostling out one another, that there arises a generation of atheists, who care not for God nor

any religion at all; and these are abominable, and in a day of vengeance they will be ranked with the grossest corruptors, as here: "those who have not sought the Lord nor inquired for him" bring upon the rear of them whom God will cut off.

> Ver. 7. Hold your peace at the presence of the Lord God; for the day of the Lord is at hand; for the Lord has prepared a sacrifice, he has bidden his guests.

To make the preceding doctrine take deeper impression, the prophet until ver. 14 resumes the threatening, and holds out the judgment as near at hand, to come on both court and chief city. He also shows yet more cause of this sentence, especially in sins against the second table.

In this verse he threatens that all their opposition to the prophets' doctrine, by defending and excusing their sins, and rejecting threatenings, should be overcome by the approaching judgment, when the Lord should make another kind of sacrifice than they dreamed of. They themselves should be the sacrifice, the Chaldeans the priests to cut them off and slay them; and as they invited friends to their sacrifices of thanksgiving as to a feast, and the priests got a portion, so the Lord would bring the Chaldeans to take the spoil, and the beasts and fowls to feed on their carcases. See Ezek. 39:17; Rev. 19:17.

1. The greatness of God's wrath against sin is not soon seen nor easily laid to heart by those who are most concerned. Therefore the Lord finds it necessary to inculcate his sentence over and over again unto them.

2. Though men going on in sin without control, will readily have low thoughts of God, yet in due time he will manifest himself to be God upon them; and as sinners take their time in walking after the imaginations of their own hearts, so God will take his time for putting things in order. Therefore the day of vengeance is called "the day of the Lord," the day in which he will appear to be the Lord Jehovah.

3. Sin, though long forborne and yet continued in, will at last bring judgment; and especially sin after a reformation ripens fast for speedy judgment. After Josiah had laboured in vain among them, then "the day of the Lord is at hand."

4. It becomes all to tremble and adore the justice of God in his strokes; and though impenitent sinners be both proud and stout-hearted when the word threatens, yet the majesty and severity of God in punishing will dash and confound

them, and will put them from all their boastings and strike them mute. Then will this be obeyed: "hold your peace at the presence of the Lord God."

5. When men tread underfoot or despise the blood of the covenant, and the ordinances which hold it out to us and are ordained as means of our partaking thereof, it is righteous with God to be prodigal with their blood, and deal with them as they have dealt with it. In recompence of their slighting and profaning of sacrifices, which were types to point out and lead them to the blood of Christ, "the Lord has prepared a sacrifice; he has bidden his guests."

> Ver. 8. And it shall come to pass in the day of the Lord's sacrifice, that I will punish the princes and the king's children, and all who are clothed with strange apparel.

He threatens that in this bloody approaching day, he will order with the profane court; with the grandees, royal family and courtiers, who abounded in prodigality, as was accomplished (2 Kings 25:18-21; Jer. 39:6).

1. When the Lord comes to plead a controversy with a land for sin, great men are found ordinarily chief in the provocation, as abusing their power and being effectual by their example to draw others to sin; and the Lord will not spare such, but reckon with them among the first. "In the of the Lord's sacrifice, I will punish the princes and the king's children," says the Lord.

2. When men, of whatever rank or quality, give themselves over to prodigality and hunting of fashions in apparel, as studying to make them their glory (though given at first as a badge of sin), then the Lord may justly reckon that among the grounds of his controversy against a land, and may punish because of it. He will "punish the princes and the king's children, and all who are clothed with strange apparel." See Isa. 3:16-26.

> Ver. 9. In the same day also I will punish all those who leap on the threshold, who fill their masters' houses with violence and deceit.

The Lord threatens in that day to punish another sin of the court, i.e. their oppressing the poor by their agents and servants, who with great insolence invaded the houses of others, as if no door could be shut against them, and came back rejoicing into their masters' houses, to furnish them with the goods they had purchased by fraud and violence.

1. As luxury, superfluity, and prodigality ordinarily exhaust men's estates, and drive them to evil shifts to uphold what they think their greatness; and as great men, and those employed by them, think that their will should be a law, and that they may take what they please without control; so the Lord will in due time appear as an avenger of all such exorbitances; for "they who are clothed in strange apparel" (ver. 8) and their agents, boldly "leap upon the threshold" of those whom they oppress; and the Lord threatens "in the same day" to punish all these.

2. As wicked inferior officers prove a court to be corrupt (Prov. 16:12), so the Lord in a day of anger will reckon not only with the authors of oppression, but with all the insolent ministers and instruments thereof. "In the same day I will punish all those who leap on the threshold, who fill their masters' houses."

> Ver. 10. And it shall come to pass in that day, says the Lord, that there shall be the noise of a cry from the fish-gate; and an howling from the second, and a great crashing from the hills.

From the court and great ones, he comes to threaten the chief city, that it should be taken by the Chaldeans; and from all parts of the city where the enemies entered (as the fish-gate in the city of David, toward the west, and the second gate, at which also the Chaldeans entered, Jer. 39:3) there should be a terrible noise of enemies assailing and killing all they met with, and of the inhabitants howling, all which should make a great echo to resound from the hilly places of the city.

1. High walls and fenced cities are no shelter to hold out divine vengeance pursuing impenitent sinners; and it will prove as a prison in which they shall be surrounded with judgments. Here the Chaldeans fall upon them in their city, on all quarters; "a noise from the fish gate, howling from the second."

2. The tumults of war are very dreadful when they meet with a guilty conscience; and neglect of repentance will in due time resolve in dreadful and woeful wailings under the heavy hand of God; for here they are threatened as a dreadful judgment and fruit of their sin, that there should be a cry,

and an howling, and great crashing, by reason of the noise
of assailing enemies and pursued sinners.

> Ver. 11. Howl, inhabitants of Maktesh, for all the merchant
> people are cut down; all they who bear silver are cut off.

He yet further threatens the inhabitants of a particular
part of the city, i.e. those who dwelt in the hollow valleys
of the city, between the hills on which most of it stood (which
places resembled a mortar, as the word signifies). Here
lived the merchants, and men abounding in money because
of trade; these are threatened, that they shall be made to
howl and be cut off. This place of the city seems to be the
same as that mentioned in Neh. 3:32.

1. When God pursues for a controversy, it is folly for
any in any place to dream of safety; "the inhabitants of Mak-
tesh," the securest and inmost part of the city, are threatened
with "howling" and "cutting down," as well as those at the
gates.

2. Former abundance of prosperity will make judgments
more bitter; and unlawful courses, by which men enhance
and heap up riches, will draw on the bitter judgment. Therefore the Lord not only threatens that "merchants and all who
bear silver" should howl, but the word "merchant," being in
the original "a Canaanite," imports that this judgment came
upon them because they had dealt rather like Canaanites
than like Jews in gathering their riches.

> Ver. 12. And it shall come to pass at that time that I will
> search Jerusalem with candles, and punish the men who
> are settled on their lees, who say in their heart, The
> Lord will not do good, neither will he do evil.
>
> 13. Therefore their goods shall become a booty, and
> their houses a desolation; they shall also build houses,
> but not inhabit them; and they shall plant vineyards, but
> not drink the wine thereof.

The Lord threatens yet further, in this taking of the city,
to take order with all atheists and epicures, who abounded
in wealth and lay secure and at ease (like wine on its dregs
when it is not moved), in their heart denying God's providence, or that he took any note of things beneath, to reward
good or punish evil. And therefore they neither loved nor
believed his promises, that they might walk in his way; nor
did they fear his justice, that they might abandon sin.

Concerning these the Lord threatens that as a man sear-
ches what is lost or hidden with a candle, so he would carefully search out their sins, and themselves to punish them for
their sins, so that none should escape; and he should search
out their goods, to give them up for a spoil. By this their
houses should become desolate, and they should be disappointed of all their expectations from their enjoyments,
according to his sentence pronounced of old in his law (Deut.
28:30-39). Hence learn:

1. Ease and prosperity slay the fool, and breed such
distempers of security and settling on the earth, that God
is justly provoked to smite. "God will punish the men that
are settled on their lees."

2. Prosperity and lack of exercise, by vicissitudes of
dispensations, is a great feeder of atheism, and an enemy
to observing and making use of divine providence. And this
again emboldens and hardens men yet more in their secure
and wicked courses; for "the men who are settled on their
lees" are also those "who say in their heart, The Lord will
not do good, neither will he do evil"; which is both the effect
of their secure condition and a ground which they lay down
for settling themselves yet more in it.

3. Secure atheists and despisers of God and his providence,
may expect that God will refute them in a language which
they will understand, and make them know his providence
upon their own expense, by effects which they shall not get
avoided. The Lord will prove his omniscience and care for
things below by "searching Jerusalem, as with candles,"
that they may not escape him and his effectual providence,
by "punishing them, making their goods become a booty
and their houses a desolation."

4. When the Lord strips a sinful person or people of any
mercies which they enjoyed, they will find upon careful
search that their enjoyment thereof has been a snare to
them, to draw them to sin; and they should read this in the
stroke. "Therefore (that is, because these things had emboldened them to settle on their lees and deny a providence,
therefore) their goods shall become a booty and their houses
a desolation."

5. The Lord will in due time prove the infallible truth of
his threatenings, however despised, upon those who dare
run that hazard; and the holy justice of God is to be adored
in disappointing men of any happiness or contentment they
expected in these things for which they hazard their souls,
and so rendering them twice losers if they will not serve

him. And in this his just procedure shines: "they shall build houses, but not inhabit them; they shall plant vineyards, but not drink the wine thereof."

> Ver. 14. The great day of the Lord is near; it is near, and hastes greatly, even the voice of the day of the Lord; the mighty man shall cry there bitterly.

The Lord until now has revealed his judgments to be near and to be caused by Judah's sin. Now, to the end that all these threatenings and the sins procuring them may have weight, and that sinners may yet (if possible) be roused up and put from all their subterfuges, he holds out this approaching day of vengeance in its terribleness, which he clears from several instances. The first is that the most courageous (much more the feeble) among them, should be frightened by it, and made to cry and weep bitterly.

1. Though secure sinners scorn all opposition from men, and put the evil day far off, and think nothing of vengeance when it is looked upon at a distance, yet God is a terrible adversary against such, and can bring evil quickly; and when it is imminent, it will be sad and dreadful; for it is "the day of the Lord," that they should not look to weak prophets or to the Chaldeans only; and "it is near, and hastens greatly"; the sound or "voice" of its approach was in their ears, that they may not dream of it as far off; and being near, it is terrible, and "the great day of the Lord."

2. Natural courage, though it may promise much and sustain many infirmities, yet will not bear out, but will faint when God pursues a controversy for sin. "The mighty man shall cry there bitterly."

> Ver. 15. That day is a day of wrath, a day of trouble and distress, a day of wasteness and desolation, a day of darkness and gloominess, a day of clouds and thick darkness.

A second instance of terribleness is that in this day the wrath of an angry God would be made manifest, by distress and trouble on men, and wasting and desolation on cities and country, and that all these calamities should be without any light of comfort. The clouds of their sin and of God's judgment should make all things black and dismal.

1. The Lord may justly for sin testify wrath against a visible church, and fatherly displeasure against his own in

it; and it will make a judgment terrible when his anger is seen and felt in it, for that is an instance of the terror of that day: it shall be "a day of wrath."

2. Though God may testify his displeasure against sin in many ways, yet such is the stupidity of men that his anger is little seen or laid to heart, until it appears in sad calamities. Therefore that day is called "a day of wrath."

3. In a time when God is pursuing a land for sin, none are to expect ease, but in some measure or other to be put to it and to taste of calamities. That day will be "a day of trouble and distress, a day of wasteness and desolation" to persons and places.

4. As judgments inflicted for sin will make a black representation of affairs, will hold out the judgment in its saddest colours, and will reveal many clouds between the sinner and God's countenance, so it is the capstone of a calamity when spiritual comfort, or some favour from God, is denied or hidden under it. When God smites and hides himself, it speaks wrath indeed; for this makes the day terrible, that when all this is on, it is "a day of darkness and gloominess, a day of clouds and thick darkness."

> Ver. 16. A day of the trumpet and alarm against the fenced cities, and against the high towers.

A third instance is that wrath, pursuing them for sin, should cause the alarm (given to stir up soldiers against them) terrible, and make their enemies successful against their most fortified places. Hence learn:

As the alarms and calamities of war cannot but be frightful and sad to the most godly (Jer. 4:19), it is a great addition to its terror when guilt makes men read God's wrath in it, especially when wrath from the Lord lets it not prove a false alarm, but makes the enemy so successful that nothing stands in his way, nor can pursued sinners find any place of safety or shelter. Being "a day of wrath" (ver. 15), this adds to the terror, that it is "a day of the trumpet and alarm against the fenced cities and high towers."

> Ver. 17. And I will bring distress upon men, that they shall walk like blind men, because they have sinned against the Lord; and their blood shall be poured out as dust, and their flesh as the dung.

A fourth and fifth instance is that the distress shall be so great because of sin, that it shall leave them destitute of all counsel, not knowing what to do, more than blind men know where to walk. And they shall be cut off with the sword, and their blood poured out in as great abundance, and with as little regard, as the dust they tread upon, and their carcases shall be left like dung on the ground.

1. It is a dreadful condition in a day of strait to be void of light to direct men; and though sinful men trust much to their own policy in a calm day, yet a day of wrath will overturn all their designs and leave them destitute of counsel, for "I will bring distress upon men, that they shall walk like blind men."

2. When judgments are accompanied with darkness and perplexity, God's hand is to be eminently seen in that stroke, and he is to be justified by our reading the bitter fruit of sin in it; for the Lord says, "I will bring distress, that they shall walk like blind men, because they have sinned against the Lord."

3. It is just with God, when he has pursued sinners with judgments in their life, to cut them off also in their iniquity, and send them out of the world to receive their full reward; yea, and to testify his displeasure on their very dead bodies. Such is here threatened: "their blood shall be poured out as dust, and their flesh as dung."

4. The greatness and terribleness of divine wrath against sin may be read in the measure of a calamity, in the ignominy of a stroke, and in God's not owning nor evidencing that he pities them in affliction; for all these are in this stroke, to be matter of terror to them: "their blood shall be poured out as dust, and their flesh as dung."

> Ver. 18. Neither their silver nor their gold shall be able to deliver them in the day of the Lord's wrath, but the whole land shall be devoured by the fire of thy jealousy; for he shall make even a speedy riddance of all those who dwell in the land.

The terribleness of this day appears further in this, that all helps shall prove vain, and their riches in which they trusted or by which they might think to ransom their lives, should not be able to deliver them from wrath, nor hinder the Lord, in his kindled jealousy, to make short work in wasting the land and consuming the inhabitants.

1. Many are the false confidences by which men think to secure themselves against a day of vengeance; and it is no easy work to refute these, that wrath may be seen in its terribleness. After all their imaginations that this evil day was far off, that it should be light, that their fenced cities would shelter them, etc., which have been declared useless in the former verses, there remains yet their riches, to be proved vain.

2. The wrath of God pursuing sin is so dreadful that no riches nor treasures, in which men trust, can ward off the stroke, nor anything else, save the blood of Christ fled unto by the self-condemned sinner; for "neither their silver nor their gold shall be able to deliver them in the day of the Lord's wrath." See Prov. 11:4; Ezek. 7:19.

3. When God's love toward his people is provoked unto jealousy by their breach of marriage-duty and their embracing strange lovers, it produces most sharp and violent judgments; and it acts as a fire which speedily consumes all before it, and with which no pact or treaty can be made; for "the whole land shall be devoured by the fire of his jealousy; for he shall make even a speedy riddance of all who dwell in the land."

CHAPTER II

Having thus threatened his sinful people, the Lord comes now to exhort them to make the right use of this threatening, by inviting the body of the people to repent, before the sentence is executed (ver. 1, 2) and the godly remnant to seek God and follow their duty, in hope of favour when the evil day should come (ver. 3). That these exhortations may be more effectual, he sets before them the sad judgments that were to come upon the nations round about, such as the Philistines (ver. 4-7), the Moabites and Ammonites (ver. 8-11), the Ethiopians (ver. 12) and the Assyrians with their chief city (ver. 13-15).

Ver. 1. Gather yourselves together; yea, gather together, O nation not desired;

2. Before the decree bring forth, before the day pass as the chaff, before the fierce anger of the Lord come upon you, before the day of the Lord's anger come upon you.

The sum of the first exhortation, directed to the impenitent body of the nation, is that though they were not a people desirous of their own good, nor worthy of any favour, yet the Lord would make offer of it; and therefore he invites them to make a serious inquiry and examination of themselves and of one another, and that they would for this end gather and collect themselves, and meet together in solemn assemblies for humiliation and repentance. They should do this immediately, before the decreed vengeance (which in God's long-suffering had been yet suspended) broke forth, and before a day of patience passed over swiftly, as the chaff before the wind; or before the day came in which they should be as chaff before the wind, and the decreed vengeance should break forth in execution suddenly and easily; and in which great and fierce anger from the Lord should inflict judgment without mercy.

1. When the Lord speaks in hardest terms to his sinful people, yet they are to read in it an invitation and allowance to come to him by repentance, and not that it is putting them away from any duty of that kind. Therefore, though the Lord had uttered his sentence as a concluded business (1:2), yet here he shows what use they should make of it, in turning to him by repentance.

2. Repentance is not acceptable where there is not a thorough and careful search and inquiry made into our own hearts and ways, and a helping one of another, in our stations, to perform that duty; and thus our consciences from clear conviction may charge upon us those sins for which the word threatens, and the sinfulness of them, and may stir up to turn unto the Lord. So the words in the original may be rendered. "Search narrowly into yourselves, and search," as men do after stubble scattered here and there, as the word is used (Exod. 5:12), or after what is lost among it; that is, search and search again, and while you are thus employed about yourself, stir up and help others to search. Such does the original construction import.

3. For stirring up to this duty of searching, and making it effectual, it is necessary that every man recollect his wandering thoughts, by which he has snuffed up the wind of his pleasure and hunted after vanities, and that the communion of saints be entertained, particularly in solemn and public humiliations. So does the word also signify, according to the translation: "gather yourselves together, yea, gather together." See Joel 2:15, 16.

4. As this duty of repentance and self-searching is of great importance and concern in all times and cases, and especially when God declares himself to be angry, so it is a duty to the performance of which there is need of much stirring up from the Lord. Such does the doubling of exhortations, "gather yourselves, yea, gather," import.

5. It is necessary for our humiliation, and for setting forth the freeness of God's love and how much he tends our welfare, that we know ourselves well. For this end it is declared here that the Lord invites to repentance a nation "not affected with desire," i.e. of turning to God or of their own good, and "not desired," or worthy to be beloved of him; the original word will import both.

6. It is a great aggravation of sin when it is general and overspreads a land, either by general corruption, or by the connivance of rulers at sins of particular persons, which brings guilt upon the whole land; or by private persons not mourning for the abominations of the time, which involves them in that guilt. All this may also contribute to commend God's kindness in following such a crew; and it may hold forth the necessity of repentance when the disease is so desperate; thus for this cause it is remarked that they were "a nation not desired," especially because of overflowing sin.

7. The Lord, in his long-suffering, does not always execute vengeance immediately upon his threatening to do so, but allows some time for bringing forth of that conceived birth (as the word in the original intimates); and thus the Lord's most absolute threatenings do not separate the penitent from hope, but rather invite him to speedy repentance. So we are taught here: "gather yourselves before the decree brings forth," as giving them time to repent, and ground of hope if they should do so. Though the Lord's eternal purposes be unalterable, yet his threatenings (which are his pronounced decree, or his sentence according to the law) when most absolutely pronounced, do include the exception of repentance (Jonah 3:4, 10). The Lord threatens so sharply in order that, upon our preventing of him, he may not execute it, as on the contrary, he promises that he may fulfill. And when his threatenings hold forth even his irrevocable purpose to send outward national judgments, in spite of the repentance of any (as 2 Kings 23:26, 27), yet repentance before it is executed is to good purpose for removing the penitent before the evil day comes, as was done to Josiah; or for moderating it to him if he sees it, as Jeremiah and the godly remnant found

(Jer. 15:11), and for taking wrath out of whatever they shall taste of the cup.

8. It is horrid iniquity to despise the patience and long-suffering of God, or to neglect the setting up of our furnace of examination and self-searching when he threatens; and it will provoke him to make his furnace of judgment so much the hotter, because it has been so long forborne. If they let "the decree bring forth," and a day of patience blow over without repentance and fanning of themselves, he will make "the day pass," and drive them as chaff, and will send "his fierce anger upon them."

9. All who believe how forcible divine wrath is, and how weak themselves are to resist, proclaim their own madness if they do not set about repentance when God threatens. Therefore it is thrice held out what this day will be: that "it shall pass as chaff," that "the fierce anger of the Lord, the day of the Lord's anger shall come upon them," as sufficient to move any who were not quite bereft of sense, to "gather together before the decree brings forth."

> Ver. 3. Seek the Lord, all you meek of the earth, who have wrought his judgment; seek righteousness, seek meekness; it may be you shall be hidden in the day of the Lord's anger.

Because there was little hope of the body of the land, that they would by repentance avert a day of anger, therefore the Lord turns to the godly remnant in the land, who are humbled and made meek under the sense of sin and God's hand, and who have studied to make conscience of their duty enjoined in the word. These he exhorts to go on seeking the Lord's face and favour, and to grow in humility, in meekness and in righteous walking, and in making use of the righteousness of Christ, as being the certain way to be hid from wrath to come, and the only way giving any ground of hope to get safety in outward judgments, though he will not make them absolutely sure of it. For this manner of speaking, see the comment on Jonah 3:9 (p. 62).

1. In declining times, the Lord has a special eye to the godly, and expects much from them; therefore leaving the wicked nation, he turns to them with exhortations and promises.

2. The truth and reality of grace will manifest itself in men's being of subdued, meek, and humble spirits, stooping

to the word, abasing themselves, trembling under judgments and being tender toward others; and in their not giving way to discouragements from duty, but stirring themselves up to seek God for himself, and adorning their profession with a righteous conversation, respecting God's commandments whatever their own natural inclinations might be. Thus the godly are here described to be "seekers of the Lord, the meek of the earth (or of the land) who have wrought his judgment," or obeyed his righteous ordinances enjoined to them.

3. Though it be incident to the godly to fall into some decay in a time of general defection, and to be discouraged from their duty by the evil example of others, yet the truly godly ought to prove themselves to be such by their perseverance, needing and seeking more of what they already have, and seeking Christ's righteousness to cover all. Especially should they be on the growing hand, if they would bear out and find favour in an evil time. Therefore in such a time this exhortation is given: "seek the Lord, seek righteousness, seek meekness," the repetition showing the urgent necessity of the thing exhorted to.

4. As it is the Lord's great mercy toward those who fear him, that he puts the remission of their sins and their eternal happiness out of all doubt, so he is further able, when he pleases, in hardest days to give them proofs of love in temporal favours by taking them into his protection, and either delivering them from trouble or moderating it. Here there is no doubt made of the first, and even the second is declared possible: "it may be that you shall be hid."

5. The Lord sees fit to exercise his dearest children with great uncertainties regarding what their lot shall be in calamities; not that they should doubt his power or good will, but that they may be sensible of the difficulty of the thing itself; that in such great and overflowing calamities the righteous shall scarcely be saved, so that it may appear to be a singular favour when God does it; that the godly, having done their duty, may yet humble themselves before the Lord, as not meriting any shelter; that they may be excited to yet more diligence; that they may learn to expect the free reward of piety in temporal things, with much submission; and that amidst all improbabilities and uncertainties, the seeker of God may learn by faith to venture much on God and rely absolutely on his goodness and tenderness, for he will not withhold any good thing from his own (Ps. 34:10; Ps. 84:11). For these causes, this exhortation is

seconded with so uncertain an encouragement, "it may be you shall be hidden."

6. Whatever uncertainty may befall those who seek God, as to temporal favours, yet they should be certain that seeking God is the shortest cut and the only way to speed, even in these things. Though they get no more than a "may be," yet upon that they are exhorted to seek the Lord, as the only way to be sure; and their "may be" puts it out of all doubt that others, who turn aside to crooked ways, may expect nothing of that kind. See 1 Pet. 4:18.

> Ver. 4. For Gaza shall be forsaken, and Ashkelon a desolation; they shall drive out Ashdod at the noonday, and Ekron shall be rooted up.
>
> 5. Woe unto the inhabitants of the sea coast; the nation of the Cherethites. The word of the Lord is against you, O Canaan, the land of the Philistines; I will even destroy you, that there shall be no inhabitant.
>
> 6. And the sea coast shall be dwellings, and cottages for shepherds, and folds for flocks.

To make the preceding exhortation more effective, the Lord subjoins a denunciation of sad judgments to come upon the enemies of the Jews upon all sides, intermixing some promises that their strokes should tend to the advantage of truth and of the church.

First he mentions the Philistines on their west coast. He threatens four of their chief cities with being solitary and desolate, with being openly and violently stormed, and their inhabitants led into captivity when it would be impossible to travel for heat, and with total extirpation. These judgments are expressed in ver. 4, with allusions to the name of the cities; and Gath, the fifth principal city of the Philistines, is omitted because it was then in possession of the Jews, or possibly because it was comprehended under the rest (as Amos 1:8).

Second, he threatens the inhabitants of the country about, lying upon the sea coasts. These were either Cherethites (of whom see 1 Sam. 30:14; Ezek. 25:16) or Philistines properly so called, who were descended of cursed Ham (Gen. 10:6, 13, 14). These the prophet threatens with his woe, and reveals God's purpose to make them desolate, that their fertile and populous country should be turned into a place of pasture (ver. 5, 6). The ground of this sentence is insinuated, for they are called "Canaan"; that is, not only of his posterity, but possessors of a part of the land of Canaan, which belonged to Israel (Josh. 13:2, 3). And these judgments were inflicted on the Philistines, partly by Pharaoh (Jer. 47:1), partly by the Babylonians (Jer. 47:2-5), and partly by the Jews themselves, after their return, and afterward by Alexander the Great, as histories record. Hence learn:

1. It is a profitable means for stirring up the visible church to repentance, and the godly to perseverance in an evil time, to consider the hand of God upon nations about, and enemies of the church. Therefore these threatenings are brought in upon the back of the former exhortations, and subjoined to them with the particle "for," as pointing out his scope in the subsequent purpose to be for their stirring up, and we may conceive the connection between the passages thus:

(a) Judgments threatened or executed upon others, ought to stir up the wicked in the church to repent. "Gather yourselves, for Gaza shall be forsaken."

(b) The godly may perceive God's tender care for them in extremities, when they look upon the full measure which he metes out to others. Seekers of God will see themselves "hid" in their troubles when they consider Gaza "forsaken" and Ashkelon "a desolation."

(c) It is an encouragement to persevere in godliness, notwithstanding any trouble, to consider that God will recompence men for all the wrongs done to the godly, and will yet restore them and make all tend toward their good. "Seek the Lord," says he, "for Gaza shall be forsaken."

2. God can, when he will, meet with those who have long been injurers of the people of God, and their inveterate enemies. These Philistines had long possessed a part of Canaan, and (as sacred histories tell) they were vexers of the church on all occasions, and now the Lord threatens to repay them in their own coin.

3. The Lord can engage his enemies in their full strength, and by his stroke undo them and put them to all disadvantages; for when he engages with the Philistines in their flourishing cities and country, he makes them "to be forsaken, and a desolation, and drives them out, and roots them up, and destroys them, that there shall be no inhabitant."

4. When God is angry, no place can promise an exemption from judgments. Strong cities, open country, and lurking holes in it, are all alike impotent before his blow; for here he threatens their cities by name, and "the nation and the land" or country.

5. There may be much woe intended and purposed against those who little apprehend it until they are made to feel it in effects; and the Lord's writing sad things against a people is the beginning of their woe, though for a time they may yet prosper. "Woe," he says, "to the Philistines," now prospering; "the hand of the Lord is against you." It foretells woe, that God had such a word or sentence in his own purpose against them, and they were visibly under woe when it was published.

6. Sin highly provokes God, and endeavours to trample his glory underfoot, and wastes souls and consciences; and therefore when he comes to punish for it, he will lay desolate the most fertile and populous land. "I will even destroy you, and there shall be no inhabitant, and the sea coast shall be dwellings and cottages for shepherds."

7. Places of great population are ordinarily places of much sin, which draws down remarkable judgments. Therefore this country is twice threatened under the name of "the sea coast," not only with relation to its fertility, but also because the gathering of many nations treasured up much sin, as fuel to impending wrath.

> Ver. 7. And the coast shall be for the remnant of the house of Judah; they shall feed thereupon. In the houses of Ashkelon they shall lie down in the evening; for the Lord their God shall visit them, and turn away their captivity.

This judgment is amplified from an event that shall follow it. When the Lord should manifest his favour to the remnant of the Jews in returning their captivity, they were to possess the land of the Philistines as a part of their own inheritance; and as the Lord's flock they were to feed and dwell there securely, even "in the evening" when it is perilous for flocks or persons to be abroad in a wasted country. This was accomplished literally in part, when at the return of the Jews from Babylon they possessed these lands; and it will be accomplished further when the Lord saves all Israel, when the inhabitants of these places are converted to the church and added to the Lord's Israel by the gospel, as is marked in Acts 8:26, 40, where Azotus is the same as Ashdod.

1. As God's covenant with a people may stand firm notwithstanding many afflictions, so that standing covenant will be forthcoming for much tenderness and restitution in due time, to the afflicted confederates, when others shall perish

in their calamities. The Lord speaks to Judah, though in captivity, by his covenant name, "the Lord their God"; and when the Philistines are gone, he promises to Judah that "the Lord their God will visit them, and turn away their captivity."

2. Covenant rights and promise rights will not fail to appear in performance, though long delayed and disappointed. This sea coast was Judah's by right; and though they were long kept out of it, yet at last "the coast shall be for the house of Judah."

3. The Lord has reserved choice mercies for his people's low state, and will do that for them then which they could not do for themselves when they were in greatest power. "The remnant of the house of Judah" shall possess the sea coast, which they could not do when they were a flourishing kingdom; and now, when they are but a remnant, yet they feed upon it, and lie down in the evening.

4. When the Lord has afflicted his church, he not only restores her, but by some special advantage he recompences her loss by trouble. This is taught in that the remnant of Judah get the land of the Philistines, to make up their hard captivity.

5. In all the calamities with which the Lord afflicts the nations, he has a singular respect to setting forth his own glory, by bringing advantage to the church and gospel by these judgments. In destroying the Philistines, he has an eye to planting Judah there, and to spreading the gospel in those places.

> Ver. 8. I have heard the reproach of Moab, and the revilings of the children of Ammon, by which they have reproached my people and magnified themselves against their border.

The next people whom God deals with are the Moabites and Ammonites, whom he conjoins in this threatening, as being both descended of Lot and so both near of kin to the Jews, and as both running together against the church and being often leagued together to that end (Ps. 83:5-7). The ground of the Lord's challenge against them is their proud scorning and reproaching of his people in the day of their affliction, and their boasting to encroach upon the church's border and to possess their land.

1. No relationship will tie the wicked to be friends of the church and the godly; but all of them, though ever so near

by nature, will run together to be her enemies. So did "Moab and the children of Ammon," though both in kin to Judah.

2. Bitter reproaches and insolent mocking of the afflicted church is a great addition to her trial, of which God will take note as a sufficient ground of controversy against the reproacher. Here it is taken notice of, as Judah's trial from Moab and Ammon, and as a ground of God's quarrel against them. "I have heard the reproach of Moab, and the revilings of the children of Ammon, whereby they have reproached my people."

3. The Lord's chastening of his people for their sins does not hinder his affection, for he will yet take notice of the wrongs done by wicked instruments, to repay them in due time. Nor do reproaches cast upon the Lord's people diminish in the slightest his regard for them, but rather increases its expression. "I have heard the reproach," says the Lord, and notwithstanding all that, yet (so much the more) they are "my people."

4. Even wicked, proud boasting and wicked plans (far more wicked deeds) against the Lord's people, their land, and their rights, will in due time be avenged by God; for it is here put upon these enemies that they "magnified themselves against their border," threatening to possess it.

> Ver. 9. Therefore, as I live, says the Lord of hosts, the God of Israel, Surely Moab will be as Sodom, and the children of Ammon as Gomorrah, even the breeding of nettles and salt-pits, and a perpetual desolation; and the residue of my people shall spoil them, and the remnant of my people shall possess them.
>
> 10. This shall they have for their pride, because they have reproached and magnified themselves against the people of the Lord of hosts.

Now follows the judgment threatened for this sin, and confirmed by an oath: these enemies should be made as Sodom and Gomorrah, not in the way of their destruction, but in God's rooting them and their memory out, and laying their land utterly desolate (as a salted land, which is barren) to bear only weeds, and that for a long time, if not forever, though there is a promise of their restoration, especially spiritual (Jer. 48:47; Jer. 49:6). And whereas they encroached upon Judah, the Lord threatens to make Judah spoil and possess their land (ver. 9), which is to be understood as ver. 7 is; and that they may know the cause of this stroke, the Lord repeats it again, that all this should come upon them because of their proud insolence and reproach of his people (ver. 10).

1. The Lord is in great earnest in saying that he will meet with the church's enemies (as he has both power and reason to do so, for he is the church's protector in covenant with her), though it be little believed, either by the enemies or by the church herself. Therefore he assures them of it by his oath, and takes unto himself titles of power and interest: "as I live, says the Lord of hosts, the God of Israel."

2. Though the Lord does not think it fit to strike every sinful nation with immediate judgments from heaven, or to make their countries utterly and forever useless, as Sodom and Gomorrah were, yet his displeasure is no less against the enemies of his people than against those whom he has so stricken; and he will in due time reveal it by desolations sore and of long continuance. Therefore his wrath on these nations is compared with that which he let forth on Sodom and Gomorrah. "Surely Moab shall be as Sodom, and the children of Ammon as Gomorrah, even the breeding of nettles and salt-pits, and a perpetual desolation."

3. Though the church may often be exposed as a prey to her enemies, yet the day may come when the church will be employed to do upon enemies that which they threatened and attempted against them. Whereas Moab and Ammon magnified themselves against Israel's border (ver. 8), now the Lord threatens that "the residue of my people shall spoil them, and the remnant of my people shall possess them."

4. In a time of judgments upon enemies, there will be need of frequent inculcating of God's controversy, if they would have a blessed use of strokes in turning to God; and that so much the rather, as they will be ready to see many things before they see their injuries done to the church, as a cause of their calamity. Therefore this quarrel is again repeated: "this shall they have for their pride."

5. Pride and insolence will not miss a fall and stroke in due time, especially when pride leads men to act sin and wrong, not out of infirmity or ignorance, but with a high hand, and against the church. "This shall they have for their pride, because they have reproached and magnified themselves against the people of the Lord."

6. A chief cause of the Lord's appearing for his reproached and wronged people is that the wrongs done to them seem to reflect upon him, as if he were not keeping covenant with them or not able to defend or redress their wrongs; and

therefore as he affects them even in troubles, so he will in due time by visible acts set out his power for them, and his love to them. Therefore this stroke is threatened, because they were insolent against "the people of the Lord of hosts"; thus both his power and interest in Israel are asserted, as being opposed by them and as being cleared in the judgment to come upon them.

> Ver. 11. The Lord will be terrible unto them; for he will famish all the gods of the earth, and men shall worship him, every one from his place, even all the isles of the heathen.

This stroke is further illustrated from an effect. When the Lord shall thus terribly plague enemies and vindicate the wrongs done to his church, he will consume the idols of the nations also, by blasting their reputation; they could not help their worshippers, but God helps his people. Thus he shall withdraw worship from them as useless things (and so famish them of their food and offerings, and make them lean); and by this means a way shall be made for spreading the knowledge of the true God, especially in the days of the gospel, in which without distinction of place (John 4:21) or of nations (Acts 10:34, 35), all the remotest nations and the isles shall serve him. And yet more particularly, in the day of the saving of all Israel, which shall be life from the dead to the generality of the Gentiles (Rom. 11:15), the fame of God's doing for them shall invite all nations to renounce their idols and serve him.

1. God is a dreadful adversary for weak man to provoke; and though he is often little regarded by the secure sinner, yet in a day of anger he will be found terrible. "The Lord will be terrible unto them."

2. As idolatry is a great cause of God's anger against a people, provoking him to smite them, so people are ordinarily so addicted to idols that they are undone before they cease to esteem them. Such is imported by the connection between the two phrases: "the Lord will be terrible unto them, for he will famish all the gods of the earth." He will terribly destroy them, for he has a mind to bring down their idols.

3. As it is a sweet fruit of judgments when they bring down idols as well as lay other things waste, so, though the Lord allows idolatry for a time, yet at last, by judgments on idolators and by mercies toward his people, he will abolish idols and exalt himself as the only true God, to be chosen

and served by the world. "He will famish all the gods of the earth, and men shall worship him."

4. It is the privilege of the New Testament and a part of the glory of Christ's kingdom, that the Lord's worship is not confined to a temple at Jerusalem, nor to the nation of Israel, but that in every place, even in the remotest isles, all nations have access to God through the Mediator; for such is here prophesied. "Men shall worship him, every one from his place, even all the isles of the heathen."

5. It is of great concern to all the churches of Christ to note, and by their prayers to help forward and hasten, the conversion of Israel, as tending to the advancement of the gospel among the Gentiles; for then this prophecy will get a new and further accomplishment (Rom. 11:15).

> Ver. 12. You Ethiopians also, you shall be slain by my sword.

The third denunciation is against the Ethiopians, who were either a nation beyond Egypt, who had served in armies employed against the church, as these other southern nations were commonly employed abroad (Nahum 3:9; Ezek. 27:10), or a people in Arabia, also descended from Cush and lying on the other side of the Red Sea, over against Ethiopia proper. These are the people usually called Ethiopians in scripture; and as they had been destroyed by Asa (2 Chron. 14:9-15) and given into the hands of Sennacherib as a ransom for Judah (Isa. 43:3; 2 Kings 19:9), so here the Lord threatens to cut them off by his sword in the hand of Nebuchadnezzar, either in his conquest of Arabia or when he subdued Egypt and destroyed those other Ethiopians among Egypt's associates, as they were (Jer. 46:2, 9).

1. Though the enemies of the church be ever so many on all sides, and ever so far away, yet God's hand is enough for them all; for here he undertakes against enemies on all quarters, and besides the Philistines, Moab, and Ammon, he threatens that "the Ethiopians also shall be slain."

2. It is a special part of reading judgments aright, to see God's hand in them, that his quarrel may be studied, that his love to his people in avenging their quarrel may be seen, that his sovereign power and providence over all the world may be adored and the stricken may know where to look for blessing and issue. Therefore it is added, "you shall be slain by my sword."

Ver. 13. And he will stretch out his hand against the north, and destroy Assyria, and will make Nineveh a desolation, and dry like a wilderness.

14. And flocks shall lie down in the midst of her, all the beasts of the nations; both the cormorant and the bittern shall lodge in the upper lintels of it; their voice shall sing in the windows; desolation shall be in their thresholds; for he shall uncover the cedar-work.

The last denunciation is against the Assyrians in the north, and the chief city of that empire, which he threatens to make desolate by his outstretched hand, and like a barren wilderness, to be an habitation for all kinds of beasts and monstrous creatures of all sorts, instead of eminent princes and the many people who frequented there. And for this end, where there had been so many stately habitations, he would pull down their roofs and leave nothing but bare walls, fit for such guests to haunt in.

1. In executing judgments, God will not forget to reach greatest enemies with saddest strokes. Therefore he sets out the judgments for Assyria and Nineveh in so dreadful and ample a way, not only to give more ample encouragement to his people (whose faith might most readily faint in this instance), but also to testify the greatness of his displeasure against them for leading his Israel captive. "He will stretch out his hand against the north and destroy Assyria, and will make Nineveh a desolation, and dry like a wilderness."

2. Though God may seem to own a prospering enemy against his people, and they may think so because of their success, yet God will in due time testify the contrary. They boasted of old that they came not up without the Lord (2 Kings 18:25); therefore the Lord will stretch out his hand against them.

3. Though sinful ways and oppression may for a time raise men up to great power and glory, and make cities and countries to flourish, yet before all is done it will lay them as low, yea, and make them more desolate than is imaginable. Such did Nineveh and Assyria feel, when "flocks lay down in the midst of her; all the beasts of the nations." And no wonder, for these creatures were no more monstrous in men's account than the former inhabitants were in God's sight.

> Ver. 15. This is the rejoicing city which dwelt carelessly, who said in her heart, I am, and there is none beside me. How she has become a desolation, a place for beasts to lie down in! Every one who passes by her shall hiss and wag his hand.

The equity of this sentence upon that city is confirmed by considering its causes. Not recounting her particular sins, he instead takes notice of the result of all her sins, and the common sin into which they all ran, i.e. her security and insolence. Being blinded with the splendour of her prosperity, she despised all other nations and cast off all fear of any change; and because of this it was righteous with God, by laying her so desolate, to make her an ignominious spectacle to all beholders.

1. It is not possible for wicked men to guide their prosperity and success in all courses well, but they will swell in pride thereby, and so provoke God yet more to anger against them; for "this is the rejoicing city that dwelt carelessly, that said in her heart, I am, and there is none beside me."

2. No matter how much wicked men, prospering in sin, have been admired by others (or have admired themselves) for their prosperity, yet divine indignation shall in due time make them as remarkable for ignominious calamity. "How the rejoicing city has become a desolation, a place for beasts to lie down in; everyone who passes by her shall hiss and wag his hand."

CHAPTER III

After these threatenings denounced against other nations, the Lord returns to speak to the church. He threatens Jerusalem for the many iniquities done in her (ver. 1, 2), especially for the sins of rulers in state (ver. 3) and of church guides (ver. 4), and confirms the equity of this sentence from God's justice and their incorrigibility, either by the word (ver. 5) or by the rod (ver. 6, 7). And because the godly would be frightened by these threatenings, therefore he subjoins many comforts to them concerning their return from the captivity and the mercies of the gospel, exhorting them to wait on God in expectation that he who punished the church would appear and punish her enemies (ver. 8), at which time he would propagate true religion and make Jews and Gentiles jointly serve him (ver. 9), would gather his people from the remotest parts of the world (ver. 10), would endue them with excellent qualifications and give them safety (ver. 11-13) and furnish them with ample matter of joy (ver. 14, 15) and of serving God without fear (ver. 16), considering his power and love (ver. 17) and what he will do for recovering their broken and desperate state (ver. 18-20).

> Ver. 1. Woe to her who is filthy and polluted, to the oppressing city.
> 2. She obeyed not the voice; she received not correction; she trusted not in the Lord; she drew not near to her God.

Since the Lord had by his prophet used all the former means for reclaiming his people, but in vain, he comes now to pronounce his last sentence against the body of that nation, and threatens Jerusalem with a woe. The general causes of this woe were her pollution through oppression and violence, and her contempt of warnings from the word, her not being bettered by corrections, her not trusting in God, but in other things, and her not entertaining communion with him who offered himself to her in the covenant.

1. God's anger declared against a people portends misery enough to them, though there were no other evidences of it; and he will not spare nor exempt his own people when they provoke him, especially those who, being most obliged to him, do yet prove eminent in defection. Therefore, as he threatens other nations, so also he threatens his own sinful people, and names Jerusalem for all, because she was chief in the desertion, though she should have been holy and a sanctuary to God; and under this woe he comprehends all the evils which afterward pursued that people.

2. Injustice and oppression is an abominable and filthy sin, especially in the church; and riches gathered that way do not give any splendour, but make men and places vile in God's sight, and obnoxious to his curse. "The oppressing city is filthy and polluted," as the crop or gorge of a ravenous bird, where all unclean things are heaped together, or as a public spectacle of infamy, as the word imports; and therefore "woe to her."

3. As disobedience unto the Lord, revealing his mind by his word, is ground sufficient for a quarrel; and as contempt of the authority of God in his word is the great cause of men's boldness in sin; so it will be a great aggravation

against sinners that warnings from the word do not reclaim them. "Woe to her who is filthy; she obeyed not the voice."

4. As rods sent upon the church will either make her better, by instructing and humbling her under God's hand, or ripen her yet more for God's woe, so obstinacy in sin under corrections is a sad aggravation thereof. "Woe to her, for she received not correction," or instruction by her correction, as the word imports.

5. God is so willing to be the stay and confidence of his people, that it is a quarrel when they will not lean all their weight upon him. And as lack of faith in God drives men to sinful and wrong courses, so this is a great iniquity before him. "Woe to her who is filthy; she drew not near to God, and she trusted not in the Lord," because she could not take pains to "draw near to God."

7. The Lord's gracious condescension and offering of himself to the visible church, to be approached in all cases, and her possession of having an interest in him, aggravates her fault in not making use of him nor taking hold of such an advantage; for it is an addition to her sin, that "she drew not near to her God"; that is, to God who was hers in offer and visible covenant, and in whom she gloried as hers.

> Ver. 3. Her princes within her are roaring lions; her judges are evening wolves; they gnaw not the bones till the morrow.

The Lord denounces this woe upon Jerusalem more especially for the sins of her state rulers, her princes and superior magistrates, who ought to have been for the praise of well-doers, and a comfort and protector to the subjects; but they were a terror, and cruel as lions, and that not against enemies but against subjects in the midst of the city. Her judges or inferior magistrates were no better than they, but were as cruel and insatiably greedy as hungry wolves, who coming out in the evening (after fasting all day) do not only eat the flesh of their prey, but gnaw the very bones and leave nothing until the morrow. See Prov. 28:17.

1. As a land ordinarily degenerates only when magistrates of all ranks are corrupt, so the sins of rulers have a special hand in drawing judgments on a nation; for when "the city is filthy and polluted" (ver. 1), then "princes and judges are lions and wolves"; and because of this a woe is denounced.

2. It is a great iniquity and abuse of God's ordinance of magistracy when the hearts of men in power are lifted up

above their brethren, and when they employ all their power for their own ends, and against those for whose good they should employ it. This was the sin of princes and judges; "they are roaring lions within her, and evening wolves."

3. It is a judgment and a presage of ruin, when rulers do not hate covetousness, but when hungry, greedy men are entrusted with affairs; when they who in their private stations could not bite and oppress, are enabled by their power and place to play the lion and wolf. Such was Judah's case; "her judges are evening wolves; they gnaw not the bones till the morrow," or, "they leave not the bones to be gnawed," or "continue not to gnaw the bones till the morrow," but devour up all.

> Ver. 4. Her prophets are light and treacherous persons; her priests have polluted the sanctuary; they have done violence to the law.

The Lord subjoins the sins of church officers, as a further cause of this judgment. He charges their false prophets, who pretended to have an extraordinary calling, with profaneness and levity in their carriage, and inconstancy in their doctrine, changing it to fit all opinions and parties, which was great perfidy. And their priests or ordinary ministers are charged with profaning the sanctuary and holy things, in ministering unto the Lord, and with perverting the true sense of the law in their ordinary doctrine and teaching of the people.

1. When God reckons with a land for sin, it is no strange thing to see those who should be means of reclaiming people, accessory to the guilt of the land and partakers in the judgment; both prophets and priests are here found guilty. See Lam. 2:14.

2. Lack of sobriety in carriage, and rashness, and inconstancy in doctrine, is a character of a false minister; it is accessory to a land's sin, and liable to sad judgments, whatever extraordinary gift the minister pretends to have. "Her prophets are light," or rash, unstable, and heady persons.

3. An unfaithful, time-serving minister, though he may please himself and others, is yet in God's account but a perfidious man, betraying his trust and the souls of men; and men will find it so in due time. Being "light," they are also "treacherous persons."

4. Every minister who would approve himself to God, ought to give himself both to deal with God on the people's behalf and with the people on God's behalf. Such was the priest's charge: to minister to the Lord in the sanctuary (in the name of the people), and to be ordinary teachers of the law to the people (in the name of God), and in both of these they failed here.

5. It is a token of sin's full ripeness and of speedy approaching judgment, when ministers dare pollute the holy things of God by going about profanely and in a carnal way in his worship and service; when their own familiarity and frequency in it, without sensible hearts, have bred a contempt for it; and when they embolden others to do the like, or tempt them to abhor God's service. Thus it was with Jerusalem, when woe came upon her: "her priests have polluted the sanctuary."

6. The holy scriptures are the revealed will of the supreme Lord, and the unalterable rule of men's duty, according to which they may expect blessings or curses; and therefore it is high presumption in men to wrest and force it to applaud their fancies, and to take their light to the word rather than coming with submission of heart to receive light from it; and so they make of scripture what they please. This is also a quarrel, "they have done violence to the law."

> Ver. 5. The just Lord is in the midst thereof; he will not do iniquity; every morning he brings his judgment to light, he fails not; but the unjust knows no shame.

The equity of this threatened woe is explained by the justice of God. God, who dwelt among them, could not pass over such gross abominations without imputation to his holiness; but he was also just in giving her fair play in this process, and not pronouncing this sentence until she was found incorrigible. This he proves from two evidences, of which the first is that though he had daily and early held forth his law by his messengers, as a lamp by which they might see the evil of their ways, and so did not fail to give them warning that they might be reclaimed; yet they proved obstinate and impudently blushed not to sin against such clear light.

1. Though a visible church, persevering in sin, may bless herself and expect great things from God's visible presence with her, yet all these privileges declare the impenitent sinner's disadvantage and his closeness to the stroke. If

the just Lord is "in the midst thereof, he will do no iniquity," i.e. in sparing her in such sin. See Amos 3:2.

2. God delights so much in mercy, and is so tender of his people, that he never proceeds to severity so long as there is another way to reclaim them or to stint the course of their sin. This abundantly justifies him when he judges; for in this also he is "the just Lord in the midst thereof; he will do no iniquity" in that he will not cast her off until other means are tried, as the following words explain.

3. It is a great favour from the Lord, and a testimony of his long-suffering, when he does not take every sinner at his first word, but follows him with frequent warnings of his danger if he goes on, and offers of advantage if he returns; for it is marked here as an evidence of God's kindness in this proceeding, that "every morning (which was the usual time of prophets' preaching, Jer. 7:25) he brings his judgment to light; he fails not."

4. Though men may pretend to acknowledge the authority of God and his word, yet it is usual that when they are mad on sin and going to ruin, a presage of it should be that the word will do nothing for them. It is marked as their sin, and a token that judgment must come on, when notwithstanding warnings "the unjust knows no shame."

5. All who are within the visible church and who acknowledge a deity, and yet dare with a high hand to sin against the clear light of the word, do proclaim themselves to be destitute of all ingenuity and given up to the plague of affronted impudence; for such "know no shame."

> Ver. 6. I have cut off the nations; their towers are desolate; I have made their streets waste, that none passes by. Their cities are destroyed, so that there is no man, that there is no inhabitant.
>
> 7. I said, Surely you will fear me; you will receive instruction, so their dwelling should not be cut off, though I punished them; but they rose early and corrupted all their doings.

A second evidence of their incorrigibility is that the Lord had often visited the nations round about, not one but many of them, and not with ordinary but with remarkable strokes, destroying their strongholds or princes (which like corner-stones, as the word imports, uphold the fabric of the commonwealth), and making such havoc of the nations that neither traveler nor inhabitant was to be found. All this, considering outward means and their duty, might have warned them to flee the sins for which those nations had been punished, and might have instructed them to fear God and reform their ways, so that their afflictions might have been kept within the bounds of fatherly correction, and they might have prevented the last stroke, of being put out of their land. And yet for all this, they were so far from turning to God that they were even worse, all their ways being not only sinful but corrupt, and bent, active and headlong in going wrong, as if it had been their study. They were as earnest to go wrong as he was to reclaim them (ver. 5).

1. The church is so dear to God, and he so tender of her well-being, that before he ruins her he will preach her duty and danger to her, upon the experience of others; for all these sad judgments on others were to inform her, that she might prevent the like.

2. Judgments inflicted on any of the world, is a document and call to others to fear God, especially those who are guilty of the same sins; yea, even the church ought to take warning from judgments on enemies, for "he cut off the nations, laid their towers desolate," so that his church might "fear him and receive instruction."

3. Though God only wise, to whom all his works are known from the beginning, cannot be disappointed of any expectation he has, yet his dealing with his sinful people, and the means he uses, are those which in reason might promise to bring forth the fruits of repentance and reformation. Indeed they oblige them to such; and therefore he subjoins this warning from his judgments on others: "I said, Surely you will fear me; you will receive instruction," speaking after the manner of men and showing what his dealing obliged them to.

4. True godliness, and an evidence of true turning from apostasy, consists in a holy awe of God, and fear because of our offending him, or of offending him again, joined with spiritual wisdom, learned from the word and from our experience of ourselves and our failings, or of others, to carry on and feed that disposition. For so is their duty here described, "you will fear me, you will receive instruction."

5. No strokes on sinners ought to discourage them, if they are penitent, from coming to God or expecting good at his hand. If they would "fear him, so their dwelling would not be cut off, though he punished them."

6. Though true godliness, or turning to God from sinful ways, will not exempt a people from fatherly chastisements

to make them more wise and their turning yet more serious, yet the penitent in these will meet with favour, considering what he deserves and what awaits those who go on in impenitence. Such is insinuated here: "so their dwelling should not be cut off, though I punished them."

7. To be delivered from going into captivity, where we should lack the public ordinances of God's worship, is a mercy which may sweeten much afftict on in our own land; it is a promise to the penitent that their dwelling shall not be cut off, though the Lord may punish them.

8. Such is the madness of men, especially where the Lord has given them over, that no example will warn them. Their security, conceit, dreaming of privileges, etc., will hide all dangers from them until they light upon them themselves; for all these warnings were not effectual, but "they corrupted all their doings."

9. The more means are essayed to reclaim a people without success, the worse will that people grow. Where means are not blessed, they leave a curse behind them; therefore since all these means, warnings, threatenings, promises, and lesser strokes were in vain, what follows? "They rose up early and corrupted all their doings"; they were vigilant, active, and earnest in going wrong.

10. It is a clear proof of incorrigibility, and an omen of certain ruin, when a people are madder upon sin after judgments have been let forth for it; for by this the Lord proves their incorrigibility, and seals this woe upon them; when the other nations were cut off, yet "they rose up early and corrupted all their doings."

> Ver. 8. Therefore wait upon me, says the Lord, until the day that I rise up to the prey; for my determination is to gather the nations, that I may assemble the kingdoms, to pour upon them my indignation, even all my fierce anger, for all the earth shall be devoured with the fire of my jealousy.

After the Lord had thus accused and left the body of the Jews under his woe, he now turns to the godly among them. They could not but be affrighted with these threatenings, and troubled with thoughts of the dispersion of the people. Therefore he gives various grounds to encourage them, some of which were to be accomplished in part at their return from the captivity, and all of them spiritually in the days of the

Messiah, besides what may be expected yet more fully at the conversion and saving of all Israel.

The first ground of encouragement is that as they had God to wait and depend upon in the time of the ensuing calamity, in which God would consume the Jews because of his jealousy over them, so there was a ground of hope that when the Lord had punished his church, he would appear against her enemies, to take the prey out of their teeth and raise up the nations to consume them, and make such havoc of them as might testify his zeal for his people and his glory, which had been violated by them. And therefore the godly were patiently to expect this day, so much the rather as all this should tend to the advancement of the kingdom of Christ, as is afterward explained.

1. The Lord's just controversy against the visible church, provoking him to abandon her, does not diminish in the least his affection to any godly remnant in it, nor make him forget them in sad times; for in the midst of all these quarrels he has a word to them.

2. God is jealous of his church and of her affection toward him, and for his church against all who trouble her. In both cases, his jealousy when provoked is terrible, and will raise up many instruments and make a great destruction; for this jealousy of God, first against the Jews (which is supposed here, and first in order to be understood) and then against her enemies (which is most expressly mentioned) will "arise to the prey," as a roaring lion; it will "assemble nations and kingdoms," to make them scourges to the Jews, and then to be plagued themselves; it "will pour out indignation and fierce anger, and devour all the earth (or land)."

3. When the Lord is about to bring forth some glorious piece of his gospel work, the church is to expect some great shakings and visitations, to make way for it. In order to fulfill what follows in this chapter, there will be "a devouring of all the earth," a casting of all into the furnace so that he may bring out his pure metal.

4. When it pleases the Lord to let judgments upon his church lead to a captivity and a leaving of them in their enemies' hand, the godly are to expect a time of trial of faith and patience, before there is a change. Such is here insinuated, that when Judah is consumed there will be need of "waiting on God" before a day of vengeance on enemies comes about.

5. Times of greatest trouble have matter of encouragement to the godly, in that they have ground of present

dependence upon God for strength and supply during the strait, and ground of future hope that there will be an end, and that vengeance will come on oppressors. They are allowed and invited to "wait upon God," until that other day come.

6. Patience is the kindly fruit of hope, and the posture in which the godly are to expect issue, and to find present troubles easy. "Wait upon me, says the Lord, until the day."

> Ver. 9. For then will I turn to the people a pure language, that they may all call upon the name of the Lord, to serve him with one consent.
>
> 10. From beyond the rivers of Ethiopia, your suppliants, even the daughter of my dispersed, shall bring my offering.

A second ground of encouragement is that these calamities on the Jews and their enemies should not make the church to cease, but that God should propagate pure doctrine, pure worship, and profession unto many people, both Jews and Gentiles, who should jointly serve him and help one another in his obedience (ver. 9). Thus a "pure language" seems to be understood, as Isa. 19:18, not secluding purity of heart among some of them but communicating it in pure language (as may appear from Isa. 6:5; Matt. 12:34; James 3:2, and from what is further propounded here). Yea, the Lord promises that he will gather them from the farthest parts of the world, to seek him and offer service to him (ver. 10). This promise is accomplished partly in his gathering together in Christ his dispersed elect throughout the world and its remotest corners (John 11:52), and these Ethiopians (or, as some conceive, Egyptians) among the rest; and partly it shall be accomplished when the Lord shall call scattered Israel from the remotest parts of the earth to serve him, and they shall bring in some Gentiles with them, as a gift to God.

1. It is matter of praise to God and of encouragement to the godly, that no matter how nations rise and fall, yet he will never lack a church, though he should gather it from pagan Gentiles and those from whom there is little apparent hope; for when "the earth is devoured" (ver. 8), he will get "many people," as the word is, and "from beyond the rivers of Ethiopia."

2. Purity of doctrine, worship, and profession is the glory of a gospel church, and a glorious work of God to make and keep it so. The Lord says, "I will turn to the

people a pure language," or pure doctrine and profession, instead of their idolatrous and blasphemous fancies and their way of following them.

3. Purity in doctrine, worship, and profession does not consist of a lawless liberty or toleration to think or say what men will, but is conjoined with and carried on by a united uniformity; and as this is the rich fruit and recompence of much trouble, so it is to be expected in the Lord's time and measure; for when after much trouble they shall have "a pure language, they will serve him with one consent," even in that pure language. See Jer. 32:39; Zech. 14:9.

4. As unanimity in the matters of God, and the free access of Jew and Gentile to serve God, is a great mercy of the kingdom of Christ, so when seekers of God are of one heart and put hand to the work, to help one another, without obstructing, it is a token of thriving service. This is also included in the promise, as a great blessing and a means of much good. "They shall serve him with one consent."

5. The true characteristics of a converted and spiritual people are their being much in prayer to God, employing and making use of him in all things, and their giving up themselves to be his servants and at his disposal; and in testimony of their subjection and thankfulness, they will put hand to his work, as they are called; they will do all as service to him, and will bring their worship, themselves, and others as they are able, to offer up to him. Thus they are here described; "they all call on the name of the Lord," when they get the pure language; they are suppliants; they serve him, and bring his offering.

6. As the Lord will not lose any of his elect, no matter how far they are scattered through the world, and will recover his own when they seem to be scattered afar off and are driven to exile, without hope or probability of return, in their own apprehension; so in particular the Lord will in due time seek after and recover his ancient people, now of a long time scattered, whereby there shall be a reviving of his service in the world. "From beyond the rivers of Ethiopia" he will seek "the daughter of his dispersed," and cause them to come, at which time there will be "suppliants and offerings, and serving of him with one consent."

Ver. 11. In that day you will not be ashamed of all your
doings, in which you have transgressed against me;
for then I will take away out of the midst of you those
who rejoice in your pride, and you shall no more be
haughty because of my holy mountain.

A third ground of encouragement is the promise of the
church's reconciliation with God, through the free pardon
of sin, and her renovation. The glory of this should rub off
the shame of her former iniquities, and should be followed
with such happiness as would take away the ignominy of
her former afflictions for sin. And particularly he promises
to purge away their conceit and carnal glory in the temple
and outward ceremonies, and to make worshipping God in
spirit and truth to be their only request.

These promises are made to the church in respect to
the elect within her, and they hold forth that eventually, at
some times, and especially at the conversion of Israel,
there may be a more general renovation of church members;
but neither do they hold forth that they shall be universally
such, nor do they prescribe that it is the church's duty to
admit none but such.

1. Greatest promises of outward things will not afford
ground for encouragement to the godly, unless with these
the work of reconciliation and renovation is going on. Therefore this is promised, to encourage the godly Jews.

2. Though the Lord's reconciled people have cause to be
ashamed of themselves and to testify their repentance by
blushing for their backslidings (Ezek. 16:61), yet being
reconciled and turned to God, they may lift up their face
through a Mediator, expecting not to be eternally confounded,
and that God will not charge them with these sins, but will
bury them, and make their future conduct rub off that reproach; and by his doing for them he will take away the
ignominious effects of their sin. So much does this promise
assure us, "in that day you shall not be ashamed for all
your doings, in which you have transgressed against me."

3. As men cannot prove their sin to be really pardoned
except by their renewed conversation, so without this there
is no taking away of the ignominy of former sinful ways.
Thus the Lord proves that they shall be a pardoned people,
and not ashamed, "for then I will take away out of your midst
those who rejoice in your pride."

4. The shameful sin of the visible church is her boasting of external privileges, and being bold to sin because of them. Her outward mercies then become her snare and stand between her and the kernel of them. This is the sin to be removed, "rejoicing in your pride" or "excellency," as the word signifies, and "being haughty because of my holy mountain."

5. As the Lord must be the worker of our reconciliation and renovation, as his making a promise about it teaches us; so when the Lord has a mind to do good and appear for a people who have lain under great ignominy and judgments for sin, he can soon reform them and make them shine in holiness, as here he promises to the church of the Jews, whose name to this day is a reproach. "You shall not be ashamed; I will take away those who rejoice in your pride."

> Ver. 12. I will also leave in your midst an afflicted and poor people; and they shall trust in the name of the Lord.
> 13. The remnant of Israel shall not do iniquity nor speak lies; neither shall a deceitful tongue be found in their mouth; for they shall feed and lie down, and none shall make them afraid.

The sanctification of the church is further commended, that no affliction, paucity, or poverty (as when they returned from Babylon) should obstruct it, but rather help it on. The Lord will empty them of all things by affliction, that they may learn to trust in God and study holiness and sincerity, which are approved in his sight; and they shall be encouraged to this by God's protecting them and keeping them in safety from violence and fear, notwithstanding their low state.

1. When the Lord corrects his church, he ordinarily makes not a full end, but leaves some to get good by these afflictions, and the fruit of them from the Lord. "I will also leave," says the Lord, "the remnant of Israel."

2. The Lord sees fit to exercise even a remnant of his people with many afflictions, after he has by their deliverance taken away their reproach, so that they may be put yet to a more serious study of holiness; for they are "afflicted, and a poor people," that they may "trust and do no iniquity."

3. Trust in God is a chief part and the root of true holiness; and the afflicted may have yet ground of hope, and may rise the more in confidence that trouble would make them humble, and carnal confidences fail. And as afflictions do

not allow us to be discouraged, but put us to trusting and immediate dependence, and do feed faith; so trust in God is ordinarily man's last shift, which he will never essay until he is emptied of all things else, and led by God to this duty; and God undertakes to work faith as well as to give the reward of it. All these are imported in this promise, as it is propounded: "I will leave in your midst an afflicted and poor people; and they shall trust in the name of the Lord," and here their holiness begins.

4. Trust in God will encourage and enable the believer to follow holiness and God's way; and though perfection is not attainable in this life, yet the believer is to prove his integrity by avoiding the dominion of sin and hypocrisy and dissimulation, and to employ God for attaining this. This is the sum of that promise, "the remnant of Israel shall not do iniquity nor speak lies; neither shall a deceitful tongue be found in their mouth."

5. As God is sufficiently able to give safety and support to his own in their weakest condition, and as the godly have the covenant right to temporal preservation when it is good for them, and are always hid in the secret of God's presence, and may attain peace and freedom from the slavish fear of trouble; so the faith or sensible experience of this protection is a sufficient motive to saints, to study holiness and keep the way of God. This is imported in the promise, "they shall feed (as his flock) and lie down, and none shall make them afraid"; and in its being subjoined, as a reason why they shall study holiness, "they shall not do iniquity, for they shall feed and lie down."

> Ver. 14. Sing, O daughter of Zion; shout, O Israel; be glad
> and rejoice with all the heart, O daughter of Jerusalem.
> 15. The Lord has taken away your judgments; he has
> cast out your enemy; the king of Israel, even the Lord,
> is in the midst of you; you shall not see evil any more.

The Lord subjoins yet further encouragements to the godly, in two exhortations directed to the church of the gospel. In these yet more of her allowance and privileges are held forth.

The first exhortation is to full joy, because of God's removing of plagues and enemies, because of his presence manifested in the midst of her and her freedom from former evils. This imports a promise that she should rejoice because of this, and that the godly of the present time might rejoice in hope of it.

1. As the true Israel in spirit, children of Zion and of that Jerusalem which is from above, and who are heirs to all the promises, have allowance and matter of complete joy above any other society, and therefore ought to entertain their good condition with thankfulness and rejoicing; so when Israel shall be converted, the church may expect that after their long silence and bitter sorrow, there will be a notable song from them. This exhortation, "Sing, O daughter of Zion; shout, O daughter of Israel," is a warrant and direction to all the godly, showing how short they often come, and a promise to Israel in particular.

2. Though sin and spiritual judgments, together with outward calamities following thereupon, and enemies inward and outward, do often trouble the church; yet in due time they shall not mar her mirth, but shall rather furnish matter of a song, when God (after he has quit the proceeding against her, and healed her spiritual judgments and plagues) shall speedily remove them and her enemies. "Sing," says he; "the Lord has taken away your judgments; he has cast out your enemies." By "judgments" we are not only to understand her outward calamities, but all her spiritual plagues accompanying sin, and all the Lord's sad sentences against her, which were the rise of the enemies' invasion and success.

3. It is matter of great joy to have interest in the true God of the church, who is the Lord Jehovah, all-sufficient to make his followers happy and to maintain his rights and theirs (Ezek. 35:10), especially when the right is made clear to believers, and the Lord is not standing afar off, but very near and in the midst of them. This may be expected by everyone who lives by faith, and is also matter of a song: "the king of Israel, even the Lord, is in your midst."

4. Though the church cannot promise herself to be wholly and perpetually free from trouble while she is within time, yet when Israel is converted she may expect not to meet with those judgments they have endured since their rejection; and the godly may expect their own competent breathing-times from trouble, and that trouble shall not hurt them, nor prove evil when it comes, and that the day shall come in which they shall be forever freed from it, which may sweeten what they meet with, that it may not hinder their joy. This is imported in the cause of their song, "you shall not see evil any more."

Ver. 16. In that day it shall be said to Jerusalem, Fear
not; and to Zion, Let not your hand be slack.

The second exhortation (which the Lord promises shall be
directed to the church, either by her pastors sent out, or by
way of acclamation from others, beholding her happy state,
particularly at their return from Babylon, and at the conversion of all Israel) is that by faith they would put away
fainting fear, and stir up themselves to serve God cheerfully. And for this end there are several encouragements
subjoined.

1. It is a usual infirmity in the godly, that their disposition comes far short of their allowance. When they are
allowed to "be glad and rejoice with all the heart" (ver. 14),
they need to be stirred up not to fear or faint.

2. The people of God are many times so mistaken of their
own case that others may see more of their good condition
than themselves, and they need the ministry of the word to
direct their thoughts, to which they should submit; for "in
that day it shall be said to Jerusalem, Fear not."

3. Faithless fainting, fear, and idleness are usual companions, which feed and entertain one another. Fear weakens
the hands from duty, and idleness feeds discouragement yet
more; therefore both are joined here: "fear not, let not your
hands be slack or faint."

4. As the reconciled people of God have no cause of
heartless fear, if they would set themselves against it; and
as it becomes them to go about any duty enjoined by God,
with alacrity and cheerfulness, so our encouragements in
God are then rightly used when they strengthen us to duty.
This much also do these exhortations, being put together,
import: "fear not, let not your hands be slack."

5. As it is the duty of faithful ministers, so also it is the
commendation of all the godly, to stir up one another to
encouragement through faith, and to cheerfulness in the
obedience of faith; for they are commendably employed if
they "say to Jerusalem, Fear not."

Ver. 17. The Lord your God in the midst of you is mighty;
he will save, he will rejoice over you with joy; he will
rest in his love, he will joy over you with singing.

The reason for the preceding exhortation, and the ground
of their encouragements, is taken from God's covenant made
with them, and his presence which was conspicuous in the

midst of them. From these grounds they might expect not only that his power should be employed for their deliverance, but that also out of his love, by which he had chosen them, he would delight and acquiesce in them, and rejoice over them, and do them good, and sweetly cherish them, notwithstanding what might be said against them.

1. The Lord's covenant with his church is not broken off by discord or affliction; and the Lord, in manifesting himself to be in covenant with her, by his ordinances (as signs of his presence) says much mercy to her, according as she needs it. The ground of all the following encouragements is, "the Lord your God is in the midst of you."

2. As the church may expect freedom from all her troubles, either by prevention, support, or deliverance, so her interest in God through the covenant makes his omnipotence forthcoming to her for that end, and she may reckon her strength by what is in him. "The Lord your God is mighty," and therefore "he will save."

3. Though the proofs of divine power let forth for the church's good do set him out above all blessing and praise, yet his love-embraces are above all and are the chief of the church's encouragements. Therefore they are added as a further degree of comfort: "he will rejoice over you."

4. Though Christ's bride is of no worth in herself, nor does he need her, yet because he has chosen her to be his bride, he will not come behind in any duty which such a relationship promises or engages to among men; but he will take pleasure to be her God, will esteem, commend, cherish and delight in her, not according to her worth, but according to the dignity which he has called her unto, and as his wife, for his love puts comeliness upon her; and he will express his delight by doing for her, as if her well-being were a sufficient recompence of all his pains. "He will rejoice over you with joy," which points at his inward delight; "he will joy over you with singing," which notes the outward expression of it; and both are borrowed from the carriage of a bridegroom to his bride. See Isa. 62:5.

5. The Lord's love so acquiesces in his people, whom he has chosen, that he does not only cherish them by many expressions of love when he takes up his rest in and with them, but he also answers all objections that might be against them, with his own free love, which has chosen them. He reckons that having loved them, he will always love them; and having let out his affection upon the unworthy, he will bear with their frailties, and not give a bill of divorce, nor

chide continually. Thus "he will rest in his love," or her whom he loves, as having gained his end when he obtains her; and in "his love" or affection toward her, which is sufficient to make him not weary of her nor reject her. Yea, as the word signifies, "he will be deaf and dumb in his love"; his love (to speak after the manner of men) will guard his ear from hearing and his mouth from uttering accusations against her, so as to cast her off or to deny her marriage entertainment, though otherwise he may humble her.

> Ver. 18. I will gather those who are sorrowful for the solemn assembly, who are of you, to whom the reproach of it was a burden.

The Lord himself takes the word out of the mouths of the encouragers, and himself applies the more general promise (ver. 7) to the broken and afflicted state of the Jews, for the encouragement of the godly remnant. He promises that he would gather and bring them again to their own land, especially those (or for the sake of those) who were mourners for the lack of solemn worship of God, as they had it in their own land, and burdened with the reproach following thereupon (Ps. 137).

1. As it is the duty of all the people of God to find God speaking in and by his word unto them, so his mind is to be found in his word and nowhere else. He himself confirms what these exhorters had said of him (ver. 16, 17) for the further strengthening of the godly; and what they said of him from his word, that he says of himself when he speaks. "I will gather," or employ my power and love to save, as ver. 17.

2. The Lord, speaking by his word, will teach and allow his afflicted people to apply general promises to their own case, as if they had been intended for them alone. Therefore he applies that general promise of manifesting power and love, to their particular strait of the captivity. "I will gather"; that is, I will employ my power and love to help you in your particular distress.

3. As the Lord's people often provoke him justly to deprive them of public ordinances and to scatter them into corners, so the lack thereof will be a sad affliction to sensible souls, as depriving them of the most lively representation of heaven on earth, as obscuring much of God's glory which is seen and spoken of in the sanctuary, and as

secluding the godly from the mutual and comfortable fellowship of another in his ordinances, and from much refreshing and help which they had by those means. Here they "are sorrowful for the solemn assembly," in which the Jews used to meet at the temple to worship God.

4. Such is the insolence and cruelty of the church's enemies that the godly may not only be deprived of solemn ordinances, where such have power, but may have their burden and grief augmented, and may be in peril of being crushed with insolent reproachings of their religion and worship. Here it is added to the former, "the reproach of it was a burden."

5. When the Lord has brought his people lowest for their sin, and enemies have gotten most of their will in crushing them, yet they are not outside the reach of his help. He can and in his appointed time will bring them out of all their captivities and troubles; for notwithstanding all these afflictions, "I will gather them," says the Lord.

6. As it is the duty of the godly in times of calamities to be most affected with what concerns God's honour and seems to allow prejudice, so those lie nearest promises for the public and for themselves also; for they who "are sorrowful for the solemn assembly, are of you," that is, your true and kindly children; and they get the first promise, "I will gather them" and the church for their sake.

> Ver. 19. Behold, at that time I will undo all who afflict you, and I will save her who halts and gather her who was driven out; and I will get them praise and fame in every land, where they have been put to shame.

The Lord confirms this gracious promise of their return, and undertakes to remove all impediments that might arise from themselves or others, to hinder their gathering and restitution. As for outward opposition, he promises to ruin her oppressors; and for herself, although by her affliction and captivity she were so crushed and broken, like a disjointed body, that she was not able to move -- yea, so scattered as the members of a body cast here and there into corners, that there is no probable hope of her gathering -- yet he promises not only to make a resurrection from the dead, and to strengthen her who halted, that she may return, and to cause the driven out to be gathered; but he promises also that by so doing he will take away the reproach in view of all people, among whom they had lurked with ignominy.

1. There is so much which the afflicted church may have in probability and sense, to object against the truth of promises, that the performance of them will be amazing and to be admired. Here we are called to admire the Lord's bringing about his purpose, notwithstanding so many seen impediments. "Behold, at that time I will save her."

2. The promises made to the church speak much woe to her opposers, and will come to effect in spite of all opposition they can lay in the way. "I will undo all who afflict you, and will save."

3. The Lord's people may be so crushed by their troubles, and disabled to do anything for themselves or their own help, and so cast out from all their enjoyments, and so scattered from the society one of another, and from having the face of a people, that it may seem impossible to sense that they shall be recovered, though there were no enemies against them. For it is a new impediment to their faith that they "halted," which disables from any activity or motion, and were "driven out."

4. Those may be brought to a very low and desperate condition by trouble, whom yet the Lord will not only preserve from ruin but will raise up (as it were) from the dead, and will bring them to a full fruition of what he has promised. "I will save her who halts, and gather her who was driven out," says the Lord.

5. Though reproach is a great addition to trouble, yet the Lord's people waiting on him may expect to have it rubbed off with advantage, and that by his mercies toward them he will make them honourable in the sight of all who despised them because of their low state. "I will get them praise and fame in every land, where they have been put to shame."

> Ver. 20. At that time I will bring you again, even in the time that I gather you; for I will make you a name and a praise among all the people of the earth, when I turn back your captivity before your eyes, says the Lord.

The Lord yet insists upon the former promise. Because it was hard to believe such a great change, being as a resurrection from the dead after so many years' burial and rotting (as it were) in their graves, therefore he repeats and, by subscribing his own name, confirms the promise of gathering and bringing them back, and of making them famous throughout the world, when he should return their captivity visibly, and to their own satisfaction.

He mentions the turning back of "captivities" in the plural (as it is in the original), with relation to their being led captives at several times, as under Manasseh (2 Chron. 33:11), under Jehoiakim (2 Chron. 36:6), under Jehoiachin (2 Chron. 36:10), and under Zedekiah, and in relation to their being scattered into several places in their captivity, from which they were to be returned as so many troops of captives, if not also to their long dispersion since the Messiah came, as well as to the former in Babylon.

1. Greatest difficulties in the way of performance of promises ought not to cause the church to doubt anything of their certainty. Therefore the promise is again and again inculcated upon these fainting Jews, as a most certain truth, whatever they had to the contrary upon which to reject it. "At that time I will bring you again."

2. One act of God's power and love manifested for his people does but make way for another to perfect it; and when the Lord begins a work with them, they may expect that he will not leave it unfinished. So much does the way of making this promise import, that when he gathers them in their exile (as he did under Zerubbabel and Ezra), he will not leave them until he safely brings them back. "At that time I will bring you again, even in the time that I gather you."

3. The Lord's appearing for a people and doing for them, is their greatest honour before the world, considering what it speaks of their interest in so great a God, what respect he carries to them in their low estate, and how glorious he will make them by doing for them; and the Lord will in due time do for his people, that he may put this honour upon them. Therefore it is here subjoined as a fruit of his work and his end in working, "I will bring you again, for I will make you a name and a praise among all the people of the earth, when I turn back your captivity."

4. The infinite fullness of God is sufficiently able to answer all his people's wants, and will not leave his work undone to their contentment, were their difficulties ever so many; for whereas they had been often led captives, and scattered into divers places, he promises, "I will turn back your captivities, and do it before your eyes," or to your full contentment and satisfaction.

5. The former proofs which God has given of his power, to give a being to what he says in greatest extremities, is

sufficient ground for the church's encouragement to lean to his promises in new difficulties. Therefore, to confirm all, he subscribes this name Jehovah, by which he had been known in their deliverance from Egypt (Exod. 6:3), as a sufficient ground for their faith in this second captivity. "I will turn back your captivity, says the Lord (Jehovah)." Of him, and through him, and to him are all things, to whom be glory for ever. Amen" (Rom. 11:36).

THE END

www.ingramcontent.com/pod-product-compliance
Lightning Source LLC
Chambersburg PA
CBHW070732030726
47601CB00005B/264